The Social History of the Unconscious

The Social History of the Unconscious

George Frankl

Open Gate Press
London

First published in 1989 by Open Gate Press
51 Achilles Road, London NW6 1DZ

British Library Cataloguing in Publication Data

Frankl, George, *1921–*
The social history of the unconscious.—
(psychoanalysis and society)
1. Man. Behaviour. Evolutionary aspects
I. Title   II. Series
155.7

ISBN 1-871871-00-X

Photoset in 10 on 12pt Times by MCS Ltd, Salisbury, Wilts.

Printed in Great Britain by
Halstan & Co Ltd., Amersham, Bucks.

Contents

Preface

I have long been aware of the paradox that while in my work as a psychotherapist I am able to help a number of individuals, society mass-produces neurotics and, moreover, shows unmistakable signs of a profound neurosis in its structure and behaviour. The symptoms of the social neurosis are painfully obvious in this century: two world wars, Nazism, Stalinism, continuing wars, political terrorism and now the threat to the life-support system of this planet. I consider the treatment of this neurosis, in which we are all involved, the supreme task of psychoanalysis. Indeed, I believe the most important contribution of psychoanalysis will emerge in its application to the social neurosis, the more so as the social sciences, both Marxist and academic, have failed to help us understand or counteract the irrational and destructive drives which dominate the behaviour of societies.

This book is intended to lay the foundations for a psychoanalytic sociology, a social science which takes the unconscious motivations of social behaviour fully into account. This may be considered a revolutionary approach to social studies, yet it is not without precedent; Freud had high hopes for psychoanalysis, not only as a treatment for individuals but also as a major contribution towards the liberation of humanity from the "pathology of civilisations". However, the difficulties of the task made him pessimistic in the end. Other psychoanalysts after him were determined to take up the challenge: Horkheimer, Fenichel, Fromm, Reich and Marcuse among others, but they also failed. However, their mistakes were manifold: they tried to align psychoanalysis with a Marxist interpretation of history, considering the economic basis of social structures as objectively given, only concerning themselves with so-called cultural and psychological superstructure, which they declared to be the valid field for psychoanalytic studies. Roheim stood out against this trend and maintained that economic and political systems are determined by the psychic structure prevalent amongst the members of a society. He believed in the universality of the Oedipus complex and patriarchy as the foundation of all cultures, a claim which, as I shall show, can no longer be upheld. If one takes the Oedipus complex as the inevitable and necessary foundation of all cultures then one condemns civilisation to be subjected to its conflicts and nightmares forever.

I resolved, therefore, to search anew for the psychic foundations of cultures, neither accepting the Marxist dogma of the economic basis of society, from which all other socio-cultural phenomena derive, nor the universality of the Oedipus complex in which Freud has remained trapped, making him lose hope for humanity. But above all, I had to declare war on the deeply entrenched conviction that reality, as we experience it, has an objective existence independent of man, and show that the reality we confront is made by man, that it is humanity which creates its own conditions and, what is more, does so largely unconsciously and then depends on the conditions it has created.

In my investigations I was drawn back to the earliest stages of man's history in the same way as the more thoroughly a patient's neurotic symptoms are explored the more definitely do his associations lead back into the past and ultimately to early childhood. Thus my work with the social neurosis led me inevitably to the long-forgotten experiences of man's childhood, his prehistory, and from there the process of 'recall' of historical events assumed new meaning: the study of history could become 'analytic interpretation'. In this process I had to refer to a wide range of specialised sciences such as archaeology, mythology (which, as Freud pointed out, are men's collective dreams), prehistoric art, the history of religions as well as modern art, and contemporary myths as they can be seen operating in politics and international relationships. Moreover, I had to explain the connection between the unconscious processes which occur in individuals with those operating in human societies. I thus had to step beyond the conventional boundaries which experts in the various sciences draw around themselves, in order to gain a comprehensive view of man's psycho-cultural development, a view that does some justice to the immense complexity and—may I say it—wonder of human evolution.

I wish to thank all those who have helped me produce the book. I am indebted to Cynthia Maccoby, Michael Sommer, Ann Measures, Jeannie Cohen, Sandra Lovell, Sigmund Laufer, Dr. Peter Randell and Elisabeth Petersdorff for their encouragement, their suggestions, criticisms and editorial labours.

I want to thank my wife, Thelma, who has typed and re-typed large parts of this book. Her sensitivity for language, and insistence that every idea should be expressed with clarity has, I hope, prevented me from indulging in specialised jargon when it was not absolutely necessary.

GF

Introduction

It is obvious that our civilisation suffers from a disease which we seem unable to understand or cure. The symptoms of the disease have been manifest throughout history and have played an important part in shaping it; the disease, however, was counteracted by regenerative forces—the visions of beauty, justice and knowledge. The conflicts between destructive and life-affirming forces, between morbidity and health, have produced a certain dialectic from which new social systems and new ideologies have emerged. We might say that the morbidity has generated compensatory responses—the civilising forces dedicated to the enhancement of life.

Utopia always had a future in the aspirations of men: while children were born and new generations emerged they would create and experience the better life or at least partake in the movement towards it. Now, for the first time in history, the future is in question; the disease shows signs of entering into the terminal stage; the momentum of the pathology is accelerating and is becoming irreversible—it threatens to destroy mankind. We are now able to enhance life to an enormous extent and to harm it—even destroy it. Man's knowledge and his technology can serve his dreams as well as his nightmares; this has always been the case but now, for the first time in history, technology has acquired the arrogance of total power; its capability for destruction has no limits and no frontiers, it encompasses the whole planet and biosphere. While we have looked forward to the progress of technology and the enjoyment of its productive capacities, we now realise with horror that it equally serves the pathological forces of destruction.

Besides the threat of nuclear warfare with its unimaginable consequences, we confront the 'peaceful' ruination of the biosphere, the exhaustion of raw materials necessary for man's sustenance coupled with the population explosion which compounds these dangers in a geometric progression. We are experiencing the pollution of the environment through industrial effluent, the spoliation of the air, the seas and rivers, the extermination of thousands of animal species and the growing disruption of biological life systems. Even traditionally life-enhancing sciences like medicine are showing double-edged characteristics by interfering with the balance of human ecology and natural selection, thereby contributing to the population explosion. The vastly increased number of children, born due to medical intervention, will become the starving millions, victims of large-scale famines, of the near future.

Apart from these problems of human survival, we are experiencing a brutalization of urban life, with a sharp increase in political violence, criminal behaviour, delinquency, and the dehumanisation of labour dictated by the imperatives of the machine, the mechanical regimentation of entertainment, and a lowering of the quality of human relationships in the anonymity of mass existence.

An ever greater number of people suffer from tension, loneliness and anxiety states, which produce a multitude of stress diseases, only held at bay to some extent by the mass consumption of drugs. We are becoming aware of an increase in neuroticism which deserves to be called an epidemic.

The fundamental question which now confronts us is whether the forces of regeneration and life-affirmation can respond with sufficient vigour to the sickness which threatens our civilisation. Are we in a position to analyse and identify the sources of the disease and encourage the social organism to adopt the measures necessary to promote a cure?

Ever since men have been able to reflect upon the suffering which they inflict on each other, they have tried to understand the causes which compel them to do so. Intelligent individuals were not content to accept the justifications of their rulers, nor were they ready to accept war or tyranny as necessary and inevitable aspects of social life. They wondered whether the constant wars between tribes and nations, the oppression of the majority of their fellow men, people's apparent willingness to relinquish their freedom and submit to the commands of religious or secular authority could be explained by some instinct, an innate religious or national sentiment or by the economic laws of production. They puzzled about man's readiness to abandon his rational faculties and regress to a state of barbarism, and whether there is a conflict between the relatively recently acquired prefrontal areas of the brain and the ancient structure of the mid-brain, representing a kind of biological dysfunction of the species. Or is there a universal conflict between Eros and Thanatos, between love and destruction, as Freud averred? Or is the class war a basic aspect of all social life and the very foundation of all historic processes, as Marx asserted?

All these speculations, and many others about the 'nature of man', no doubt recognise certain aspects of human life, but it is extremely doubtful whether they produce a satisfactory explanation of the causes of men's social conflicts. And indeed, the 'solutions', which some explanations have given rise to, have intensified the conflicts and have been used as justifications for tyranny and violence. Are we then to relinquish any hope of arriving at a fundamental concept by which the many phenomena of man's social behaviour can be satisfactorily understood? Is it necessary to give up the search for the causes because all previous attempts have been inadequate? This surely contradicts the spirit of science and the instinct of inquiry.

If there is one thing which all human cultures, societies and civilisations have in common it is that they are the product of the human mind. This may appear as a tautology, a self-evident statement, for there cannot be a culture without a mind, and there is no society without a culture, but it is a truth which we are constantly inclined to forget. We tend to consider social behaviour to be conditioned by external circumstances and regard ourselves as victims of 'objective reality'. But any study of man's social reality, the external conditions as well as our responses to them, must acknowledge that it is humanity which creates its conditions and, what is more, does so largely unconsciously and then depends on the conditions it has created.

THE MIND IN REALITY

All social facts, both the material structures as well as the rules, laws, customs and conventions, are artefacts or ideal facts subsumed under the terms 'culture' or 'civilisation'. They are modes of human self-expression objectified in the norms and structures of society. As Robert Musil has aptly put it: "One might say that man becomes himself only through self-expression, and the forms of his self-expression become manifest in the forms and structures of society". Or, as Marx has said: "Man's nature is characterised by praxis and the reality he confronts is his own product".

While it is true that social reality conditions our actions as well as our thoughts, a student of society must never forget the mental processes which have gone into the making of social reality. Society represents the mind of man that has become objectified and appears as fact. Every social fact is a factum, i.e. a made thing. As by mind we mean the thoughts, fantasies, ideals, values and emotions of man, we must regard the facts of society as objectivations of mind, internal processes externalised into objective forms.

Beginning with the simplest tool made, or the simplest path cut in the wilderness, or the simplest hut built, and ending with all the gadgets, machinery, domesticated animals, palaces, cathedrals, universities, museums, all the cities and villages, all the pictures, statues, books, all the energies harnessed by man—heat, electricity, atomic fission—all this makes up the material culture or civilisation of humanity. Civilisation is made up of the totality of the biophysical objects and energies that are used as media for the objectivation of meanings, values and norms. Physically and biologically there are no human organisms that are kings, popes, generals, scientists, labourers, peasants, merchants, criminals, heroes, saints, and so on. All these and thousands of other 'meanings' are superimposed upon biological organisms by the socio-cultural world, where groups and persons function not only as physical objects and biological organisms but mainly as mindful human personalities, as the representatives, creators and agents of symbolic meanings and values. To paraphrase John Locke: "There is nothing in society which is not also in the mind of its members". Or, as Sorokin has observed: "Every social group is built around and contains a set of cultural meanings as its heart and soul, as its unifying bond and its reason for existence".[*]

---

[*] P. A. Sorokin: 'Sociological Theories of Today' (Harper & Row, 1966).

The cultural values of organised social groups give meaning to the active pursuits and the roles adopted by its members. Anyone, therefore, who wishes to undertake a scientific study of society and who does not take into consideration the ideational or cultural dimensions of social facts does not understand society. If he merely focuses on objective phenomena without reference to their mental-cultural meanings he is like a man who upon perceiving a Corinthian column sees no more than a piece of stone, nothing but a succession of sound waves in a symphony. However meticulously he might subject the natural properties of the stone or the system of sound waves to physical or statistical analysis he will not understand anything at all about Greek architecture or about music, for the stone and the sound waves are only the means to create an imaginative representation. Contrariwise, however, he who considers nothing but ideas and values in the life of society, who ignores the hard facts of their embodiment in economic and political reality, is like someone who ignores the instruments which are played in a symphony or the stone used in the creation of architectural beauty. It is the stone moulded by the craftsman's skill and effort, the poet's imagination, the architect's cultural values and his use of mathematical calculations which together create the Greek temple; it is man's imposition of his imagination and his skill upon the natural materials which create the facts of civilisation. As Sándor Végh, the eminent violinist, has written: "Stradivarius chose the maple and pine in such a way that the hidden qualities of the wood became perceptible, of course only to the musical ear. Although scientists have analysed the wood and the lacquer, the art of making violins remains elusive. Stradivarius sought out the soul of the wood and liberated it". [*]

A religious value superimposed on a little stick transforms it into a sacred totem; two sticks put across each other represent the symbol of the Cross; with a piece of cloth on a stick we have a national flag which is an object for which life is sacrificed. It is obvious, therefore, that values, symbols, myths and ideas permeate human actions and the structure of society.

Anthropological studies have made it abundantly clear that the myths which predominate in cultures have a decisive influence upon the consciousness, judgments, perceptions and behaviour of their

---

[*] Sándor Végh: 'Music as Experience' (Eranos Jahrbuch, 1960)

members. In the field of epistemology, i.e. the philosophical investigation of knowledge, Immanuel Kant, probably the greatest philosopher of the Western world since Plato, has shown that men do not perceive reality as such, as if it were a thing in itself, but that their perception of things is determined by innate a priori ideas, the categories of time and space, causation, mass, extension, among others. Psychoanalysis has added a new dimension to Kant's categories of the understanding by showing the importance of unconscious determinants such as complexes, fixations and fantasies upon men's perceptions and judgments of reality. On the socio-cultural level, we must recognise the impact of myths, the collective fantasies shared by the members of a culture, upon their perception of reality, their judgments and behaviour. Culture can be said to be the public expression of private fantasies of individuals. In providing a common catharsis it also acts as a bond between individuals and provides them with a sense of identity. Perhaps more than anything else, a culture provides its individuals with the security of a consensus for modes of perception, valuation and the interpretation of phenomena. Neither as individuals nor as members of society do men experience reality as it is but as they perceive it. And the perceived reality is permeated by the myths and symbols shared by the members of a culture or, in complex societies, by members of a variety of subcultures. Mythological and religious fantasies as well as political ideologies largely determine the perception of reality.

It is perfectly true that men have to adjust to the external world in order to survive just like any other living organism, but the world to which men have to adjust is made by men and is the material embodiment of their mind. Apart from the satisfaction of biological needs which he shares with animals, man lives in a universe not of things but of symbols. There can be no question that man is a culture-producing, symbol-orientated, symbol-using, symbol-dominated animal throughout.

There has been a very considerable upsurge in the study of symbolism by social psychologists, but their concept of symbols frequently lack the depth of psychoanalytic exploration. They usually fail to relate social symbolism to its roots, i.e. the unconscious foundations of mythological structures and fantasies. Psychoanalysts, while investigating the emergence and developments of symbols in the psyche of individuals, their manifestations in dreams, poetry, art as well as in neurotic and psychosomatic symptoms, have made many attempts to apply those findings to the symbols and myths of cultures. Psychoanalytic anthropologists like Geza Roheim, Money Kyrle, Erik Erikson, and anthropologists like Malinowski and Clyde Clukhom, who were influenced by psychoanalysis, traced the formation of cultural symbols to childhood experiences, modes of infant rearing and the conflicts of the libido shared by members of certain societies.

A psychoanalytic sociology, therefore, will have to investigate how the myths and symbols of societies originate and the manner in which they determine the behaviour and the perception of their members; it will devote itself to investigating how the unconscious becomes manifest in the artefacts and symbols of a society.

I am convinced that the most important achievement of psychoanalysis is yet to come through the light it can shed on previously unknown mechanisms in the behaviour of societies. But it is important to acknowledge some fundamental problems which one encounters in such an enterprise. Some of these problems were clearly recognised by Freud and defined by him on a number of different occasions. In his book, 'Civilisation and its Discontents', he wrote:

> If the evolution of civilisation has such a far-reaching similarity with the development of an individual, and if the same methods are employed in both, would not the diagnosis be justified that many systems of civilisation, or epochs of it, possibly even the whole of humanity, have become 'neurotic' under the pressure of civilising trends?...
>
> The diagnosis of collective neuroses, moreover, will be confronted by a special difficulty. In the neuroses of an individual we can use as a starting-point the contrast presented to us between the patient and his environment which we assume to be 'normal'. No such background as this would be available for any society similarly affected; it would have to be supplied in some other way. And with regard to any therapeutic application of our knowledge, what would be the use of the most acute analysis of social neuroses, since no one possesses power to compel the community to adopt the therapy? In spite of all these difficulties, we may expect that one day someone will venture upon this research into the pathology of civilised communities.

Freud wrote this passage in 1930. Since then mankind has experienced the consequences of the social pathology through the terrorism of Nazi and Stalinist dictatorships, the massacre of 15,000,000 soldiers, 20,000,000 civilians, incarceration of more than 20,000,000 in concentration camps, and the devastation of wars on a scale unprecedented in history. Since the end of the Second World War, there has not been a moment without wars occurring in some parts of the world. Now we confront the possibility of nuclear destruction: destruction of the life-system of our planet.

I am very conscious of the immense complexities of the disease afflicting civilisation and of the difficulties of adopting a suitable therapy, but the seriousness of the condition may persuade the patient that a therapy is really necessary and arouse in the therapist a new determination to extend to the utmost his therapeutic knowledge and skill. I believe that the mind which has created the conditions for human destruction can also overcome them, particularly as more men are becoming aware of the appalling dangers of the social malaise and of the need for a cure if we are both to preserve life and to acquire a capacity to enjoy it.

Part 1

1 Psychoanalysis as a Social Science

The idea of applying psychoanalysis to the social pathology immediately confronts us with the question how psychoanalysis can be applied to society as it clearly is an individual therapy—a personal transaction between a patient and analyst—and derives its findings from the study of individuals, and how its teachings can contribute anything to an understanding of social problems.

It is widely assumed that because psychoanalysis is an individual therapy and its theories were developed out of the therapy of individuals it has nothing to say about society and, furthermore, as many Marxists assert, that it is the product of capitalist society and expresses the world-view of a decaying bourgeoisie.

In recent years there have been many efforts to correct the view that Freud neglected and disregarded cultural and social factors in the analysis of psychological phenomena. This accusation was directed against a man who began with, and invariably returned to, the basic proposition that the drama of the self is always carried out against the social background, starting with the family, who as early as 1908 wrote a long essay on the effect of cultural repressions on mental illness, who in his later writings addressed himself almost exclusively to cultural problems and insisted that all psychology was group psychology, and who in the last summary and revision of his thinking ('New Introductory Lectures on Psychoanalysis') stated clearly that there were only two branches of science, the human sciences, i.e. psychology, pure and applied, and the natural sciences. He was not only aware of but took great care to emphasize the fact that all aspects of civilisation, all its myths, aspirations, taboos, fears and conflicts are in some measure reflected in the mind of an individual. In his 'Group Psychology' Freud stated that: "The contrast between individual psychology and social or group psychology which, at a first glance, may seem to be full of significance, loses a great deal of its sharpness when it is examined more closely... From the very first, individual psychology is at the same time social psychology as well".

Freud repeatedly committed himself to the proposition that sociology, dealing as it does with the behaviour of people in society, cannot be anything but applied psychology, and Talcott Parsons, the American sociologist, acknowledged that Freud had introduced in his psychology an explicit recognition of the social structure in which the individual lives. Lionel Trilling has observed correctly: "For the layman, Freud is likely to be the chief proponent of the whole cultural concept... His psychology involves culture in its very essence; it tells us that the surrogates of culture are established in the mind itself, that the development of the individual mind recapitulates the development of culture".

In 1935, at the age of seventy-nine, Freud wrote: "My interest, after making a lifelong detour through the natural sciences, medicine and psychotherapy, returned to the cultural problems which had fascinated me long before when I was a youth scarcely old enough for thinking. At the very climax of my psychoanalytic work in 1912, I had already attempted in 'Totem and Taboo' to make use of the newly discovered findings of analysis in order to investigate the origins of religion and morality. I now carried this work a stage further in two later essays, 'The Future of an Illusion' (1927) and 'Civilisation and its Discontents' (1930). I perceived ever more clearly that the events of human history, the interaction between human nature, cultural development and the precipitates of primeval experience, are no more than a reflection of the dynamic conflicts between the Ego, the Id and the Superego, which psychoanalysis studies in the individual, are the very same processes repeated upon a wider stage".

It is an odd delusion on the part of positivist sociologists and psychologists as well as Marxist critics to charge a thinker more deeply steeped than themselves in the heritage of cultural history with blindness to the effect of social influences upon human life. Characteristic of their often cynical misrepresentations of Freud's thoughts are the many jokes and jibes which are meant to be taken seriously concerning Freud's reactionary indifference towards society. There is, for instance, the story that a sign hung in Freud's consulting room with the inscription, 'Social sufferings are not treated here'. It may not be sufficiently known, certainly not by his cliché-ridden critics, that Freud translated one of John Stuart Mill's books in 1880, with chapter headings, 'The Emancipation of Women', 'The Worker Question', 'Socialism'.

Fromm has pointed out that: "The object of psychological investigation for Freud is the socialised human being immersed in his social relationships; environment and the social conditions of life play a decisive role in Freud's concept of psychological development and are fundamental for his theoretical understanding of the human being. Freud was certainly concerned with the biophysiological function of drives, but he has shown the extent to which these drives are modifiable, and that the modifying factors are to be found in the environment, in social reality".

Freud was not merely concerned with the renovation of psychiatry but with a reinterpretation of all psychic productions pertaining to culture, from dreams through art and morality to religion and ideology. Psychoanalysis is concerned not merely with the interpretation of the neurosis of individuals but also with the interpretation of culture.

Ever since 1900, when his 'Interpretation of Dreams' appeared, he proposed that "dreams are the dreamer's private mythology and myths the waking dreams of peoples". He not only considered that the development of the human psyche is always acted out against a family background but that the child's environment is deeply affected by culture, its taboos and its myths. He made it possible to trace the link between culture, family and the individual psyche and, in turn, laid the foundation for an understanding of how a culture is produced.

That Freud considered psychoanalysis essential for an understanding of society is very clearly expressed in his essay, 'The Question of Lay Analysis': "As depth psychology, the science of the unconscious, psychoanalysis has become essential to all sciences which are concerned with the development of human culture and its great institutions like art, religion and social organisation. I believe that it already has contributed considerably to those sciences, but these are only small contributions to what it could achieve if cultural historians, workers in religious psychology, linguistics, etc., were to come to understand the tools which the new methods of psychoanalytic investigation put at their disposal. The application of psychoanalysis to the therapy of neuroses is only one of its many applications; perhaps the future will show that it has not been the most important".

To those who steadfastly rejected psychoanalysis as a bourgeois science, I would mention that Leon Trotsky in his essay 'Literature and Revolution' declared that, "It is quite wrong to turn one's back on Freud and to consider psychoanalysis as contradictory to Marxism". The dogma of the counter-revolutionary nature of psychoanalysis has been deliberately propagated by Stalinism in its reactionary endeavour to block the cultural changes which are inevitable in true socialism. The Stalinist reaction has made a system out of the condemnation of psychoanalysis and has tried with all possible arguments to consider it as unacceptable to Marxism and to brand it generally as a counter-revolutionary imperialistic doctrine. It is well to remember that the Stalinist counter-revolution has shown that psychoanalysis as a critical theory is unacceptable to any authoritarian regime.

Against the reactionary dogmatism of Stalinist ideologues, Siegfried Bernfeld pointed out that psychoanalysis is a dialectical science: "It corresponds in its discovery of the history of the human psyche with Marx's historical theory of class society. Psychoanalysis helps us to gain insight into the interaction between social processes and psychological reactions to them and to throw light on the dialectic between productive relationships and allied ideologies as transformations of the psychic structures of man. It upholds the theory that man makes his own history but under certain given conditions which include psychological conditions". The American Marxist, Paul A. Baran, said: "It must be amongst the highest tasks of Marxist theory to take up Freud's work at the point where he left it and to reintegrate his discovery and his new theory concerning human actions".

The most radical application of psychoanalytic ideas to society was formulated by Wilhelm Reich: "The work of mass psychology must not remain in the shadow of political economy but political economy must be in the service of mass psychology. The needs of man do not exist for economic policies but economic policies are there to serve the satisfaction of human needs".

With regard to the question, whether psychoanalysis can contribute anything to an understanding of social problems, one must admit that the social structure which Freud mostly dealt with in his analysis of individuals was the family. He did, however, show how the psychic processes engendered by the family structure are carried forward into society and are reproduced in its symbols, its myths and institutions. The child's images of parental authority, its fears and emotional conflicts, as well as love and security, are transferred to society and elaborated in its culture. It may be considered as the chief task of a psychoanalytic sociology to investigate how this process occurs.

We might say that civilisation represents the social dimension of psychic events and the individual mind represents the psychic dimension of social events. It is no longer enough to say—as most sociologists do—that we react as individuals to the demands, rules and pressures of society; it is necessary now to give attention to the symbolic significance, to the psychological meanings of social systems. Freud has remarked that dreams are the private myths of individuals and myths the public dreams of cultures. Fundamental myths become elaborated into religion, art, drama and philosophy, which, in turn, influence political ideologies, institutions and laws. Social activities, like work, property relationships, class conflict and political practice, reflect these cultural images, which frequently operate on levels beyond the control of rational judgment, just as dreams cannot be controlled by reason. History provides plenty of evidence of some force at work which defeats reason and with depressive regularity determines the behaviour of society with the force of a compulsion. Here indeed is a dialectic, but it is not one of external processes operating in nature, history or economics but inside the mind of man.

Psychoanalysis has often been accused of looking backwards, stressing the past as an iron law which determines man's conduct. It is true that to a great extent psychoanalysis considers people as the product of their history, but that is not the same as upholding the authority of the past and thereby limiting the capacity for freedom, as Fromm has implied in his criticism of Freud. One cannot, however much one aligns oneself with freedom and self-determination, deny the historical processes which influence our minds. Moreover, it is just when we repress the impact of the past upon our thoughts and attitudes that it becomes a compulsive force. We can, however, transcend the past and free ourselves from its bondage to some extent if we become aware of its influences and subject them to conscious valuation and judgment. The degree to which the ego can subject necessity to a searching criticism is the measure of its capacity for freedom. When Freud said, "Where id was there shall ego be", he also implied that where compulsion reigned there shall freedom be.

While it is not difficult, particularly in our time, to discern pathological traits of society, the application of the psychoanalytic method to society encounters difficulties which often appear insurmountable; the sheer complexity of the task; the intellectual difficulty of finding the right parameters in which the problems of society and the concepts of psychoanalysis can meet; how to formulate psychoanalytic concepts in such a way that they manifestly apply to the values and ideologies of a society. Psychological influences in economics, politics and industry have often been pointed out, but it is very difficult to define these influences in a manner which economists, technologists and politicians, as well as 'the man in the street', can recognise as meaningful to themselves. The habit of considering social conditions as objectively given is deeply ingrained. The subjective conditioning of objective structures and, in particular, the unconscious conditioning of social reality is a daunting proposition because it is so contrary to our habits of mind.

In order to liberate ourselves from the social compulsions, which appear as objective reality, we must make ourselves conscious of the psychic determinants of our social behaviour and our social institutions. As every neurotic person if he is to be cured of his symptoms must acknowledge that they do not merely exist as something given but are the manifestation of some drives or desires in him, however bizarre or painful they may be, so we, as social beings, must learn to acknowledge the drives and desires in us which operate in societies. The resistance against our conscious identification with the social pathologies, the unwillingness to admit that we ourselves are their causes, is very considerable. We do not, as civilised beings, wish to admit that we are driven by savage and brutal desires, that we want to fight and oppress, and that we are responsible for the dark and horrible side of our society. We would consider such an admission as an injury to the illusions which we have about ourselves. It certainly takes courage to look at the reflections of our psyche in society, to see it as a mirror of our neuroses and pathologies. But once we can recognise the pathological manifestations of society and admit responsibility for them we can begin an authentic enquiry into their causes. The separation of social actuality from psychic processes, just as much as the separation of symptom from the subjective self, is false consciousness, a fundamental aspect of alienation.

The assumptions and habits of social institutions perpetuate this false consciousness, they reinforce the split between the living subject and external reality. We are still at the stage where the products of the mind of man, civilisation and its material artefacts, appear to exist independently of the mind, confronting it as an objectively given reality. The creator of the artefacts of civilisation appears to have forgotten his own role in their creation. Men have forgotten, i.e. repressed the mental images and fantasies which have gone into the making of the environment. "Symbolic structures, God, Church, Nation, Party, economic systems, can govern man and human behaviour more powerfully than biological reality or organismic drives. This is the basis of the most sublime achievement of man; it is also the cause of all the follies of human history. Thermonuclear bombs are not only the ultimate weapon but the ultimate of symbolism run wild in science, technology and politics".[*]

It is a major task of psychoanalysis to investigate how the projections of an individual become hostile, how the unconscious part of his mind, appearing to operate outside him, can become a danger to him. It must investigate the processes by which men project and externalise their fantasies and desires and create symbolic structures in society, how they can split themselves off not only from their own mental activity but from the environment they have produced, and how the externalised part of themselves, i.e. their civilisation, can turn against them and become a destructive force. In the psychotherapy of individuals we repeatedly have to point out to patients that many aspects of their lives which they consider to be entirely due to external circumstances, objective conditions outside their control, are in fact produced by themselves, by parts of their mind of which they are not aware. In the same manner, psychoanalytic sociology will have to show that what

---

[*] Ludwig von Bertalanffy: 'Robots, Men and Minds'.

we consider objective conditions are, to a large extent, the productions of that part of our own minds of which we do not appear to be conscious. To learn to appreciate that it is we ourselves, our own thoughts and our own fantasies, who are the causative agents of our reality can be a responsibility which we do not wish to shoulder; but if we wish to achieve a measure of maturity as well as liberation from major psycho-cultural diseases, we must recognise ourselves in them, however unpalatable and frightening this may be. The point which psychoanalysis has to bring across to patients is that the liberation from disturbing symptoms necessarily involves the acknowledgement of their own part in them.

While it is the fundamental task of psychoanalysis to reunite the individual with those parts of his mind which he has repressed, it is the task of a psychoanalytic sociology to reunite men with those parts of their mind which operate in society.

THE OEDIPUS COMPLEX AND THE INTERPRETATION OF CULTURES

Freud made his first systematic attempt to link anthropological material with his psychological theories and, in particular, to apply the concept of the Oedipus complex to culture in general in his book, 'Totem and Taboo'. Jung's observation of the analogies between the mental processes of neurotics and of primitive people led Freud to a close study of the mythologies of totemism. In four essays, which were collected into one volume, he showed that a dread of incest was even more marked among primitive people than among civilised races and had given rise to very special measures of defence against it. He was attracted to totemism, the first system of organisation in primitive tribes, a system in which the beginnings of social order are united with a rudimentary religion and the implacable domination of a small number of taboo prohibitions. The being that is honoured is ultimately always an animal from which the clan claims to be descended. Many indications pointed to the conclusion that every culture, even the most highly developed, had once passed through the stage of totemism. Freud's starting-point was the striking correspondence between the two taboo injunctions of totemism, i.e. not to kill the totem and not to have sexual relations with any woman of the same totem clan, and the two elements of the Oedipus complex, the desire to kill the father and take the mother as wife. He came to equate the totem animal with the father; in fact, primitive people do this explicitly by honouring it as the forefather of the clan.

The analysis of early animal phobias in children often showed that the animal was a substitute for the father, a substitute onto which the fear of the father derived from the Oedipus complex had been displaced. This enabled Freud to recognise the killing of the father as the nucleus of totemism and the starting-point in the formation of religions.

Theodor Reik and Geza Roheim took the line of thought which Freud developed in 'Totem and Taboo', and in a series of works extended, amplified or corrected it. Freud himself made many attempts at forming a closer connection between social psychology and the psychology of the individual in works such as 'The Ego and the Id' and 'Group Psychology', among others. He recognised that it is only a step from the fantasies of individual neurotics and the dreams of ordinary people to the imaginative creations of groups and cultures as we find them in myths, legends and drama.

The creations of the great dramatists were the imaginary gratifications of unconscious wishes, just as dreams are. They represented primeval, i.e. universal desires, usually of an unconscious nature, but they differed from the narcissistic products of dreaming insofar as they were calculated to arouse interest in other people and were able to evoke and gratify the same unconscious wishes in them too. They brought into the open the conflicts and complexes of people everywhere which they had repressed, yet were able to recognise or experience to some extent through the drama and the productions of great poets, painters and sculptors.

Sophocles had brought the naked incestuous wish fantasy of the child out into the open in 'Oedipus Rex', and had clothed it with as much explicit horror as any anxiety dream. In Hamlet the wish to lie with his mother is overlaid by layers of repressions and can only be detected by interpreting the symptoms which these repressions produced. Throughout the play Hamlet hesitates to accomplish his task of revenge upon his father's murderer. Shakespeare stated neither the cause nor the motives of his hesitation, and until Freud turned his own Oedipal eye on Hamlet's dilemma no one had successfully interpreted the reasons for Hamlet's tortured inertia. Freud interpreted Hamlet's depression and inertia: Hamlet is able to do anything but take vengeance upon the man who did away with his father and has taken his father's place with his mother, the man who shows him the repressed desires of his own childhood. The loathing, which should have driven him to vengeance, is thus replaced by self-reproach, by conscientious scruples which tell him that he himself is no better than the murderer whom he is required to punish. We can here translate into consciousness what had to remain unconscious in the mind of the hero.

When Freud finished 'Totem and Taboo' in 1914, he considered it as his greatest and perhaps last good work, and said he had not written anything with so much conviction since the 'Interpretation of Dreams'. Nevertheless he was soon beset by misgivings and doubts, possibly caused by his realisation that this book would create a sharp and unbridgeable division between psychoanalysis and all religious organisations or his anxiety about the validity of having posited an historic event—the killing of the father by a band of brothers—for which there could be no empirical evidence. When Jones and Ferenzci asked how the man who had written the 'Interpretation of Dreams' could now have such doubts, Freud replied: "Then I described the wish to kill one's father, now I have been describing the actual killing. After all, it is a big step from a wish to a deed".

After 'Totem and Taboo' Freud put aside his excursions into cultural and social topics for a number of years but took them up again in his essays, 'Beyond the Pleasure Principle' (1920), in which he first formulated his concept of the death wish—the great adversary of Eros—followed by 'Group Psychology' and 'The Analysis of the Ego' (1922), 'The Ego and the Id' (1923) and in 1930 'Civilisation and its Discontents'. In this work he applied the concept of the Superego as the most important element in the foundation of societies. This book may be seen as the consolidation of the theories first put forward in 'Totem and Taboo' and the clarification of the sense of guilt in culture and its development into conscience. Having formulated previously the destructive instinct as a manifestation of Thanatos—the death wish—he could now clearly show its conflict with Eros—the libido—and explained the sense of guilt as arising from the clash between the two fundamental forces in man.

He declared the aggressive drive to be an innate disposition in man constantly in conflict with the demands of culture, which is a manifestation of Eros and aims at bringing together human individuals, then families, then tribes, then nations into one great unity, that of humanity. These masses of men need to be bound to one another libidinally; necessity alone, the advantages of common work or a sense of common interest would not hold them together. This concept of society sharply contradicts the notions still widely held among academic sociologists that society is a group or a human population, who live in a certain environment to which they have to adapt in order to survive, i.e. that they are bound by a common interest such as the pursuit of work necessary for survival or defence. They interpret culture as representing an organised body of rules guiding people's communication with each other, their behaviour to one another, and the tasks which they have to perform. It is my opinion that these concepts may suffice to explain the existence of clubs or associations devoted to certain purposes but do not explain the bonds that exist in a culture and in a society, bonds which frequently contradict practical interests and inhibit the performance of rational tasks and often compel members of a group to behave in a manner that obviously contradicts all rational considerations.

SUPEREGO AND CIVILISATION

What means does civilisation use, asks Freud, to hold in check the aggressiveness that opposes it, to make it harmless, perhaps to get rid of it? The answer is that aggressiveness is introjected, internalised, and it is taken over by a part of the Ego that distinguishes itself from the rest as the Superego, and now, in the form of 'conscience' exercises the same propensity to harsh aggressiveness against the Ego that the Ego would have liked to enjoy against others. The tension between the strict Superego and the subordinate Ego we call the sense of guilt; it manifests itself as the need for punishment.

There are, as Freud has observed, two sources for feelings of guilt; that arising from the dread of authority and the second one from the dread of the Superego. The first one compels us to renounce instinctual gratification, the other presses over and above this towards punishment, since the persistence of forbidden wishes cannot be concealed from the Superego. The Superego continues to observe and watch us inside ourselves and it takes notice not only of our deeds but also our wishes; it carries on the severity of external authority which it has succeeded and to some extent replaced. The threat of conscience carries on the threat of authority.

In the process of introjecting the external authority into ourselves we identify with it and together with it we turn against ourselves and punish ourselves for the instinctual wishes and drives which we harbour. The relation between Superego and Ego is a reproduction of the real relations between the Ego and an external object. Remorse and guilt are the result of the very earliest primal ambivalence of feelings towards the father. The sons hated him but they also loved him. After their hate against him had been satisfied by their aggressive act, their love came to expression in their remorse about the deed, set up the Superego by identification with the father, gave it the father's power to punish as he would have done for the aggression they had performed, and created the restrictions which should prevent repetition of the deed. And since impulses of aggression against the father were repeated in following generations the feelings of guilt persisted too, and were further reinforced every time an aggression was suppressed anew and made over to the Superego. It is not really a decisive matter whether one has killed one's father or abstained from the deed; one must feel guilty in either case, for guilt is the expression of the conflict of ambivalence, the eternal struggle between love and the destructive instinct.

When mankind tries to institute wider forms of communal life, the same conflict continues to arise. Since culture obeys an inner erotic impulse which bids it to connect mankind into a closely knit unit, it can achieve this aim only by producing an ever-increasing sense of guilt. That which began in relation to the father continues in relation to the community. If civilisation is an inevitable course of development from the group or the family to the group of humanity as a whole, then an intensification of the sense of guilt—resulting from the innate conflict of ambivalence, from the eternal struggle between love and aggression towards the father and his representatives in society—may swell to a magnitude that individuals can hardly support.

Freud was perfectly aware that most readers would find his emphasis upon guilt in civilisation exaggerated, and he points out that the sense of guilt produced by culture is not perceived as such and remains to a great extent unconscious or comes to expression as a sort of uneasiness or discontent for which other motivations are sought. The religions, at any rate, have never overlooked the part played by the sense of guilt in civilisation; what is more, they all come forward with a claim to save mankind from the sense of guilt which they call sin.

It is hardly to be wondered at, that towards the end of his essay 'Civilisation and its Discontents' Freud declared himself to be sympathetic to those who feel that when one surveys the aims of civilisation and the means it employs one is bound to conclude that the whole thing is not worth the effort and that in the end it can only produce a state of things which no individual will be able to bear. He allows himself to plumb considerable depths of pessimism and declares that he has no thought of rising up as a prophet before his fellow-men, and bows to their reproach that he has no consolation to offer.

'Civilisation and its Discontents', which can be considered as the last major and systematic excursion into the psychoanalysis of culture apart from Freud's last book 'Moses and Monotheism', combines the theory of the death instinct with the universality of the Oedipus complex. It aroused a furore of arguments among psychoanalytically orientated socialists and became a kind of watershed that was to divide the pessimists from the optimists, the conservatives from the revolutionaries.

THE REVOLT AGAINST FREUD'S PESSIMISM

Many psychoanalysts had viewed the theory of the death instinct or Thanatos with considerable scepticism, considering it as an unnecessary speculation to which Freud himself did not give the status of a scientific theory, as an intellectual indulgence of a great mind who feels the need sometimes to break loose from the self-imposed bonds of scientific discipline. They considered that in any case it does not make much difference in the clinical work of psychoanalysis. While many psychoanalysts now do not take this idea very seriously, socially-orientated psychoanalysts like Reich and Fromm, for instance, considered it to be a serious obstacle in the application of psychoanalysis to socio-cultural matters and at the same time as a contradiction to Freud's theory of sexuality.

Wilhelm Reich considered 'Civilisation and its Discontents' an unmitigated disaster. This was not only an emotional or temperamental reaction to the pessimism which he discerned in Freud's attitude but a refusal to accept what he considered to be a fundamental contradiction to Freud's earlier thinking. The question as to whether aggressive-sadistic or masochistic self-destructive drives are fundamental instincts innate to man or acquired characteristics, the result of the denial and block of the libido, is indeed fundamental to psychoanalytic theory and its concepts of culture. Reich, probably more than any other psychoanalyst, took this problem to be crucial for a psychoanalytic sociology.

If the destructive drives are considered to be some kind of instinct that operates in individuals and societies, then one would have to consider the repressive nature of societies as inevitable and uphold the necessity of authoritarian and hierarchic social structures. This Reich believed to be fundamentally contrary to the spirit and theory of psychoanalysis; he was convinced it was contrary to what Freud had intended and that it was the product of the resignation which had overtaken Freud in his old age due to his disillusion with men who had for decades attacked him or misunderstood and debased his hard won insights. As Reich observed: "The world could no longer deny the facts of unconscious psychic life. So it began anew its old accustomed game of debasing what it could not destroy. It gave Freud a great many pupils who came to a table all set for them and who did not have to work hard for what they got. They only had an interest to make psychoanalysis socially acceptable. One after the other they sacrificed the libido theory or diluted it". If his disciples could not make the compromise between the theory of sexuality and their own resistances to it, they either dropped their association with Freud or started their own more 'sensible' schools. Breuer and Stekel ceased to co-operate with Freud; Adler and Jung and Rank started their own schools. The Ego-psychologists later minimised the libido theory and the importance of the unconscious. Until 1940 Reich considered himself to be one of the very few real Freudians, and he stood aghast at the compromises with the forces of repression which Freud made in his old age.

Whether Freud's postulate of a death instinct arose from his deep disillusionment with mankind's incapacity to acknowledge its unconscious compulsions or whether it was one of those dispositions of very great minds to endeavour to understand universal laws which operate in the world and determine the phenomena which they have studied is hard to say. Einstein in his later years used to say: "I want to know how God created this world. I am not interested in this or that phenomenon, in the spectrum of this or that element. I want to know His thoughts—the rest are details". Einstein had a considerable sense of humour and may have made reflections of this kind without taking himself too seriously. It is, however, true that he never ceased to work on the General Field Theory, which was to have achieved The Great Formulation, the discovery of the One Law that determines everything. Maybe Freud's concept of Eros and Thanatos had seemed to him a universal law by which everything could be explained and the rest mere details. Freud remained sceptical towards the solutions through socio-political changes, and his scepticism seems amply justified in our time. And Freud had not seen the last of the manifestations of man's destructiveness and savagery; he died just before the outbreak of the last war. However, Reich, Fromm, Horkheimer and Marcuse, and others, were still inspired by the possibilities which psychoanalytic insights could provide for a struggling humanity; they could not adjust to the fatalism of a universal death instinct, nor to the proposition that the Oedipus complex is the inevitable foundation of all civilisations.

2 Is the Oedipus Complex Universal?

'Daddy, what an ass you are!' This was the final sentence to an argument which I had with my youngest daughter, aged five. I had not been able to convince her or to sway her opinion... I ceased arguing and reflected. I tried to imagine what would have happened had I thus addressed my father some forty years ago. I shuddered and sighed. Fate was unkind in making me appear forty years too soon.

Four hundred years earlier, for such a reply a child would have been beaten, put into a dark room, tortured or disciplined into death or mortal annihilation. Four thousand years ago, perhaps, in the Bronze Age, a blood-thirsty patriarch would have killed it outright. But forty thousand years back, or thereabouts, (I am not very strong on dates or hypotheses), the matrilineal father might have smiled on his offspring even more indulgently than I was able to do, and without that wry twist on his face which comes, I suppose, from undigested patriarchal traditions. In any case, among my present-day Stone Age savages of the South Seas, I have heard children address a father as frankly and unceremoniously, with the perfect equivalent in native of the English, 'You damn fool!', while he argued back without any show of patriarchal dignity.*

MATRIARCHY AND PATRIARCHY

In the 1920s, a famous debate took place between Ernest Jones and Bronislaw Malinowski concerning the universality of the Oedipus complex. On the basis of his field-work in the Trobriand Islands,

---

* Bronislaw Malinowski: 'The New Generation' (Allen & Unwin, 1930)

Malinowski came to the conclusion that the Oedipus complex, as formulated by Freud, is only one among a series of possible 'nuclear complexes' which originate from the family structures predominant in certain societies.

In 1923, Malinowski wrote that "Freud's fundamental conception of the Oedipus complex contains a sociological as well as a psychological theory". "The psychological theory", says Malinowski, "declares that a very great part of man's mental life has its roots in the sexual life of children, which comes to be repressed by the paternal authority and the restrictive atmosphere of patriarchal life. Thus a parricidal complex emerges in children, particularly during puberty, and it remains an important drive in the unconscious mind of patriarchal men".

The sociological implications of this theory indicate that throughout the development of humanity there must have existed the institution of individual family and marriage, with the father as a severe, nay, ferocious patriarch. Freud himself assumes the existence at the outset of human development of a patriarchal family, or horde, with a tyrannical and ferocious father who repressed the sexual claims of the younger men.

Malinowski opposes this view with his own findings from anthropological researches among various primitive races. "When we come to examine in detail the original constitution of the human family—not in any hypothetical primeval form, but as we find it in actual observation among present day savages—some difficulties emerge. We find, for instance, that there is a form of matriarchal family in which the relationship between children and progenitors does not exist in the typical form as required by Freud's hypothesis of the 'Oedipus Complex'. Taking as an example the family as found in the Coral Archipelago of Eastern New Guinea, where I have studied it, the mother and her brother possess all the legal 'potestas'. The mother's brother is the ferocious matriarch, the father is the affectionate friend and helper of his children. He has to win for himself the friendship of his sons and daughters, and he is frequently their amicable ally against the principle of authority represented by the maternal uncle". Malinowski found that none of the taboos and repressions of the Oedipus Complex exist in the matriarchal family of Eastern New Guinea. The taboo of incest is mainly directed towards the separation of brother and sister. Thus we have a pattern of family life in which authority and sexual taboos appear in a manner which is different from that found in the patriarchal family.

The husband is not regarded as the father of the children in the sense in which we use the word; physiologically speaking he has nothing to do with their birth, according to the ideas of the natives, who appear to be ignorant of physical fatherhood. Children, in native belief, are inserted into the mother's womb as tiny spirits, generally by the agency of the spirit of a deceased kinswoman of the mother. Her husband has then to protect and cherish the children, to 'receive them in his arms' when they are born, but they are not 'his' in the sense that he has had a share in their procreation. The father is thus a beloved, benevolent friend, but not a recognised kinsman of the children. He is a stranger, having authority through his personal relations to the child, but not through his sociological position in the lineage. Real kinship, that is identity of substance, 'same body', exists only through the mother. The authority over the children is vested in the mother's brother.

In our own type of family, Malinowski continues, we have the authoritative, powerful husband and father backed up by society. We have also the economic arrangement whereby he is the breadwinner and can—nominally at least—withhold supplies or be generous with them at his will. Amongst Trobrianders, on the other hand, we have the independent mother and her husband, who has nothing to do with the procreation of the children, and is not the breadwinner, who cannot leave his possessions to the children, and has socially no established authority over them. The mother's relatives on the other hand are endowed with very powerful influence, especially her brother, who is the authoritative person, the producer of supplies for the family and whose possessions the sons will inherit at his death.

If we examine the consequence of matriarchal organisations in terms of instinctual repression and particularly taboos on sexuality, then we find a very profound difference from patriarchal patterns of sexual repression. In Melanesia there is no taboo on sex in general. At an early age children are initiated by each other, or sometimes by a slightly older companion, into the practices of sex. Naturally at this stage they are unable to carry out the act properly, but they content themselves with all sorts of games in which they are left quite at liberty by their elders, and thus they can satisfy their curiosity and their sensuality directly and without disguise.

They indulge in plays and pastimes in which they satisfy their curiosity concerning the appearance and function of the organs of generation and, incidentally, receive a certain amount of positive pleasure.

Melanesian children are fond of 'playing husband and wife'. A boy and girl build a little shelter and call it their home; there they pretend to assume the functions of husband and wife and, amongst those, of course, the most important one is that of sexual intercourse. At other times a group of children will go for a picnic where the entertainment consists of eating, fighting and making love. A very important point about this infantile sexuality is the attitude of the older generation. Parents do not look on it as in the least reprehensible. Generally they take it entirely for granted. The most they will do is to speak jestingly about it to one another, discussing the love tragedies and comedies of the child world. Never would they dream of interfering or frowning in disapproval, provided the children show a due amount of discretion, that is, do not perform their amorous games in the house, but go away somewhere apart in the bush. But above all the children are left entirely to themselves in their love affairs. Not only is there no parental interference, but rarely, if ever, does it come about that a man or woman takes a perverse sexual interest in children, and certainly they would never be seen to mix themselves in the games in this role. Violation of children is unknown, and a person who played sexually with a child would be thought ridiculous and disgusting.

Wilhelm Reich observed that: "With the exception of the incest taboo, there is no sex-negating morality among the Trobrianders. On the contrary, a clearly affirmative Ego develops and a sex-affirmative Ego-ideal. As sexuality is free, the incest taboo cannot be considered a sexual restriction, since abundant possibilities for gratification of a sexual nature remain".

Malinowski's anthropological observations have since been confirmed by other anthropologists. They provide ample evidence that the Oedipus Complex is not the inevitable pre-condition for the evolution of cultures but, at the same time, they verify Freud's concept of infantile sexuality. These observations clearly refute the reasoning of opponents of psychoanalysis who have steadfastly, and often passionately, denied its validity on the grounds that the theory of infantile sexuality is based on the fantasies of neurotic individuals. Such objections can now be seen in their true light, namely, as the repressions of patriarchal individuals masquerading as scientific empiricism.

The evidence provided by Malinowski and others also shows that where the repressions and taboos of patriarchy do not apply, infantile sexuality is openly manifested and freely practised. This does not only confirm the reality of infantile sexuality but also the mechanisms of repression operating in cultures which are subject to the Oedipus complex and its patriarchal Superego. The proposition, however, that the Oedipus complex precedes and is a condition for all civilisation rests upon the mistake of equating patriarchy with civilisation.

In 1924, Ernest Jones wrote a paper in reply to Malinowski's views in which he defended the classical psychoanalytic theory of the primacy and fundamentality of the Oedipus complex.* In support of his hypothesis, Ernest Jones draws to a considerable extent upon the material from the Trobriand Islanders, but differs from Malinowski in regard to the central theme and reaffirms Freud's theory of the Oedipus complex as a fundamental, in fact, primordial phenomenon. While he recognised Malinowski's field data as in themselves interesting, he did not think that they pointed to the need for an important theoretical revision of the psychoanalytic framework. He asserted that matrilineal social organisations can be seen as a defence against the father-son ambivalence which is universally characteristic of the Oedipus complex. He argues that the apparent ignorance of the father's role in procreation is due to a repression of the hatred towards the father by repudiating the father's part in coitus and procreation and, consequently, softening and deflecting the hatred against him. The attitudes of awe, dread, respect, and repressed hostility, which are inseparable from the idea of the father image, are transferred upon the maternal uncle, who becomes the scapegoat, so to speak, upon whom all the aggression and fear can be heaped, thus making it possible for the father to lead a friendly and pleasant existence within the household. In this way we have a 'decomposition' of the primal father into a kind and lenient actual father, on the one hand and a stern and moral uncle on the other. In other words the combination of mother right and ignorance of the processes of procreation (as distinct from famili-

---

* Ernest Jones: 'Psychoanalysis and Anthropology', 1924.

arity with sexuality) protects both father and son from their rivalry and hostility.

For Ernest Jones the Oedipus Complex remains fundamental and the matrilineal system a mode of defence against the primordial Oedipus tendencies. The chief point at issue here is that Jones regarded the Oedipus Complex as the cause, and the whole social structure as its effect.

The question whether the Oedipus Complex, with its instinctual repression and resulting neuroticisms is a necessary condition of all cultures, or whether there can be a social order able to safeguard the instinctual needs of man without sexual repression and neurotic conflict, has divided psychoanalytically orientated anthropologists and sociologists into two opposing camps.

On one hand we have Malinowski, Reich and Fromm among others, affirming this possibility and pointing to matrilineal societies as an example and as model for a non-repressive culture and, on the other side Freud, Ernest Jones, Geza Roheim and Erik H. Erikson upholding the inevitability of instinctual repression as a pre-condition of all possible cultures.

Reich and Erich Fromm maintain that a non-repressive social order can exist, and that it is our task to transform civilisation so that it permits sex affirmation and instinctual gratification; that such a society could solve, for the first time, some of the problems which oppress men's lives, and which transformed a large part of human history into a battlefield of sado-masochistic conflicts.

Among the anthropologists who were entirely devoted to Freud's cultural theories Geza Roheim was probably the most brilliant as well as the most thorough investigator. It was his ambition to make psychoanalytic anthropology into a new scientific discipline, and he applied psychoanalytic categories to anthropological investigations both as a theoretician as well as field-worker in a single-minded and relentless manner.

In the spring of 1928 Princess George of Greece (Marie Bonaparte) financed a field trip to enable Roheim to undertake the first psychoanalysis of primitive people. He undertook this trip which took him to Australia and the Normanby Islands largely in order to refute the claim of anthropologists such as Malinowski that the Oedipus Complex is not universal and, in particular, that it is absent in matrilineal cultures. As a psychoanalyst, Roheim initiated a new method in anthropological field work. He made the usual attempts to observe social structure, economic institutions and public ritual, but he devoted by far the largest part of his time and energy to analysing individuals. He maintained that in order to understand a society thoroughly, we must study it in its individuals.* To accomplish this task Roheim employed several different techniques. First, he attempted to psychoanalyse individual primitives largely by means of the interpretation of their dreams. Individual analysis was complemented by a general study of the sexual lives of the natives. And, finally, Roheim adopted from Melanie Klein the technique of play analysis which provided an excellent method for observing the all-important processes of childhood personality formation. In consequence of his field researches Roheim developed his ontogenetic theory of culture which contended that cultural differences were a product of infantile traumas. Each culture has certain prevalent patterns of child rearing which produce infantile traumas and conflicts characteristic of that culture. The infantile traumas experienced by the members of a culture and shared by them evoke certain typical reaction formations, certain modes of repression, sublimation, fantasies, certain types of Superego and, above all, certain characteristic symbols which create myths, religions, moral concepts as well as political and economic ideas. The imagery and the fairy tales of childhood and the shared mythological fantasies of adults provide members of a society with a common understanding of the world and of their relationship to each other; they provide the foundation for their collective consciousness and common evaluation of events, of their rights and their duties.

Roheim considered the political and economic structures of a society not as something objectively or merely externally given but as the product of psychic processes, symbols and myths projected upon the outside world. In contradistinction to the Marxist psychoanalysts like Reich and Fromm, who have struggled for years to achieve a synthesis between Marx and Freud, Roheim considered the Marxist view of the fundamentality of economic conditions to be grossly inadequate. Considering the complexity and power of psychological processes and their overriding influence on men's perception and experience of the world, he ridiculed the idea originally derived from Montesquieu that behavioural and cultural

---

* Geza Roheim: Psychoanalysis of Primitive Cultural Types.

differences could be entirely traced to environmental differences. On the contrary, he adopted a self-consciously anti-Marxist stance and declared Marx's notion of economic conditions as the substructure and cultural psychological processes as their superstructure to be thoroughly naive and dogmatic.

It is interesting to note that many of those psychoanalysts who in the 1920s and 1930s opposed the Freudian concept of Thanatos as well as the universality of the Oedipus complex were Marxists. They held that the Oedipus complex as well as the so-called death drive were psychological phenomena brought about by social conditions, and that it would be erroneous to understand them without reference to socio-economic forces in society. Reich, Fromm and Bernfeldt, upheld the Marxist view that cultural and ideological processes were based upon the economic structure of society. In contradistinction to the so-called vulgar Marxists however, they were convinced that the psychological processes which psychoanalysis had uncovered represented the link between economic base and cultural superstructure; the secret roots of cultural consciousness and political ideology.

In his Marxist period, Reich saw the development of the human psyche and, in particular, the formation of character as a result and the reflection of the prevailing social order: "In class society the ruling class secures its position with the aid of education and the institution of the family, by making its ideologies the ruling ideologies of all members of the society. But it is not merely a matter of imposing ideologies, attitudes and concepts on the members of society. Rather it is a matter of a deep-reaching process in each new generation, of the formation of a psychic structure which corresponds to the existing social order, in all strata of the population. Scientific psychology, then, has a sharply defined task: it has to discover the means and mechanisms by way of which social existence is transformed into psychic structure and with that, into ideology. One has to distinguish the social production of ideologies from their reproduction in the members of the society. To study the social production of ideologies is the task of sociology and economics, to study their reproduction in the members of society is the task of psychoanalytic characterology. Characterology has to study the effects of the immediate economic situation (food, housing, clothing, work process), as well as the effects of the so-called social superstructure, that is, of morality, laws and institutions on the instinctual apparatus; it must define as completely as possible the many intermediate links between 'material basis' and 'ideological superstructure'. Ever since society was split into the owners of the means of production and the owners of the commodity working power, every social order has been established by the former, with disregard or against the will of the latter. Because this order forms the psychic structure of all members of society, it reproduces itself in people".

As Reich turned away from Marxist ideology he came nearer to Roheim's ontogenetic theory of culture, and they shared an insistence upon the significance of child-rearing practices for the formation of cultural processes. However, he continued to maintain his opposition to the notion that the very existence of culture is based on the repression of the instincts. He agreed with Freud that the culture of today is based on sexual repression, but he insisted on asking the next question: Is cultural development as such entirely based upon sexual repression and could it not be that it is only this culture, i.e. patriarchal culture, which is based on the denial of natural instincts? He maintained that Freud's discovery of infantile sexuality and of the processes of sexual repression was, sociologically speaking, the first beginning of an awareness of the denial of sex which had existed for thousands of years. The period of authoritarian patriarchy of the last four to six thousand years has not only suppressed natural sexuality but also created the secondary, perverse sexuality of the human being of today. It has also created an economic structure dedicated to the exploitation of men and the creation of class society.

The instinctual energy repressed by patriarchal culture has produced authoritarian structures elaborated and consolidated in modern Nation states, in their class divisions and economic systems dedicated to the exploitation of human labour for profit, and in the competition between Nations and the compulsion to wage wars. Both Reich and Fromm became convinced that capitalism merely utilised the deep-seated authoritarian and repressive forces which it found operating in society. The authoritarian social system and the submissive attitudes of the masses were not caused by capitalism but were the necessary pre-condition for the operation of capitalist economics and its social relationships.

These debates between Freud, Jones and Roheim on the one side and Malinowski, Reich and Fromm on the other have clarified the proposition that it is not culture as such but more specifically patriarchal culture which demands instinctual renunciation. The libido energy repressed by this culture has on the one hand been transformed into the symbols and aims of civilisation, with its religious aspirations, its art and its political ideologies, and on the other hand, into destructive compulsions: the duality of Heaven and Hell, of Sundays and Workdays, of Ideal and Reality and the Sacred and Profane, which characterise civilisation as we know it: the dialectic between the yearning for human co-operation, peace and universal morality and the rage that finds its outlet in the quest for power over others, tribal as well as national paranoia and its unremitting compulsion for warfare.

The need to submit to authority and wage wars against other nations is accompanied by the urge to rebel against the own authority, often by supporting the enemy—the other authorities. This polarity of patriarchal culture is epitomised by the soldier and the revolutionary, the good citizen who, acting in obedience to his nation, kills its enemies, and the rebellious and disobedient citizen, who is intent upon destroying the authority of his own nation and proclaims universal peace and friendship towards its enemies. They are the permanent poles of the patriarchal conflict, the constant dialectic between obedience and rebellion, between nationalism and class war.

The psychological processes operating both in individuals as well as in societies can thus be seen not as universal and necessary characteristics of men as a species but of men as members of patriarchal culture. This does not invalidate in any way the observations of psychoanalysis but relates them to the fabric of patriarchy. The observations of psychoanalysis apply to the psychic processes of a culture which has been predominant for thousands of years and whose fundamental characteristics are shared by all members, whatever nation or class, religion or political party they may belong to. That the mechanism of the Oedipus complex has general validity, is due to the fact that patriarchal culture has become universal in our time insofar as it has in effect conquered all other cultures.

The question arises whether the contemporary matriarchal organisations, as found among a number of primitive societies such as the Trobriand Islanders, are the survivals of an ancient culture of matriarchy that has preceded the culture of patriarchy; whether indeed one can speak of a matriarchal period in human history which was defeated and replaced by the patriarchal order; furthermore one can ask, why did this transformation between the two cultures occur and how did it happen? Can we find any evidence for an historic conflict, or battle, between matriarchy and patriarchy, and what changes in the psychological, social and economic structures resulted from it? While there is plenty of anthropological evidence for matriarchal structures in various primitive societies existing at present or, at least, up to very recent times, this does not make it necessary to assume that this type of culture reigned supreme in an ancient period of man's social evolution and that it historically preceded the culture of patriarchy.

THE BATTLE BETWEEN MATRIARCHY AND PATRIARCHY

It was the Swiss historian, J. J. Bachofen, who in his monumental work 'Mother Right' set out to prove the existence of an ancient matriarchal culture and its supercession by patriarchy. He regarded the transformation from matriarchy to patriarchy as the most significant event in the history of civilisation. In his wide-ranging studies of the folklore, religion and rituals of the Cretans, Egyptians, Athenians and many Asiatic peoples, he gathered evidence for the predominance of Gynocratic or matricentric societies in ancient times. Furthermore, he drew our attention to the drama of the Ancient Greeks as particularly illuminating presentations of the conflict between the two cultures.

Aeschylus and Sophocles can be considered not only the greatest of the Greek playwrights but in their dramatic proclamations of the values of patriarchy as among the most powerful and impressive dramatists of the Western World. Aeschylus' 'Oresteia' and Sophocles' 'Oedipus' represent two different aspects of patriarchal culture, each of fundamental importance. The first, written forty years before the other, is almost entirely concerned with overcoming the demands of matriarchal morality and with the struggle for superiority between the mother and father in the moral and juridical order of society; whereas the latter, having seen the victory of patriarchy, sets out to propound its most powerful taboos, namely, those concerning the sexual bonds between mother and son. Both dramatists propagate the necessity for men to be weaned from their dependency upon their mothers, first in terms of law and morality and second in terms of emotional and sexual bonds which have to be overcome if the new civilisation, the new world-view, is to remain victorious.

It is interesting to note that Freud almost never mentions the 'Oresteia' of Aeschylus, although he was obviously acquainted with it, as if he wished to avoid having to take notice of the struggle between matriarchy and patriarchy which it presented; it would have made it necessary for him to acknowledge that patriarchal culture was neither universal nor inevitable but had to achieve its supremacy in an historic battle against a much older culture whose precepts and taboos were of a different order. As Bachofen has stated: "The advance from the maternal conception of mankind to a paternal conception was the most important turning-point in history which brought with it fundamental changes in the psycho-social orientations of human beings".

We have seen from the investigations of contemporary matriarchal cultures that they are governed by a gynocracy, that is, a blood-bond between the members of a family or group to their mothers. Being the mother's offspring unites members of a group into a community, whereas the father is considered as a friend, guest, helper, without any significant legal importance for the group's cohesion. It is a community of blood relationship that relates the children to the mother, the members of the group to the womb from which they have sprung.

The blood-bond symbolises the love between the mother and her offspring, promoting a sense of brotherhood and equality, whose governing principles are not fear or sacrifice but love and compassion. Bachofen himself graphically describes these traits: "The relationship which stands at the origin of all culture, of every virtue, of every nobler aspect of existence is that between mother and child; it operates as the divine principle of love, of union, of peace. Raising her young, the woman learns earlier than the man to extend her loving care beyond the limits of the Ego to another creature and to direct whatever gift of invention she possesses to the preservation and improvement of the other's existence. Woman at this stage is the repository of all culture, of all benevolence, of all devotion, of all concern for the living and grief for the dead. Yet the love that arises from motherhood is not only more intense but also more universal; whereas the paternal principle is inherently restrictive, the maternal principle is universal. The idea of mother-hood produces a sense of universal fraternity among all men, which dies with the development of paternity. Every woman's womb, the mortal image of the earth mother Demeter, will give brothers and sisters to the children of every other woman; the homeland will know only brothers and sisters until the day when the development of the paternal system dissolves the undifferentiated unity of the mass and introduces principle of articulation".*

"The matricentric complex", as Fromm has remarked, "is characterised by a feeling of optimistic trust in mother's uncondi-tional love, far fewer guilt feelings than those shown by patricentric individuals, a far weaker Superego and a greater capacity for pleasure and happiness. Along with these traits there also develops the ideal of motherly compassion and love for the weak and others in need of help".**

On the other hand the good and benevolent mother goddess can turn into a ruthless Fury if the law of the blood is offended against. The benign and kindly Demeter turns into the Furies, the Erinyes, divinities personifying the rage of the mother against the trans-gressor of her laws. Aeschylus and other Greek dramatists have shown that the concept of justice which prevailed among the pre-Olympian cultures was based upon the principle of revenge. It was the function of the Furies to hound the offender in his dreams and in his imagination, and to pursue him until vengeance was executed. Their horrible aspect and relentless cruelty were sharply exposed by Aeschylus in his 'Oresteia'. Apollo makes a devastating attack upon the inconsistencies and inadequacies of their code of justice; while they will punish a son who does not take revenge for any harm done to his mother and punish equally a son who kills her, they will ignore the guilt of a wife who kills her husband because he is not her blood relation. This is an intolerable position as it implies a deep contempt of the marriage bond which was fundamental and sacred to the new order; it also shows that the Furies' concept of justice is based upon the blind demands of instinct and is incapable of taking into consideration the com-plexities of individual cases. Moreover, under their dispensation, a

---

* J. J. Bachofen: 'Myth, Religion and Mother Right'.
** Erich Fromm: 'The Theory of Mother Right and its relevance for Social Psychology' (1970).

single murder may lead to an insoluble blood feud and an endless series of murders in successive generations. On the whole the old religions provided no safe moral guide, the quest for justice received no solution from the ancient mother goddesses.

In the 'Oresteia', Aeschylus shows how the rule of revenge becomes a ruthless and inescapable fate that haunts society, and he sets out to show a way by which the ancient concept of justice and its chain of violence can be replaced by a higher code of law and morality, governed by reason and persuasion, by intellect rather than the blind forces of instinct. He intends, furthermore, to prove to the citizens of Athens that this new code of law is associated with the rule of the father, with the emergent patriarchic culture. In the first play of the Oresteia, Clytemnestra kills her husband Agamemnon in order to gain revenge for his murder of their daughter Iphigenia. He had sacrificed her to the goddess Artemis in order to assure his success in the war against Troy. By this act he outraged Clytemnestra's motherhood and by his ten years absence in wars and conquests, which he deemed more important than the needs of his wife, he also outraged her femininity. Clytemnestra becomes a murderess, a Fury, a witch, and her son Orestes kills her to avenge the murder of his father.

The third play of the trilogy confronts the problem of justice which centres around the crime and guilt of Orestes. It has to be established who is more important in the family, in society, mother or father. The traditional dominance of the mother under the gynocratic order has to be broken and the superior importance of the father in the family, and in the state, unequivocally established. His claims to a higher level of intellectuality and his capacity of reasoned persuasion had to be illustrated by a rational victory over the instinct-dominated demands for revenge. The representatives of the new order had to be seen not merely to be more powerful but on a higher level of rationality. Not violence but holy persuasion had to assure victory in order to validate the new dispensation. The Furies represent the old order, while Apollo and Athene represent the new. The former haunt and pursue Orestes and demand his blood, whereas Apollo defends him. The Furies claim that his crime is much more horrible than that of Clytemnestra for in killing his mother he outraged the laws of blood, whereas Clytemnestra's crime is less serious for her murder of her husband did not violate the blood-bond since the husband is not a blood relation.

In the climax of 'The Eumenides', in the trial scene, we have a long argument between the Furies and Apollo on the respective rights and status of mother or father in marriage and parenthood. Apollo states succinctly the case for the father and tries to show that the traditional ideas of the blood-bond between mother and child are incorrect:

Apollo: This too I answer; mark the truth of what I say.
          The mother is not the true parent of the child
          Which is called hers. She is a nurse who tends the growth
          Of young seed planted by its true parent, the male.
          So, if Fate spares the child, she keeps it, as one might
          Keep for some friend a growing plant.

After Athene has cast her decisive vote in favour of Orestes, thereby defeating the claims of the old order, the Furies threaten to revenge themselves upon Athene:

Chorus: The old is trampled by the new!
          Curse on you younger gods who override
          The ancient laws and rob me of my due!
          Now to appease the honour you reviled
          Vengeance shall fester till my full heart pours
          Over this land on every side
          Anger for insult, poison for my pain—
          Yes, poison from whose killing rain
          A sterile blight shall creep on plant and child
          And pock the earth's face with infectious sores.
          Why should I weep? Hear, Justice, what I do!
          Soon Athens in despair shall rue
          Her rashness and her mockery.
          Daughters of Night and Sorrow, come with me,
          Feed on dishonour, on revenge to be!

Athene implores them to accept the new law, declaims its virtues and offers them an honoured abode in a sacred cave below the ground:

Athene: Let persuasion check
          The fruit of foolish threats before it falls to spread
          Plague and disaster. Calm this black and swelling wrath;
          Honour and dignity await you: share with me

A home in Athens. You will yet applaud my words,
When Attica's wide fields bring you their first-fruit gifts,
When sacrifice for childbirth and for marriage-vows
Is made upon your altars in perpetual right.

...And I tell you this: if you
Now make some other land your home, your thoughts will turn
With deep desire to Athens. For the coming age
Shall see her glory growing yet more glorious.
You, here possessing an exalted sanctuary
Beside Erechtheus' temple, shall receive from all,
Both men and women, honours which no other land
Could equal. Therefore do not cast upon my fields
Whetstones of murder, to corrupt our young men's hearts
And make them mad with passions not infused by wine;
Nor plant in them the temper of the mutinous cock,
To set within my city's walls man against man
With self-destructive boldness, kin defying kin.
Let war be with the stranger, at the stranger's gate;
There let men fall in love with glory; but at home
Let no men fight.

Thus 'holy persuasion' and respect for the commands of reason is to replace the old forms of justice dominated by the blind forces of revenge, and democracy—as we understand it—was born.

After having extolled the ancient virtues of matriarchy, Bachofen goes on to remind his readers of the spiritual superiority of the patriarchal system: "In matriarchal cultures we have confinement to instinct and the demands of nature, in patriarchal culture we have intellectual and spiritual development. In the former we have unconscious lawfulness, in the latter individualism. In the former we find exultation in the abandonment to nature, in the latter we find exultation above nature, a breaking of the old barriers and a powerful striving of Promethean life replacing the constant rest, peaceful pleasure and eternal infantilism. Here man breaks through the bonds of his childhood and lifts his eyes to the higher regions of the cosmos".

Who can, however, fail to reflect that two thousand five hundred years after the birth of Greek democracy, the ancient fantasies of blood tie and its politics of revenge continue in various guises to defy Athenian justice? The ancient mother goddesses have been driven underground but not finally vanquished. As long as patriarchal cultures are based upon the repression of mother-orientated instincts, Demeter will continue to lure man's romantic imagination and the Furies will demand revenge against the domination and authority of the Fathers. They wait in their underground lairs, in the unconscious regions of man's mind to erupt upon the surface whenever the patriarchal structure shows signs of weakness; then they will emerge and strive to acquire once again domination over the thoughts and actions of men. The mother-dominated dreams of the childhood of humanity continue to exercise their appeal upon the mind and upon the body-politic, whether it be in the dreams of the classless society—the modern version of the country of milk and honey where bountiful mother-nature provides for her children and fulfils their needs without discrimination or, on the other side, as the politics of revenge which provides ideological justification for destruction and terror. The Furies emerge in the political arena in the form of fascist nationalism as well as revolutionary terrorism; the one intent upon the destruction of the enemies of the Nation who threaten its soil and violate the bonds of blood, the other committed to destroy and liquidate Capitalist exploiters who have deprived men of their birthright to enjoy the wealth of the Earth.

The bonds of blood and the sanctity of the soil—the national territory—have found their ultimate expression in the obscenities of Nazism. The cry for revenge against the polluters of the pure blood of the race, against the inferior races who "infiltrate the life-cells of the Nation and destroy all that is strong and healthy", and who threaten the purity of the motherland have led to a demand for the annihilation of Jews, Gypsies, Capitalists and Bolsheviks—all those who threaten the Nation from within and from without. These were the fantasies which motivated a great Nation to follow an insane Leader, who managed to express the dreams of the deep, the images which have survived over the Millennia in the underground regions of civilised Nations. Blood and soil—the ancient call of Demeter—which has turned into the rage of the Furies, still rings in our ears as the ultimate abomination of the twentieth century.

Barely has the world recovered from the bloodbath--the Holocaust—the murder of some thirty million people, the destruction of towns, and countries, and from a deep injury to the self-respect of Western Civilisation and, once more, the horrible cry of the Furies is heard. For they have infiltrated the revolutionary movements and transformed them into instruments of terror; revenge against the capitalist system and imperialism inspires terrorist movements to bring "poison and sterile blight" upon society.

Everywhere the principles of freedom and rationality have degenerated into the forces of revenge, the ancient cry of the Erinyes erupting through the thin veneer of Apollonian justice. While purporting to promote socialism, with its claims of being the highest form of western rationalism, the ultimate development of its philosophy and ethics, the rulers of Russia use socialist revolutionary movements as an instrument for the defence and expansion of the power of Mother Russia. It is no longer the class consciousness of the educated workers and intelligentsia that is seen as the avant-garde of world socialism. In a political directive written in 1977, E. C. Pyrlin, the chief expert on Russia's Near East policy, stated that: "Arab countries would evolve towards communism not through class conscious rejection of capitalism but through anti-imperialist nationalism". His essential message was that, if properly handled, Arab nationalism could be harnessed to Soviet policy objectives. The shift towards the emphasis upon nationalistic and revanchist sentiments in the battle for socialism is illustrated by the 'Work Plan', issued by the K.G.B. to its recruiting agents in the Middle East. It details the qualities agents should look for among potential spies: hostility to imperialism, national and nationalistic feelings, and the personal motivations of fear and revenge.

We must recognise, however, that it is not only the female goddess who can undergo the transformation from a loving to a hating divinity but that the divine representations of patriarchy are subject to similar transformations. The patriarchal ideal of the free and just man, the man free to exercise his will, and to realise his innate potential, governed by reason and respect for others, can degenerate into barbarism where freedom is seen as a licence to deny the freedom of others, where the activation of one's will means the negation of the will and dignity of one's fellow men.

We have seen how the myth of the blood-bond became the battle-cry of the Nazis; but what made their deeds so particularly horrible was the employment of the tools of scientific objectivity which treated the murder of millions of human beings as a cold-blooded scientific enterprise. Their scientific modes of destruction were a thousand times more horrible than the rage of ancient religions. They transformed men into numbers and statistical entities upon whom destruction could be visited without any awareness of their human dignity.

The whole globe now is a battleground of the ancient instincts, applying scientific parameters for the manipulation of millions in a monstrous game of global competition between a few tribal organisations expanded into superpowers, applying the logic of games theory, statistical probability, and the "acceptable rate of dispensability of human populations". We can thus see the image of the rational and protective male degenerate into the barbarian who exercises his reason to dominate others or to destroy them. While the nations of the world proclaim the principles of Athenian justice and democracy, with science and technology proclaiming the victory of patriarchal reasoning they can serve to destroy everything that is rational. Science and technology have come to represent instrumental reasoning, i.e. reasoning directed towards the domination of nature and of human beings to gain power over them and to manipulate them. While instrumental reasoning is, or rather pretends to be value-free, it frequently serves goals which are contrary to reason. It can serve the instincts of gynocracy as well as the patriarchal males' barbaric pursuits of power; it can serve Fascist or Communist dictatorships; it can be the hireling of business or of state bureaucracies, and it can be used to manipulate human beings in order to force them into submission in the name of freedom.

The study of an ancient matriarchy, which preceded patriarchy but continues to exercise a powerful influence upon it, has shown that there is not only a patriarchal Superego but also a much older matriarchal Superego, and that, furthermore, the matriarchal as well as the patriarchal Superego can degenerate and become dominated by aggressive-destructive drives. The mother can turn into the witch and the father into the devil; witch and devil can combine to dominate the mind of individuals as well as the culture of societies, where the ideals of human love are mocked and replaced by the excitement of sadism. The question as to how the protective, loving and all-providing mother-goddess turns into a witch remains to be investigated, and it possibly presents one of the most challenging problems for psychoanalysis. But there is no doubt that the witch exists in the unconscious mind of men as she exists in the underground of our culture, casting her shadow on memories of the lost paradise of childhood and disturbing the visions of Utopia.

3 The Origins of Culture

While Freud considered the Oedipus complex as the universal and necessary foundation for the evolution of cultures, we have seen that it is the product of patriarchy and that patriarchy is not the only possible form of social organisation. Anthropological researches have increased our awareness of the immense variety of cultures, and archaeology has unearthed a vast amount of evidence of social and religious systems of a distant past of which nothing was known in Freud's time. There is now little doubt that matriarchal societies not only existed up to very recent times but that historically they preceded patriarchy. Indeed, it appears that patriarchy is a relative newcomer in man's cultural history. In subsequent chapters I shall review some of the evidence concerning the antiquity of socio-cultural developments, but let us here consider some of its implications.

There must have been long periods lasting hundreds of thousands of years before patriarchal or matriarchal cultures emerged, when myths and religions, as we understand them, were not yet established in the minds of men but, nevertheless, they had already developed the ability to work, to conduct collective forms of worship and to populate the universe with the symbols of their imagination. If, however, we are to make an attempt to formulate a single principle upon which all cultures can be based, then it would be the principle of externalisation.

We have pointed out in an earlier chapter that it is a fundamental characteristic of man that he externalises his mental processes by reproducing them outside himself in material symbols and cultural ideas. This process of externalisation of man's psychological mental activities is fundamental to all cultures; it precedes patriarchy and matriarchy, and commenced with the emergence of the human being as a species about one million years ago. It is a characteristic of man that he is a culture creator, and there are no human beings without a culture.

While Hegel and Marx spoke of externalisation (Veräusserlichung) as an aspect of alienation, I use the term to describe a fundamental human capability to work and to create his own environment, thus transforming biological evolution into cultural evolution; the mind takes over from biology as the agent of evolution. Man's capacity for work and to make tools has long been recognised as the fundamental quality that characterises the human being and sets it apart from the animal kingdom. But this characteristic has been taken for granted, as if it somehow appeared on the evolutionary scene ready-made, and its psychobiological development, the reasons for its emergence, has received very scant attention. How this basic human characteristic developed is however of enormous importance for a proper understanding of human cultures and also of the psyche of individuals.

Due to the enormous expansion of the prefrontal areas and of the visual area of the cortex, man can have an image of an experience even if it does not actually happen, he can see himself doing something even if he is not actually doing it. He can experience sensations and impulses in his mouth, hands and fingers, for instance, and enact those impulses in his imagination. He can conceptualise and visualise possible or potential actions and anticipate future situations and deal with them in his imagination. (The future exists in the present as an imaginary condition and in turn the present is influenced by the images of the future.) Thus he can engage in a great number of different activities in his mind, compare their usefulness, and choose the best one before he commits himself to action. The enormous value of this capability from the point of view of natural selection and adjustment to the environment is quite obvious. It has indeed allowed man to make adjustments and modifications of behaviour in a few minutes or even seconds, which would take other organisms subject to instinctual responses many thousands of years of natural selection.

However, man cannot only initiate his own natural selection by doing experiments in his mind, he can also experience his own impulses and motor sensations in objects, that is to say, he can project his peripheral and motor sensations upon external objects. He can not only imagine his fists gripping and his claws tearing but he can project these images and their sensations upon objects and imagine them capable of such actions.

As he wishes his fingernails, which are so important for cutting, piercing and scratching, to be firm and powerful, he can identify certain stones as potential fingernails, visualise them as symbolic claws and see them doing the claws' work even more powerfully and efficiently than his own. Thus, certain stones will acquire the vitality of his own organs; he can externalise the sensations of his own cutting and tearing organs upon such objects and make them into tools. Similarly he can project the urges and sensations of his fists and his forearms upon other types of stones. He will make a stone to represent his fist and he will make a handle to go with the stone in the image of his forearm, and he will produce a hammer or a club. So, he will invest external objects with the emotional experiences of his own motor organs, he will recognise a stone as a potential claw or fist. This 'recognition' can be seen as the objectivation of concepts. In the stone there is hidden, as Plato would have said, the idea of the tool, the essence of the tool, which the worker or sculptor has to bring out of the stone.

The ability to 'recognise' a human motor organ in a stone or a stick implies the ability to project the sensations and impulses of peripheral organs upon external objects. The projection of subjective sensations upon an object imbues the object with subjectivity; it will be perceived as being alive and endowed with impulses and sensations. (Needless to say, these processes of visual as well as sensory projections are unconscious; what a man is aware of is the act of recognition.) In the making of the tool man recreates an organ in the material object and endows it with life. A spear represents flight; it represents an arm that follows its own impulses and becomes free from the body; the spearhead represents the claw that tears at objects, the tooth that penetrates; spear and spearhead represent the satisfaction of the movement of flight and the power to penetrate the flesh of the quarry or an enemy.

However, these processes of projection and externalisation are not confined to the sensations and images of the motor organs but equally apply to the deeper emotions and psychological processes; man can recognise them in a wide range of natural objects, in living and inanimate things. Here we must say a few words about symbolisation and symbols.

A symbol represents both concepts as well as urges and feelings made recognisable in the form of visual images. Every emotion and every idea subjectively experienced finds its visual representation in a symbol. Man will make efforts to reproduce these symbolic images by means of drawing, painting, sculpting and building, and he will also seek to find representations of his symbolic images in external objects of nature; trees, flowers, the sky, the sun, clouds, meadows, clearings in forests symbolise states of mind which we project onto them. A tree can be seen as a powerful and proud being symbolising the unyielding strength of a male, a flower the delicate maiden tentatively presenting her erotic sensations to the world; delighting in its delight and celebrating by its colours the excitement of yearning and desire, it can be brazen or blushing with shyness, and vulnerable and delicate by its openness, liable to be threatened by the violence of passion and the insensitive possessiveness of man.

A whole host of fantasies and, indeed, unconscious complexes and fears are projected upon the objects of nature. According to the state of mind or character of the onlooker, a flower can be also the symbol of dangerous sensuality of the voluptuous and teasing female, the exciting colours and sensual shapes threatening the austere spirituality of the male; it can be a threat as well as a celebration according to the states of mind of an individual or the cultural values dominant in a society. A tree, as we have said, can represent the mind and character of the well-rooted and secure male, asserting his strength and unflinching powers to the world, but it can also represent by its branches the horrifying arms and claws of a vengeful monster or witch. It is said, however, that a tree is a phenomenon of nature, not possessed of a mind and fantasies, composed of wood, roots and leaves, and that it has nothing at all to do with such projected fantasies. This empirical point of view may be perfectly true, and if it has dominance over the mind of a person who sees the tree then he will deny all its symbolic emotional aspects, he will see it as a scientific phenomenon or, if he happens to be a merchant, as a source of revenue which can be statistically or economically evaluated or, if he is a friend of the earth, as an essential provider of oxygen for living organisms on this earth and, as such, to be protected from commercial exploiters.

While such people would consider themselves to be entirely empirical it would be difficult to deny that they do project their own particular conceptual and emotional attitudes on the tree. Even the strict empiricist cannot entirely obliterate the symbolic meanings of a tree or flower which will re-emerge in his dreams or pre-conscious fantasies.

Indeed, we can say the animistic world-view with its spirits and souls, fairies and monsters no longer appears in the conscious mind of man. Having long been ousted by religions and scientific cultures it continues to lead an underground existence, mostly on the unconscious level but occasionally re-awakened by artists and mystics.

Thus man is an organism that can externalise itself. He can be inside himself and outside himself. What is more, he can view and think himself from outside himself. (What Hegel has called the objectivity of the spirit or the God who can have a view of man, are manifestations of self-externalisation.) Man can feel himself in the things he creates and he can, in turn, be alienated from the things he has created and become a stranger to them. Externalisation is the basis for toolmaking and work, animism, totemism, God-worship and ideologies.

Self-externalisation is possibly one of the most extraordinary capacities of human beings, one that definitely differentiates them from all other animals. It would be intriguing to ask just how and when this capacity in the ape, who became man, emerged and developed. In so far as externalisation is basic to the toolmaking ability of man, we can trace it back to the Middle Lower Pleistocene, to Homo Pithecanthropus erectus and Homo Pekinensis. These two races, who belonged to the same species, are reckoned to have lived in Java and China between one million years and seven hundred thousand years ago. They are widely considered to be the first known members of the species 'Homo' and were definitely toolmakers. Also the volume of their skulls was far superior to any known previous species, ranging from 750 cubic centimetres in the earliest Pithecanthropus to 1,150 in the later Homo Pekinensis. In so far as I link the toolmaking capacity to the process of externalisation, I would say that these early men developed externalisation processes and, in so doing, laid the foundation for the further mental and physical development of the human species.

As a tool is an objectivation of an urge or impulse, so the sound expressing an emotion will become an object representation of an emotion. Thus certain emotions or needs would be externalised in certain sounds, and would be recognised by these sounds. Human sounds would begin to 'exist' in the world, and a proliferation of sound symbols, each binding a definite emotion or intention, and a whole system and structure of sounds, an increasing complexity of sounds, will gradually emerge as 'objects', i.e. words, presenting an ever wider range of emotive meanings. As man has learnt to handle the environment by means of tools, he has also learnt to handle his needs by means of oral expression, communication through sound tools, sound objects and to use and elaborate them eventually into language. Wittgenstein in his flashes of genius considered words as tools, as use objects, and frequently asserted that the meaning of a word lies in its use. But he failed to understand that tools symbolise impulses, represent drives, and give them expression. I do not wish here to indulge in theories of language but merely to throw out a suggestion that with the powerful stimulus to conceptualisation which emerged with toolmaking, the ground would be laid for language formation. I think it is true to say that without the capacity to make tools, i.e. the capacity of externalisation, language could not have arisen.

PREHISTORY AND THE UNCONSCIOUS: THE ARCHAEOLOGY OF THE MIND

But we want to ask what made this evolutionary jump, the emergence of culture and, therefore, of humanity, possible. We now know a fair amount about the climatic and ecological changes that occurred at that time, but we know next to nothing about the psychological, the psychosomatic processes which took place in the mind of our ancestor destined to become human. Of course, we cannot psychoanalyse our early ancestors in order to understand their psychological responses to the changes in their environment, but the insights we have gained from psychoanalytical studies of contemporary individuals and especially of the earliest years of their lives, their psychological prehistory, so to speak, may provide us with a conceptual tool by which we can interpret the archaeological evidence and make some reasonable inferences about the psychological experiences of primitive men. Such comparative studies can in turn enhance our understanding of the deep and mostly unconscious motivations of modern man and his societies.

Freud has often spoken of psychoanalysis as the science of men's prehistory, as the archaeology of the mind. By this he meant the study of a person's earliest psychic development, the prehistory of the individual, in so far as the early stages of his development lie beyond his consciousness, beyond his awareness of his own history. But he also linked the prehistory of individual developments with the prehistory of the species, and considered the interrelationship between the history of the species with the history of the individual as one of the important biological foundations of psychoanalytic theory.

During the late 1890s Freud sought to relate the predominant fantasies which he found among most of his patients—the so-called primal fantasies—to a prehistoric reality, and came to formulate his concept of a prehistoric content of neurosis. The fundamental neurotic traits which appeared to be common to humanity could be traced back, he felt, to our common prehistory as part of our phylogenetic endowment (phylogenesis—the evolution of the species.) He broached this issue at some length in his 'Introductory Lectures' (1916–17): "I believe that the primal fantasies, as I should like to call them, are a phylogenetic endowment. In them the individual reaches beyond his own experience into primeval experience and points where his own experience has been too rudimentary... I have been repeatedly led to suspect that the psychology of the neuroses has stored up in it more of the antiquities of human development than any other source".

Freud's eagerness to provide an historical and phylogenetic explanation for certain aspects of mental disturbance was not entirely the result of his own speculations but was largely influenced by Darwin's work on child psychology and the researches done by his successors. Indeed, in 1897 Freud exclaimed: "It is interesting that writers are now turning so much to child psychology. Today I received another book on the subject by James Mark Baldwin. So one still remains a child of one's own age, even with something one had thought was one's very own".

Darwin's observations on the emotions of children had a direct influence on Freud. Darwin's evolutionary concern with documenting the mental continuity between man and lower animals led him as early as 1838 to propose the 'natural history of babies' as a fruitful topic for future enquiries. He kept a detailed, and to begin with, day by day record of his first-born's mental and behavioural development for at least the first years of life. When the family grew (eventually to ten children, eight of whom survived infancy), Darwin studied the comparative rate of development exhibited by his various children's mental faculties.

It was fully in keeping both with the growing interest in child development in the latter part of the nineteenth century and with this field's intimate relevance to evolutionary theory that Darwin decided to publish these observations in the first formal journal of psychology, 'Mind', founded in 1876. 'A Biographical Sketch of an Infant' (1877) traces the early development of motor phenomena, the emotions (notably anger, fear, pleasure and affection), reasoning capabilities, the moral sense and the ability to communicate. When Darwin took his two-year old son to the London Zoological Gardens, he was surprised to observe the child's fear of larger and more exotic animals. "May we not suspect", Darwin conjectured, "that the vague but very real fears of childhood, which are quite independent of experience, are the inherited affects of real dangers and abject superstitions during ancient savage times?" Darwin's position on inherited childhood fears was later reiterated by the American psychologist and ardent Darwinian, G. Stanley Hall, in his 1914 publication 'A Synthetic Genetic Study of Fear'. Freud, in turn, enlisted the support of both Hall and Darwin in likewise arguing that many childhood fears, especially phobias, are phylogenetically endowed. Among those of Darwin's successors who had a particular influence on Freud we might mention George Romanes (1848–94).

In 1888 Romanes published a study on child development entitled 'Mental Evolution in Man', which was read and carefully annotated by Freud, probably during the early 1890s. His main objective in this work was to demonstrate to psychologists man's naturalistic descent from ape-like progenitors. Romanes was a whole-hearted supporter of Ernst Haeckel's famous biogenetic law, according to which the development of the species is recapitulated in the development of the embryo, and beyond, that the psychological development of the race is to a great extent recapitulated in the psychological development of the individual.

It was a short step for Freud to maintain that the prehistoric experiences of our race are reproduced in the unconscious layers of the individual mind. Freud's implicit endorsement of the biogenetic law—ontogeny (the development of the individual) recapitulates phylogeny (the development of the species)—constitutes perhaps the least appreciated source of a prior biological influence in all psychoanalytical theory. In his 'Introductory Lectures on Psychoanalysis' Freud wrote: "In forming our judgment of the two courses of instinctual development, both of the Ego and of the libido, we must lay emphasis on a consideration which has not often hitherto been taken into account. For both of them are at bottom heritages, abbreviated recapitulations of the development which all mankind has passed through from its primeval days over long periods of time. In the case of the development of the libido, the phylogenetic origin is, I venture to think, immediately obvious". The American psychologist, James Mark Baldwin, put the case for the biogenetic law in evolution succinctly in his book 'Mental Development in the Child and the Race' (1895) when he wrote: "The infant is an embryo person... and he is in these early stages plainly recapitulating the items in the social history of the race... the embryology of society is open to study in the nursery."

Freud was familiar with the work of Baldwin and referred to it briefly in his 'Three Essays on the Theory of Sexuality'. Freud's conviction that there is an historical and phylogenetic explanation for many aspects of mental disturbances was clearly shown in an hypothesis he set forth in a letter to Ferenczi written in 1915: "There is a series of chronological starting-points in patients which runs thus: anxiety hysteria, conversion hysteria, obsessional neurosis, dementia praecox, paranoia, melancholia, mania. This series seems to repeat phylogenetically an historical origin. What are now neuroses were once phases in human condition. With the appearance of privation in the glacial period men became apprehensive; they had every reason for transforming libido into anxiety."

We see here that Freud explores three distinct but interrelated concepts:

1)   The phylogenetic basis óf some fundamental psychological processes which he found in the analysis of individuals.

2)   The biogenetic law which proclaims that the development of the species is recapitulated in the development of the embryo and, beyond that, that the psychological development of the species is to

a great extent recapitulated in the psychological development of the individual, in particular, that the prehistoric experiences of our race are reproduced in the unconscious layers of the mind.

3) That the anxieties experienced by our ancestors during the ice ages continue to have a major impact upon our minds and are repeated in our primal fantasies and neurotic conditions.

As far as the application of the biogenetic law for an understanding of individual and social psychology is concerned, I want to say that I accept it as an important theory or, rather, as an hypothesis which still needs a lot more evidence before it can be fully accepted, and I intend to contribute to the evidence. But while I think we can trace many definite analogies and interactions between the two dimensions of evolution—phylogeny and ontogeny—one must not view ontogeny as simple reproduction of phylogeny. For the development of an individual's personality is deeply influenced by the culture in which he is reared, and it is possible to find wide divergences in the patterns of child rearing in different cultures, and within those cultures there are great variations in the character of the parents and their attitudes to the child.

While the genetic characteristics of the human species are reproduced in every individual, it is an important peculiarity of man that there is a wide range of individual variables in the unfolding of his personality. The influence of culture is superimposed upon genetic inheritance in the development of a person's psychological and behavioural characteristics, and there are many variations in the character development of individuals within a culture; the more complex or advanced cultures become, the greater the scope for personality differentials.

A culture does not only reproduce itself in each individual, but each individual in turn reproduces his culture. But in his own psyche he also reproduces its conflicts and contradictions. In his attempts to resolve those conflicts within himself he plays an important part in the transformation and development of his culture.

We are now in a far better position than Freud was at the turn of the century to attempt a reconstruction of man's psychological development, the origins and evolution of cultures and social organisations. Recent investigations into the life of Primates and the discoveries of archaeology have disclosed a vast amount of new information concerning the life of our early ancestors. We can, furthermore, look at the artefacts, tools, paintings and sculptures as symbolic manifestations of their cultures and subject them to psychoanalytic interpretation. In this way we may be able to obtain deeper insights into the mental characteristics of early men, their family relationships, their communal life and their myths and beliefs.

While in historical studies we tend to think in terms of centuries or at most millenia, we now enter into an area that spans periods of time extending over hundreds of thousands of years. I shall therefore don not seven-league boots but ten-thousand-year boots in order to cover the eons of time involved in this journey.

Part 2

4　*Beginnings*

ON LEAVING THE FOREST

One of the major criticisms levelled against Freud's theory of the primal father murder, i.e. the killing of the father by a band of brothers, is that apart from being a rather far-fetched idea it was based upon his belief in the existence of a patriarchal horde as the original condition of man's social existence. Following a suggestion by Darwin, he proposed that men originally existed in a condition which he calls the 'primal horde': a single tyrannical father dominating the family group, enjoying the favours of a number of females and excluding the sons as soon as they achieved sexual maturity.

Many modern writers claim that this theory is now repudiated by recent studies in social anthropology and, particularly, the investigations into the life of Primates. It is pointed out that the errors of many prevalent notions about the underlying causes of human behaviour, about human drives and impulses, might have been avoided if research into the lives of Primates had been carried out a century or so ago. Robin Fox of Rutgers University said that Freud recognised what most biologists and few psychoanalysts recognise today, namely, the importance of basing any theory about the origins of human behaviour on the behaviour of other Primates. Unfortunately, the best sources available to Freud were highly coloured and unreliable. John E. Pfeiffer observes: "The only evidence Freud had during the early nineteen-hundreds consisted of second- or third-hand tales about gorillas. Their basic social unit was supposed to include a single dominant male, a number of females whom he monopolized, and younger males continually trying to gain access to the females and continually being out-fought. Using such material, he conceived of a 'primal horde', the original human family made up of an all-powerful, jealous and aggressive Jehovah-like father who maintained a harem and drove his sons out of the household when they became sexual rivals, thus providing the basis for Oedipus and Electra complexes".[*] The observations of Schaller and others do not support these notions. Gorilla bands usually contain more than one adult male; the head of the hierarchy may be completely unconcerned when other males copulate with females, even those males who have only recently joined the troop, and younger males are not driven off. In fact there seems to be a very high level of tolerance towards the sexual activities of young males in the gorilla troop, and aggression of any sort is rare.

While, therefore, Freud was right to draw attention to the fundamental group structures of the great apes in order to find clues to the origin's of man's social complexes, the knowledge accumulated since his time makes it necessary for us to reconsider his ideas about the origins of social structures. In any case, the development of the Oedipus situation cannot be traced simply to the conditions which exist among the higher Primates as there are some fundamental differences between them and man. Apart from the obvious genetic and psychological differences between the species, there are two factors which are of particular interest:

1 The gorilla is a forest dweller, finding shelter in the foliage and making his nest in it.
2 He is entirely vegetarian, providing his sustenance by foraging for plants, berries and the bark of trees.

Men, on the other hand, have inhabited from earliest times the open lands of the savanna and tundra and had to become carnivorous. It is one of my main propositions that man emerged as a species when he had to leave the forest and face a world denuded of trees and forest foliage, when the plains no longer provided him with vegetarian sustenance and became barren. Both the shelter as well as nourishment of the forest disappeared and the savanna became increasingly arid, and men's ancestors had to become hunters of animals more powerful than themselves.

---

[*] John E. Pfeiffer: 'The Emergence of Man', (Thomas Nelson, 1970).

It can be said that humans are forest creatures to the extent that their basic structures, brains, sense-organs, their limbs and reproductive systems evolved in the forest. Later developments, namely, life in the open country called for modifications and elaborations of these structures rather than totally new ones. Thus the arboreal existence of the ape ancestors of man has been a necessary pre-adaptation for the emergence of human characteristics. It was the achievement of the human species to transform its basic Primate characteristics when such transformation became necessary.

In the evolution from Primate to man we can observe a number of stages: the transformation of the environment from huge unbroken forests into fertile open land—the savanna—and gradually over the millennia the erosion of the savanna and the need for man to hunt not merely occasional small animals but large animals, to become a big game hunter in order to survive.

It has been estimated that the broad sub-tropical forests which extended uninterruptedly from the west coast of Africa to the West Indies, and from South Africa to Scandinavia, from the southern tip of Australia to Siberia, began to be invaded by the savanna some twenty-five million years ago. Grass spread amongst the trees, and dry plains emerged as wide as oceans. It was the beginning of geological upheavals which started during the Miocene period of the Tertiary and culminated in the cataclysmic transformations of the Ice Ages during the Pleistocene. The Primates and apes of the forest have spent much of their time in the shade, leading enclosed lives inside 'green caves' of leaves and branches. The vegetation of the forest provided both shelter, protection and sustenance, just as it continues to do for the chimpanzees, orang-outangs and gorillas of our world. They scampered along tunnel-like trails through the underbrush, leapt and swung high in the canopies of tall trees and generally avoided the bright uneasy places where savanna grasses encroached upon the edges of the wood. But while our gorillas are being threatened by the still-encroaching plain, artificially produced by modern man in his relentless quest for agricultural produce, and cannot leave his ancient habitation, some fourteen million years ago a new type of Primate appeared along the irregular borders of forest and savanna. This new Primate ventured out into the open spaces, rich in grass and tender shoots, perhaps chasing and catching small animals. He probably took greater and greater chances as food supplies near to the trees became exhausted and went further into the savanna. "Evolution often works most intensively at the edge of things, where the two environments intersect, when something very different lies close at hand and the lure of novelty is strongest".*

These creatures were primitive pre-man, pre-human apes who were certainly much smaller than the gorilla. The fact that these forest dwellers took up life on the ground indicates that they were less fully committed to the life in trees than chimpanzees for instance. They did not have, or had lost, the special limb and shoulder structures which permitted highly advanced branch-to-branch swinging. Remains of such a pre-human ape were found in India and dated about fourteen million years ago. He was given the name Ramapithecus. Not many Ramapithecus specimens have been recovered so far, less than a dozen in all, but that is enough to serve as a basis for speculation about early man's evolution.

While fairly sudden ecological changes occurred during the Pleistocene and gave rise to the extreme climatic changes of the Ice Ages which forced the Primates to face an extremely inhospitable and dangerous environment, we now know that transformations of a less catastrophic kind occurred much earlier. These transformations were of a milder and more gradual nature, the erosion of the forest was much more limited and the plain land, the open savanna, was not a frozen tundra devoid of vegetation, but open grassland, rich in shrubbery, providing plentiful nourishment to a vegetarian species ready to adapt to life in the open. This kind of terrain offered two main types of habitation for apes: islands of residual forests in which specialised tree-dwellers lived their entire lives, and fertile grassland mingled with semi-arid savanna where other Primates had to spend a large part of their lives on the ground and learned the advantages of walking erect. Chimpanzees and gorillas, or rather their ancestors, remained in their island forests and developed into their present form entirely adapted and, at the same time, limited to arboreal existence, while men evolved in the plains. However, whenever possible these earliest ancestors of man returned to the wood to sleep in the shelter of the trees. When the trees were no longer available, they chose places where predators could not follow easily, perhaps spending the nights on ledges of cliffs

---

* John E. Pfeiffer: 'The Emergence of Man', (Thomas Nelson, 1970).

facing the cliff wall, as some baboons do in our time. During the day they ventured into the open grassland or semi-arid regions exploiting every available ounce of food. That meant, among other things, covering an increasingly wide area when vegetation was sparse. They increasingly used digging sticks and pointed rocks to get at water-containing tubers and other berried food. The rocks and digging sticks could also have served as weapons to ward off carnivores which came their way.

An apparent contradiction arises when we consider the size of their teeth, especially the canine teeth, which provide a significant clue as to how they lived. Most Primate species have large canines and put them to good use. The baboon, for instance, another Primate whose ancestors turned from tree-dwelling to life on the ground, will face an opponent by opening his mouth wide and flashing a set of huge and sharp canines. This elaborate show of his weapons is a symbol of warning and enables him to avoid any further trouble, and usually his opponent gets out of his way. When threats and warnings fail however, these teeth may go into action. They are a baboon's most formidable weapon and, in the last analysis, his social order in the troop depends on how well he can fight and his canines symbolise his prowess.

But it is known that Ramapithecus was not equipped with such large canines, they were comparatively small and had shallow, small roots. Indeed, he was the first pre-human ape known to us who did not possess natural weapons. Since the survival of a species depends on vigorous, offensive and defensive capability there must have been some reason for this significant development. L. E. Simmons observed: "These hominids were not feeding and fighting the way apes feed and fight; they certainly would not have used their teeth as effectively as apes in shredding up plants and in aggressive displays against predators. Indeed, it seems likely that their hands played a major role in food getting and defence. Furthermore the extensive use of the hands implies that they walked upright".*

Thus the small canines mean that Ramapithecus had other means for defence and aggression which would have given him a new and superior mode of survival in the environment of the savanna. The interest of this new form of adaptation lies in the fact that it was an

---

* L. E. Simmons: 'The Early Relatives of Man', Scientific American, July, 1964.

innovation which provided the basis for the further evolution of man's ancestors. He adopted a two-footed gait and developed a certain capability to walk upright. What were the advantages of this form of locomotion against its obvious disadvantages? An animal balancing on two feet can be easily knocked down, is more conspicuous when it comes to escaping from a predator and, above all, imposes considerable strain on the lumbar region making him easily exhausted. But the advantages must have outweighed the disadvantages; indeed they must have been very great to outweigh the drawbacks and awkwardness of bipedalism. We can observe that Primates do stand erect for short periods of time under certain circumstances as, for instance, when they want a better view of the surrounding terrain. Male baboons frequently stand up on their hind legs in order to keep track of the rest of the troop. This behaviour has been cited in support of the 'reconnaissance' theory of human bipedalism. The theory is that savanna-exploring hominids were frequently killed by lions and other predators lurking in tall grasses and that evolution put a premium on standing erect as a way of spotting predators at a distance and avoiding them.

Besides these advantages there is another factor, namely, the display or bluffing behaviour by which animals make themselves more frightening and more formidable in emergency situations by increasing their apparent size. Puffer fish double or triple their body size by inflating themselves into globes; birds ruffle their feathers and puff out their chests and spread their wings wide; cats arch their backs and their fur stands on end. (Humans emphasise their aggressive image by inflating their chests and stiffening their backs).

But the self-expansive 'display' instinct has taken another step with Primates once they can stand up and free their hands from the need for locomotion, namely, the ability to reach out for something external, something not part of their body which would make them appear bigger and more formidable. They would have picked up branches or clumps of tall grass, or perhaps long bones and waved them about to enlarge their body image. This activity is common among contemporary chimpanzees and gorillas. When they are aroused they often grab a nearby stick or branch, rear themselves up to their full height and swing it about in a vigorous flailing motion. In this case we can say that the branch or stick becomes a part of the narcissistic self-image, giving the animal a greater appearance of power and providing increased capability of self-expansion. An interesting example of this is reported by Mrs van Lawick-Goodall, which she felt to be strangely ritualistic. A big male chimpanzee may become tremendously excited, break a branch off a tree, brandish it about and rush down a mountain slope (often on two feet) dragging it behind him. Then he rushes back up the slope and repeats the action several times. Sometimes other males will join the fun in a mass 'branch waving display', calling loudly, tearing off and waving branches, hurtling themselves to the ground from the trees.

The advancement of the use of tools no doubt was enhanced by the hominid ape's ability to stand erect and to walk on two feet for a few minutes or even longer. Bipedalism increased the freedom of the hands and provided more time for acquiring new manipulative skills. It also resulted in a more continuous and panoramic view of the savanna, an increased ability to see things occurring and to detect and anticipate dangers. One can also speculate that the erect posture helped to discourage the most dangerous predators—the big cats. George Schaller, who has observed tigers in India and lions in Tanzania, comments on this possibility: "Big cats hunt by lying in wait or approaching stealthily and bounding on the victims back, and they bite at the neck. Man, being bipedal, does not furnish a good target, a good horizontal plain for the cats to jump on. Perhaps that is one thing that deters them today and deterred them in the past."

There is no doubt therefore that the ability to walk erect at least for some distance was a decisive advantage for an ape forced to live in the plain. It freed the fore-limbs from the necessity of propulsion and opened up new areas of skill for the hands, for the handling and manipulating of objects and the increased use of objects for the purposes of self-display, for food-getting and for attacking animals. However, Ramapithecus, the pre-human of fourteen million years ago, was still essentially a vegetarian like his cousin, the ape. He gained a large proportion of his sustenance from the fruits and grains and grasses of the savanna, and only occasionally had to kill animals. These animals he killed were small prey, and he took good care to avoid the larger animals. Also he would probably have tried to keep close enough to the forests to spend an occasional night in them, and he could still regard the forest as a refuge from the rigours of the plains. In other words he would not, at that time, be exposed to the ultimate loss of forest shelter or edible vegetation.

But Ramapithecus laid the foundations which made the emergence of homo erectus possible, for the emergence of a species which could meet the challenge of an ecological catastrophe and become human.

Before this happened many developments took place both in the transformations of the habitat and in the evolution of hominids, all paving the ground so to speak for the emergence of man.

John E. Pfeiffer has observed that: "Ramapithecus stands alone, a face or rather the shadow of a face seen in the distance. His successors like his predecessors are still elusive. Practically nothing is known about his development during the period between fourteen million and about five million years ago, the biggest gap in the story of evolution". The geological and ecological transformations which occurred during those ten million years however are much better documented. Human evolution proceeded during times of unprecedented geological unrest, producing a dwindling of the seas and a further spread of savanna, semi-deserts and deserts.

A burst of archaeological activity after the end of the last war provided ample evidence for a large and varied population of pre-human hominids generally subsumed under the name Australopithecus Africanus who lived between one and a quarter million and two and a half million years ago, i.e. during the end of the Pliocene and the early part of the Pleistocene.

The African sites uncovered just before the war, and much more intensely since then, in the areas of Tang, Sterkfontein, Makapansgat, Swartkrans and Olduvai in particular, the veritable treasure house of the Olduvai Gorge in Northern Tanzania, and the southern shore of Lake Rudolph in Northern Kenya, disclosed an abundance of fossils belonging to different varieties of species, all embraced under the generic term Australopithecus. There is no doubt that Australopithecus was a meat eater, probably a general feeder like ourselves, and not entirely dependent on vegetable food as were the apes and earlier hominids. There was a species among Australopithecines, namely, Paranthropus, who lived at the same time but who was entirely vegetarian and became extinct when the forests disappeared and the plains became barren.

It is likely, as Professor Dart, one of the first discoverers of the fossils of Australopithecus (indeed it was he who first gave them this name) has suggested, that the African man-ape used tools in the sense that we have described earlier; he used antelope jaws lined with teeth for scraping and the bone of its legs for clubs, as well as smaller dagger-like bones. There is a lively controversy among palaeontologists concerning the ability of Australopithecus to shape tools out of raw stone, i.e. whether he was a tool maker as distinct from being a tool user. Neville Mason of the University of the Witwatersrand in Johannesburg examined 20,000 stones collected at Makapan. A number of them looked as if they were worked tools, but after considering the assemblage as a whole he realised that there was no solid evidence for the presence of artefacts. Nature had done the shaping, such as it was. Recent discoveries made at the bottom of the Olduvai Gorge contain what appear to be stone implements. These materials have rough, irregular surfaces and do not show clearly where flakes and chips have been knocked off. They seem highly individualistic in the sense that they cannot be classified readily and are not shaped according to a few standardised traditional patterns. While they presented a great surprise to palaeontologists, it is not at all clear to what extent they have been shaped by nature or by more or less accidental non-organised human activity. It was left for later, larger brained hominids to advance to the level of organised toolmaking as distinct from tool using.

However, there is another aspect of Australopithecus which gives an important clue to the evolutionary advances made by these species, namely, the structure of his foot. The feet of the Olduvai hominids, as they are called, belong to a later period of Australopithecus and were discovered by the Leakeys in the Olduvai Gorge. They are remarkable because they show distinct similarity to ours. They confirm what has been deduced from earlier studies of pelvic bones that Australopithecus could walk upright. The structure of the foot also hints at the beginnings of fundamental changes in mother-infant relationships and in social organisation. Infant monkeys have gripping feet, half hands with mobile and opposable big toes designed to bend around and cling to the mother's hair as she moves along with the troop. Australopithecus infants had feet already so specialised for walking that clinging was no longer possible for them. Presumably they had to be carried in their mother's arms and required more attention, a situation which may have helped to create conditions favouring a unique human development. The women would find the need to cradle their infants in their arms to be a very considerable impediment in keeping up with the troop, and, on the other hand, the troop, habitually covering large distances and facing the necessity to move quickly, at times would find the child-carrying females an impediment to its mobility. So they had to create home bases where women and children could stay in relative safety while the troop members went out in search of food. The notion of leaving a group of females and infants behind is totally foreign to ape troops, who generally move as a single unit. Such separation of roles was probably initiated by Australopithecus, and it is likely that he established home bases to which the other members of the troop could return. It is easy to see that this was a decisive step, a significant transformation in the social organisation of man's ancestors.

Mary Leakey, in her intensive and painstaking investigations of 'living floor sites' in the Olduvai region, found that many sites contained a large number of unworked and otherwise undistinguished stones; but gradually it became apparent that these stones were arranged in a definite pattern. The pattern revealed piles of rock in a rough semi-circle around a saucer-shaped area, perhaps a crude wall which may have served as a wind break. The area of the 'living floor' is about fifteen feet in diameter and is thickly covered with shattered pieces of rock, bone and choppers. They obviously served as tools for the job of smashing bones to get at the marrow. Practically every bone that could yield marrow has been smashed. Adjacent to this area is a concentration of bones which do not contain marrow and is believed to be a kind of garbage heap. Between this heap and the 'dining room' is an arc-shaped area which could have been used as a wind-breaker of stones and branches because it lies directly in the path of prevailing winds. The barrier would have helped to protect the hominids from predators, a strategy still used today by native tribes.

The site is definitely a home base from which hominid troops ventured out into the savanna to collect edible vegetation and to hunt small prey. Thus Australopithecus established a new kind of stability, a centre for family and group associations, the place where traditions and skills could be developed to a degree unknown to previous hominids. With the separation of roles between the more active and mobile males and the mothering females, and probably other members of the group who because of their youth or old age or sickness perhaps could not join the expeditions, a separation of labour would have emerged and the hunting activities of the species would have received a new impetus to mark a higher level of competence. Having a relatively secure home base it was possible to range further in search of food when the rainfall declined and the land turned into semi-desert. Indeed, Australopithecus hunted regularly and he was beginning to change nature, modifying things, however slightly, and moving towards an increasing measure of independence.

It is likely, as we have observed, that early hominids obtained an appreciable proportion of their nourishment from the meat of small game for some million years, and the practice was firmly established by Australopithecus over two million years ago. However, if meat eating had never involved more than small game-hunting, the course of evolution would have been considerably less spectacular and more in the tradition of evolution by genetic rather than cultural change. The most advanced species existing today would not be the human being but a hominid breed, a small-brained small-time toolmaker such as Australopithecus. Homo erectus and Homo sapiens would not have developed.

We have been looking back at the stage in evolution when the basic upright, ground-walking human form, the hunting of small animals, the use of tools and some basic rudiments of toolmaking as well as the building of home bases had been developed, but before brains had become significantly larger than those of the early hominids. We are now entering upon the decisive period during which an evolutionary transformation emerged almost suddenly and once again meet Homo Pithecanthropus erectus, our courageous ancestor who, by braving the Ice Ages, transformed the hominid strain into the strain of Homo and made it possible for us, who are his descendants, to ponder about him.

A MILLION YEARS AGO

During the seven million years of the last period of the Tertiary, namely, the Pliocene, the earth's climate had been generally warm and stable. Then a new period began with the Pleistocene, about 2 million years ago, when the weather became colder and eventually, about 1,500,000 years ago, a frozen blanket of ice and snow began to cover large areas of the planet, developing into glaciers of continental proportions. These vast glacial sheets, perhaps a mile thick in places, came down over much of Europe, Asia and North America, and, pushed by the cold and ice, subarctic zones moved down towards the equator. There is evidence that in England glaciers started at London and in Western Europe at a line from Amsterdam to south of Berlin and Warsaw, while they came down to the Caspian Sea in Asia. The earth had entered a period of extreme climatic pulsations in marked contrast to the peaceful sameness of the Pliocene. After each of the cold phases, of which there were four, there was a return to higher temperatures—the interglacial periods.

During the glacial periods, when the northern continents were covered by ice and snow or by a subarctic barrenness, many thousands of species perished, including many of the anthropoid apes and hominids. But it is in the archaeological layers belonging to the Middle Pleistocene, more specifically towards the later period of the first glaciation, that the earliest tools and skeletal remains of man were found. No tools go back to the early Pleistocene, beyond the layers associated with the Villefranchian fauna of the Middle Pleistocene; it is in these layers that the so-called Olduvian (core) tools were found—pebbles with flakes struck off along one side to make a sharp edge. These are the earliest known tools and, as I have said, can be definitely dated as belonging to the latter part of the first glaciation.

Pithecanthropus erectus and Homo pekinensis and probably Heidelberg man were the inventors of tools, the first toolmakers, as distinct from the tool users like Zinjanthropus, Australopithecus, Paranthropus and other hominids; we must ask what enabled them to respond to the challenge of the Ice Ages and to succeed in mastering an unbelievably hostile environment. We must ask particularly: What enabled them to externalise their organs and by transforming them into tools achieve a sudden increase in their power to adjust to the environment? It is in my opinion relevant to apply to this question insights gained from the study of the impact of acute deprivation upon the development of infants.

We know from the study of the early development of the individual that acute deprivation anxiety in infants greatly intensifies oral-aggressive and sadistic drives, producing powerful urges to bite, to tear and to penetrate the cold, indifferent or elusive surface of the mother's breast—the primary object. An increase in anxiety causes a flow of energy to the jaw musculature and to the teeth or gums, producing increased stimulation of the gripping and biting impulses, and soon fantasies, dominated by teeth, claws, or knives, or their equivalents, appear in the mind of the child. Such oral-sadistic impulses and fantasies continue to operate in adults and are plentiful in dreams.*

If we assume the existence of an historic (or more precisely, prehistoric) period during which the man-like beings—the hominids of the Pleistocene—were confronted by ecological crises which deprived them of their habitual sources of nourishment and shelter, thus arousing in them extreme states of anxiety for prolonged periods, then we can also assume that such states of chronic anxiety would lead to a sharp intensification of their oral-aggressive sadistic urges. The natural transformations which occurred with the onset of the Ice Ages would represent such an ecological crisis, bringing with it a traumatic sense of deprivation, a sense of terror and also a sense of disorientation. The pre-humans could be expected to respond to these fears and extreme sense of insecurity with outbursts of sadistic, oral-cannibalistic rage, which would be combined with a fearful sense of inadequacy of their existing organs. It is obvious that their weapons of aggression, i.e. their organs were insufficient to cope with the requirements of a radically changing environment. They were also inadequate to discharge the aggressive libido aroused, leaving an undischarged quantum of energy. In other words, the teeth and claws of our pre-human forefathers were not sufficiently powerful to discharge the large amounts of aggressive urges which appeared in them. The surplus libido of aggression would be channelled into fantasies of an aggressive nature and they would be externalised in the creation of weapons and tools.

These processes, particularly those of externalisation and tool-making, require three pre-conditions:

1 A prolonged period of radical changes in the ecological environment and subsequent intense states of tension and anxiety.

---

* I provide a detailed description of these processes in my book, 'The Unknown Self'.

2   That our ancestors' natural organs of aggression were insufficient to discharge the aggressive drives which were aroused by these states of anxiety.
3   That their brain was capable of intense fantasy activity and expanded sufficiently to create symbols and recognition of symbols in external objects.

This point specifically implies that the brain was capable of absorbing the surplus libido of aggression and discharging it by means of fantasies and their projection into external artefacts. In other words, the hominid ancestors of man would have to be creatures with a fairly large brain and retarded or degenerated organs of aggression, due to a prolonged existence in a period of stability and relative peacefulness, who were suddenly subjected to a period of crises and intense anxiety: an intelligent and peaceful hominid ape made terrified and angry. The situation of the Ice Ages presented precisely such conditions.

The earth, which for tens of millions of years was covered with vast forests, became cooler and the forests sparse. The hominids of the early Pleistocene were already adjusting themselves to moving on the ground with an erect posture and swinging gait, with the leg muscles supported by a stiff-arched foot. As the forests receded further during the Pleistocene the erect posture became extremely useful and even necessary, as the brachiating arms no longer found support in the trees and their branches. The pelvis became stronger and the lumbar span began to point upwards instead of forwards, thus carrying the torso into position above the hip joints and legs. There is no doubt that the evolution of the foot, legs and torso towards an ever more upright stance accompanied the thinning of the forests all through the Pleistocene and created the hominid who could deal with the complete disappearance of trees at the onset of glaciation. We must, however, assume that none of our ancestors was able to walk upright for long periods of time. Australopithecus, for instance, must have used his arms repeatedly for clasping, in order to steady himself on branches. However, the crucial test of survival came when trees became very sparse or extinct and the ability to walk erect for long periods, to be able to stand, walk and run without any need for brachial support became imperative. The species which could pursue its activities without brachiating support altogether was obviously at a very great advantage. There is no doubt that the Primates or hominids depending on brachiation became either extinct or managed to emigrate to equatorial zones. So when the Ice Age came some hominid species learnt to keep themselves erect and walk across the barren tundra. But the availability of food and shelter also became sparse.

The hominid would look around for trees and shrubs and for the customary diet of fruit and nuts and would see only a vast barren expanse. His instincts to seek shelter among the trees and shrubs, to lie down on leaves to rest and sleep would be denied to him. Wherever he looked would be rocks, frozen earth or ice, with scarcely a fruit-bearing tree anywhere. No supports and shelter, none of the usual nourishment to satisfy his hunger. He faced acute discomfort, freezing cold and starvation. Fortunately, however, his ancestors had learned to attack animals with sticks and animal bones to provide themselves with an occasional carnivorous diet. Now, being deprived of vegetarian nourishment, he had to rely on this skill and develop it to the utmost. It was his only means of survival. He became a carnivorous predator, a killer ape. Besides the ability to hunt, walk erect, manipulate objects with his hands and focus his eyes and mind on them, a fairly large cortical association area of the brain singled him out as a potential survivor of the ecological catastrophe of the Ice Ages. The ability to become a completely carnivorous hominid was the test for his success as a species.

His erect posture was now necessary, and it enabled his eyes to range far into the distance beyond the clasp of his hands, and he would know that he must observe before he was able to handle. He has to hesitate before he reacts to an object, he learns to weigh up in his imagination the dangers or rewards which an object presents to him, and he imagines the manner in which he can handle it. He learns to delay responses. This capacity to weigh and deliberate on what it perceives before responding, the inhibition of reflexes and the channelling of action through the higher cortical functions involving the association areas of the brain in all important motor reactions, became not only a necessity in the new environment but also the most potent factor in the radical expansion of the brain which accompanied the process of becoming human.

The capacity of a high level of generalisation and abstraction from actual concrete stimuli, characteristic of the higher cortical formations, was thus greatly emphasised and acquired decisive importance. In the species Homo we find a large area devoted to associations between the various sensory and motor centres, and thus the emphasis is transferred from reflex actions to thinking, or, at least, the formation of patterns of actions from stored associations. The old sensory and motor centres enable an animal to respond, to see things and do things, whereas, to put it simply, in the association centres man remembers what he has seen and done and imagines what might be seen and done. The speech system began to be included in the structure of the voluntary movements and actions. He could think 'I want' or 'I have to do a certain thing' or 'I don't want to' or 'I mustn't do it', and his movements would reflect those thoughts.

Our carnivorous hominid ancestor not only increased his capacity for attention and for the connection in his mind of signals from the outside world with memories of previous experiences, he not only elevated attention to an activity in which direct responses are excluded or delayed, he also communicated the process of attention to others by language. Language became a presentation of events, and this presentation in turn became a stimulus for motor reactions.

There was always a straining outwards for signals and the need to interpret them. The intervals between need and gratification, between stimulus and reaction, became longer. Instead of the quick responses to familiar stimuli characteristic of an ape and the short cycles between need and gratification, signal and response, there would be long periods of tense inactivity, that is, motor inactivity, while the senses are alert and the association areas actively experimenting with possible modes of action.

In those long periods of intense observation and attention, the hominid's mind would be filled with fantasies of attacking distant animals which he can observe. He would know that his objects of prey are far more powerful, swift and aggressive than he. He would be frightened, angry and restless, and a concentrated rage would come into his eyes, a certain look which we can but very rarely see in apes.

His pituitary glands will release increased quantities of adrenalin into his blood stream, tightening up his musculature and tensing his posture. His erect posture will be greatly reinforced by wariness and tension, and it will also increase his aggressive fantasies and his determination to attack. Symbols of powerful teeth and claws will fill his imagination and he will see a tooth in every stone and a claw in every pebble, and he will make a tooth and a claw out of stones and pebbles and with these new powerful organs will move up to his prey and attack them and become their master. Once he has learned the satisfaction which these tools give him he will spend more and more time making them. He will thus remake himself into a new species, whose artefacts become his natural equipment. To survive in the new environment the hominid had to become a carnivore. He became a killer despite his inadequate natural equipment for attack.

If one could imagine an anthropoid ape with an upright stance and stereoscopic vision geared to distant observation, one could assume that in the course of natural selection he would have developed his fangs and claws into efficient organs of aggression, and a new powerful anthropoid carnivore would have emerged. It is unlikely that he would have developed the capacity to make tools. Instead of developing artefacts he would have developed his own organs to cope with the danger around him. Instead, the hominid developed his brain, his manual dexterity and the ability to make tools and became human. He could not, and did not have time to develop natural organs to a size and strength to cope with the new situations which required exclusively carnivorous habits.

Apes have intelligent front teeth; they are good nibblers with incisors and strippers of bark with the canines, and they also do a great deal of investigating and manipulating with the projecting mobile lips. Their incisors project forward and the canines are large; the strongly projecting front portion of the jaws widens at the front. Such a dentition is geared to the coarse vegetable and fruit diet of the anthropoids, with the canines being important for opening the tough rind of many of the fruits and also for tearing the bark off trees. No doubt such teeth served also to threaten animals even of the same species, and other animals. A gorilla in a rage is a formidable sight, and the first thing that happens is a great show of his incisors, particularly his canines (this is usually enough to scare anybody subjected to this exhibition). There is no doubt that in rage his teeth are libidinised for attack and could, if exercised, make most powerful weapons. Already, however, in this intelligent ape the show of the organs of attack takes the form of a symbolic ritual which, accompanied by the beating of his chest, screaming and stamping his feet, is understood by others, i.e. felt in all its fearful power, and suffices to scare them away. He does not need his enormous strength and his teeth in order to kill, it is enough to scare other animals or rivals, as he is a vegetarian.

The human teeth, adapted merely to chew what is brought to the mouth by the hands, no longer have the facility to express large amounts of aggression. For attack and aggression they are pitifully inadequate, even though we still bare our teeth and particularly our small canines in a snarl when angry. Already in Pithecanthropus erectus we find the molar teeth much smaller than those of an ape, although they are still massive compared with those of Homo sapiens. His canines are no longer pronounced and are all level with the other teeth. The dental arch is much smaller and, rather than projecting forward, broadens out at the sides. The teeth, therefore, are no longer a useful weapon of aggression or even attack of any kind, having been adapted not to attack but to receive objects from the hands. It is the hands which have to exercise the function of aggression, but there is no doubt that he soon found they were no match for the vicious claws of carnivorous animals.

We have assumed that man's capacity of externalisation must be based upon the existence of a brain capable of higher cortical functions. If we consider the internal capacity of the skull as the most serviceable measure of the size of the brain, then we find that in the large apes it is about 500 cubic centimetres, very little more in Zinjanthropus and Australopithecus, about 900–1000 c.c. in Pithecanthropus, and 1,450 in contemporary man. This is the measure of the brain explosion which occurred in less than $1\frac{1}{2}$ million years. What, however, is most significant is that in this trebling of the size of the brain by far the greatest increase took place in the association areas of the cerebral cortex. It may be surprising to notice that the Australopithecus brain was not much larger than that of the highest apes, but his brain was already differently organised, and it is upon the basis of the new pattern, namely, the emphasis on the association areas rather than the increase of the sense and motor areas that man's brain developed.

The Australopithecenes, with their relatively small front teeth and fairly erect posture, developed a high capacity to manipulate objects with their hands. Their hands had a far greater range of movement than that of our ape ancestors, and this means a far greater range and facility for experimentation than was possible for the apes whose lips and teeth were skilled and sensitive. With the addition of a pair of stereoscopic eyes, watching and taking note of what the hands are doing, the storing of manual behaviour patterns in the cerebral cortex, and the constant discovery and invention of new skills, we can see that a much faster rate of brain increase was now possible. The increase in the cortical areas, which we can observe in Pithecanthropus, means a large increase in memory and, above all, in internal imagery of possible actions and situations, an enormously enhanced capacity of internal perception and presentation more or less independent of actual sensory stimuli.

The first man, probably Pithecanthropus, could imagine events and could react emotionally to these internal presentations more or less as much as he would to external stimuli. He could have wish-fulfilment fantasies, he could imagine dangerous animals being hunted by him in all sorts of possible ways, he could master emotional pressure such as fear and hunger by enacting in his fantasies the conquest of the prey or threatening beast. And under the pressure of hunger and anxiety, he would imagine himself with powerful weapons symbolising teeth and claws, and he would associate these images with stones and other solid objects around him. He would, on seeing a stone, recognise in it the imagined weapon and shape it accordingly. He would, therefore, transfer his image outside himself and make it real by means of work.

But the externalisation of urges and their symbolic images through work is only one of the many aspects of externalisation. Once the externalisation of the emotions of aggression and defence had been achieved by means of tools and weapons, the gates were opened for the externalisation of a variety of fantasies and emotions. These psychic experiences would be seen to exist in the world outside: 'exist' is outside. We have already remarked how sounds, made to represent certain emotions and experiences, came to exist and, by existing, became language. Emotions of love and hate, security and anxiety, destruction and restitution, guilt and sacrifice would find symbolic presentations in fantasy images, and these symbolic images would be thought to exist outside man—out there in the world. Symbols representing a great number of emotions, good and bad, frightening and reassuring, would begin to populate the world of man. The drama of his conflicting emotions, presented in symbolic imagery, would be experienced as if they took place in the world outside, the battle of emotions would appear to be enacted by the spirits, ghosts and monsters fighting his battles. Man would no longer be alone. He would not face the unknown universe by himself; the ghosts and spirits would both protect him and threaten him, fighting his battles and teaching him how to act. He would recognise himself in the spirits which he projected into the world and would acquire a sense of identity and security in relating to them.

Once man had learned toolmaking and created language the spirits could be represented in signs and symbols both graphically as well as verbally; a new world of meaning and drama would emerge, and culture, as we know it, would be born. Culture signifies the capacity to populate the world with ghosts, spirits and myths, to communicate them to members of a community and relate to them collectively through common worship and ritual. By means of cultural symbols members of a community share their emotional experiences and find communion with each other.

Ghosts and spirits also represent people whom we have known and of whom we think. Every person we remember and visualise becomes a ghost in so far as the thought image of him is externalised as having existence in the world outside. Just as our parents appear to us as living people in our dreams after they have died, primitive people would ascribe a continued existence to the apparitions of their dreams and fantasies. They would imagine the deceased to exist in another realm and find ways of communicating with them by means of sacred evocations, signs and incantations. So ghost worship would begin, facilitated by words and names, by appropriate signs and graphic symbols. Eventually, the name pronounced would be an invocation of the ghost, a ritual, a magic act. In fact the ghost would be in the word which pronounces his name.

Primitive man would have learned to appreciate the importance of his mind. His mind would become highly libidinised; it would be the most important organ in his battle for survival, and consciously or unconsciously he would feel it to be important. Thus primitive man may have realised that the ghost resides both in his mind as well as in the world outside, and in order to communicate with or possess the ghost of an ancestor he would eat his brain. We devour the brains' of our teachers; we 'pick their brains' and 'digest' them. But what we as Homo sapiens express symbolically, early man enacted. He made a hole in the skull of his ancestors, took out the brain and ceremonially devoured it. By doing so he absorbed the strength and skills of his ancestral ghost and reassured himself of his assistance and love. He introjected the loved ancestor.

The first remains showing signs of culture and ritual were discovered in the caves of Choukoutien, the habitation of Homo pekinensis (to be more exact, one of his habitations which has been discovered). Great numbers of the skulls of Homo pekinensis were found there with holes made in exactly the same place. Many skulls were laid out in circular patterns, and one must assume that they did symbolise something to the mind of old Homo pekinensis. There is little doubt that these holes enabled them to remove the brain from the skulls and devour the ghost who dwelt in it. This was probably a communal feast, a primitive version of the Christian mass, the partaking of the host and the wine, i.e. the symbolic eating of the body and drinking the blood of Christ. It represents the same mechanism which later operated in the totem feast, namely, identification of the members of a culture with the totem by ceremoniously eating its body and thereby absorbing its powers, its skills and its mind.

Thus early man regained the security which he had lost when he had to step beyond his instinctive orientations and entered into a world dominated by mental images and symbols and produced his own organs for survival. His mind replaced natural selection, his imagination and skills replaced, or rather, supplanted his instincts as the agent of his evolution. Having lost the security of his instincts he entered into a universe dominated and directed by his mind, the world of images, symbols and artifices of his own making.

HUNTERS AND HOMEMAKERS

The hunter, and particularly the big game hunter, has to learn to inhibit his spontaneous movements and to control his reflexes; the long periods of immobile observation of the movements of prey would put an emphasis upon memory and calculation, which, in turn, increases the memory units of the brain—which John Young of University College, London, calls 'mnemons'.

Elizabeth Marshall Thomas, who has spent much time with Bushmen, points out that "in an area of hundreds of square miles, they know every bush and stone, every convolution of the ground, and have usually named every place in it where a certain kind of veldt food may be even if the place is only a few yards in diameter".* They do not read nor write, but they learn and remember. If all their knowledge about their land, and its resources, were recorded and published it would make up a library of thousands of volumes. Such knowledge was as essential to early man as it is to these people.

John Young's studies indicate that the mnemon may be the fundamental building block of all memory systems including the larger and more intricate system of the cortex which evolved as early hunts ranged more widely and had to draw increasingly upon past experience in coping with new problems. Evolution favoured the survival of bands and individuals whose memories tended to be longest and most capacious. It is one aspect of the mnemon that it is a unit involving the inhibition of undesirable behaviour and this emphasises the basic relationship between memory and self-control and domestication. Restraint did not come naturally to the hominid. Every choice, every course of action performed for the future benefit of the group had to be learned and remembered; it also implied the increased capacity to restrain the impulse for immediate response and gratification. The hunt demands patience and waiting. Waiting for the prey at water-holes, waiting for an animal to look away as you stalk it, to becoming immobile so that the animal should not notice you when it looks in your direction, and waiting after the kill so that you do not devour all the meat on the spot but save most of it for the others waiting at the home base. Man is the only Primate that shares food and saves it for later occasions. These demands of the hunting culture changed man's ancestors physically, psychologically and socially. Above all, they affected the transformation and growth of certain parts of the brain. They not only dramatically increased the overall size of the brain but especially the higher association areas of the cortex, which co-ordinate and analyse the unceasing flow of messages coming from the sense organs and trigger appropriate action on the basis of these analyses. But more than anything else they necessitated the expansion of the frontal lobes. These, as we have remarked earlier, deal with the anticipation of events, with plan-

---

* Elizabeth Marshall Thomas: 'The Harmless People', Knopf 1959.

ning and imagination and a consciously perceived and imagined sense of purpose.

Human beings take in an enormous amount of information through their senses, most of which is irrelevant to their purpose at any given moment and thus is blocked from reaching consciousness or motor discharge. In order to put sensory information to meaningful use and to make it recognisable we must relate it to past experiences and to a sense of purpose. Memory of the past and the imaginative anticipation of the future provide an understanding of the meaning of present experiences and stimulate action to promote the desired goal.

But with the development of cortical activity and the general increase in brain size, the process of maturation becomes delayed. Humans, and even pre-human beings, remain infants and depend on their parents, particularly the mother, for increasingly long periods in proportion to the complexity of their brain structure and the need for learning to co-ordinate reflexes and to acquire the skill accumulated by their culture.

We have seen that Australopithecus developed home bases mainly for their mothering women and children. With the prolonged helplessness of the infant and need to be protected by the mother, the home base itself has to become more permanent and protective, and provide more secure shelter from predators. An added and very important incentive for this would be the increasingly cold climate which emerged during the Pleistocene. Not only mothers and children but the grown homo erectus needed shelter from the climate, and had to be able to return to it from his hunting expeditions.

Early hominids, like their fellow Primates, lived mainly exposed to the elements. Sometimes on cold or stormy nights they may have been driven to seek cover under overhanging cliffs where they huddled together in a world still dominated by other animals. Sometimes bad weather would have driven them into caves; or they would have entered these caves during the day to obtain water or to get out of a scorching sun. But if they huddled under rock shelter or even entered caves for short periods, then it was to avoid momentary inconvenience of weather, knowing that it would not last long and they would return to their normal habitation in the open plains.

But Middle Pleistocene man had no such expectation of the

imminent improvement of the weather—it remained freezing cold for generation after generation, and the shelter of a cave became a necessity.

More than any other element of nature it was fire which provided early man with warmth and with a sense of security from dangerous predators. He brought fire to the places where he established his home bases, he created zones of warmth and light in his caves, and achieved a way of keeping the harsh elements, the night and the prowlers, at bay and freedom to explore new territories with harsh climates. Man's ancestors first put fire to work on a regular basis to keep themselves warm in the Arctic and subarctic zones of Europe and Asia. No hearths have yet been found in Africa.

There is no doubt that man's ancestors first obtained fire ready-made from natural sources, that he was a fire-user before he became a fire-maker. He could have encountered accidental fires started by lightning in dry bush or grassland. Occasionally in damp environments coal or shale-oil deposits might be ignited by spontaneous combustion. Perhaps hunters camped near such fires as a natural resource like game or water or shelter. Having learned the attraction of fire, they would leave those fireside camps once the flames began to peter out, and maybe they would take the fire with them. It would have to be kept burning, and one could speculate that they had a fire-bearer as do some present day Bushmen—perhaps one of their older members who was responsible for carrying and guarding embers and who breathed the embers into flame when the troop found a new place to live. But there is no evidence for any of this.

In any case, while early man lived in sub-tropical or mild climates, he had no overriding need to use fire. Remains of a fire-bearing hearth appear on the caves inhabited in colder places and colder times. (Among the earliest known fireplaces are those discovered in the Escale Caves in France dating some 750,000 years ago, being largely contemporary to the fire-bearing hearths found in the caves of Peking man).

The invention of firemaking enabled early man not only to obtain an artificial source of warmth but also to keep predators at bay, to chase them out of the caves which they inhabited and to keep them out. The caves were originally occupied by powerful and long-established carnivores like bears, hyaenas, wolves and probably tigers, and these animals had to be chased from the caves before man could come to occupy them; and he had to make sure of keeping them out by having a fire burning near the entrance. Fire enabled Peking man to take permanent possession of his caves at Choukoutien, and it initiated the cave-dwelling culture of the Ice Ages. Apart from providing warmth and defence against large predators, the security of a more or less permanent home, fire also provided light. It increased the length of the day; the hours after dark became hours of leisure in which ancient man could plan more and more complex activities. The fireside became an institution, a cohesive force bringing members of the band closely together, old and young. Individuals too old to hunt became important because they remembered things beyond the memory of the others, they increased the memory store of the group by telling of things long past; the old man could relate to them old adventures and skills and he provided a sense of continuum between past and present. His stories would become the core of mythology, a system of sentiments which gave a deeper dimension to the psychological cohesion of the group. He reinforced the imagination by which the concrete experiences were integrated with things of the spirit. He became the link between men and their ancestors, and he made their life and their experiences real to the present generation. And when the old man died, they ceremoniously consumed his brain and assured themselves that his store of memories would live on and his myths would be perpetuated.

The internal mental life which prevents the past from disappearing and preserves it in the present as a part of existence thus became enormously enhanced and so did the mental representation of a wide range of feelings. Fire, for instance, became not only a natural object but the symbol of security and salvation in times of freezing despair and danger. Men did not only carry the fire-making ability around with them on the hunt but they imagined it in their minds as the symbol of warmth and light, transforming the cave into a welcoming shelter one could return to after the hunt. It represented the image of a home, the mother's protection, the woman's embrace and her welcome.

With the increased differentiation between the sexes, the woman, staying for longer periods in the cave as the period of dependency and helplessness increased among the offspring, became more and more associated with home, with the image of protectress, and with love.

The longer the infant needs its mother, the longer and more intensely the mother needs a reliable adult male to support her, making the formation of new and stronger male-female bonds necessary. When infants are dependent for years instead of months, survival is impossible without radical changes in established patterns of behaviour, particularly sexual behaviour. Indeed it is interesting to note that with the disappearance of the oestrus cycle among human beings, a closer and at the same time a more personal relationship became established between men and women.

The typical pattern among mammals involves regular bursts of sexual frenzy which takes precedence over all other activities. At every ovulation, or immediately after, all non-human females come into oestrus or 'heat'. Sexual activity is so concentrated and intense during such periods that it tends to interrupt the care of the young as well as all other activities. This type of sexual attraction ensures effective reproduction among mammals which have rapidly maturing offspring, but not among Primates. If all the females in a Primate troop were subjected to three or four days of sexual mania every month or so, their helpless infants would die of malnutrition or be killed by predators. Natural selection brought about a modification in monkeys and apes to the extent that oestrus ceases during the later part of pregnancy and the early part of nursing. Man is the only animal in which oestrus has disappeared altogether.* This development probably took place about a million years ago with the emergence of homo erectus. A new reproductive process was being established, and oestrus went by default in the same way as large canine teeth may have gone with the habitual use of tools and weapons.

The female of the species became sexually receptive at practically any time. Such extended sexual responsiveness also extended her attraction to the male, and the extended or rather continuous stimulation which the female exercised helped to tie the male more closely and securely to the mother and child. The irresistible sexual drive during the periods of oestrus among non-human Primates is essentially beyond the individual's control. Its presence and absence are determined by the automatic turning on and turning off of sex hormone secretions, which is biologically conditioned. Under such conditions the sex act among monkeys and apes and

---

* John E. Pfeiffer: 'The Emergence of Man'.

presumably early hominids tended to be fairly impersonal and mechanical. With the absence of oestrus, the sexual urge came under a measure of voluntary control, it became possible to select the time and place for intercourse, and to show personal preference for the mate. Such personal preference would emerge for the first time in the history of living organisms and make the male-female relationship more enduring. This was the beginning of the history of love, at least, love in the human sense. We can speak here of the beginnings of a spiritualisation of sexual relationships in so far as the sexual desire is directed to an individual, i.e. to a person whose presence and whose attraction would be carried along in the mind, be represented in imagination, and desire would find its representation in fantasy. The female ceased to be merely a biologically determined sexual object, but became an individual not only desired but also loved, not just responded to at certain particular moments but whose presence would be perpetuated in the man's imagination. Personal feelings and choice were superimposed upon biological necessity, and attraction between two people began to matter in the bonding of man and woman. The desire for the woman, who was associated with home and family, transformed the cave from being merely a shelter against the elements and dangerous predators into a symbol of emotional pleasure. It created a new bond between the members of the troop and united them in a symbol of unity, a narcissistic extension of the self to the 'we', the extension of the narcissistic libido into a communal libido.

But here we come once again across the problem of the dominant male. When we speak of the psychological element in sexual relationships, of the male desiring the female and vice versa, making a powerful bond between them, we introduce the elements of possessiveness and jealousy. This does not mean that the powerful male who feels himself responsible for the protection of the troop could only establish one-to-one relationships with a female; he would be attracted to a number of women in the tribe and, being their protector, consider himself their possessor. He would be jealous of other males and the young males would threaten his harem and challenge his power. We can observe harem groups or one-male breeding groups among gibbons of the plains, and many students of early man have referred to them as showing many similarities to early human societies.

According to the anthropologist Clifford Jolly there is an important resemblance between Gelada baboons who live on the plains and humans, namely, the common characteristic of a one-male breeding unit. The Gelada baboon's social structure is described by J. H. Crook as follows: "The 'one-male group' is the reproductive unit of a Gelada population. It consists of a large adult male, a group of females including both mothers and non-maternal animals in all stages of the oestrous cycle, variable numbers of juvenile animals, infants and babies, and an occasional sub-adult male often almost totally grown but not sexually mature. In areas where the population is widely dispersed, such social units are the commonest observed associating inconstantly with small groups consisting wholly of large sub-adult males and mature males not possessing 'harems'. These 'all-male' groups likewise move independently from other units and show considerable cohesion over several weeks". [*]

Such a social structure is precisely that which Freud termed 'the primal horde' and which he considered to be the original condition of human society. We have here the same despotic adult male who monopolises a group of females to the exclusion of the younger but sexually mature males; these are chased out of the family circle and form a group of brothers (the all-male group), who form a close association of predators or hunters, while the adult-dominant male stays at home guarding his women.

In the baboon society, as well as in the society of the primal horde as envisaged by Freud, we find a dual structure in the social organisation, namely, the one-male breeding unit of the dominant male exercising his despotic powers, guarding his females and keeping the young males, his sons, out of his 'bedroom', his empire, and making it necessary for them to roam outside forming close associations of cooperative hunting and foraging units. This dual structure would lay the foundations for the father-murder by the band of brothers when their sexual needs for women became irresistible and the elimination of the tyrant the only means of gaining access to them.

---

[*] J. H. Crook: 'Gelada Baboon Herd Structure and Movement', Symp.Zool.Soc. London 18, 237–258, 1966.

THE PRIMAL COMMUNITY.

The harem society of the Gelada baboons shows psychological traits among its members which are in many ways comparable to that manifested among human beings dominated by the Oedipus complex. It shows a remarkable degree of mistrust and anxiety, with considerable aggressiveness erupting frequently in fights and much jealous irritability. The dominant male repeatedly has to assert his authority in an aggressive manner, is often engaged in fights with younger males and, although no one has as yet reported an act of father-murder, he does have to relinquish his dominant role when he grows old and is unable to match the aggression of younger males. Ritualised rivalry among the young determines the emergence of the new leader. While there is little doubt that modern man shares many emotional characteristics with the baboon, even though they are largely repressed from civilised consciousness, this does not necessarily mean that man's human ancestors of the Pleistocene lived in societies similar to those of baboons and governed by the Oedipus complex. Indeed, there have been a large number of important circumstances in the life of homo erectus which would have made this type of group structure most unlikely.

The exclusion of the young males from the father-dominated group, involving their expulsion from the protective security of the cave and hearth around which life revolved, would have been impossible for they would not have survived the rigours of climate and the danger presented by powerful carnivorous predators. Hostility of the dominant male and a rejective attitude of the females would have transformed the cave from being a symbol of libidinous pleasure and warmth into a symbol of rejection and anxiety. If he were deprived of the assurance of a warm and affectionate welcome home from his sojourns in the hostile world outside, he would have perished from cold and anxiety. It would have been essential for him to carry in his mind a sense of belonging to his community, a feeling of cohesion and mutual affection, to sustain him in his activities of big-game hunter during the Ice Ages. Furthermore the role of the dominant male as the leader of the hunt would have made it necessary for him to participate in the hunting expeditions and to act as teacher and inspirer to the younger members of the troop. He would be a member of the all-male group of hunters, form a close emotional tie with them as their leader, and encourage them to establish a sense of identification with him. He would therefore have had to avoid the conflict between the all-male group and the one-male group; the sons would have to identify with the dominant male without suffering anxieties about his enmity and jealousy and without fear of rejection by the females in the troop. This means that, not unlike the gorilla troop of our time, the dominant male would have taken a very tolerant attitude towards the sexual needs of the young males, and allowed them to share in the erotic attractions exercised by the females, thus reinforcing the warmth and unity of the home and of the group.

We cannot judge what amount of sexual repression would have existed among the young males in order to be accepted by the old male, but whatever its degree, the aggression aroused by it would be deflected on to the hunt. Indeed the very nature of the hunt would absorb any residual aggression and permit erotic feelings to be directed towards the group. The erotic drives would be expressed as a bonding force within the home, and aggression would be directed outwards, producing the paramount sentiment of the warmth and love inside as against the cold and aggressive world outside. And in fact the outside world needed every bit of aggression he could summon for the pursuit of the hunt and sustenance, and the inside world needed every bit of warmth and pleasure to make man, i.e. our ancestors, able to survive under almost impossible conditions.

Indeed, the process of externalisation, which we have described as the essential characteristic of the genus homo, found here its most important application; homo erectus literally had to externalise his aggressive power and direct it to the world outside by means of new artificial organs of attack in order to survive. Homo erectus ceased to be a species that lived entirely in the world outside, in the world around him, he was no longer entirely a part of nature.

He had to turn against nature and enforce his will upon it; he had to manipulate and change it, and escape from it whenever possible into his self-made environment which he called home. And he had to generate warmth and love in this environment to protect himself from the dangers which confronted him outside. Home and world became two distinct and separate entities.

Thus a duality would emerge in the consciousness of homo

erectus, not a duality between the group of young men and the father or dominant-males but a duality between the close bonds of home and the world of danger outside. Indeed, the bonds of warmth and affection between the members of the group would be the most important factor which enabled him to succeed in his struggles against the world outside, with the dominant-male acting as protector and leader giving reassurance to the younger males. There is no doubt that if the father-figure became too old to exercise his functions as leader he would be replaced by another or others, but there is no need to assume that such changes in leadership would be the result of internecine struggle.

The new leaders would either simply take over the functions and responsibilities from the old or they would, if the opportunity arose, find new caves and take some women with them and found new groups. While then the group would greatly depend upon the skill and strength of the leading males as well as on their love in order to survive, we can speak of a paternal community rather than a patriarchal tribe to describe their social structure. Patriarchal tribes would arise at a later stage under quite different conditions.

While, therefore, the paternal community structure prevailed among Homo erectus we would find little signs of the Oedipus complex. Deprivation anxiety would predominate and aggression would be entirely directed outwards. And the libido of narcissistic and sexual contact would be encouraged in order to counteract fear.

There is another important factor which would have considerably reduced the motivations for an Oedipus complex and that is the short period of sexual delay and relative absence of a latency period in primitive man. The gap in modern man between the first puberty at the age of five or six years and the second puberty at thirteen or fourteen is largely due to a delay in cultural maturation. Psychoanalytic investigations have shown the latency period to be a period of sexual repression during which the young male has to acquire the skills and knowledge of his culture before he can fend for himself and be accepted as a mature member of the male community and ready to procreate and be responsible for a family. He has to wait eight years or so during which he has to recapitulate by training and learning the cultural attainments of his race. Those eight years represent a condensed acquisition of the hundreds of thousands of years during which man learned to read, write, think in numbers, to acquire the skills of work, know about the properties and behaviour of material objects, about the history of his people and the geography of his environment, and to master the rituals and ceremonies of his culture.

During this period the boy has to submit to and identify with the males, the teachers, in order to learn from them, to become one of them and be accepted by them. In this purpose of identification with the males his heterosexual needs become repressed and homosexual patterns of male relationships occur in the form of identification with and introjection of current patterns of maleness.

In homo erectus the amount of new skills and knowledge to be acquired were relatively few (we must emphasise however the word 'relatively' because already for the young homo erectus the efforts towards the acquisition of current skills and knowledge must have appeared formidable), making the cultural maturation lag fairly short. In fact we can measure the complexity and advances of a culture by the length of the latency period. The higher and more complex the culture, the longer the latency period and the more prolonged and intense, sexual repression. In homo erectus the element of sexual repression would hardly occur, first of all because infantile eroticism would have been encouraged or accepted for the sake of libidinous bonding within the group, and secondly because maturation delay would not be a major factor in their development. The process of skill acquisition and identification with the grown-up males would not entail sexual repression. In other words, young males did not have to leave the bedroom—the home (bedroom and home being the same)—upon reaching sexual maturity, and he would not have to repress his sexual desires while he acquired the skills of his culture.

Maybe it is one of the paradoxes of human life that while man's early ancestors had to face the most difficult and hostile conditions, he attained a sense of security and warmth in his home never to be regained in later stages of his evolution. His identification with his fathers would have been of an expansive, loving kind, and the aggressive-sadistic component of introjection, so important in later, patriarchal cultures, would be absent. He would not have developed the sacrificial complexes derived from the guilt of having slain the father, either in deed or in fantasy. His culture, therefore, would certainly have been pre-totemic, it would be based chiefly on the perpetuation of the parental ghost by means of the ceremonial eating of his brain after death. The ceremonial of eating the brain of the departed ancestor and the laying out of skulls in a circle, depicting both the magic circle of home as well as the continuum of life, would have predominated as a cult, not only among homo pekinensis but among all homo erectus species. (We have to wait for further palaeontological discoveries to provide evidence for this concept.)

We have stayed for some length with pithecanthropus erectus (homo erectus), in order to understand and reconstruct his mode of life and the structure of his groups, because he was most probably our true ancestor, creating the foundations for our human characteristics, and, furthermore, he existed for a very long time, probably over a period of some 600,000 years. Putting it differently, we humans lived as homo erectus for over half of our whole evolutionary existence and, therefore, are bound to have many of his traits ingrained in our psycho-biological system; he thus represents an important part of our collective unconscious.

The psychological characteristics engendered by the nature of his group life continue to exercise a profound influence upon the deep structures of our social instincts. The division between the world inside—the security and warmth of the home—and the cold and dangerous world outside, in which the males have to fight against powerful and frightening predators, between the world of one's community, family, tribe, nation, and the perennial enemies outside continues to dominate our social existence.

It has been important to discover that humanity did not start with the Oedipus complex, and existed for a long period without it. The Oedipus complex, therefore, does not need to be considered as the mainspring for man's social existence, the foundations for society and culture, as Freud averred. Looking at the group structure of homo erectus, we can see that it was neither patriarchal nor matriarchal and will be justified in calling it the Primal community. While the community depended upon the leading male for survival, he did not exercise tyrannical powers but inspired a sense of emotional security and cohesion in his community.

We leave our heroic ancestor, and move on in our sojourn through man's prehistoric evolution. We must move forward a few hundred thousand years, but as we pass them on our way we shall salute the later members of homo erectus—Heidelberg man, Steinheim man, Swanscombe man, the man from Arago, Verteszöllös, and many others who lived through the second and third glacia-tion—till we arrive at the third inter-glaciation, in order to look at a new species, namely, Neanderthal man.

NEANDERTHAL MAN: ANCESTOR WORSHIP AND THE ORIGINS OF TOTEMISM

Neanderthal man made his appearance during the end of the last interglacial period, about 110,000 years ago. Most of his tools were flakes of flint struck from a core and trimmed into projectile points, knives and scrapers, which made up the Mousterian com-plex. With his new methods of flake striking and edge chipping, Neanderthal man initiated a revolution in the art of toolmaking which enabled him to produce sophisticated and very efficient flaked tools, such as one-bladed and double-bladed knives, sharp axes and scraping tools, as well as microlithic or miniature blades set into handles to be used as spearheads so delicately pointed that they could easily penetrate the hides of thick-skinned animals. Neanderthal man became a most efficient hunter, well-adapted both in his physique as well as in his technology to the arctic conditions of the last glaciation, and he spread in large numbers over many parts of the globe.

By the onset of the last—the 4th or Würm—glaciation, about 80,000 years ago, the Neanderthals had established themselves as the dominant human species, extending without interruptions across Europe into the Near East, Central Asia and China. The record of this era demonstrates man's extraordinary ability to adapt, to live practically anywhere and under any conditions. Indeed, the last glaciation probably presented the most severe climatic conditions of the whole Pleistocene era. Ice descended upon the British Isles and upon Europe, and came down over the Alps and beyond, into the region south of the Alpine mountains. This turned Central Europe into an arctic province.

However, these extremely cold conditions brought about a considerable lowering of the levels of the seas and rivers due to the absorption of the waters by the ice, exposing large numbers of caves, and Neanderthal man made good use of them. With his ability to make fire fairly easily and his efficient weaponry, he took possession of the caves, protected them from ferocious animals, and managed to achieve a reasonable degree of comfort and security. The exposed cliffs and caves provided abundant raw material for his tools as well as shelter. His tools also enabled him to make clothing out of the furs and hides of animals. But survival would have been impossible without reserves of food and fuel.

The chief hunting-grounds may have been snow tundras, wide, flat areas swept by icy winds where the snow might only be a foot deep and edible grasses grew beneath it. Today in Canadian arctic and subarctic regions such places provide a major source of food for herds of caribou, and similar conditions would have helped to maintain herds of reindeer, wild horses, woolly rhinos and bears in the time of Neanderthal man.

The quantity of tools found in Neanderthal caves is truly astonishing, and, moreover, they reveal fairly regular patterns in their characteristic and design. Different layers contain different tool kits which hint at variations of technique during different periods. 19,000 tools were discovered at Combe-Grenal, one of the richest deposits of Neanderthal remains located in the area near Les Eyzies. In a site near Rouen 2,000 tools were found similar in characteristics to those uncovered in Israel near the Sea of Galilee. A staggering number of Neanderthal tools have recently been collected in south-east China near the Great Wall as well as in sites along river banks in the Crimea and other parts of Russia. One of these dwelling sites contained large deposits of bones of horses, rhinoceros, caribou and brown bears, 27,000 pieces of flint and 15 hearths. More than 50 prehistoric sites have been discovered in north-west Greece in recent years with large tool assemblages with a high proportion of microlithic or miniature implements.

Apart from the astonishing wealth of implements discovered in Neanderthal caves, the arrangement of the caves and their 'furniture' can be considered even more significant as they indicate the importance of cultural and religious rituals in the lives of Neanderthal man: flagstone floors, work tables, benches and altars as well as burial places with their own ritualistic implements. Man had begun to face the mystery of death, both for the animals killed in the hunt as well as for himself. He conducted funeral rites and entertained ideas about the continuation of existence after an individual's death, and he wanted to ensure that the deceased would enter his new existence well provided for. The Neanderthals were, as far as we know, the first species of man to conduct proper burials accompanied by rituals and ceremonials. Instead of identifying with the ghost of the ancestor by eating his brain, a ritual enacted, as we have seen, by Homo erectus hundreds of thousands of years earlier, the dead were given tools and weapons and other possessions as well as food supplies to take on their journeyings into the land beyond—the external land of the spirit.

We can get a flavour of the imagery which prompted early man to conduct funeral rituals if we consider the rituals of Ainu, a strange race of primitive men who live in the northern islands of Japan—Hokkaido, Sakhalin (now belonging to Russia) and the Kuriles. They are semi-nomadic, palaeo-Siberian fishing and hunting as well as Stone Age planting people whose culture shows signs of great antiquity. When a funeral ceremony is performed, the master of the family becomes the celebrant. "You are a God now", he says to the corpse, "and without hankering after this world, you are to go now to the world of the Gods where your ancestors abide. They will thank you for the presents that you bring. And now go on quickly! Do not pause to look back". The celebrant puts a pair of leggings on the voyager's legs, a pair of mittens on his hands. "Take care not to lose your way. The old goddess of the fire will guide you alright. I have already asked her to do so. Rely on her and go your way with care. We have made a fine staff to help you on your way. Take hold of it firmly at the top, and walk securely minding your feet, lifting and lowering them as you raise and lower the staff. You have plenty of food and drink. Look neither to the right nor left, but go on quickly and delight your ancestors with your presents. Do not keep remembering your brothers, sisters and other relatives in this world. Go your way and do not yearn to see those that are here. They are safe and sound under the care of the old goddess of fire. If you go on yearning for them, the folks there will laugh. This you must understand. You must not behave in such a foolish manner".

Unlike the evidence provided by our primitive contemporaries whose ritual acts can be observed, and whose myths are told by the elders, archaeological excavations rarely provide direct information about the feelings and ideas of our remote ancestors. Usually we have to use our intuition in order to reconstruct the ideas and thoughts that lie behind the material evidence. (However, the study of contemporary representatives of primitive cultures enables us to gain some understanding of remote periods of human evolution. And now and then the past leaves artifices whose cultural significance cannot be mistaken.)

The many burial sites discovered in caves inhabited by Neanderthal man provide ample evidence for his concern with life after death. At Le Moustier a boy of about fifteen or sixteen years old had been buried in a cave. He had been lowered into a trench, placed on his right side with knees slightly drawn and head resting on his forearm in a sleeping position. A pile of flints lay under his head to form a sort of stone pillow, and near his hand was a beautifully worked stone-axe. Around the remains were wild cattle bones, many of them charred, the remains of roasted meat which may have been provided to serve as sustenance in the world of the dead.

One spring day about 60,000 years ago members of his family went out into the hills, picked masses of wild flowers and made a bed of them on the ground, a resting-place for the deceased. Other flowers were probably laid on top of his grave, still others seem to have been woven together with the branches of a pine-like shrub to form a wreath. The flowers and the tools given to him show the love bestowed upon the deceased and the security provided for him by the tools and food enclosed in his grave.

In southern France, in a cave at La Ferrassie in the Dordogne, the remains were unearthed of two Neanderthal adults and two children who had been ceremonially buried. One of the elders, probably a woman, had been placed in a crouched or flexed position in a cavity dug into the floor, legs pressed against her body and arms folded upon her breasts, an attitude that can only have been brought about by binding tightly with thongs before the corpse stiffened. The other adult, probably a man, also lying on his back, had his head and shoulders protected by slabs of stone. The two children, lying supine, were in shallow graves, and close by were holes with the bones and ashes of a wild ox, the remains of an offering of some kind.

Also in the Dordogne, at La Chapelle-aux-Saints, an individual of about fifty was placed in a small natural depression orientated east and west and accompanied by a number of shells, some Mousterian flints and the remains of a woolly rhinoceros, horse, reindeer and bison. We may assume that laying out the body orientated towards the rising and setting sun shows that solar symbolisms representing the ideas of birth and death as well as rebirth were established in the minds of Neanderthal man.

A remarkable piece of ritual has recently been reported from the cave of Teshik-Tash in Eastern Uzbekistan where a buried child was closely surrounded by a ring of five or six pairs of goat horns still attached to their parent skulls and pushed point downwards into the floor.

A penetrating insight into the psychology of Neanderthal man is provided by one of three skeletons from the cave of Shanidar, situated at a height of 2,500 feet in the Zagros Mountains in southern Iran. The subject, thought to have been killed by a fall of stone from the roof of the cave, was a man, an arthritic one-armed cripple who had attained the age of about 40 or 50 years. Careful study of the skeletal remains have shown that the right arm and shoulder had never fully developed and that the arm had indeed been amputated below the elbow. Furthermore, examination of the teeth confirms that unlike those of other Neanderthalers they show signs of marked wear as if they had been used to remedy the lack of a right arm. The fact that an individual so disabled from childhood should have been able to live to what must have been regarded for that period as an advanced age shows a degree of concern for the individual far transcending anything shown in animal societies. Indeed, having regard to the rigorous conditions of life and the small number of potential meat winners in each social group, the care shown to this cripple, who presumably had to keep close to the cave and can hardly have shared in hunting activities, reflects a degree of humanity not always displayed towards one another by members of civilised societies.

There is an ambiguity in the burial rituals which we should not overlook. The flexing of the lower limbs in the cave of La Ferrassie which would have been brought about by binding the lower limbs with thongs seems to have been widespread Neanderthal practice since it has been noted as far afield as Kiik-Koba in the Crimea and Mount Carmel in Palestine. There has been speculation whether this practice indicates a desire to symbolise the foetal position or whether it was intended to prevent the dead person from coming back in order to haunt the living. However, we can assume that the tight binding with thongs of the lower limbs shows a defence mechanism—a need to inhibit the dead. The concern for a dead person's future journey and his continued safety in the other world is accompanied by apprehension that his ghost may return. The burial ceremony of the Ainus related above ends in the following manner: "After the celebrant has finished his instructions and assurances to the deceased, the coffin is not carried out through the door but a part of the side of the house is taken away and repaired before the mourners return. The ghost then will not know how to get back in. Or if the one who has died is the mistress of the house, the whole dwelling is burnt. Into the grave go jewels, ear-rings, kitchen knives, pots, pans and ladles, weaving looms and other such if the departed was a woman—swords, bows and quivers if a man. And when the burial has been completed, the mourners leave the grave walking backwards, lest, turning, they should be possessed of the ghost of the deceased; and they are holding weapons in their hands—the women sticks, the men their swords—which they wave back and forth for their defence".* This ambivalence between concern for the dead man's safety in his future journeys and the fear that he may return to haunt the living indicates not only the notion of eternity but also of guilt. It means that the ritualistic assurances and prayers for his safety serve to ensure his goodwill towards the living, so that he should be grateful and think well of them and not harbour any resentment and come back and punish them. In other words, we can find reasons to think these rituals already served to ward off fears that the dead individual would blame the living for having in some way been responsible for his death by harbouring death wishes towards him or harming him in any way. The ghost represents both our love as well as our aggressive urges; the frightening ghost is a representation of our destructive urges projected upon the dead, he represents our bad conscience, our frightening Superego, whereas the loving ghost represents our good conscience, our loving and protective Superego.

These early burial rites then show both man's concern for his fellows as well as propitiation of guilt feelings. They show the beginnings of the concept of the good ghost and the bad ghost, the imaginative representation of the good and the bad Superego and the mechanisms of propitiation.

---

* Joseph Campbell: 'The Masks of God: Primitive Mythology' (Souvenir Press, 1973).

It is significant that Neanderthal man almost always buried his dead in his caves, or later, during the warm spell of the fourth glaciation, in the compounds of his camps. The ties of community were so profoundly developed that he could not bear to cast the dead person out of the community, though his ghost was known to have moved on to another world. In the ceremonial assurances of his future life, the mourners partake in his continued existence thereby alleviating the shock experienced by his loss, and at the same time overcome the fear that he might return and punish the community for any death wishes which it may have harboured against him.

While in earlier times mourning took the form of introjecting the dead by eating his brain so that he continued to live in the mind of his community, the new form of mourning employs the process of projection in so far as the fantasies of the dead person's journey are acted out in imagination and by material symbols such as tools, weapons and food which ensure his future well-being. Thus man's desire for continued existence and well-being is projected upon the departed person and he becomes an actor in the imaginative drama of the afterlife; he affirms man's quest for eternity. Thus projection and symbolisation became established in early man's culture and greatly enlarged the world of his imagination.

The ambivalence between the bad ghost and the good ghost, the processes of projection as well as propitiation and restitution find further expression in the widespread rituals of animal sacrifice and primitive totemism which played a large part in the culture of Neanderthal man. The records provide rich evidence for these cults. More than any other animal it was the cave-bear who figured in his totem worship. These animals had to be driven out of the caves before man could move into them and they were killed by the hundred and eaten. Indeed, they were a major supply of food. They were most probably considered as the original inhabitants of the caves, their original owners so to speak, and the caves would have retained some of the bear spirit. A mountain cave in eastern Austria contained a rectangular vault holding seven bear skulls all facing the cave entrance, while a site near Regoudon in southern France represents perhaps the most elaborate bear cult burial known. It included a skeleton, stone drains, a rectangular pit covered by a flat stone weighing nearly a ton, and the remains of more than twenty bears. A cave in Germany, Petershöhle near

Velden, which was excavated from 1916 to 1922, had closet-like niches in the walls which contained five bear skulls as well as his leg bones. We see here altar-like edifices upon which the remains of cave-bears were laid out to be worshipped in some way or at least kept as monuments to their continued existence. The object of the hunt, which was killed and eaten, had to be propitiated so that its anger would not have entered into the hunter. While the bear was killed and eaten his good spirit would remain and continue to populate the hunting grounds and the caves. He would be offered back his home and given sanctuary, and his spirit would pervade the cave and reassure its inhabitants.

Man depended on the animal of the hunt, and it played a large role in his imagination. The animal was important, desired and even loved as the provider of man's sustenance. The slaying of the animal was necessary in order to provide food, but this food had to be freed of the animal's anger and its suffering, and its good libido had to be assured. It had to be good food, not angry food. The spirit of the slain animal had to be propitiated so that it would love the hunter and enter into him as a good spirit. Man had to be sure that the internal object was good and not angry, accepted and accepting. Furthermore, man had to be assured that by eating the dead animal it would not disappear but that its existence would be perpetuated. By ritualised representations of the spirit of the dead animal it would remain forever and continue to provide security. The animal would be inside the man and outside him, and by being assured of its special status it would become a good and protective spirit.

However, Neanderthal man has left us no man-made relics of his worship, but we must assume that ceremonial dancing and singing would have accompanied the rituals of propitiation. Being unable to carve images or paint, Neanderthal man would have laid out the skulls and bones of the bear in a ceremonial manner, danced around them, probably accompanied by some ritualistic chanting, thus assuring himself of the animal's goodwill and its eternal existence.

But here the question forces itself upon our mind why the old form of ritual introjection as practised by homo erectus no longer sufficed for Neanderthal man, why indeed he had to conduct ritual worship of a primitive totemic kind, and what caused the intensification of his guilt feelings which made propitiation cults necessary.

We must assume that a degree of repressed aggressiveness existed in Neanderthal man which can be held responsible for the intensification of the ritual acts of propitiation and restitution. There is considerable evidence that aggressive behaviour, acts of violence in the sense of man killing man, became increasingly frequent in the life of Neanderthal man.

Remains of some kind of mass killing were found in a rock shelter overlooking a river in northern Yugoslavia, where investigators recovered 500 bones and bone fragments representing at least a dozen individuals. A number of the bones are charred, suggesting that cannibalism occurred, while other bones show definite signs of having been cut. The mass killings hint at organised fighting among neighbouring bands, a possibility strengthened by findings in other Neanderthal sites—a flint projectile point in a rib cage, a pelvis with a spear hole in it, and skulls bashed and penetrated in various ways. These are other signs that Neanderthal man had become 'more human', developing aggressiveness directed upon other communities. It is possible that we encounter here the first signs of organised warfare.

What caused this aggressive urge which had to be repressed and transferred upon members of other communities while members of his own community and his animals of the hunt had to be protected from it? We can find a clue to this problem in the emergence of a latency period, the need for sexual repression and the resulting aggression towards the Superego, perhaps the first beginning of an Oedipus complex in early man.

The very success of Neanderthal man's technology, the increased complexity of his tools, made it necessary for the young men to spend more time in the acquisition of skills. There would be more emphasis on learning and training the young, and sexual maturation delay would be prolonged, necessitating a latency period. This would demand in turn a period of sexual repression and arouse conflicts between fathers and sons much more pronounced than in earlier periods of man's evolution. Perhaps we can say that the very advances of the technical perfection of Mousterian tool cultures were responsible for sexual repression. In this way, sexual conflicts, aggression and guilt became part of Neanderthal's psycho-cultural character, and we must expect cultural restitution rituals to emerge in order to master these conflicts.

While the cults of propitiation and restitution of the dead and of the animals killed in the hunt indicate a great leap forward in man's imaginative capability (Neanderthal man had an astonishingly large brain—from 1,200 to 1,600 c.c.), he left no relics of painting or carved figures, or other representatives of deities. He probably lacked the ability to transform the images of the spirit into paintings or statues, and had to be content with their representation through the actual remains of the dead person or animal by putting them into graves or altar-like structures.

If we look at the skull of a typical Neanderthal man we find that the frontal areas of his brain are much smaller than those of Homo sapiens, while the parietal and occipital lobes at the rear top and rear area of his brain are quite large, indeed, as large if not larger than those of Homo sapiens. It has been found that the anatomical divisions of the cortical regions of the brain correspond approximately to particular functions which control the bodily activities, processes of sensory information and intellectual activities. While the frontal and pre-frontal lobes of the cortex are the areas responsible for the activity of intelligence, the capacity of foresight, planning, anticipation, purpose-direction, experimentation and the concept of rules related to abstract ideas, the parietal and occipital regions determine the co-ordination and control of sensory input and output, visual imagination, body sense and body awareness.

We must assume that Neanderthal man's capacity to entertain abstract ideas, his ability to plan ahead and experiment, was limited. But having a large parietal and occipital brain he would be capable of a high degree of visual imagery and of projecting his own body sensations on to these images; he would be able to identify with his images, and feel them as having the same sensations and motivations which he experienced himself.

He would be capable of animistic thinking whereby objects of nature acquire a soul and the sensation of being alive. On the other hand, however, he would not be capable of performing the task of shaping inanimate objects to make them represent his imagery, he would not be able to sculpt or paint. He would only to a limited extent be able to experiment with new possibilities. Thus innovation would rely on concrete manipulations, on his actual experience with objects, and he would not be inspired by concepts of general laws or by abstract ideas governing the behaviour of things. François Bodes, an archaeologist who has done more detailed work in the classification of Neanderthal tools than possibly any other investigator, was impressed not only with their craftsmanship but also with the fact that the Neanderthal craftsmen were working in an almost automatic fashion, as if they had perfected their technique and then stopped inventing.

Thus we may assume that while Neanderthal man arrived at a stage of high work efficiency and bodily adaptation to his arctic or subarctic environment, initiated religious imagination and ritual, and entertained animistic concepts about his environment, he had not reached the stage of religious ideas involving the concept of deities. For this achievement in the maturation processes of the human species we must thank the appearance of a new race, Cro-Magnon man, the first true human, the first man who was physically and mentally just like ourselves. The arrival of Homo sapiens in the European continent was as sudden and dramatic as it was decisive for man's evolution. It heralded not only the greatest advance in man's development but also one of its great tragedies, namely, the Neanderthal catastrophe.

5   Homo Sapiens Emerges

During the warm period of the Würm glaciation, a period which occurred between 40.000 and 25.000 years ago, one of the most astonishing events of human prehistory took place. After a reign of some 70.000 years, during which time he spread over most of Europe and Asia and large parts of Africa, Neanderthal man disappeared almost suddenly to be replaced by a new kind of man, namely, Homo sapiens. This 'Neanderthal catastrophe', as it has been called, and the emergence of Homo sapiens in Europe within a very short time—by some researchers considered to be a few thousand years, by others even a few hundred years—has caused much puzzlement. The question as to how and why Neanderthal man became extinct and where Homo sapiens came from has occupied many archaeologists and anthropologists and has been the subject of much heated argument.

It is generally recognised that this new species, our own direct ancestors, were invaders in Europe, for there is no other explanation for the abrupt change in the physical and cultural properties of the new inhabitants of the area. There would clearly not have been time for Neanderthal man to evolve into a significantly different species.

The generic term given to the first representatives of Homo sapiens in Europe is Cro-Magnon, after the cave of Cro-Magnon near Les Eyzies where his remains were discovered in 1875. Subsequently many other sites were discovered belonging to the early representatives of this species particularly in Combe Capelle, Les Eyzies, and many others in the Dordogne valley. Les Eyzies has been called the prehistoric capital of Europe because it is the centre of a region especially rich in sites and artefacts relating both to Neanderthal as well as Cro-Magnon man. During the warm spell of the Würm glaciation, the valley of the River Vézère as well as the Dordogne were a concentration point for game. Forests of spruce, oak and ash blossomed with strips of vegetation which attracted reindeer, bison, great numbers of rodents and later flocks of sheep. There was ample supply of game, and water was plentiful and the forests provided wood for the new man who knew how to fell them with his polished axes.

Cro-Magnon man has been described as tall, handsome, with regular features, high forehead, a prominent chin, small teeth, delicate face bone, without the huge brow ridges that characterised Neanderthal man and all his predecessors. There is no doubt that he was of a Caucasian racial stock. If one looks at the only painting known so far of this man—a small bas-relief at Angles-sur-l'Anglin—one is astonished at the break with all earlier types of man. The straight and high forehead, absence of pronounced brows, straight and narrow nose, white skin with black hair and black beard gives us the modern white man. His tools and implements represent a revolution in technology; they show that the makers of these tools could strike off a flake from a core in such way as to get a knife-like blade; these blades were marvellously delicate, their knives thin and sharp, their spearheads follow a precise pattern expressing a symmetrical concept which we still regard as perfect for spearheads and arrowheads. They made spears, blades, knives, scrapers and polished axe-heads in stone compressed and beaten to an exquisite sharpness and thinness which is unrivalled in any palaeolithic culture. Furthermore, they used bones from horses and stags, and ivory from mammoths from which they made pointing drills, arrowheads and needles. The new culture of tool-making is called Aurignacian and it is not only an improvement on the old—it is an evolutionary jump in the quality of tools. Perhaps their most important technological invention was a tool called the burin. This was a special kind of chisel or graving tool which made it possible to manufacture tools of bone, amber and ivory of a precision and efficiency that surpassed by far anything man could do before. Once a hunter carved a spearhead out of ivory or stag horn it would not break easily, while a comparable head of flint would shatter at its first contact with animal bone. Aurignacian man could tie thongs to his spearhead by boring holes in it and fasten it to the shaft. He could carry a supply of these spearheads with him and thus be able to kill a great many animals before having to return home for new weapons. The burin is indeed a key tool for Cro-Magnon culture, a tool-making tool and its basic shape and principle is still used in our time as the cutting knife for machine tools. It is the prototype of all machine tools. Besides the importance of the burin for creating far more efficient hunting tools it made possible the development of a whole host of household utensils out of bone and stone, but above all it made possible the manufacture of needles and pointing drills which in turn facilitated the art of clothes making and hut making from animal skin. It enabled man for the first time in his history to create permanent artificial homes which could provide warmth and protection and replace the caves.

On levels belonging to the Aurignacian culture in Europe as well as in Asia we find symmetrical and smoothly constructed floors with pillars of stone on the corners and edges to support a roof. These hut foundations are quite regular and contain a hearth in the middle. They were constructed to form an encampment of several of such huts plus one or two larger structures resembling the longhouses found up to recent times in the Pacific, i.e. Borneo Sumatra, some parts of Africa as well as among nomadic tribes of Siberia.

Man had clothes now to provide warmth; he knew how to make fire anywhere; he would carry warmth around with him, both as clothes as well as the knowledge and ease of firemaking. In his compounds he had developed a division of labour unlike anything known before. For the first time the hunter did not have to make all his own tools. Those less physically fitted for hunting were no longer useless: they stayed at home in the compound and specialised in toolmaking, and the old did not have to die because they could no longer hunt, but they could use all their accumulated experience and knowledge to improve the techniques and skills of the race. So the hunters were provided with excellent tools and could use all their ability in the hunt, and they vanquished all before them. In Solutre in France they killed 100,000 horses, and at Pedmost in Czechoslovakia they killed 1000 mammoths. The Neanderthals, able and powerful as they were, could not match the new man in efficiency of the hunt.

MATRIARCHY: THE ORIGINAL CULTURE OF HOMO SAPIENS

Besides the technological advances of his Aurignacian culture, Cro-Magnon man introduced a completely new dimension into human civilisation. Out of ivory and stone he created statues in great numbers, mostly representing female figures, and he carved abstract and realistic patterns. A new ability to concretise symbolic concepts emerged here—art, as we know it. There is no doubt that this new dimension of symbol presentation was motivated by a new type of psychological preoccupation, facilitated by the new technology. The burin did not only enable man to enhance greatly the precision and the efficiency of his tools but also to make precise and delicate engravings and sculptures.

The sculptures mostly depict females, often with grossly exaggerated sexual features, and there is no doubt that they were cult statues. It is interesting that they usually have no feet and their legs end in a point. This has been assumed to indicate that they were stuck in the ground to preside over some household shrine. They do not represent individual women, for their faces are deliberately left blank, but can be taken to represent symbolised concepts of fertility, security and plenitude. From the great number of almost exclusively female statuary, as well as from the structures of the compounds which resemble quite closely those of recent matriarchal civilisations, we can confidently assume we here deal with a matriarchal culture. Thus Homo sapiens not only introduced a revolution in technology and the invention of artificial habitations but also the social and psychological structure of matriarchy.

In the new habitations women had begun to play a much more important role—they became productive in their own right. The higher levels of technology provided women with a much wider range of activities, and they would take over a larger area of socially necessary work than ever before, including the growing of fruit and vegetables—they were the initiators of horticulture. With the refinement of hunting tools men would venture out further afield and remain away for longer periods, and women would stay behind in the compounds, no longer merely tending to the children and waiting for the men to return but would be making utensils of all kinds. With the invention of the needle they would sew clothes and make roofs for the huts out of animal skins. These activities would emphasise the importance of females in productive activities.

In the new hut communities women would come into their own right, as one might say, discovering for themselves a host of new skills and responsibilities. While we can appreciate, therefore, the increased importance of the female, how can we explain her worship? One simple explanation would be that we worship those upon whom we depend, we give them power over us and endeavour to propitiate them in order to secure their goodwill and their continued supply of the things we need.

Even Freud has remarked that we submit to those who can supply our needs and we love them if they grant us our satisfaction. This is quite true, but to explain the 'religion' of matriarchy in this way and perhaps to introduce further the Marxist explanation that those who own the means of production are our masters would be far too simplistic even while true on one level. In order to gain a better understanding of the emergence of the new culture, we must go back to the question as to where Homo sapiens came from, what kind of social structure he developed, and what psychological motivations could have occurred to motivate the emergence of matriarchy.

We know that he appeared in Europe during the mild period or interstadial of the Würm glaciation, about 35,000 years ago. With the advent of warmer weather different kinds of animals had appeared, replacing the mammoths and woolly rhinoceros and other game which had predominated during the cold climate. Wild cattle, fallow deer, elk, bison, buffalo, aurochs and other herd animals grazed in green wooded valleys which rose from the coastal plains and extended into the foothills of the mountains. Herds became larger, and their movements through the valleys were mass movements. For the hunters, risks increased as well as opportunities. These now extinct animals should not be imagined as the docile cud chewers of today's farmyards. They were fierce, fast and big (some of the bulls measuring $6\frac{1}{2}$ feet high at the shoulder), and quite capable of fighting back. Their successful pursuit demanded large-scale hunting methods involving the co-operation of a number of bands.

The milder climate had enabled Neanderthal man to emerge from his cave and live in encampments of primitive tents, constructed from shrub wood with skins laid out on top, and to roam further afield for his hunting expeditions. However, his form of hunting was limited to the pursuit of single animals by a single band consisting of members of his community, involving maybe half a dozen individuals.

WHERE DID HOMO SAPIENS COME FROM?

The advance towards large-scale co-operative hunting methods developed amongst other people who lived far from the glaciers, who experienced warmer climates much earlier than their cousins on the Eurasian mainland. While the milder climate emerged in Europe and large parts of Asia some 40,000 to 35,000 years ago it had become warmer 20,000 years earlier—about 60,000 years ago—in the Middle East and Southern Asia. People living in these areas had the opportunity to engage in large-scale hunting methods on a community basis for hundreds of generations, to produce radical changes in their social organisation and new methods of living.

They had taken the first major steps towards the fully-fledged tribe, an association of a number of families held together by new types of rituals and symbols, shared practices and purposes including co-operative hunting and warfare. Their religious ideas were of an altogether more abstract kind and were symbolised by sculptured and painted images.

It is therefore towards these regions that we must look for the transformation from Neanderthal to Homo sapiens.

Work in Middle East caves—especially those at Mount Carmel —has thrown much light on the development of the early post-Mousterian industries and may help to show more clearly the process by which the change from Mousterian to Aurignacian cultures took place.

At Tabun on Mount Carmel, and other caves in the area, various stages of the Mousterian tool cultures were discovered, and the cave at el Wad continues the sequence up to the Aurignacian. Subsequent excavation at other sites showed there were in fact thick deposits between the Mousterian and what is referred to as the Levantine Aurignacian. These intermediate deposits are particularly well preserved in the rock shelter of Ksar Akil near Beirut, with over sixty feet of archaeological deposit of which fifteen feet lay between Mousterian and the Levantine Aurignacian. These layers indicate the existence of a culture of transformation—an evolutionary period—which linked Neanderthal with Cro-Magnon man.

The remains found at Mugharet-es-Tabun and Mugharet-es-Skhul near Mount Carmel in Israel are of particular importance. From these and other sites in Israel have come a number of skeletons which show positive characteristics of both Homo sapiens and Neanderthal man. They are thought to have lived during the time of the Würm glaciation—before the warm interstadial. These discoveries provide a genetic link between early Neanderthal man and modern man. Many skeletal remains from the sites in Israel show clearly developed characteristics similar to those of modern man. The thigh bones are straight, quite long, and can easily be distinguished from the short, slightly bent thigh bones of 'classic' Neanderthal man. The brow ridge is still fairly prominent, but there are already signs indicating that this species is changing and starting to take on characteristics of modern man. The vault of the skull of some of the Israel Neanderthal men is high, the occipital region is full and rounded and the lower jaw shows signs of developing a chin. This type was slightly taller than Neanderthal man, and the volume of the best preserved skull from Mugharet-es-Skhul is about 1,500 cubic centimetres.

The remains discovered in the years from 1933 to 1974 in Djebel-Kafzeh near Nazareth belong to a similar type of man. A particularly well-preserved skull has a volume of 1,560 cubic centimetres and new discoveries have proved strong similarities to Homo sapiens.

In other sites in the Middle East, Blade and Burin industries come within the range of Aurignacian cultures. These typologically early Aurignacian industries can be dated to between 52,000 and 42,000 years ago—long before they appeared in Western Europe.

The fairly plentiful human bones found in these caves are also intermediate between Neanderthals and men of our own kind, reaching almost from one to the other.

The cave of the Kids, Mugharet-es-Skhul, was one of anthropology's great finds; it contained ten buried skeletons in different states of repair and in a densely cemented matrix. Skeletally they were tall, strongly built but straight-limbed, and so were quite unlike their hulking contemporaries of the west. There were faint suggestions of skeletal relationship to Neanderthal, such as relatively short forearms with somewhat bowed radius and ulna, but in most aspects they approached closely to Homo sapiens. Indeed, it would be correct to regard them as coming within the range of modern man.

There can be little doubt that in these fossils we are witnessing the actual evolution of Homo sapiens from Neanderthal man before his grand entrance into Europe. While Cro-Magnons replaced western Neanderthals fairly suddenly in Europe and mixed with them very little, there was a much more widespread and looser relationship between the various races in the Middle East and Southern Asia. Thus we can assume that Homo sapiens evolved in the Middle East during a period some 20,000 years before he arrived in Europe. (Recent calculations, using thermoluminescence (T.L). suggest that Homo sapiens evolved in the Middle East even earlier, but these calculations have not yet been confirmed.)

THE DEVELOPMENT OF THE HOMO SAPIENS BRAIN

The increased skills in toolmaking, the manipulation of these tools, the complexities of social organisation which replaced instinctual bonds of the family cave, the rules needed to govern social life, the symbolic representation of deities and religious ideas made an expansion of the cortex and in particular the frontal lobes of the cortex inevitable. It was no longer sufficient to have an internal image of the immortalised ancestor and animal of the hunt; these images were externalised into permanent symbolic representations and their meaning had, in turn, to be recognised.

The visual representation of divinities gave religious worship a new sense of conviction and magic, and this was needed in order to provide cohesion and identity to the larger communities. The more complex social structures also needed new rules to co-ordinate man's activities, an increased capability for generalisation and the conceptualisation of laws. Man thus transformed the vicissitudes of chance into the assurance of certainty, the profane into the sacred, and the image of the sacred gave new status and meaning for his life. He would gain a new sense of identity and recognise himself in the artefacts of his religion.

The skill required for such representations and recognition

depended on the possession of the frontal cortex of the brain which not only controls the higher mental functions like intelligence, learning and purpose direction but also motor adaptations to mental processes and images, and to reproduce them by means of manual manipulation. The frontal lobes of the cortical brain enable man to create objects which represent mental images, to reproduce his images in objects and to invent new meanings through new mental combinations and representations. Intelligence provides an internal environment that acts as a feedback mechanism, it is the structuring activity, it creates structures and, in turn, generally produces organs which obey the structure and function of the intelligence. Intelligence is not derived from reflexes hereditarily acquired and perpetuated in circumstances that repeat themselves; it arises at times when changed circumstances make habitual reflexes inadequate. When the needs of a situation transcend the framework of instinct or of habitual associations, the subject gropes for new response patterns. This takes place not merely by trial and error in physical action but by the remoulding of internal anticipations and cognitive experimentation of new possibilities and new types of association. But the groping for new types of responses is not non-systematic or subject to chance solutions, it needs the awareness of an end to be attained.

In 1933 Claparède wrote: "No groping is altogether incoherent because its function is always to attain some end, to satisfy some need, it is always orientated in some direction... In the lower forms of thought this direction is still very vague, very general. But the higher the mental level of the seeker becomes, the more the awareness of relationships is strengthened and, consequently, the more specific becomes the direction in which the search for the problems' solution must take place... Thus every new groping tightens a little the circle within which the next gropings will occur... Groping is, consequently, the agent which permits the discovery of new relationships".*

Now the question arises where we can find the origins of direction and the conceptualisation of ends which direct groping as well as experimentation. It is obvious that mostly these are not conscious but derive from a symbolic configuration (Gestalt), which may express an emotional drive. The emotional drive and its

---

* Edouard Claparède:'La Genese de l'hypothese' (Archives de Psychologie) 1933.

symbolisation lies at the root of purposiveness. More precisely, it is the libidinous primacy expressed in fantasy and symbolic imagery which produces a sense of purpose which, in turn, gives direction to new action, experimentation and new constellations of thought. The intelligence, being an instrument of the Ego, is therefore directed by the libido primacy which dominates the individual and his culture.

When we consider the infantile stages in the development of the libido we find that the child at first perceives the world in the form of part objects. Before the mother acquired an image of a whole personality she was an object represented by her organs of gratification. The breast is the centre of the infant's needs and the focus of its attention (and although the libido of the breast expresses in many ways the character, the conflicts and attitudes of the mother, it is nevertheless as a breast or nipple that she manifests herself to the child), and later her skin and her embrace is perceived as the object of narcissistic gratification. It is only at the later stages of narcissistic development with the beginning awareness of a sense of the self, of a primitive Ego, and the onset of the anal primacy accompanied by the projections of the narcissistic self outwards that concepts of the whole person, both of the self as well as the mother, appear.

With the capacity to produce self-images out of material shapes the child acquires the ability to externalise its narcissistic self-awareness into an objective representation. Such an external, objective self-image acquires the quality of permanence and indestructability. In this way the Ego processes and Ego identity become strengthened and reinforced. At this time the mother also acquires the attributes of a whole object. Her various erotogenic zones on which the infant depended—separate worlds so to speak—become co-ordinated into a whole person imbued with an Ego and a sense of permanence. When the child arrives at a concept of the self as an Ego, enabling it to speak and think of itself as 'I', it also begins to understand that the mother thinks of herself in the first person. She emerges as a separate person, with her own narcissistic needs, interests and activities. Her separateness will become a source of anxiety to the child, and it will engage in endless games depicting mother's disappearance in order to abreact its anxiety, and to receive from her assurances of her continued presence and attention. If these games and fantasies fail to provide reassurance, then they will continue in the form of symptoms as, for instance, asthma, or clutching possessiveness producing a wide range of muscular tensions as well as compulsive rituals which demand meticulous execution and the fulfilment of certain conditions which symbolise the return of the mother's attention and love. However, besides the numberless games, rituals and symptoms in which the child engages (symptoms often being games that become 'frozen', irresistible and unavoidable), a more successful way of assuring itself of mother's presence emerges with the onset of the anal projective stage.*

Having acquired the ability to assure itself of a new sense of identity by means of self-projection and the manipulation of material objects into a self-image, the child will apply this method to ensure the continued existence and proximity of the mother: it will create images and pictures and shape her into figurines and forms which symbolise her. In this way the child can exercise its own powers to assure her presence and will no longer be passively dependent upon the vicissitudes of her moods or upon external circumstances which distract her attention. The child's skill and imagination would ensure her presence and the permanence of her protection.

SYMBOLISATION AND MYTH

When a child plays with material objects and attempts to form them into various shapes it gains pleasure and satisfaction from the exercise of its skill and the handling of materials. But we must bear in mind that in its play the child attempts, often unconsciously, to represent images and fantasies which occupy its mind. (Indeed, play therapy as developed and employed by Melanie Klein in her analysis of children is based on this need in children and provided for the skilled observer insight into their unconscious conflicts and complexes). The material may consist of clay, mud, sand, plasticine, etc., and the child knows that, but in its play the material becomes endowed with a spirit which reproduces the world of imagination. The emotional charge of the fantasy image is transferred on to its material representation, the libido of the image goes

---

* See: 'The Unknown Self'.

into the object and in this way the symbolic shape or artefact acquires a life of its own. It may become a fairy or a witch, a friend or an enemy; a circle may represent the womb, the cave, the territory, the unity and wholeness of mother's protection; a line may symbolise a division of the self from the other, or a square denote order and obedience. Just as the small child beholding its faeces perceives them as vibrating with the vitality and libido of its internal self revealed, so it will perceive the various symbolic objects as being possessed by a feeling of being alive. The make-believe world of childhood is the game of belief and ecstasy. This is a primary, spontaneous device of childhood, a magical device by which the world can be transformed from banality to magic, and its inevitability in childhood is one of those universal characteristics of man. As Joseph Campbell remarks: "It is a primary datum of the science of myth which is concerned precisely with the phenomenon of self-induced belief".*

In a paper, 'On the force of the demonic world of childhood', Frobenius illustrated his thesis in this way: "A professor is writing at his desk and his four-year old little daughter is running about the room. She has nothing to do and is disturbing him. So he gives her three burnt matches saying, 'Here, play!' And sitting on the rug she begins to play with the matches, Hänsel, Gretel and the witch. Some time elapses during which the professor concentrates upon his task undisturbed. But then suddenly the child shrieks in terror. The father jumps. What is it? What has happened? The little girl comes running to him showing every sign of great fright. 'Daddy, daddy', she cries, 'take the witch away! I can't touch the witch any more!'" An eruption of emotion, Frobenius observes, is characteristic of the spontaneous shift of an idea from the level of the emotions to that of reality-consciousness. The match is not a witch, nor was it a witch for the child at the beginning of the game. The process therefore rests on the fact that the match has become a witch on the emotional level, and the conclusion of the process coincides with the transfer of this idea to the plane of consciousness and reality.

The magic of the child's play is enacted in cultures and experienced as religious myth. "The myth", as Thomas Mann has observed, "is the foundation of life, the timeless schema, the pious

---

* Joseph Campbell: 'The Masks of God'.

formula which life flows into when it reproduces its traits out of the unconscious". In the Roman-Catholic mass, for example, when the priest quotes the words of Christ at the Last Supper, he pronounces the formula of consecration, first over the wafer of the Host—'For this is my body'—and then over the chalice of the wine—'For this is the chalice of my blood, of the new and eternal testament: the mystery of faith, which shall be shed for you and for many unto the remission of sins'. (The bread and the wine become the body and blood of Christ, and every fragment of the Host and every drop of the wine is the actual living saviour of the world. The Sacrament is not conceived to be a reference, a mere sign or symbol to arouse in us a train of thought, but is God himself, the creator, judge and saviour of the universe).

But let us return to Cro-Magnon man. There is no doubt that with the development and growth of the pre-frontal lobes of the cortex he was able to make abstract representations of his imagery and his feelings, and to make combinations of them. But what were the emotional needs which could be held responsible for the mother complex that prompted Cro-Magnon man to make numberless statues and statuettes of female goddesses signifying the cult of the mother, the culture of matriarchy?

THE CULT OF THE MOTHER GODDESS

With the increase in size of the settlements and the greater complexities of social life, women took over a wide area of responsibility and engaged in varied activities so that children would no longer find their mother's attention undividedly centred upon them. The new woman of Homo sapiens communities became an individual in her own right, a separate person so to speak, she was no longer wholly a mother but a person with responsibility to society.

She became absorbed by the larger responsibilities of the village society, and the child as well as the man had to share her with other members who were instinctively strangers to them. The narcissistic need to be surrounded by the mother's libido and her attention would be subjected to the trauma of separation and insecurity. Memories of these traumas of separation would remain in the mind of the grown Homo sapiens. On his return from the hunt he would no longer receive the undivided welcome of the cave home, pervaded by the woman's libido and symbolising her embrace, but instead would have found women active and busy organising the life of the village compound, working at a variety of tasks, and absorbed to a large extent in the community of women who organised the village in the absence of men.

So, both child and man, the child in the man, would be overtaken by the urge to re-create the lost magic of her love and her presence, and he would shape images of her and surround himself with the libido which they represented. In this way the spirit of the mother would be omnipresent again and cast its protection upon the home. The intimate union with the female experienced in infancy and prepetuated in the cave community was lost in the larger and complex world of compounds and villages and had to be re-created by symbolic representations.

By playing with material shapes man plays with the mother and satisfies his need for her—he re-creates her—and she would be with him forever, his creation, his possession. And Homo sapiens made images of the woman emphasising her sexual characteristics to assure himself of the permanence of her libido. And also, having lost the intimate, instinctive sense of his own identity of which he was assured in the close circle of the cave and the spontaneous and unquestioned recognition by the mother, having become one of the many in the new large habitations, he reassured himself of his narcissism and his identity by making sculptures and symbols of himself. He created Ego artefacts as a mirror for his own identity; he painted his body in various colours and abstract designs in order to affirm his individuality as well as his belonging to the new community. He adorned himself and made himself a new skin in order to compensate for the deprivation of his narcissistic libido. Cro-Magnon people used cosmetics and made the earliest known jewellery. They wore clothes decorated with rows of coloured beads, ivory bracelets, necklaces of pierced teeth and fish vertebrae. These elaborate decorations were related to a general increase in the complexity of society, to the rise of mass hunting methods. Jewellery, as John E. Pfeiffer has observed, may have done more than beautify. It may have helped to identify the clan or the status of people associating in groups too large for individuals to know one another by sight or name.

Object deprivation as well as narcissistic deprivation not only found a measure of compensation in the creation of mother-images and narcissistic adornment; the libido which has lost its intimate union with the primary object, the mother, would forever seek to find her in the world around; the child as well as the man will be prompted to rediscover the mother in natural objects and perceive them as symbolic representations of her presence. He will look for her everywhere and recognise her everywhere, the yearning for her libido will direct the senses to perceive her, and his imagination will convert natural objects into feminine symbols; hillocks and sand dunes, valleys and meadows, flowers and the sparkle of lights in rivers, lakes and waterfalls will represent her body and its manifold libidinous sensations, forests and shrubs symbolise her hair and open glades surrounded by dense forest re-create the magic of her femininity, her sanctum—the holy of holies.

However, man not only perceives the symbolic presence of the mother and her attributes in the objects of nature but the whole of nature appears to him as a manifestation of her presence and her power. Having lost the enveloping security of the maternal cave, he reproduces it in his imagination. He draws its circle around him to encompass not only the new habitation which thus becomes a new mother-protected community but also the world of the hunter outside. Thus, the whole of perceived nature, the sky and the horizon as well as the earth and all the things that grow and live on it are surrounded by her libido and her presence and she guards over him. The plants and trees, flowers and rivers that spring from the earth are a new extended family, they are her children manifesting her vitality and her libido. The world will be populated by fairies, sprites, spirits and gnomes. The sunshine, the verdure of spring and summer will be perceived as an expression of mother's joy, while the cold and the snow, the endless ice and frozen stillness will, no doubt, express the mystery of her withdrawn quietude.

The image of the mother would be projected onto nature and life, and her spirit, her all-enveloping wholeness, would be worshipped and men would depend on her power not only in childhood but all through their lives.

We might wish to draw attention to an important factor which would have contributed to the spiritualisation of nature and her identification with mother. The life of the young child, and even of the infant, would have been a life outdoors during the warm period of the interglacial, that formative period of Homo sapiens. In the open compound the women would foregather in the courtyard (an open space surrounded by huts), and the mothers would feed their infants under an open sky close to scenes of nature. Thus the infant, upon looking up at its mother, would see the circle of sky surrounding his mother, as well as trees and hills and meadows as part of her image. In this way the heavens and aspects of nature would be suffused by the libido of the mother, becoming an aspect of her, and remain in the unconscious as a symbol of motherhood. These impressions of infancy would be ingrained in the imagery and assume an aspect of the holy, the magic of the maternal presence. Also, when the child is a little older and moves about more freely, it would play in open meadows enveloped by sky and could use tree trunks, stones, earth and all kinds of material things in play. It would experience its urethral excitement in the flowing brooks and rivers, it would encounter the dark mysteries of forests, the shadows and bright sunlight, and the world would be dominated by the mother's presence. While mother would no longer be close to him and attend to him single-mindedly as soon as he could crawl, or walk, or play, he would continue to feel her presence and re-create it in his mind and experience her libido in his natural environment and in the objects of his games.

So, on the one hand she would no longer be as close to him as in the cave, she would cease to be in close bodily contact with the child from an early age as she pursues her various activities, but the child would have introjected her in his mind and her spirit would be present and extend to the boundaries of his world. Also one must bear in mind that the child lived in a woman-dominated world while the father was absent for long periods on the hunt.

It is of particular interest that Cro-Magnon man painted his most magnificent paintings in the most inaccessible and hidden parts of the cave. These paintings, as found in Altamira, Lascaux, Pech Merle and other places, depict scenes of the hunt and its chief animals; they are dedicated to the spirit of the mother-goddess and are placed in her sanctuaries, her symbolic womb, as gift offerings to her so that she should give birth to them and make them become real in the world. The image of the wonderful and desired animal would be given to the mother so that she can introject them and reproduce them in her womb and then project them outwards for the satisfaction of man's needs. For if she loved him she would make his wishes come true and out of the womb, symbolised by the deepest recesses of the cave—life and wealth would emerge.

During the later periods of Cro-Magnon man, particularly among Magdalenian man whose paintings achieved the highest peak of artistic perfection, a new glaciation had set in and once more snow and ice covered the landscape. But Homo sapiens had made enormous advances both in technology and culture and his method of the large-scale hunt and village communities remained established. Although some of the communities used caves once more for occasional habitation, they mostly lived in man-made compounds with well-constructed huts similar to those still used by Siberian hunters and North American Eskimos. Indeed, Cro-Magnon man's compounds, his huts and clothes would have been similar to those of his contemporary cousins, who are still arctic hunters. The large caves in whose recesses he painted the scenes and animals of the hunt, those marvellous temples of his art and religion, may have been inhabited at times, but the main sanctuaries containing his masterpieces would have been largely inaccessible, sacred chambers which remained separate from the profane occupations of daily life.

Now let us look at the available evidence for these theoretical constructs about the life and culture of our Homo sapiens ancestors. The theories I have proposed are based on the following assumptions:

1 That Homo sapiens originated between 60,000–40,000 years ago in the Middle East and Southern Asia, where the warm periods of the interglacial arrived earlier than in Europe and other northern areas.

2 By the time Cro-Magnon arrived in Europe he possessed a brain very similar to that of modern man.

3 That his large-scale, co-operative hunting methods created settlements consisting of a number of families. In this way primal communities founded on the family or enlarged family gave way to complex social organisations which had to be held together by new cultural symbols of identity.

4 He developed graven images, a wide variety of sculptures and paintings which had a sacred, symbolic meaning and were objects of worship.

5   His culture was of a matriarchal order and his communal organisations were based on the authority and power of women.

Do the archaeological and palaeontological finds relating to the period of human evolution between 60,000–20,000 years ago justify these assumptions?

The chief classification of early Homo sapiens is derived from their toolmaking technology representing major cultures with the following approximate durations in Europe:

Perigordian   — named after the region which includes Les Eyzies. More than 35,000–c. 22,000 years ago.
Aurignacian   — named after the Aurignac site in the Pyrenees. About 35,000–20,000 years ago.
Solutrean   — named after the extensive open-air site near the village of Solutré in east-central France. 20,000–c. 17,000 years ago.
Magdalenian— named after the La Madeleine shelter about three miles from Les Eyzies. 17,000–12,000 years ago.

THE ART OF THE CAVE TEMPLES

While Cro-Magnon evolved a new and original art form, we can recognise distinct variations during the successive epochs of its history. The most outstanding product of the Aurignacian period and its eastern European and Russian branches—the Gravettian —were without a doubt figurines of women and animals. Apart from a remarkable but unique figure of a man carved from ivory and accompanying a ceremonial male burial at Brno in Czechoslovakia, the human statues and figurines were all female. Some of these were symbolic in form but the great majority were realistic at least as far as the trunk was concerned. The emphasis was undeniably sexual; the figures were usually shown naked, pregnancy was often indicated and emphasis was laid on breasts, buttocks and thighs. By contrast the head was usually left featureless even though hair might be indicated by one convention or another.

While the Aurignacian mural paintings were linear and some-what stiff, though by no means crude or incompetent, most of the bone, ivory and stone figurines were of consummate elegance. These figures have been found in immense numbers from the Pyrenees right across Europe and Russia to Lake Baikal in Siberia, indicating a common culture of the mother goddess and showing astounding similarity in technique. Among the most famous of them is the Venus of Willendorf—a statue made of stone and found in a Gravettian site in Austria. Traces of paint suggest that she was covered with red ochre. The precise depiction of the hair contrasts with the absence of a face.

A female figure made of a mixture of clay and powdered bone with prominent hips and large breasts was found in Dolní Věstonice in Czechoslovakia. Like many figures it tends to taper towards the legs. A number of mammoth ivory figurines come from Kostienki in south Russia. A most interesting head of a woman was also found in Dolní Věstonice. Unlike the majority of these Venuses her facial features are clearly defined and beautifully executed in a realistic manner. An exquisitely carved head of a young woman with long plaited hair draping towards her shoulders and somewhat stylised face comes from Brassempouy in France. These are just a few of thousands of carved female figurines found in an area that extends over thousands of miles across Europe and southern Asia covering the habitation of Aurignacian and Gravettian peoples between 40,000 and 25,000 years ago.

During the late Aurignacian period a number of female figures were found carved in relief. The famous Venus of Laussel was carved on a large slab of limestone which was probably attached to the shelter wall. She is a most impressive big woman with large hips and breasts, holding a bison horn in her right hand. Similar engravings on limestone slabs are known in the French Solutrean. In southern Spain the late Solutrean site of Parpallo has produced many painted and engraved stone plaques in the style very similar to those of the north.

Many palaeontologists have divided prehistoric art into home or mobile art, and cave or parietal art, i.e. sculptures, carvings or paintings which were kept in the home and carried by men whenever they changed abode, and such paintings and sculptures which by their very nature became part of a cave. The sculptures and engravings mentioned above, would be designated as home art and generally belonged to an earlier period than the great paintings in the cave temples of France, Spain and other areas.

While the mostly female sculptures of the Aurignacian represent a peak of man's artistic achievement in his capacity to make exquisite 3-dimensional representations of his deities, there is no doubt that the highest advance in prehistoric art was achieved by Magdalenian man and, in particular, his cave paintings. However, earlier Aurignacian wall paintings have been found in northern Spain and France, and it is possible that cave paintings of the Aurignacian people of eastern Europe and Russia are waiting to be discovered.

The artists who produced the paintings and engravings in caves as well as the sculptured statues, displayed considerable versatility, and, considering the means at their disposal, the results they achieved were of an extraordinarily high order. Engravings varied greatly in depth and strength and presumably were cut by flint burins or engraving tools. The figures in sculptured friezes were thrown into relief by cutting into the limestone and finished off by being rubbed smooth and, in some instances at least, were painted. Painting was carried out by means of the finger being dipped in pigment, by the use of some kind of brush, by means of a pad of feathers or fur, or by blowing from the mouth or through a pipe. The only pigments to survive are minerals, including ochres for reds, browns and yellows, and manganese for black.

Here we come to a phenomenon which has mystified generations of archaeologists and anthropologists. The great majority of cave paintings and engravings of the West European Magdalenian culture are located in deep chambers of the caves, often with difficult and tortuous access routes. It is significant, however, that long before the high art of the cave paintings reached their peak in the deep sanctuaries of the Magdalenian cave-temples, we find engravings and paintings of animals as well as humans which are fully exposed to daylight or at least lit by it indirectly and readily accessible. Here the artistic representations were open to public gaze, part of domestic life or at any rate easily open to inspection, part of the living environment and not hidden from it. They do not appear to be accompanied by the sense of mystery and secrecy like those of the later Magdalenian paintings.

What could have motivated this practice not shared by his ancestors, what were the psycho-cultural developments which drove Magdalenian artists to paint their masterpieces in deep and almost inaccessible places? We have said that man makes artistic representations of the object of his libido if he has ceased to be in close contact with it and he has experienced a trauma of separation. The mother who has become separate from the child is reproduced in stone or other material in order once again to become part of his reality. We may say that the female figurines and carvings of Aurignacian people represented a sacred symbol which however was present in the open light of day and essentially devoid of mystery. Why then the mystery which has come to surround the artistic products of Magdalenian people? What has motivated the great artists of the Magdalenian culture to paint his masterpieces in the invisible and hidden recesses of the caves?

We might approach a clarification of this problem if we consider that the mystery ritual of Magdalenian culture was an expression of a process of reparation, of providing the mother with the most desired objects so that she would be satisfied and loving and ready to protect man. This implies that the Magdalenians began to experience a sense of guilt as well as anxiety in their relationship to the mother goddess, a sense of separation and estrangement far exceeding that of the earlier cultures. The beginnings of tension between mother and child, men and women must have occurred to an ever-increasing degree—maybe some 18,000 years ago—inspiring Magdalenian man to create his great works of art as a sign of devotion to her, an act of restitution towards the maternal Superego.

There is no doubt about the feelings of sanctity associated with his art chambers, their hidden location deep inside the caves, practically inaccessible to ordinary people who resided in the cave or in settlements nearby. The works of art were mostly hidden deep in the mountain-side, free from the scenes of daily life. To give some examples:

The first traces of cave art discovered at Niaux in France were located over 500 yards from the entrance. The finest panels of black outline paintings, associated with the clay figures on the floor, were as much as 612 yards inside and could only be reached after a long uphill and downhill tunnel had been negotiated. Other examples of cave art in this region were found up to 1,120 yards from the light of day.

At Arcy-sur-Cure, a relatively small cave can only be entered through a tube-like tunnel about 100 metres long and only just big enough for a man to squeeze into. One has to go in head first, wriggling about salamander fashion over the muddy floor. This is very hard work with solid rock all round and one's face an inch or so above the mud and sometimes in it. (The archaeologist, Henry Breuil, one of the great explorers of prehistoric art, became stuck in this cave and had to be pulled and shoved through it; it was one of the last caves he ever explored). Imagine the difficulties under which the Magdalenian artists had to work in such conditions. Why he chose to work in these conditions remains one of the most challenging problems in the study of prehistory. He frequently painted his masterpieces in areas which were not only difficult to get to but were cramped and forced him to work in awkward positions, tight and cramped corners, or the edges of narrow platforms above a deep pit, or at the bottom of a pit from which he had to scramble up again to find his way out, like in one of the caves of Lascaux.

There are many such places and while some are quite large and easily lit up by lamplight, it is significant that in practically all of them entry can only be made by a long and often tortuous route. While this has rightly been regarded as one of the most baffling aspects of prehistory, it may also provide the key to an understanding of the symbolic meaning of the cave sanctuaries. Their deep secrecy as well as the narrow passage which lead to them combine to create an image of the maternal womb and the passage of the vagina that leads to it. The male has to wind his way through the vaginal passage of the goddess in order to reach her sacred chamber; he has to offer her his passion and the fruit of his passion so that she would transform it into new life.

We know from the analysis of individuals that the fantasy of entering bodily into the mother's body through the vagina plays an important role in the unconscious mind of many men, particularly if their masculinity has not been readily acknowledged by the mother and he has been made to feel a sense of genital inadequacy. If the mother appeared to him as huge, forbidding and distant, and his malehood not accepted by her, then the whole body is transformed into a penis symbol, it becomes a body penis. The fantasy of the penis entering the vagina is transformed into a fantasy of the whole body penetrating the mother, to gain complete acceptance by her as well as orgastic gratification. We find here a combination of narcissistic and genital eroticism. However, there is another primacy of the libido which is involved, namely, the anal libido; the gift offering of the whole self, becomes associated with the narcissistic faeces accepted by the mother. What he has to offer her is not merely the product of his genitality but the material embodiment of his soul, i.e. the products of his artistic creativity, his sculptures and his paintings.

Yet there is still another association with the great efforts he has to make to work himself through the passage to enter into the mother. The effort needed in order to achieve penetration rests on the same principle as that which we observe during the oral primacy, when the child has to make great efforts to gain gratification from the nipple, has to bite and penetrate into the breast in order to find the mother's libido and communion with her. When we cannot gain gratification through outside contact we must attempt to achieve inside contact, and the very effort of doing so becomes libidinised and a source of pleasure. Thus the very difficulty of forcing one's way through the narrow passage, the dangers and discomforts of entering into the sanctuaries are themselves a libidinous gratification. This gratification becomes ritualised into sacred activity, and only those privileged and capable to carry out these hazardous tasks are worthy of making the great offering to the mother and placing it in her sanctuary; they are the privileged and the elect; they are the artist and the priest, the magicians who overcome all the resistances of the Superego; they penetrate into the mother's libido and release it from the armour which surrounds it. In doing so, the priest-artist not only finds gratification for himself but for the whole community. By his efforts and his sacrifice he overcomes the resistance of the mother goddess, forces her to relinquish the barriers which she has erected around herself and once more allow her libido to flow to her children.

The very difficulty of access and the distance of her chambers, their isolation from ordinary life symbolised the extent to which the mother has become distant from the child and the degree to which men have felt deprived of their intimate relationship with the woman in the new surroundings. It is not merely a question of genital relationships which, for all we know, may have been as regular as ever, but above all the narcissistic sense of unity and mutual belonging. Men no longer felt as close to her ever since the intimacy of the cave was broken by the complexities of the new society. And only the artist, the priest, capable of penetrating the distance, of making his way through the barriers, was capable of entering into her sanctum and to establish that union which man had lost. Not only does the artist-priest reveal in his work the soul of his fellow-men and offers it to the goddess on their behalf, but he must experience hardship and loneliness to fulfil his purpose.

It has always been so with the artist: unless he has the fortitude to bear the burdens of his task and the sense of isolation, be it in the poverty of his garret or the loneliness of his work, he will not be able to achieve the full realisation of his art. Often 'the ordinary people' who are afraid to penetrate the sanctum of the mother-goddess, who are adjusted to the repressions which society has imposed on them, will resent his audacity and all too often ostracise him. He not only has to overcome his internal taboos but also the taboos of society; he has to conquer his own fears and the fears of his community.

We are reminded of Kafka's wanderings to find the elusive Castle, both in his tortuous novel as well as in his tortured life, with the difference that Kafka's Castle was on a mountain, the sanctum of patriarchal power, whereas for early Homo sapiens the sanctum was that of the mother hidden in the depth of the underground. Whereas the former is in the over-world, the latter was in the under-world.

The caves of Altamira, Lascaux, Niaux, Pech Merle, Teyjat, Font de Gaume and many others, all are resplendent with animals of the hunters' most desired possessions. If we create the image of ibex. These animal paintings obviously are magic representations of the hunters most desired possessions. If we create the image of an object it becomes alive to us and represents the living which we desire or fear. The omnipotence of our imagination makes it real; its soul is in our power and subject to our will. Thus art and magic combine to bring about the realisation of our desires or ward off our fears. But the magic act finds its apotheosis in the approval of the gods, for the power of the Ego can be destroyed and its wishes brought to nought unless the Superego, the God, gives his blessing. So the magic act has to be accepted by the omnipotent being, indeed it has to be offered to him, or her, for the power of creation and of fulfilment resides in the divinity. As the child offers not only symbolic representations of its soul to the mother but all the things it produces to gain her approval and finds reassurances in her pleasure, so the Magdalenian hunter places his products in her cave for her approval and her pleasure.

The hunter who paints animals reproduces in his act of creation a sense of identity with the animal of the hunt. The ice-age hunter adopted animal characteristics, he disguised himself as an animal to remain unrecognised as long as possible by the herd. He wore a mask topped by antlers or horns and draped himself with the animal's fur which he carried on his back. Stalking the herd in this manner he would cause the least possible disturbance and get near enough in order to discharge his arrows before being discovered. Stalking in animal disguise is still the normal method which hunting people employ in our time and it must have been the typical method used by Magdalenian man, particularly during the glacial periods.

Now it is interesting to notice that during the later periods of Magdalenian culture, particularly during the glaciation of the late Würm period, pictures representing men's identification with the animal appeared in the sanctuaries of the caves.* Some of these figures masked in animal disguises performed dancing movements apparently engaged in identifying themselves with the prey. Especially fine examples were found in the caves of Trois Frères in the French Pyrenees. The man wears a horned mask of bison from which the skin hangs with the tail swinging to the rhythm of the dance. In another cave, rendered all the more impressive by its dominant position, surrounded by engraved bears, bison and horse and reindeer, a large engraved figure picked out by black paint is shown wearing the tail of a wolf or horse and a mask consisting of the antlered head of deer or reindeer with large eyes and long ears. This picture has been called 'The Sorcerer' and is one of the most famous expressions of Magdalenian art. In his identification with the animal the hunter enacts its movements and its behaviour in a kind of dance, the man representing the spirit of the animal. There is no doubt that by the time of late Solutrean and Magdalenian times certain individuals acted out the animal magic and dance and became sorcerers, the personification of the spirit of the animal. In acting out the animal he has power over it and assures the success of the hunting tribe. He is a new kind of priest, the dancing

---

* After the warm 'interstadial' which lasted in Western Europe from 35,000–25,000 B.C., the cold period of the Late Würm glaciation returned, and continued till 10,000 B.C.

priest—the sorcerer—as distinct from the painter-priest. Quite apart from being an essential person in the ritual of the hunt he soon acquired all kinds of powers: to heal the sick and the wounded, to drive out evil spirits, to avert the evil eye, i.e. to protect people from the malevolent Superego, to foretell the future and to interpret dreams, and to avert dangers which may befall individuals or the community. In the pictures painted of him he descends into the cave and by communing with the Goddess in the sanctuary he returns to the surface imbued with special divine powers. He became a shaman, a healer and a priest mediating between man and the Mother God.

In these figures bedecked with animal skins and all kinds of amulets that had symbolic powers and crowned with horns and antlers we can recognise the prototype of our devil whose home is in the underworld and whose powers for good or evil keeps man in awe and fear. Only in our time of patriarchy the underworld, the home of the mother-goddesses has become the abode of hell and the goddess and her priest assumed the role of the evil one.

We can see that the offering of the animal to the Goddess became transformed into an offering of the human being in the shape of the animal, and the priest-sorcerer became her servant, and by this contact with her he acquired great powers among his fellow men.

We are obliged to ask how the masterpieces and their symbolic gift offerings placed as they were in the secluded and hidden sanctuaries would be known to the community; for what would be the point of carrying out such elaborate magic on behalf of the community if apart from the artist-magician no one would be able to see those masterpieces and experience their powers.

It is likely, as has been suggested by a number of writers, that the caves were used for initiation rites. When we consider that the artist discloses his wishes to the Goddess, bares his soul to her, so to speak, on behalf of his community, then every member in some way partakes in his effort. Even while men may regard the sanctuaries as sacred and secret, they would know about them, and it is likely that they would enter into the temple at crucial times in their lives particularly during initiation ceremonies. It is therefore highly probable that at the moment of initiation the young man would experience the artist's courage to penetrate into the secret abode of the goddess and his ecstasy of communion with her, prove himself to be worthy of being a man, to receive her blessing and to re-emerge into the compound as a fully fledged member. The rites would be conducted by the priests and sorcerers, resplendent in their attire, animal skins, antlers and amulets of all kinds.

The awesome image of the priest and the darkness and shadows and eerie setting of the cave in which the sacred animals emerge out of the walls would produce a trance-like state, a sense of hallucinatory revelation which would have an overwhelming impact upon the young man. He would feel the spirit of the underworld revealing itself to him and his normal Ego defences would break down in this dream, which would engrave itself ineradicably on his mind. A hint of prehistoric initiations was discovered in the Tuc d'Audoubert cave in the French Pyrenees. A stream enters into the cave and leads into a passage that opens up into a hall with a pond in it and white stalagmites and stalactites. At the other end of the hall there is a deep slope or chimney, followed by a tunnel several hundred yards long leading to a large circular room with two clay statues of bison in the centre. Near the centre is a clay area with small heel prints in a circle as if children and adolescents had danced there around the bison. The initiation rituals of Magdalenian man did not necessarily take the forms prevalent in later initiation rites of patriarchal cultures where genital circumcision and all kinds of mutilations occurred symbolising phallic restitution and sacrifices. We can assume a different kind of initiation, namely, initiation as communion with the sacred spirit of the underworld, the boy's capability of serving her by identifying with the hunter's prowess, and making gift offerings to her. The overall feeling of being accepted by the goddess in her secret chambers would be the major significance of these rituals.

THE CRISIS OF MATRIARCHY: THE GODDESS BECOMES A WITCH

Towards the end of the Magdalenian period changes take place in the nature of the paintings and engravings. They become more angular and stylised, the rounded outlines of the paintings and circular, wave-like shapes of abstract engravings, which are plentiful in Middle Magdalenian times, give way to harsher forms: lines symbolising spears and arrows, and javelins piercing animals, straight lines, squares and triangles replace the much more harmonious symbols of earlier times. The feel of the artistic imagery becomes altogether more tense, aggressive and restless. The animals are shown with spears stuck into them, wounds gaping and dripping blood. The hunters are shown as pin men without flesh and colour. Aggressive-sadistic images replace the serene symbiosis between hunter and animal.

There is little doubt that these images represent a transformation of the benevolent, protective and loving maternal image into an angry mother-goddess; she becomes mean and resentful, evoking anxiety, tension and phallic aggressive drives among men.

In one of the later paintings at Lascaux we find a fantastic kind of animal with two long straight horns pointing directly forward from its head, while its heavy stomach hangs nearly to the ground. We have here the representation of a female animal whose species is entirely unclear, endowed with phallic-aggressive characteristics. The benevolent power of the animal gives way to a threatening aspect and its dangerous nature is emphasised. There is another uncanny painting at the bottom of a deep shaft in the same cave—a most difficult and awkward place to reach—of a large bison bull eviscerated by a spear that has transfixed its anus and emerged through its sexual organs. A prostrate man lies before it wearing a bird mask, his erect phallus is pointing at the pierced bull and beside him stands a staff, bearing on its tip the image of a bird. It is likely that we see here signs of an emergent phallic aggressive primacy. In the first of the two paintings we get the impression of a threatening female animal with phallic weapons, whereas in the second we see a much more complex representation of a conflict between man and the mother goddess. The bull has been pierced through the anus and the spear comes out through his genitals, and both the horns of this animal as well as its protruding spear-penis has obviously killed the prostrate man. On the other hand, the man wears a bird's mask, the symbol of the aggressive female, while the staff with the bird at its tip either stands there or lies on the ground beside him. We must assume that it is standing there stuck in the ground. But it is interesting that the staff is obviously his totemic symbol representing the angry mother goddess, and the man with a bird's head is a sorcerer. In this picture the bull is a victim as well as aggressor, for it is obvious that although he has been the victim of an assault, the spear that has attacked him also emphasises his phallic anger and he either has killed the sorcerer (who identified with the mother goddess) or rendered him helpless; but the staff with the bird on top still seems to stand there ominously affirming the continuing power of the goddess with the beak.

This painting belongs to a period classified as Magdalenian IV, i.e. late Magdalenian, dating about 12,000 B.C. During this period pictures of harpoons and spears grow more common. The animals are depicted with spears stuck into them, often with blood dripping from the wounds. However, the wound marks are often highly ambiguous and are hard to distinguish from female genital symbols. Leroi-Gourhan* asks whether we are really dealing here with representations of weapons and sympathetic magic of animals being killed in the hunt. When we consider the variants of the spear and the wound marks we become aware that they represent forms of the male and female signs. In other words, it is highly probable that palaeolithic men were expressing something like 'spear is to penis as wound is to vulva'. Thus a panel at Bernifal showing a horse and a wounded bison is found to be equivalent to a panel in which are shown a woman (represented as a quadrangular sign) and a man (symbolised as a barbed arrow sign) accompanying these animals. It is not particularly surprising that the wound itself has been assimilated to a female representation, since we know that throwing weapons express male symbols. While in early and middle Magdalenian cave art we frequently find that male and female animals of the same species are represented side by side, or one behind the other, in the later Magdalenian periods male and female animals are facing or opposing each other, and the feeling is no longer one of co-ordination and harmony but of confrontation.

At Teyjat and in southern Italy bulls and cows follow one another; in other caves they are side by side. We find many stag-hind pairs, male and female reindeers, male and female deer. These represent an ideal composition of the unity of the sexes, like the paired male and female signs. It is also interesting to note that in this period one rarely finds animals attacked by spears or arrows and very little traces of blood coming from wounds, whereas in the later paintings they are increasingly more frequent; there is an increased emphasis on phallic-aggressive signs and the vulva represented as a wound, pierced by a spear or an arrow.

The phallic representations express an aggressive reaction to a

---

* André Leroi-Gourhan: 'The Art of Prehistoric Man in Western Europe' (Thames and Hudson, 1968).

threat of rejection or castration. Whereas in the Oedipal situation of patriarchal man these castration threats stem from the angry and jealous father, in the matriarchal setting the Superego threat comes from the mother who resents the boy's masculinity and wants to rob him of his special and desirable endowment. The envious and angry mother-woman evokes a number of responses in the boy: on the one hand fear and self-assertive phallic aggression, on the other hand a need to propitiate the woman's anger by offering his penis to her and seeing her as a phallic woman. The whole of late matriarchal culture is pre-occupied with making reparation to the angry goddess and to abreact the fear which she instills in man.

The character of magic changes from sympathetic magic to contagious magic, and we may call it avertive magic. While contagious or hostile magic expresses man's desire to inflict harm or to kill a threatening animal, a hostile human being or enemy, avertive magic means the ritual of averting a threat which arises from an angry divinity. The chief purpose of such magic is to avert the danger of castration. Such rituals are still practised among primitive tribes in Australia. A magic known as the 'pointing-bone' has been described by Geza Roheim, who writes: "Black or hostile magic is predominantly phallic in Australia ... the sorcerer before he actually 'bones' his victim makes him fall asleep by strewing in the air some semen or excrement which he takes from his own penis or rectum. He holds the bone under his penis as if a second penis were protruding from him. The man who is being 'boned' has a dream which announces the boning to him: first he sees a crack or opening in the ground and then two or three men walking towards him within the opening. When they come near they draw the bone out of their body". If we are to interpret this dream, which is apparently a kind of collective recurrent dream among these people, then we would first of all recognise the opening in the ground as the vagina of the earth goddess. The two or three men emerging from the opening with an elongated phallus would be a reversal (a frequent aspect of dream processes) of the male phallus entering into the vagina, but then it would become the woman with the penis coming forth and threatening the man. In the subsequent ritual the men strive to reassert the power of their penis and by making it artificially elongated they would assure themselves of their masculinity.

In the homosexual act of sodomy men reassure each other of the security of their maleness and overcome the threat of castration by the aggressive goddess, the angry and frightening mother. The Pindupi tribes of Australia abreact the fear of castration by a ritual in which several men hold a pointed bone with both hands, and bending down with their bottoms pointed backwards pass the magical bone just beside the penis. The 'victim' is asleep and the bone goes straight into his scrotum or rectum.

"Women also make evil magic", Dr. Roheim continues, "through the agency of their imaginary penis. Luritja women cut their pubic hair and make thereof a long string. They take a kangaroo bone and draw blood from their vagina. The string becomes a snake which penetrates into the heart of their victim". (It is of considerable interest that these rituals amongst women of primitive cultures also emerge frequently in dreams of contemporary women and it is therefore easy enough to reconstruct their meaning. The penis, envied by the women and taken into their possession, becomes an aggressive and hence guilty penis, it symbolises a man's castration, and is therefore a danger to him. Such women, who frequently suffer from depressive guilt symptoms, harbour fantasies of being witches, a danger to men and, therefore, rejected by them. However, in times of patriarchal crises such women strive to be accepted as the norm of femininity, the revenging female helping to bring down the domination of the males).

The great period of prehistoric art came to an end with the end of Magdalenian culture some 12,000 years ago. The records provide us with convincing evidence for its demise. Occupation layers at major Magdalenian sites are thick and extend far beyond the area in front of caves and rock shelters and contain many tools and utensils. They represent the remains of a stable, powerful and prosperous people. By contrast the layers on top of the most recent Magdalenian deposits are meagre. They are so thin that early explorers missed them and contain far fewer tools including characteristically flat harpoons. They are the remains of a shrinking and unsure people, the so-called Azilians.

The Magdalenians had flourished in the midst of bitter glacial conditions, the last glaciation of the Würm, but they could make nothing of the new conditions, the continuing retreat of the glaciers, making reindeer and the other animals of the hunt which they depicted in their magnificent paintings less and less abundant.

The species of grass which had adapted to glacial conditions and provided food for the Arctic animals followed the glaciers north, the reindeer and bison followed the grasses, and many hunters followed the animals or moved to coastlines and lived on other herd animals and seafood. They became a different race. The Azilians were descendants of those who remained behind, and they did as best they could, but they were no longer able to uphold the ancient traditions of Magdalenian art, the great inspiration had gone out of their lives.

The great Magdalenian culture soon disappeared from the world but the angry mother-goddess gained ground among men and her reign spread to other cultures and other races. The conditions which transformed the protective and life-giving mother into a witch-like divinity continued to prevail in the societies of Homo sapiens and brought about cultures dominated by the rituals of blood sacrifice.

We could be justified in assuming that this dramatic transformation of the image of the goddess had as its basis a change in the attitudes of the actual mothers. We have found that the frightening Superego emerges out of a sense of frustration and fear in the child, the formation of aggressive drives which are then projected on to the mother. However, this anger in the child is caused by its own frustration due to an inadequate supply of libido in turn caused by the mother's restraints and inhibitions, her neglect of or distance from the child, sometimes even by her resentment of it. Now what causes the mother to adopt such negative, libido-denying attitudes? Usually it is her own sense of deprivation either brought about by taboos imposed by a culture or by lack of erotic gratification and attention from her husband. Frequently this sense of being neglected by the man will make her angry towards him, an anger that usually has its roots in the anguish she felt as a girl towards her rejective or frequently absent father. Her son feels her anger, becomes angry with her and then projects his anger on the mother and she acquires the image of a frightening witch.

We have seen that the seeds of a conflict between the sexes were already present during the high Magdalenian culture, caused by the mens' loss of intimacy with their women in the large compounds. This conflict would have become increasingly exacerbated until it became a culture crisis.

The combined effect of greatly enlarged compounds, the growing power of women in them and their new found activities and responsibilities, the greatly enhanced efficiency of the weapons of the hunt and the longer lasting sojourns of the men in the hunting grounds away from the village settlement combined to produce not merely a sense of separation between men and women but also an estrangement between them. Mutual affection between man and woman ceased to act as a cohesive force, a bond that held the community together; indeed the structure of the community disrupted these affectionate bonds, with the result that women became on the one hand more powerful in the villages and on the other hand more frustrated and resentful. The men sensing their women's pre-conscious anger would have made themselves more independent of them and founded homosexual bonds in the male groups of the hunt, and these communities of males became more self-contained and integrated. This in turn would have made women even more angry and envious till they assumed an image of the witch, the hating and vengeful goddess in the imagination of the men. She acquired the image of the angry, maternal Superego. However, while the matriarchal sentiments, the concept of the spiritual power of the woman still retained dominance in the mind of men, they would have become frightened of her anger, her powers over life and death would have become dangerous and threatening.

There are many stories and myths of the transformation from the benevolent mother-goddess into a dangerous witch amongst ancient people in many parts of the world; they are too frequent and widespread to ignore, and obviously reflect a psycho-cultural event, a major transformation, during prehistoric times. Among the Ona people of Tierra del Fuego, for example, there is a legend which has been summarised by Lucas Bridges in the following way:

In the days when all the forest was evergreen, before Kerrhprrh the parakeet painted the autumn leaves red with the colour from his breast, before the giants Kwonyipe and Chashkilchesh wandered through the woods with their heads above the tree-tops; in the days when Krren (the sun) and Kreeh (the moon) walked the earth as man and wife, and many of the great sleeping mountains were human beings: in those far-off days witchcraft was known only to the women of Ona-land. They kept their own particular Lodge, which no man dared approach. The girls, as they neared womanhood, were instructed in the magic arts, learning how to bring sickness and even death to all those who displeased them.

The men lived in abject fear and subjection. Certainly they had asked, what use were their weapons against witchcraft and sickness? This tyranny of the women grew from bad to worse until it occurred to the men that a dead witch was less dangerous than a live one. They conspired together to kill off all the women; and there ensued a great massacre, from which not one woman escaped in human form. Even the young girls only just beginning their studies in witchcraft were killed with the rest, so the men now found themselves without wives. For these they must wait until the little girls grew into women. Meanwhile the great question arose: How could men keep the upper hand now they had got it? One day, when these girl children reached maturity, they might band together and regain their old ascendancy. To forestall this, the men inaugurated a secret society of their own and banished forever the women's lodge in which so many wicked plots had been hatched against them. No woman was allowed to come near the Hain, under penalty of death. To make quite certain that this decree was respected by their womenfolk, the men invented a new branch of Ona demonology: a collection of strange beings—drawn partly from their own imaginations and partly from folklore and ancient legends—who would take visible shape by being impersonated by members of the Lodge and thus scare the women away from the secret councils of the Hain.

Among the Yahgans also, the southern neighbours of the Ona but a very different people, much shorter in stature and devoted not to hunting in the hills but to fishing and sealing along the dangerous shores, there was the legend that formerly their women had ruled by witchcraft and cunning. "According to their story", states Mr. Bridges, "it was not so very long ago that the men assumed control. This was apparently done by mutual consent; there is no indication of a wholesale massacre of the women such as took place among the Ona. There is, not far from Ushiaia, every sign of a once enormous village where, it is said, a great gathering of natives took place. Such a concourse was never seen before or since, canoes arriving from the furthest frontiers of Yahgan-land. It was at that momentous conference that the Yahgan men took authority into their own hands". And Mr. Bridges concludes: "This legend of leadership being wrested by the women either by force or coercion, is too widely spread throughout the world to be lightly ignored".*

---

* Quoted in 'The Masks of God' by Joseph Campbell (Viking Press, New York).

Writing of an ancient reign of goddesses, Jane Ellen Harrison observed that in the field festivals and mystery cults of Greece numerous vestiges survived of a pre-Homeric mythology in which the place of honour was held, not by the male gods of the sunny Olympic pantheon, but by a goddess, darkly ominous, who might appear as one, two, three, or many, and was the mother of both the living and the dead. Her consort was typically in serpent form; and her rites were not characterised by the blithe spirit of manly athletic games, humanistic art, social enjoyment, feasting and theatre that the modern mind associates with Classical Greece, but were in spirit dark and full of dread. The offerings were not of cattle, gracefully garlanded, but of pigs and human beings, directed downward, not upward to the light, and rendered not in polished marble temples, radiant at the hour of rosy-fingered dawn, but in twilight groves and fields, over trenches through which the fresh blood poured into the bottomless abyss. The beings worshipped were not rational, human, law-abiding gods, but vague, irrational, mainly malevolent spirit things, ghosts and bogeys and the like, not yet formulated and enclosed into a godhead.[*]

----

[*] J. E. Harrison: 'Prolegomena to the Study of Greek Religion' (C.U.P. 1903).

6 Patriarchy

THE REVOLT AGAINST MATRIARCHY AND THE BEGINNINGS OF AGRICULTURE

At the end of the last glaciation, Magdalenian man followed the retreating glaciers and his animals of the hunt, to the Low Country, the British Isles (which were at that time still connected to the continent), northern Germany, Scandinavia and that great sweep of subarctic Russia, to the Urals and beyond. At the same time, some moved southwards and mixed with the people who had for millenia lived in Northern Africa. These two migrations, the northern and the southern, came to produce the chief cultures of Western civilisation during subsequent millenia.

Out of the northern migration developed that great complex of Scandinavian cultures, with their rock engravings and their megaliths, culminating in the Teutonic and Slavic myths. We have spoken of the pin men, human figures depicted in thin and usually straight lines, during Late Magdalenian and Azilian cultures. We find such engravings of human figures in rock carvings in Scandinavia, and especially male figures with long thin legs, the body drawn as a circle, often with four spokes which hold the circle together much like a wheel, the head of a goat, genitals with an erection, and wielding a hammer with a very long handle. These are obviously fighting men and precursors of the Nordic legendary myth of the Edda with its great god Thor wielding his hammer and a wheel-like body. The phallic characteristics are highly emphasised in these pictures and reinforced by the long handle of the hammer or axe as phallic weapons.

A whole assembly of men pursuing a wide range of activities, wielding hammers, throwing spears, unleashing arrows from their bows, blowing trumpets, and all endowed with erect phalluses, as well as fighting ships and sun symbols, are depicted in rock carvings in Fassum, Sweden. These and similar works of art covering a long span of time obviously show the male triumphant.

On the southern stage of man's post-glacial habitations and migrations we find a large number of somewhat similar representations of the human figure, although the art of this region represents a mixture of earlier North African cultures with an indigenous south-west European culture, particularly of Spain. They all have thin elongated bodies, while their legs are strongly emphasised and thicker than those of their northern compatriots. It is an art of rock painting and engraving alive with vivid little figures, bowmen hunting and fishing, ritual and sacrificial scenes, dancers and groups of women intent on some activity, lively scenes of human figures of a wonderfully vivid stick-man style developed with a sense for the rendition of active and intense movement.

Whereas the Magdalenian art of the caves represented the timeless atmosphere of the divine animals, the embodiment of the eternal mother goddess who in her deep chambers performs the mysteries of creation, here we have an atmosphere of life on earth and the ritual acts of living communities. The emphasis is upon the intensity of human pursuits; the hunters strain their bodies with the bow and follow the arrow and the spear as if it were an extension of themselves. Indeed, we find in these paintings and engravings a wonderful rendering of men's feelings for their weaponry. Not the shaman now but men in the group are the embodiment of the holy power.

It is interesting to note that these pictures are not in caves but on rock surfaces above ground. They must have been part of the daily life of the encampment, vivid reflections of man's actual pursuits in which he could recognise himself as the active agent intent upon the pursuit of his goals. As such they represent an emancipation from dependency upon the eternal mother and the transfer of libido towards narcissistic affirmation of man's powers, and his exercise of mastery over the environment.

The heartland of this new style was the grassy land of North Africa where today is only desert but which of old was a great pasture full of game. The type station is Capsia (Tunisia), hence the name Capsians for these people. Besides rock paintings of elephants, giraffes, rhinos and running ostriches, giant human forms with heads of jackals or asses, we find already the symbols of lions on cliffs lit up by the sun, and men standing in postures of adoration with uplifted arms before great bulls or before a ram with a sign of a sun-disc between its horns.*

While most archaeologists state that nothing is known of the early history of this culture, its earliest forms, known as Lower Capsian, reach back as far as the Aurignacian period. It seems likely that the Capsian people were descendants of early Homo sapiens races who moved west from the Middle East into the rich pasture lands of Northern Africa, while others came to settle in Europe. When, at the end of the ice ages, many of the European Homo sapiens migrated north and created the wide sweep of Teutonic and Slavonic cultures, others, who were left behind, namely, the Azilians, moved southwards to the shores of Africa, joined the southern branch of Homo sapiens and became part of the Capsian culture. There is some evidence for the theory that Capsians gradually moved eastward and created the neolithic cultures which came to flourish in Palestine, Sumer, Assyria and Mesopotamia and Southern Turkey—the Fertile Crescent, where wheat grew wild.

The art of these Middle Eastern people, known as Natufians, shows many striking similarities to that of Capsian art, and one can speculate on the affinities of their respective cultures. The Natufians of the Middle East not only showed many similarities with Capsian culture, they also shared many of their physical characteristics. Like the Capsians they were of moderate stature, averaging about five to five and a half feet in height, having long heads with retreating foreheads. They hunted with clubs, boomerangs, spears, bows and arrows and delicate harpoons. They wore beads, discs shaped from ostrich shell, feathers, bracelets and girdles of perforated shells. (It is of interest to note that during the fourth and fifth millenia B.C., a great number of ornaments made of ostrich shell were found in Sumer).

Soon they were to use the wild grains they found for farming plantations and founded the agricultural civilisation. The most important species of grain cultivated in early times in south-west Asia were barley, emmer and einkorn. To judge from the present

---

* This, some 5,000 years before they appeared in Egyptian mythology.

distribution of wild species and from traces recovered from early archaeological sites, it looks much as if the process of domestication went forward at more than one centre in this as in other regions. The best stands of wild einkorn, from which the two-grained cultivated form derives, occur in south-east Turkey. Wild emmer grows most vigorously in the Upper Jordan Valley, and this may have been the centre of domestication and its origin rather than Turkey, Iraq, Iran and proximate parts of the USSR where it grows more sporadically.*

But before organised agriculture became possible, the men had to take over organisation of the communities and wrest its leadership from the women. There can be no doubt that organised farming as it began in the Middle East some ten or eleven thousand years ago—agriculture in our sense—was an activity organised and carried out by men as distinct from vegetable plantations and smallholdings on the fringes of villages which had been cultivated by women for millenia past. The agriculturalists established new myths and sciences based on observation of the rhythms and laws of nature, and as agriculture emerged as the chief source of sustenance, the centre of the economy and culture, men gained a dominant role in the life of society. But this ascendancy of men cannot be simply explained by the advent of agriculture. The psychological foundations for the emergence of agriculture can be found in man's phallic assertive drive to gain supremacy over the women and mother nature, to penetrate her, to make her yield and submit to him and receive his seed.

MEN LEARN TO DOMINATE THE EARTH MOTHER

Bachofen and many others after him, such as Sir James Frazer, Jane Harrison, Leo Frobenius, and Father Wilhelm Schmidt, have provided rich evidence for early matriarchal systems in many parts of the world. However, they connected matriarchy with nomadic and early agricultural stages of evolution. The mythologies belonging to this age represent, in their view, agricultural man's profound understanding of the mystery of female power symbolised by the Mother goddess Earth, the originator of all life and growth. It was

---

* Grahame Clark: 'World Prehistory' (Cambridge University Press).

a world which, as Bachofen tells us, "was held together and given form by that mysterious power which equally permeates all earthly mothers, the love of mothers for their young; and the blood kinship of the matriarchal family was the fundamental starting principle of the social order". But rather than connecting this matriarchal vision of human community with agriculture, we would do well to consider that in agriculture it is the seed, man's particular contribution to life, which assumes central significance, becomes the active and causative principle; it is the man who inspires and fecundates the Earth Mother; he makes her dependent upon him for the realisation of her life-giving potentials. It is not so much the worship of the earth which dominated the imagination and rituals of agricultural people, but the dominance of the man who enables the earth to bring forth the life which he plants into her. It is he who arouses her passion, her reproductive powers, and she depends on him for her fulfilment.

It is widely assumed that in matriarchal cultures people were ignorant of the connection between sexual intercourse and reproduction, a state of ignorance which has shrouded man's consciousness of his paternity and made the role of the father towards his children relatively unimportant. In patriarchy this role becomes at last quite clear and is strongly emphasized.

With the onset of agriculture men challenge the mother's right of succession, they demand the right of self-perpetuation through their offspring; they assert their primacy as the productive and reproductive agents of life. The aggressive drives of men, developed and shaped over the millennia in the pursuit and killing of game, turned towards the earth. The phallic weapon of the male could now penetrate the earth; he inserted his seed into her and produced new forms of life, new forms of nourishment; the Earth mother would be subservient to him, the receptacle of his life-giving powers. J. J. Bachofen has called this the Dionysian stage of human development: "Its mythologies are of the Sun-god at the zenith, masterfully fertilising the earth as the phallic power. The Dionysian father forever seeks receptive matter in order to arouse it to life".*

The symbolic representations of this victory can be found in the painted and engraved images as well as in the immense number

---

* J. J. Bachofen: 'Mother Right'.

of myths of Neolithic peoples. Indeed, the expressions of men's struggles to liberate themselves from domination of the mothers find their most dramatic expression during the high culture of early patriarchy. Just as individuals can remember dreams depicting deep conflicts only when they are to some extent mastered by the Ego, so the deep conflicts of a culture can find elaborate and dramatic catharsis in art and mythology when they are already mastered, when men achieved mastery in society. The powers of the goddesses and their sacrificial demands continued to occupy the imagery of patriarchal cultures over the millenia, finding their most vivid expression in Greek mythology. The symbolic representations of the dangerous goddesses, the battles between Greeks and Amazons, play a large role in their art and drama, and there seems to be no end to the tales of mutilation, castration and murder.

One of the most important aspects of the emergent patriarchal culture, one that had the most profound importance upon its social structures, is the concept of property and the emergence of authoritarian, hierarchic systems far beyond anything experienced in matriarchal societies. Once more we must stress that the property system and the emergence of social classes is not just the result of economic interests. Not only agriculture but also its property structure and its class divisions were determined by profound psycho-social motivations and particularly the dominance of phallic drives. They transformed the earth into a sexual object to be penetrated, dominated and possessed. By their fertilising labours men claimed to possess the earth, make it their own—it became their property. While in matriarchal societies the hunter provided nourishment and sustenance, the women were in possession of the villages, of the huts and the utensils they produced. By providing for his families and for the village, the hunter received welcome and warmth, security and sexual gratification, but he did not have ownership either of his wife and children or of his home and the ground which it occupied. Neither did he have authority over the village, nor was his name perpetuated by his offspring. It is only when the earth had to be penetrated and fertilised in order to yield sustenance, and became dependent on the activities of the farmer, that men became owners of the land they dominated, and thus also obtained power and authority over the family and village. They became lawmakers and law enforcers, and the earth as well as the women depended on them. In this way the patriarchal family represents man's ownership over the territory which he masters and plants, it means ownership of his wife and all the offspring which she brings forth—his property bearing the seal of his name. It is the man now who embraces the woman, encircles her with his arms and protects her.

TOWNS AND FORTIFICATIONS: THE CULT OF POWER AND PROPERTY

While it is true that the circle, the hut, the house, the village, the city represent the female symbol—enclosure, security and nurture—they acquire a dual meaning. The circle of the town is not merely a female symbol in patriarchy, not merely the womb of the goddess but also man's embrace of her and his power of protection and ownership—the house, the storage pit, the granary—they are protected by his strong arms symbolised by the walls which come to surround the settlements. Some of the earliest agricultural settlements are not only built in the round but surrounded by walls. We may say that agriculture, property and urbanisation are a natural sequence. Indeed, it is one of the most startling discoveries of modern archaeology that almost as soon as agricultural settlements were built they were fortified and turned into citadels. The most important finds of early neolithic man were very ancient settlements that had not been villages but cities. At Jericho a city was established some 8000 years B.C., which had the civic organisation to construct a massive defence wall and had developed techniques for the cultivation of wheat and barley. Agriculture and not just the collection of cereal food was the basis for its urban economy and its social structure.

The Natufian culture arrived in the Middle East, above all in Palestine, around 9,000 years B.C. It is interesting that no direct genetic links have been established between its people and the people of the mesolithic Kebaran culture which preceded it. Could this not be a sign that the Natufians were in fact the same people as the Capsians who migrated from northern Africa to the Middle East? However this may be, the Natufians established a large number of settlements on open ground overlooking lakes and marshes or near powerful springs as at Jericho. Sickles and sickle blades, querns and mortars and pestles give evidence of reaping, preparation and storage of cereals. Clay-lined storage pits imply the conservation of surplus food. This culture has been called

Proto-Neolithic as it was most probably dependent on the reaping and collecting of wild wheat and barley; it is also clear from the tools and weapons found that hunting and fishing still provided the population with a substantial part of their nourishment.

The most important settlements of this culture of transition between hunting and agriculture in this region were found at Eynon. This village contained about fifty round houses with diameters of up to 7 metres, arranged around an open central area which contained a number of plastered pits, probably for the storage of food. The entire village covers at least two thousand square metres. While, as we have said, much of their cereal food consisted of wild growing grain, there were found a number of picks—phallic shaped stone implements—which were probably used for a primitive kind of ploughing, as well as sickle blades and other agricultural instruments. It is probable that the earliest attempts at ploughing and sowing occurred among these people.

There is evidence that the Natufians were the first inhabitants of Jericho as they left behind what has been considered a mysterious structure, which Kathleen Kenyon, the archaeologist, who was largely responsible for the discovery of Jericho, considered to be some kind of totem pole. This particular structure is built on virgin ground, right at the bottom of the mound of rubble that represents the many layers of habitation which has extended over a period of some 10,000 years. This 'totem pole' has been dated to 8,000 B.C. Near the base of this mysterious structure or shrine, harpoon heads, characteristic of Natufian craftsmanship, were found, which links the Natufian not only with the earliest beginnings of Jericho but also with other peoples in this region and beyond to southern Anatolia and the Zagros mountains. There is no break between the earliest Natufian settlements at the site of Jericho and the new town which arose about 8,000 years B.C. It can be assumed without a doubt that the almost explosive growth of Jericho into a walled city was due to the development of agriculture and the capacity to produce and store surplus food. The new town consisted of round houses built of mud-brick on stone foundations; the floors were well below the level of the ground outside and entry was through a door with wooden jambs and down several steps.* The wall around Jericho was a solid, free-standing structure, built of boulders

---

* James Mellaart: 'Earliest Civilisations of the Near East'; 'The Neolithic of the Near East' (Thames & Hudson).

brought from a river bed half a mile away. It is six foot six inches thick at the base and its foundations rested firmly on bedrock. Outside the wall the prehistoric builders had carved out of solid rock an enormous ditch, 27 feet wide and nine feet deep. How they could have made this excavation in Jericho's withering heat remains a puzzle. There would hardly have been more than 2,000 or 3,000 inhabitants on the ten acres that made up Jericho 10,000 years ago. But perhaps an even more remarkable discovery than the wall and the ditch was a solid stone structure, tall enough and massive enough to have graced some of the great medieval castles of France.

This tower is more than thirty feet in diameter at the base and even today its ruins stand more than thirty feet high. Carefully built into the centre is a flight of steps going down to a horizontal passage at near bedrock level. The passage leads to a door at the eastern end of the tower. A water channel from the top of the tower drains into a series of curvilinear enclosures built up against its north side. A similar enclosure has most probably been used for the storage of grain. The tower then combines the functions of pumping the water from the well to feed the town and fields around it, the storage of grain, and as a look-out tower and battlement—a central part of the defence system.

Besides being the centre of an agricultural area, there were other sources which contributed to the wealth of this city. Trade must have played a large role in its economy as it commanded the resources of the Dead Sea: salt, bitumen and sulphur—all useful products in early societies. Obsidian, nephrite and other green stones from Anatolia, turquoise from Sinai and other metals were found in the remains of the tower. No doubt there were many workshops where these metals were used for implements of all kinds, and warehouses where they were stored and traded.

The city encouraged the development of a large variety of skills, and its human composition became more complex. In addition to the farmer, shepherd and fisherman, many other crafts entered the city and made their contribution to its existence: the miner, the metal worker, painter and sculptor, the woodman and weaver. From these types, which originated in the villages, still other new occupation groups developed: the soldier, the merchant, the banker, the courier and clerk. Thus the new urban existence co-ordinated a large number of skills and produced an enormous expansion of human capabilities in all directions. However, the foundation for these wide-ranging activities was the development of agriculture and the accumulation of surplus products beyond people's immediate requirements, the concept of property and the deliberate production of surplus commodities for the purpose of trade and exchange. In order to make these activities possible a set of values must be assigned to each commodity beyond its immediate use; rules to govern trade and exchange must be enforced. Such enforcement of rules depended upon the existence of authorities whose decisions were commonly accepted.

Moreover, the prodigious labours involved in the erection of massive fortifications and other public activities imply a central authority to plan, organise and direct the work of a large part of the population and an economic surplus to pay for it.

The city not only brought more people, more strangers together in one place, varied their activities, their skills and responsibilities, it also created a new concept of authority and new institutions to represent it. The ruler or king could command the services of large numbers of men and organise them for collective labours on an unprecedented scale. Man-made mountains of stones or bricks, pyramids and ziggurats arose in response to royal command; whole landscapes were transformed and bore in their strict boundaries and geometric shapes the impress of an inflexible human will. There is no doubt that without this new dimension of obedience to the king and men's readiness to offer their labours and even their life to him, our civilisation could not have evolved.

The invention of the city brought with it the invention of large-scale warfare quite different in nature and scale from anything known before. From the very first days of the cities of the plain in Mesopotamia, Ur and Uruk, Eridu and Lagash fought each other for territory, for leadership, for control of trade routes. After a long period of perpetual but indeterminate quarrelling they fell victim to a larger movement of violence. The earliest imperial adventure of which we have the full record—that of Sargon of Akkad—added a new dimension to military power and armed conflict.

We are entering here upon known territory; history is beginning to emerge in terms which are familiar to us. But the psychologist cannot merely take this pattern of history for granted as some kind of self-evident process inherent in man's social existence and unfolding itself from the beginning of civilisation to our times. We must ask what it is that makes man submit to a central authority, to the ruler, the priest and the king, what it is in the nature of our own psyche that makes us respond to the call of warfare, discipline and self-sacrifice. Neither the economic processes which underlie the accumulation of wealth, of trade and exchange, specialisation, the division of labour and the emergence of social classes, nor the forces of nationalism or religious convictions can in any way be taken to be fundamental to the development of human history. Underlying these processes there is a psychological process which gave rise to patriarchy and expressed itself through it.

THE DIVINITY OF KINGS

We can sum up the factors which have led to the formation of patriarchy and the emergence of the paternal Superego in this way: men had fled from the threat of the mothers to the love of the father and developed a Superego on the basis of a de-sexualised, sublimated homosexuality. It represents an escape from the fears of the sadistic, maternal Superego to the phallic assertiveness of the male community determined to vanquish and dominate the mothers, in consequence transforming the earth into a male-dominated, male-dependent object. Thus agriculture, property and possessions developed, producing fortified urban communities. But how did kings emerge? What compulsion made men raise certain individuals to situations of unquestioned power, to glorify them and submit to them?

We could simply answer this question by saying that men of great power symbolise every patriarchal man's fantasies of omnipotence and give it full expression. Men project their desire for power and possessions upon certain individuals, glorify them as kings, serve them, and identify with them to partake in their glory. This represents a process of projection and identification for, on the one hand, each man sees himself as a man of power and of property and, on the other hand, he is prepared to sacrifice and enslave himself to the image of omnipotence vested in the king. The labourers who toiled at the fortifications and the soldiers who sacrificed their health and their lives in the battle of their king, split off the fantasy of glory and projected it upon the 'great authority' whose glory, in turn, is reflected upon the citizen who serves him.

There is a dual aspect of the father's authority, namely, his authority in the family and his submission to his king and his God. By his submission to a kingly and divine authority, the father identifies with them and represents their powers. Similarly we find that the ruler of patriarchal communities does not merely exercise his powers by means of his personal influence or capabilities but by the charisma that is bestowed upon him by his special relationship with spirits and divinities. He is himself the subject of the divinity, he serves it and by doing so he identifies with its power, i.e. introjects it. This relationship of the father figure with the superior power thus can be seen to operate on three levels at the same time:-

1 Every male is a father of his offspring, an authority to his family.
2 He submits to his king and in doing so partakes of his power.
3 The king, in turn, stands in a special relationship to the divinity, that magic spirit that ultimately represents the image of omnipotence.

In this way *every* male partakes in the powers of the omnipotent spirit, identifies with it and gains fulfilment for his manic, phallic-narcissistic fantasies. The male submits to the king, the king submits to the deity and in this way the abstract image of the all-powerful male rules society.

We may look at some contemporary primitive societies to illustrate this process. There is no doubt that the beginning of kingship is to be found in the role of the magician, the combination of ruler and shaman. The role of the shaman has been of very considerable significance in the structuring of culture as he is the prototype of priests and divine kings. The name comes from Siberia where he is also called Tahid. He is a very important figure amongst the Eskimos and the Laplanders, but in Siberia there were also women who were shamankas. The climate, the landscape and the life of these northern hunters, with whom we may include the Ainu of northern Japan, is, as we have indicated earlier, closer to that of Upper Palaeolithic man in Europe during the last ice-age than any other living today. Only the great animals have disappeared, the mammoths, rhinoceros and cave-bear.

Moreover, all the religions of the arctic areas have in common the shaman's techniques of ecstasy, the soul flight, the activities of guardian spirits, the use of drums as a means of exultation, and above all the companionship and conversation with birds and animals in their special language, the healing powers and mastery of fire. During his initiation the shaman has generally met an animal which reveals to him its language. The shamanic session begins with an appeal to the guardian spirits and conversations in secret language; then follow drumming and dancing in which movements of animals and birds are imitated.

Religious life revolves around the shaman, who alone has access to the spiritual powers, and in the veneration shown to certain places where men have felt themselves to be in touch with mysterious forces. We have observed the priestly role of the great cave artists of Magdalenian times who mediated between man and the maternal goddess, and we find that among contemporary Eskimos shaman and medicine man are also their chief artists.*

What above all characterises the shaman is his freedom to come and go between heaven and earth, his special friendship with animals whose language he speaks, and his companionship with divine spirits.

We have later-day echoes of the palaeolithic shaman in the stories that surround the desert Fathers and Celtic hermits with their familiar beasts, culminating perhaps in St. Francis, endowed with the great spiritual powers of the shaman.

Geza Roheim upheld the view that the world over, primitive societies can be called a pharmacocracy, a rule of the wizard or shaman. Summarising the evidence of the role of the shaman in primitive societies in Australia, Frazer wrote: "On the whole then, it is highly significant that in the most primitive society about which we are accurately informed it is especially the magicians or medicine men who appear to have been in process of developing into chiefs".** Roheim comments: "Considering the evidence brought together by Frazer for the ascent of the magician, we must say that this seems to be the regular path to monarchic rule. For although cases might certainly be found in which a paramount person in a savage community owed his influence to the strength of his arm, his sagacity or even his wealth, it is easy to show that the

---

* N. K. Sandars: 'Prehistoric Art in Europe' (Penguin Books, 1968).
** J. G Frazer: 'The Magic Art' (1911).

historic kings of ancient civilisations really derived their power from men who represented the link between the worlds of mortals and immortals. Everywhere in antiquity the ruler of a community wields supernatural powers and appears to be a representative or incarnation of the deity".*

In the ancient kingdoms of Sumer, Sin, the moon-god, was said to be king of heaven, who rules on earth with his crown. The moon-god chooses the king and confers his sceptre upon him. Hammurabi, the great lawmaker of Babylon, calls Sin his creator and himself a scion of royalty created by Sin

It is, however, the identification of the king with Tammuz that demands special attention, both on account of its antiquity and because Tammuz seems to have been not a specific deity but one of many—the representative of a type of divinity with whom Sumerian, Syrian and Egyptian kings were identified. He is the fecundity of the country, the master of the country's vital power. He is also the faithful son, the son and consort who on his death is mourned by his mother and probably also revived by her. When she mourns for him it is not for him alone, it is "for the plants which do not grow, for the flocks which do not produce; there is no grain, the fish will not spawn, the tamarisk refuses to grow. Life itself disappears with the Lord of Life". The kings of Uruk regarded themselves as the chosen consorts of Ishtar. These kings were, everyone of them, a Tammuz (consort = Tammuz), or a Gilgamesh (Gilgamesh = the cosmic man), and both these figures seemed to combine and mean the same. Tammuz and Ishtar do not signify any particular god or goddess but every god or goddess who played the role of son and his bride, the bride being also his mother. The leading feature in the character of the ancient Sumerian kings and their Semitic successors was their marriage to a goddess who was also their mother.

If we study the nature of kingship of neolithic times we find an extraordinary similarity with the priestly role of the Magdalenian artist. The king's magic power derives from his special relationship to a mother-goddess, with the significant difference that she is now in a state of dependence towards him, adoring him and regarding him as the source of life, the king of heaven, the sun whose

---

* Geza Roheim: 'Animism, Magic and the Divinity of Kings', (Routledge & Kegan Paul, 1972)

radiance bestows happiness and fertility upon the earth. Instead of the priest descending into the cave sanctuaries in the deep regions of the earth, he is now above her and his reign is in the heavens—he is the sun or moon bestowing his life-giving powers to her, and not only the goddess but all living things on earth depend on him for their well-being. Apart from his fertilising powers, the narcissistic element is manifest in his universality, he populates the heavens and covers the earth from "one end to the other". This manic-narcissistic aspect of the patriarchal male's psyche is fully manifested in his gods whose powers and potency are without limits, free from restraints and inhibitions to which ordinary mortals are subject.

It is precisely this freedom from inhibitions which is the chief characteristic of the new gods. Having overcome their dependency upon the big mother, men give full rein to their fantasy of possessing her sexually, of being the sole recipient of her love and admiration. But of course not every member of the community can be thus chosen; sibling rivalry demands a favourite, and every man's wish to be the favourite of the mother is projected upon one particular individual who then becomes the embodiment of all men's pre-conscious fantasies of erotic and narcissistic wish-fulfilment. He reflects in his person the collective fantasies of the males, and all glory is heaped on him, and in his worship men vicariously affirm their own desires. At the same time, however, men identify with the other men of the community, being bound to each other by the sublimated homosexual ties of the ancient hunting group and to their leader who provided a sense of direction and purpose to their collective pursuit. But while the leader of the hunt shared the home and the women's love with the other males of the group on their return to the cave or home base, the new king, by contrast, stays at home in his palace, collects the gift-offerings of the agriculturalists and the artisans and receives the spoils of war; he guards his possession and his women and he is the chosen favourite of the goddess. His very glorification gives him power not only over the mothers and the home but also over the men of the community.

THE CULTURE OF THE OEDIPUS COMPLEX: PATRIARCHAL PARANOIA

The king transformed the cave home into a palace which he claimed as his own, keeping all other men out of it with the exception of a few courtiers and guards. The castle became the personal fortress of the king as the fortified town is the collective fortress of the urban community. We see here a new type of ruler emerging who is much closer to the dominant male of baboon communities who tyrannises the young males, frightens them into submission and demands sole right of possession over the females. The king in his castles with his privileges, his wealth and divinely ordained powers, glorified by men as the embodiment of their collective fantasies, aroused at the same time their envy and their hatred. They envied him for his presumption and his wealth and they hated him for his power over them. The ambiguity between adoration of the ruler and aggressive feelings towards him not only produced the profound conflicts of the Oedipus complex but also the structure of class divisions in society.

While the king represents the ambitions of phallic manhood, the men of the community are split off from the powers which they had vested in him and become his servants. They want to kill him in order to regain for themselves that sense of power and dignity which they had vested in him, but at the same time they have to protect him from these urges of regicide; they develop elaborate rituals to restore and glorify the king whom in their fantasies they have killed, and ascribe to him the right to punish them and demand their sacrifice. It is by such sacrifices that men are liberated from their guilt feelings and it is the king's obligation to provide outlets for men's self-sacrificing needs. For the king's power, representing the manic fantasies of patriarchal man which have been projected upon him, is in turn introjected as the Superego, and becomes part of the ego as "My king and my country". Service to king and country, and self-sacrifice in peace and war become redeeming acts and they liberate men from their bad conscience and reassure their ruler that not only do they not want to kill but that they love him. For he represents them and speaks for them; he builds palaces, temples and tombs for himself on their behalf, and fights battles to enlarge his kingdom for the greater honour of his subjects.

The largely unconscious battle between citizens and kings, the subsequent feelings of guilt and rituals of propitiation are enacted in every family in the battle between sons and father. The Oedipus complex did not in fact start in the family but in society or rather, let us say it developed in society and in the family to become an interacting feedback process. Therefore the Oedipus complex exists in each individual, in the family and in society.

The many romances of the fairy prince reveal to us the rescue of the mother or daughter figure from the powers of an evil tyrant. In these tales of defiance the hero liberates the mother—the lady— from the possessive father, enabling her once more to enjoy her libido and bestow its blessings upon the community. The young man's difficult task of setting the lady free from her bondage is expressed in such tales as 'The Sleeping Beauty' and the thorns which surround her, the flames encompassing Brunnhilde, climbing slippery glass mountains, the ripping open of garments, forcing entry into rocks, etc. Such actions obviously symbolise the sexual act: by breaking down the walls, gates, locks and barriers and liberating her from her inhibitions, the hero not only defeats the Superego that has imprisoned the mother but gains her love and reciprocal sexual fulfilment.

But the Superego erects a number of defence mechanisms in order to safeguard its powers and its representatives, the kings, gods and totems. Indeed, we can say that the king uses the internal authority of the Superego in order to maintain his social power, and the Superego uses the social power of the king in order to maintain its internal authority.

One of the most important psychic and political defences of the king and the Superego is the process of displacement, whereby the aggressive urges which are directed towards them are deflected onto alien kings and gods, the rulers of other communities who then come to represent a permitted object of aggression. The own Superego encourages citizens to discharge their aggressive and hostile urges upon the 'other', the 'alien' Superego, and by so doing ensures the continuation of its own powers. To kill enemies becomes an outlet for the forbidden murder of the own father or ruler and therefore a virtue; every enemy killed is an act of loyalty, an affirmation of love towards one's ruler or king. Every king will strive to set an example of this virtuous act of aggression by his ability to kill large numbers of his enemies. It is really quite extraordinary how kings and generals have boasted about the large number of enemies they have slain and tortures inflicted on them. Every slain enemy represents an act of regicide not committed, it is an act of protection of the king, an affirmation of one's loyalty to him.

Our father who loves us must be protected from the father of the other tribe who threatens to destroy us. Thus the conflict between the impulses of love and hate is transformed into a conflict between the own and the other tribe. But in the same way as the repressed sexual and aggressive energies constantly press for entry into consciousness, and thus become a threat to the Ego and a source of anxiety, so the alien tribes and their gods, upon whom we have projected our own repressed urges, represent a constant threat to our tribe and to our god. The Superego then has to be protected from the attacks of 'the others', it has to be glorified and affirmed, made more and more powerful and defended against the enemy. And all the spiritual powers, the powers of the will and of faith, as well as the material powers at the command of a civilisation, all the weapons and arms provided by technology must be devoted to this task, no matter whether a civilisation calls itself scientific or theocratic or anything else. For in the same way as the repressed Id impulses attempt to gain access to the Ego and threaten to break through its defences, so the enemy Superego representing those Id impulses will constantly strive to penetrate the defences of the tribe or the nation and attempt to take possession of its soul and its territory. The tribe will, therefore, constantly feel threatened by the enemy and inevitably become paranoid. Thus 'tribal paranoia' is a universal condition of patriarchy.

Just as the sons have to defend the father and his representatives on earth, the ruler, the king or the party against the enemy without, so they have to defend God, the Father, against his enemies within, the sinful thoughts and the evil that resides in the soul. "I acknowledge my transgressions and my sin is ever before me" (Psalm LI, 3). We appeal to the omnipotent being to release us from our guilt and our wickedness and we glorify him and sacrifice ourselves to him that he should be pleased and convinced of our repentance: "Hide thy face from my sins and blot out all my iniquities" (v. 9). "To the Lord our God belong mercies and forgiveness, though we have rebelled against him" (Daniel IX, 9). "O Lord, correct me, but with judgment; not in thine anger, lest thou bring me to nothing" (Jer. X, 24). "Our Father which art in Heaven, hallowed be thy name. Thy kingdom come. Thy will be done in earth as it is in heaven. Give us this day our daily bread. And forgive us our trespasses, as we forgive them that trespass against us. And lead us not into temptation; but deliver us from evil: for thine is the Kingdom, the power, and the glory, for ever and ever. Amen". (The Lord's Prayer). "Dearly beloved brethren, the scripture moveth us in sundry places to acknowledge and confess our manifold sins and wickedness; and that we should not dissemble nor cloake them before the face of Almighty God our heavenly Father; but confess them with an humble, lowly, penitent and obedient heart; to the end that we may obtain forgiveness of the same, by his infinite goodness and mercy". (All these prayers are quoted from the Book of Common Prayer of the Church of England).

But it is not enough for us patriarchal sinners to beg God's forgiveness in prayer: we have to defend him from the external enemy and take up arms against the heathens, the non-believers, who are eternally determined to destroy him and his representatives on earth. The unity of the cross and the sword, submission to God and unbending strength in face of the enemy are the dual characteristics to which patriarchal man aspires as the highest virtue and undeniable duty. Of course there is an enormous variety of totems and gods, tribes and nations, religions and ideologies; they share the fundamental conflict in the mind of patriarchal man which finds expression in his political reality. We are now in a position to define a number of important stages in the evolution of patriarchal culture. These evolutionary stages in the history of Homo sapiens have become dimensions of the mind which continue to operate as the deep motivations of social behaviour:

1 The transformation of the mother goddess into an angry witch.
2 The emphasis on phallic-aggressive primacies in order to dominate the witch and make her once again give forth life and love.
3 The emergence of agriculture, the glorification and deification of the king as the embodiment of male power.
4 The emergence of fortified towns, property rights and the class structure of society.
5 The development of the Oedipus complex and the attempts towards its resolution in the myths, religions and politics of patriarchal civilisations.

We have seen the first signs of the angry mother goddess during the late Magdalenian period and the emergence of phallic-sadistic fantasies in its cave paintings as well as in the paintings and engravings of Azilian, Capsian and Scandinavian cultures; we have traced the beginnings of agriculture and of fortified cities and the consolidation of patriarchal rule. Side by side with these psycho-cultural transformations we have also followed another theme, namely, the continuity of Homo sapiens' evolution from his earliest origins in the Middle East some 60,000 years ago and his arrival in south-west Europe some 40,000 years ago, the northern and the southern migrations at the end of the ice age, and the migration across northern Africa, to return to the Middle East some 11,000 years ago where he found natural growing wheat, developed agriculture and built the first cities. These developments can be seen both as responses to environmental changes, as a pursuit of suitable climatic-ecological conditions as well as psycho-cultural transform-ations which, on the one hand, are conditioned by environmental factors and, at the same time, motivate men to respond to them in a particular way.

In this way we follow the external as well as the internal trans-formations of Homo sapiens, we follow his ecological-geographical movements as well as evolutionary changes in his mind and his culture, and we emphasise that the two are constantly interwoven in a mutually conditioning feedback process. And so we establish a hypothetical model of Homo sapiens' evolution that follows a line of descendence from Cro-Magnon man to Magdalenians, to Azilians, Capsians and the Natufians of the Middle East who initiated the patriarchal and agricultural revolutions and laid the foundations of what we call civilisation.

This theory of the continuity of evolution differs from the theory of diffusionism as advocated by Gordon Childe and long upheld by most palaeontologists and prehistorians, maintaining that civilisa-tions originated in Sumer and Egypt and spread from there to other regions. We shall see that these civilisations represent relatively late developments of patriarchal culture. Long before Egypt, Sumer and Babylon appeared on the scene of history, patriarchal man built many great cities, spread the art of agriculture, industry, trade, complex social organisations and a rich tradition of culture and religion across many parts of the Middle East and Europe.

We have spoken of Jericho as probably the very first city known, but there is evidence that after the first one thousand years of its existence it suffered a decline, largely due to climatic changes which produced very hot and dry conditions and made the growing of cereals increasingly difficult. While, nevertheless, the town continued to be inhabited largely due to its leading position as a trading and manufacturing centre, it is likely that many of its inhabitants and many farmers of the surrounding regions moved north in search of moister climates suitable for the agriculturalist. Now we find that in the uplands of northern Mesopotamia and the Zagros Mountains and in particular southern Turkey wild growing wheat existed with a much higher level of rainfall than encountered in the Palestinian lowlands of 7,000 B.C. We may thus venture to suggest that people migrated north from Jericho and brought with them not only their agricultural skills but also their culture.

It is noteworthy that from about 6,500 B.C., spreading over a period of about 2,000 years, most towns were located in the uplands in the northern areas of the Middle East which were suitable for the growing of cereals and also provided minerals necessary for the making of tools, utensils and decorations, and provided opportunities for agriculture, manufacture and trade.

THE VULTURE AND THE BULL

In 1960 James Mellaart discovered a prehistoric town at Çatal Hüyük in southern Turkey which turned out to be of great interest to the student of prehistory and also to the psychoanalytic sociologist. Its many shrines and sanctuaries provide us with a unique opportunity to gain some insight into the fantasies and conflicts which occupied men's minds during the early stages of patriarchy.

While we have observed the first signs of the transformation of the mother goddess into a witch during the late Magdalenian stage of matriarchy, we find in Çatal Hüyük some of the most intriguing manifestations of these fantasies. Çatal Hüyük dates back to about 6,500 B.C., and is, if not the oldest known prehistoric town, certainly the largest yet discovered. Its economy was based on irrigation, agriculture and cattle breeding, trade and industry. A study of the crops has shown that domestic emmer, einkorn, wheat and barley were grown, the latter two cereals having developed into important food crops as a result of irrigation.* Vegetable fats were

---

* Helbaek: 'First Impressions of the Catal Hüyük Husbandry' (Anatolian Studies XIV, 1964).

obtained from the seeds of conifers, acorn, pistachios and almond. Other fruit included crab-apple, juniper berries, hackberry and capers. Dogs and cattle were domesticated, sheep were known but were not fully domesticated. Domestic cattle provided the people of Çatal Hüyük with ninety percent of their meat as well as being an important means of transport. One should undoubtedly add such foods as the following, which leave no archaeological traces: dairy products such as milk, butter, cheese; green and root vegetables, onions, garlic; fruit juices, hackberry wine and beer; also grapes, pears, walnuts, figs and pomegranates which grew wild in Anatolia. Olives, however, do not appear before the fourth millenium B.C.*

The population of Çatal Hüyük was of mixed origin: Euro-Africans, who probably descended from the palaeolithic Capsians formed about fifty-nine percent of the inhabitants, proto-Mediterraneans and a third group of brachycephalic Alpines (this, as we shall see, is of particular interest). Conservative estimates suggest that in its heyday Çatal Hüyük may have had one thousand homes with a population of something like 6,000. The town controlled not only the surrounding plains, which were vital for its food supplies, but also trade in surrounding areas. Many smaller towns and villages would owe their origin and their livelihood to the market which the large population of Çatal Hüyük would provide for their produce and the trade it stimulated.

Homes were closely built against each other though there were some courtyards. There were no streets and all communication was at roof level. Access to the house was through a hole in the roof which was reached by a ladder and this hole also served as ventilation and escape for the smoke from the hearth. The furniture was part and parcel of the house: a bench, a series of platforms used for work and sleep. Many storerooms contained grain bins of various types. To the outside the city presented a wall, the back walls of houses serving as fortification in much the same way as medieval towns in Tuscany. Even though there were no fortifications on the scale of Jericho, the walls presented by the backs of houses were evidently sufficient defenced against marauding bands from other cities; the many injuries and head wounds discovered among the skeletal remains give evidence of frequent warfare.

---

* James Mellaart: 'The Neolithic of the Near East' (Thames & Hudson, 1975).

The people of Çatal Hüyük buried their dead beneath the sleeping-platforms in their houses and shrines, which strongly suggests that the dead were still regarded as part of the family and, moreover, were kept within the protection of the walls, i.e. not exposed to the world outside. Their burial customs were unusual in that their dead were exposed to birds of prey and insects who removed the flesh, and after excarnation were wrapped in cloth. This method of letting birds of prey eat the flesh of the dead has a double significance to their culture. This custom has no doubt something to do with considerations of hygiene in view of the fact that the dead were buried inside the houses; it would, however, have been over-determined by a sacrificial compulsion whereby the dead ancestor is given in sacrifice to the mother-goddess in order to satisfy her oral sadistic urges and to propitiate her rage. The goddess is represented by the bird of prey, a vulture, confronting and attacking a headless human being, the head, as it were, having been devoured by her:

> The nightingales are singing near
> The Convent of the Sacred Heart,
> And sung within the bloody wood
> When Agamemnon cried aloud ...

as T. S. Eliot has observed 8,000 years later. In such paintings the men of Çatal Hüyük would also abreact their castration anxieties and by presenting the act of castration provide catharsis for their fears. Indeed, the huge vultures painted on blank walls seem to form a central aspect of their religious art.

Of the 139 buildings studied by James Mellaart no fewer than forty were shrines or sanctuaries. These shrines were of the same plan and structure as the houses but were distinguished by their superior decoration and content. They were grouped within a complex of buildings and four to five houses were served by one shrine. This shows the intense spiritual life of the people and their deep preoccupation with the resolution of their psychological conflicts.

There is good evidence that Çatal Hüyük owed its importance not just to its material prosperity but as a religious centre. Its gods and its shrines served as a spiritual focus for a large surrounding area. People from neighbouring villages would flock to the city in order to worship its deities.

Among the many sculptures of religious significance in the shrines and houses we find female figurines with pointed legs and stalk-like body with a beaked head, as well as animal figures frequently covered with stab marks indicating their use in sympathetic magic during ceremonial hunting rites. It is interesting to note that these primitive female figurines never appear inside the shrines but are buried away in the wall brickwork. This indicates their symbolisation of evil spirits, as it is a very ancient custom upheld up to recent times to hide figures representing evil spirits in the walls of buildings so as to prevent them from emerging and casting an evil spell or evil eye on the inhabitants. By having been thus imprisoned and made harmless, they also act as protective spirits against evil powers outside. Besides these figurines there are many statuettes carved from stone or clay which were found in the shrines as cult figures. These figures—both male and female—show distinct and highly emphasised sexual characteristics—large breasts, vulvas as well as phalluses. Frequently the female statuettes are depicted with a bird-like head, a beak as nose, and a narrow, aggressive, threatening aspect. They represent old women, crones and witches. These statuettes are often placed in groups, thereby indicating their association and relationship. An old woman, a bird of prey and a confident young male represent the witch, and the young god. A young female with leopard in blue limestone, and an old female with leopard and a boy riding a leopard form another group. The leopard represents the symbol of vital power, which is associated with the young female as well as with the old mother goddess, and also with the boy who rides it. But by riding it he is in charge of the vital power and dominates it just as he dominates the old goddess and the young woman. Male figures frequently ride animals often represented by bulls.

A great many shrines have huge vultures painted on their walls decapitating human bodies, but these symbols are countered by large carvings of bulls' heads with great horns emerging from opposite walls in plaster relief. These bull heads often form the centre-piece of an elaborate altar-like structure with pillars and large boulders at the base and top. There can be little doubt that these bulls' heads, which often appear in pairs with a small or young bull head placed on top of the large head, represent male power, father and son, king and citizen guarding the city from the threat of the devouring vultures. As if to reinforce this theme of the guardian bull, the protector of man from the spirit of the dangerous vulture goddess, the sleeping-platforms are surrounded by pairs of enormous horns. These horns, mostly of aurochs, are embedded on the edges of the sleeping-platforms and are obviously meant to protect the sleeper from the dangerous Queen of the Night; they would act as a formidable barrier against the monsters which threaten to invade his mind while asleep and unable to defend himself against them.

There is also a group of sculptures which depict man's descent from the mother-goddess while at the same time showing his position of power and dominance. This theme is presented by sculptures of female deities giving birth to horned bulls or other animals, always characterised by exaggeratedly large horns. Here the birth of the male, fully equipped with the symbols of masculine power, represents his release from the bondage of the mother and his rebirth as a fully equipped male. We have observed rebirth ceremonies in the initiation rites of many people where the mother brings forth the young male as a full member of his community and hands him over to the fathers. The power of the goddess is not denied here nor has her worship ceased, but she is confronted by the power of the male. While she gives birth to the young God, she relinquishes her dominance over him and entrusts him to the male community, to the male Superego to which she must herself submit. While she has to relinquish her dominant position in the community she gains dignity as the mother of the God, and she continues to exercise her influence through him. Her once all-powerful spirit now resides in the son and acts through him.

This theme of the inheritance of the ancient powers of the mother-goddess was to become a major subject of Egyptian mythology; it had considerable influence on its social structure insofar as those who retained the mother's magic became kings; they assured their superior status by symbolically marrying the mothers. The kings of Egypt broke the taboo on incest, they married their sisters, which symbolised marriage to the mother, and while openly acting out the Oedipus complex by committing what was to ordinary people the supreme sin, they showed their superiority over them, they established the aristocratic order, the bond of divine rulers.

PREHISTORIC CIVILISATIONS OF EUROPE.

But before I turn to the emergence of the kingdoms of Egypt and Sumer, I should like to point to recent discoveries of a flourishing European civilisation which antedated the great Middle Eastern kingdoms by two or three millennia. These discoveries, made only during the last twenty years, make it necessary to revise our ideas concerning the development of civilisations, as they have shown that farming cultures and many urban centres existed in Europe as early as 6,000 B.C., and mineral technology, large-scale mining and working of copper and iron was practised about 4,000 B.C. This culture of ancient Europe developed its own patterns of religious art, particularly an art of sculpture which was in many respects unique. However, Europeans would hardly have developed agriculture independently, entirely on their own initiative, since many of the plants and animals involved were introduced from the Middle East. Apart from the small-seeded einkorn, Europe lacked natural growing cereals to provide the seeds necessary for organised farming. It is also significant that the European farmers used the same kind of reaping-knife and quern for harvesting and milling as their Asiatic contemporaries. The sheep and goat, which predominated among the earliest livestock maintained by European farms, had no wild predecessors there and must have been introduced in their domesticated form. One can, therefore, assume that the Europeans acquired the art of farming from the Middle East and, in particular, from Anatolia. This assumption gains credibility if we consider that maritime movements were well established and there would have been no difficulty for the people of Middle East civilisations to cross the ocean from Anatolia, or even from Palestine, to sail upon the Aegean Sea and spread their culture into the Balkan regions. The most important route by which the art of the new economy was introduced into Europe was by way of the Aegean, Greece and the southern Balkans, and spread from there into central, southern and eastern Europe. The initial phase of this migration can be dated to 6,000 B.C., and was at first confined to Greece and the southern Balkans. The first expansion beyond this initial zone occurred during the fifth millennium B.C., and centred upon eastern and middle Europe.[*]

---

[*] Grahame Clark: 'World Prehistory' (Cambridge University Press, 1977).

If these dates are correct, and there is no reason to doubt this, then the farming communities of south-eastern Europe were contemporary with those of Çatal Hüyük and Jericho, and, therefore, a fairly regular movement of people, of grain, domesticated animals and implements could be assumed to have taken place.

The Neolithic culture of south-eastern Europe left remarkably homogeneous artefacts, including distinctively painted bowls, jars and a vast array of sculptured figures and statues. Wheat, barley, lentils and peas were cultivated and among domestic animals sheep and goats were most numerous. The tells created by the accumulation of artefacts attest the permanence of these farming communities.

By around 5,000 B.C., there were many large settlements occupying as much as twenty or more acres, mostly along river terraces. The houses were of two or three rooms and organised into streets. These settlements were urban centres rather than villages.*

What is of particular interest to us is the evidence of large numbers of sculptures, of masks, bird-like female figurines and phallic worship among these people. Although they were able to depict the human form in a fairly realistic manner, the large majority of their sculptures extending from between 6,000 to 4,000 B.C. were rendered in a mask-like form. We might ask what motivated these people to hide the human face behind masks, and what meaning did the marks represent to them. We have seen how the sorcerers of Magdalenian times were depicted in animal attire (which in fact can be considered as masks) as identification with the chief animals of the hunt, whose power and characteristics they absorbed by dressing up to look like them. That these 'masquerades' are clearly forms of identification with the admired animal is fairly obvious, but the masks of the old European cultures are much more strange. Most of the facial masks were almost disc shaped and flattish in front, with two eyes pierced through from the back of the head; another type of mask had very prominent cheek-bones with elongated chins, producing an inverted triangle effect, and no mouth. On some of the earliest masks the flat, circular face had only a small nose barely breaking the flat surface. The triangular masks with huge cheek-bones often had sharp

---

* Marija Gimbutas: 'The Gods and Goddesses of Old Europe' (Thames & Hudson, 1974).

prominent noses. Other masks represented stylised forms of animal heads—mostly of rams.

There is no doubt that the masks express an ideal type, whether it be derived from the spirit of an animal or a state of mind. If we look at the flat, circular surfaces of the early masks, what strikes us is their bland imperturbability which denies all emotive expression—it is impervious to anxiety. The other most prominent type—the triangular mask emphasising prominent cheek-bones with powerful, elongated chin—represents on the other hand an image of aggressiveness. The absence of the mouth represents invulnerability, an emotional and relentless determination, the blank area where the mouth should be gives the impression of tightly pursed lips in an attitude of controlled anger and defiance.

Why should these people present such images and attitudes in countless sculptures and sculpted masks? If we consider that these masks almost entirely depict male figures then we might conclude that their culture was largely concerned with the males' determination to assert their power over some danger, either by a studied blandness and imperturbability or by a show of relentless, unshakeable strength. Of course, there were a large variety of ideal types expressing many different emotions but they are dominated by the two conventions mentioned, i.e. the two dominant states of mind.

We have seen that the late palaeolithic priest and sorcerer faced the mother-goddess in her cave in the form of an animal, and we can assume that the man of 'old Europe' faced the world through a mask, a stylised emotion which must have been of dominant importance. But what is he facing? Is it once more a goddess whose anger he was to confront and whom he has to dominate?

The clue to the question can be found in the many female figurines. Almost all are sculpted with very pronounced bird-like features having a long and narrow beak-like nose, a narrow face whose elongated shape gives an impression of a bird of prey. Some of the beak noses are long and sharply pointed, others have the shape of a duck's beak and others still that of a vulture. Indeed, we here encounter once more the angry goddess, the vultures of Çatal Hüyük and, indeed, we shall continue to encounter her in later civilisations.

We can see that the circular face of early European sculptures as well as the triangular faces are phallic faces determined to defy the maternal Superego, to dominate her and to penetrate her, to overcome any resistance offered to man by the goddess of the earth. Indeed, the phallic primacy of those earliest European agriculturalists is amply evidenced in their sculptures. Marija Gimbutas wrote that, "The whole group of interconnected symbols, phalluses, ithyphallic man, God-man and bull-man, represent the male stimulating principle in nature without whose influence nothing could grow and thrive. This family of symbols goes back in its origins to the early agricultural era, to the same period when the goddess of vegetations was born. Charging bulls, bull heads and horns alone, bovine heads with human eyes and ithyphallic men are already known to the eastern cultures of 6,000 or 7,000 B.C. Shrines at Çatal Hüyük include large bull figures in wall frescoes and sculptured bull heads and horns. Around the Mediterranean the bull and he-god play a prominent part in religion from the seventh millennium onwards. The phallic figurines from the Natufian and pre-pottery sites in Palestine demonstrate the persistent importance of phallic symbols in agricultural societies".*

While it is true that the phallic symbols represent the male-stimulating principle in nature, without whose influence nothing would grow and thrive, we must not forget that they also represent men's early struggle to assert their dominance as the life-stimulating agents. Indeed, one can speak of a phallic obsession among 'Old European' cultures. From about 6,000 B.C., phallic representations are found in all places in cultural groups of old Europe. They were fashioned in all sizes from miniature to the exaggerated. Decorations and shapes vary from the naturalistic to fantastic; some have a cap or circumcision and opening at the top; others are geometrically decorated by painting or incision; still others spiral upwards like snakes. A clay phallus from Thessally is painted cream, its naturalism enhanced by reddish-brown bands, having a broad incision at top. There is one enormous marble phallus painted with meanders at top and bottom. From the Vinca and Lengyel regions come clay or bronze phalluses decorated with idols symbolising snakes. There are instances where heads of snakes or frogs appear at the top, while many others imitate snakes. Some of the most interesting are those with human facial features on the top, reminiscent of the circular faces described earlier. Indeed, the representation of the phallus as a person, or as a face, is widespread

---

* ibid

in all patriarchal cultures, and even in the Middle Ages it was a common habit to have a face painted on cod pieces. More dramatic representations of men's phallic assertiveness and excitement are found in sculptures and paintings of ecstatic dancers with goat or bull masks—the archetypal Dionysus. There can be little doubt now that the origins of the Dionysiac festivals lie not in Greece but in Anatolia and south-east Europe, and the old discussion as to whether they originated in Thrace, in Crete or Asia Minor is pointless as they were common to Neolithic cultures from about 6,000 B.C.

We have observed earlier that a proportion of the inhabitants of Çatal Hüyük were brachycephalic Alpines whose roots were in the Balkan and Austrian regions of Europe. This indicates that already during the early stages of Anatolian urban civilisations movements to and from Europe occurred, and also explains the contemporaneousness of European farming cultures with those of Anatolia. While we can safely assume that during those migrations seed grain was brought into Europe, and agriculture became established in the south-east and the Balkan areas soon spreading into Central Europe, the hunt remained for millennia the prominent culture of northern Europe and the agricultural and patriarchal revolutions occurred much later there. This accounts for the continued influence of matriarchal cultures in north-eastern Europe and Russia.

While agriculture was not quite so widespread in the Alpine regions of Central Europe as in the south-east, their patriarchal revolution found expression in large-scale mining and metal working industries. The impulse to penetrate and dominate the mother-goddess which gave birth to agriculture here took the form of entering into the depths of the earth and labouring among its precious contents. By 5,000 B.C., these Central European miners had developed a metallurgical industry based on the ability to mine and smelt copper ores as well as to forge and shape them. That copper was mined, smelted and made into a wide range of implements at this time is shown by the multitude of copper dagger blades and perforated copper axes found in the Salzburg region and in Carinthia. These mining processes in Austria and also Rumania were carried out on a very large scale. It has been estimated that hundreds of workers worked in teams and spent a large part of their lives in mining activities, much of it underground, and we can speak here of a highly organised and complex metallurgical industry. The organisation of great numbers of men, working according to a plan, subject to industrial discipline and a central authority reminds one of the urban discipline of the early citadels of the Middle East. If we are to explain how these miners came to submit to the disciplines of organised labour and how the planners acquired authority to direct the lives of hundreds of men for the purposes of production, we meet with a peculiar problem.

There is no evidence that they worshipped kings or rulers, nor do we have any evidence of fortified cities, the usual symbols of patriarchal authority among Middle Eastern civilisations. Nevertheless, we have to assume that there existed some kind of authority and some kind of compulsion which directed large numbers of people to labour in mines, to co-ordinate the work of the miner with those who melted the ore and those who practised the craft of metal working transforming the ore into tools, weapons, utensils and, above all, ornaments. Moreover, it is obvious that these products were exported all over south-eastern Europe and as far as the Middle East in exchange for farming products and other commodities.

Apart from the organised planning and direction which these activities demanded, there must have been a psychological motivation which impelled these people to perform their arduous tasks and subject themselves to the disciplines and restraints which they required.

A clue to this question is perhaps provided by the Old Testament which accorded the metal workers, the Canaanites and Kenites, with magical powers. They were the forerunners of the alchemists, the archetypal Vulcan (the husband of Venus), the ancestors of the great Greek sculptors who transformed dumb matter into idealised images of the human form. The miner and the smith mimic the birth-giving powers of the mother. The phallic gratifications of forcing entry into the earth were accompanied by the gratification of labouring among her treasures and to bring out into the open what was hidden inside her. In doing so the metallurgist also entered into a special bond with the earth-mother; she allowed him to enter into her deepest regions and to acquire the knowledge of her mysteries. And he brought forth the hidden treasures and shaped them in his image, and thus his product was not only the symbol of the mother's magic but of his narcissistic self. These products and specially the large number and variety of ornaments he made were in great demand among the agricultural people who had left the security of matriarchal bonds and had entered into the strange new world of patriarchal rule and needed narcissistic reassurance and affirmation of their identity.

The arts of metallurgy spread from the Alpine regions to the Saalfeld area of Thuringia, whose products were characterised by a high silver content. Ornaments and particularly dagger blades and axes made of this material were their speciality and they entered into a trade network which carried them east to Silesia and south-east into the Rhineland. Metallurgical arts spread from Austria and southern Germany over the plains of northern Europe to the still early neolithic regions of Denmark and Sweden, whose craftsmen eventually created an indigenous culture of metal working. We can see an outburst of productive activity, the birth of a work ethic which became a fundamental characteristic of European civilisation.

The men of 'Old Europe' thus originated what Marx considered to be the characteristic of man's 'essential humanness', namely, the urge to produce and create material objects, to reproduce his self-image in material form. There is no doubt that the products created by man acquired a high value and were used in trade and exchange, and thus gave rise to activities which are subsumed by us under the term economics. But while the value of objects is determined by their desirability, the desirability of objects is determined by the symbolic meaning they represent, the type of psychological needs which they express and fulfill.

Even up to recent times whole continents were converted into European dependencies due to the native's irresistible fascination for the glittering artefacts, often cheap beads and imitation jewellery, offered to them by their 'civilised conquerors'. Even use objects like sewing machines were valued and desired by so-called primitive people, not for their utilitarian purposes but their apparently magical properties. Most 'primitives', having acquired their magic sewing machines, would continue to do their sewing by hand but would feel proud of their new possession, and like them we endow magic or divine characteristics to machines and ascribe to them a value which often far transcends their utilitarian advantage.

While the priests of urban civilisations of the Middle East derived their sacred aura from the divinities they served, and the people, in turn, acquired their sense of identity and security through the priest and the gods, the metal workers of Europe did not need gods and kings in order to be assured of their identity; their leaders represented in their person the collective aspirations of craftsmanship and were given authority to coordinate their labours. They did not build citadels for the glorification of kings, their habitations—often fairly large—were not fortified, and they had a tradition of moving freely in pursuit of their craft, and wherever they went they were regarded with a sense of reverence. When the Israelites first encountered the Canaanites they felt frightened of their magic art of ironworking and they had to rely on the greater magic of their God to overcome their fear.

We see the emergence of a dialectic interaction between the cult of the metallurgist craftsmen of Europe, the cult of productive labour as an end in itself, and the great religions of the Middle East which used the craftsman's skills and his products for the glorification of their gods. But as the Middle Eastern empires spread their influence, the European ancestors of the Renaissance humanists, of the scientist and engineer, fought to retain their authentic culture against the empire-building godworshippers, and in various ways established an international fraternity, which sometimes took the form of secret societies, to counteract the power of gods and kings. They were the ancestors of the Greek sculptors, of Michelangelo glorifying the human being and liberating his mind and his body from submissiveness to religious myths, and the genius of Leonardo da Vinci celebrating the free expression of all human faculties and their sensual embrace of the mysteries and actualities of the natural world, of the Enlightenment and its affirmation of reason over the tyranny of the Superego.

There is no doubt, however, that the establishment of patriarchal rule, the culture of the Oedipus complex, reached its first full expression in the empire states of the Middle East and from there spread, over the millennia, into most parts of the world.

7 Of Gods, Kings, and Empires: Mesopotamia and Egypt

THE EMERGENCE OF THE SUMERIAN KINGDOMS

At around 5,300 B,C., a large part of Çatal Hüyük and of other Anatolian cities were destroyed by fire, caused most probably by earthquakes which were widespread in this area and in other parts of the Mediterranean at that time. It is likely that many of the inhabitants left their destroyed homes and emigrated to the east in search of habitations suitable for agriculture. They formed new communities which spread along the well-watered southern foothills of the Turkish mountain ranges, from the Euphrates river in the west to the Zab river in the east, and soon played an important role in the culture of this area, which came to be known as the Halaf culture. As its beginnings can be traced back to about 6,000 B.C., it would be wrong to assume that the Halaf culture was founded by immigrants from Çatal Hüyük or other Anatolian cities; it is, however, likely that they had a decisive influence upon it. By the late sixth millennium a large number of religious symbols and artefacts appeared which clearly show an Anatolian imprint. Wall paintings and engravings of enormous bulls, bull horns and occasionally rams indicate the reappearance of the Anatolian bull cult. Also many of the small motifs, such as the hourglass and double axe, leopard paintings, etc., are very similar to those which were popular in Çatal Huyuk. However, these old Anatolian motifs were applied to gaily embroidered textiles, obviously an indigenous Halaf product

From about 5,000 B.C. onwards, Halaf pottery underwent a decisive technical improvement and the early Halaf styles and techniques were abandoned. We now notice an abundance of metals and precious minerals in the manufacture of pots, plates and a great variety of ornaments. Real masterpieces of ornamental art, such as beads, plaques and vessels appeared, cut from obsidian ore imported from the north, and widespread use of natural copper and lead.

Eventually there appeared a very high level of metal production from melted copper, lead and bronze. Trade was evidently well organised and extensive among the Halaf communities. Obsidian was imported from Lake Van areas, copper and lead from southern Turkish and Iranian mountains, and even Indian Ocean shells were imported via the Persian Gulf.

It can be said with confidence that never before had one culture traded in such a wide area. Their religion, dominated by the bull cult, as well as their craftsmanship in metal-working, weaving and advanced pottery, clearly show the influence of Çatal Hüyük and other Anatolian cities like Haçilar and Can Hasan.*

Contemporary with the 'Middle Halaf' culture, from about 5,200 B.C., another important cultural region emerged some two hundred to three hundred miles to the south-east, namely, the Hassuna and Samarra cultures of northern Mesopotamia. There is reason to believe that they originated from the areas bordering on Turkey, in other words, from the Halaf cultural territory. Hassuna lies near the Tigris river and Samarra is on its shores, and it may be a likely conjecture that people from the Halaf region, which included the upper reaches of the Tigris, sailed down this river and established settlements along its banks. From about 5,000 B.C. new types of pottery appeared there, far more developed in technique and design than anything produced there before. It came to be known and famed as Samarra pottery. Metalworking became an established art, and it would not be surprising if Anatolian and European metal smiths had a hand in it.

Their designs show many similarities with the products of the Middle Halaf culture, particularly animals painted on pottery, plates and plaques containing numerous motifs of bulls' heads and horns. While the Halaf people executed exquisite pictures of large birds with rich plumage, designs of vultures in full flight, antelope and deer whose horns intimate sun symbols between the horns,

---

* James Mellaart: 'Earliest Civilisations of the Near East', and 'The Neolithic of the Near East' (both Thames & Hudson).

Samarran art is of a more lively, more dynamic pattern. We see here less of the traditional confrontation between the female and male principles and instead an attempt towards their harmonisation, a new concept of unification. The Samarrans show their animal and human figures in a circular form at the same time indicating the four points of the compass and revolving anti-clockwise. In one plaque we see four deer with long straight horns gyrating around a tree, in another four long plumed water birds each gripping a fish in its beak. On a cup we see four women, their long hair streaming in the wind as they gyrate—surrounded by a ring of scorpions. Circling goats and many other animals, women whose long hair intertwining creates the shape of a swastika, express a worship of the vibrant powers of life, the circle of the recurring seasons and the image of a central point of energy around which nature revolves.

A familiar example is that enigmatic symbol, the Maltese cross, which originally represented four he-goats running around a drinking pool. Besides a number of phalluses carved in stone, we find them painted in many shapes and guises usually on tops of pots and vases, again creating the image of a rotating circle.

What is of particular significance is the large number of highly sophisticated painted clay female figurines with elaborate coiffeur, painted or tattooed, and having coloured garments. They differ from Halaf women, who were always modelled either without a head or a head sketchily indicated as a mere bulb of clay, as if the artist dare not provide his goddess with a recognisable personality. In Samarra, by contrast, her head is highly elaborated and carefully groomed as if to emphasise her personality—her idealised image. It seems therefore that the male had reached a degree of confidence which enabled him to represent the female goddesses in an ideal form as an object of his care and admiration.

Agriculture had reached a stage which employed large-scale irrigation which, in turn, indicates the establishment of centralised control and direction of labour and a high level of organisation in the mastery of the environment. Samarra settlements were located in areas whose annual rainfall was insufficient for farming. Irrigation methods therefore had to be employed in order to make agriculture possible. Given this ability among people of the Samarran culture, they could nourish the light and stoneless alluvium soil with the waters of the Euphrates and Tigris and make it rich and fertile. Having discovered their ability to transform the desert into good agricultural land by means of irrigation some of them sailed further south on the rivers with their ships and founded new settlements or brought new life into ancient and primitive habitations until they reached the Persian Gulf, built large cities and laid the foundations for the great Mesopotamian empires:

> And the Lord God planted a garden eastward in Eden; and there he put the man whom he had formed. And out of the ground made the Lord God to grow every tree that is pleasant to the sight, and good for food. And the river went out of Eden to water the garden.' (Genesis ii, vv.8–14).

Only, it is more likely that it was man himself who utilised the waters of the rivers in order to make the earth fertile, to bring forth food and vegetation and to assume mastery over the land and its produce. And he made God in his own image and saw his powers and skills reflected in a heavenly being.

The oldest town, perhaps the first of this land, was Eridu. It was also the most southern in Mesopotamia, probably lying on the shores of the Persian Gulf whose coastline at that time extended some one hundred miles further north than it does now. (So far nothing has been discovered in the far south that indicates settlements that lie to the south of Eridu). Recent excavations at Eridu have brought to light the remarkable fact—probably unique in the annals of archaeology—that no less than eighteen temples were built here one above the other on a single site.

The earliest temple found at Eridu—that of level 11—stood on a platform approached by a ramp, which was later extended. It was a complicated structure with mud brick walls strengthened by external buttresses. It is the oldest built temple ever to be discovered and contains elements which have persisted through to our time. It consists of a rectangular shrine which seems to have been divided in two zones by partition walls. At one end is a niche made to contain a mud brick pedestal and an offering table. Here we have, as it were, the layout of the typical Christian church: narthex, nave and chancel containing an altar. The temple of Solomon had exactly the same tripartite arrangement: portico, holy place, and holy of holies. The temple of level 9, of the same type but better preserved, was complete with altar and offering table in a similar position. The best example came from level 8: it is measured over 20 metres in length by about 12 metres in width. The furnishing of the temple has its special significance; men felt that when the God deigned to dwell on earth they should not appear before him empty-handed: offerings were indispensable. Two structures in baked brick were set up inside the sanctuary. One of these, in the apse, served as pedestal for the God, the other, in the antecella, as the offering table. That such a lay-out was employed at Eridu makes it clear that there existed an organised religion, that their God had his habitation in the temple, and the temple in turn sanctified the town and made it into a holy city.

The people of Eridu thus created the cultural foundations which came to characterise the whole of Mesopotamian civilisation: the sacred city whose economic, social and religious life was centred upon the temple and its priests. The cults of the temples and social rituals had a decisive influence upon social structure and gave rise to large cities which were dominated by the splendour of its public buildings, both religious as well as administrative, representing the power of its gods and its kings.

That large towns existed at this time, about 4,300 B.C., is evidenced not only by the many fine buildings uncovered but also by the large cemeteries. The cemetery of Eridu contained more than one thousand graves, and many other cemeteries of comparable size were discovered belonging to other cities in southern Mesopotamia. The monumental temples were constructed in mud-brick (which makes its first appearance), often on stone foundations and they dominated the cities from the top of ancient mounds or artificially built hills, the origin of the ziggurats. The outside of the buildings were ornamented with elaborate projections and recesses which remained in character with all later sacred buildings in Mesopotamia. The most monumental temples, arranged in three wings around a central court, were found at Tepe Gawra, and it illustrates even better than Eridu the tremendous advances made in this period. The intense religious feelings which gave rise to so much care and labour to its sanctuaries is unquestionable.

But what do we know of their gods? What do we learn from their figurative art in respect of their spiritual-religious imagery? While we are here still in a proto-literate culture we have once more to rely upon their representations of divine figures to give us a clue to their spiritual imagery. The structure of their temples, the pedestal and the offering table on which burnt remains of ritual gifts were found indicate that they worshipped a god, or gods, and that they made offerings to him. We may be able to reconstruct this god from the nature of the sculpted figurines and paintings which they left behind. The figurines were sculpted in clay and we find a large and varied assortment of both male and female images. The females are quite different from the earlier 'great mother' types. They are slim, always standing upright, sometimes holding a child, sometimes with hands resting on hips, their bodies picked out with touches of paint. The heads are no longer amorphous as in the Halaf cultures but have a pronounced snake-like aspect crowned with wigs made of bitumen. These snake-like heads have puzzled prehistorians but if we look at them carefully we cannot but be impressed by the ferocious aspect and recognise the bird of prey reminiscent of the goddesses of Çatal Hüyük: eyes are set wide apart, almost at the side, the beak-like nose producing an aspect of dominant ruthlessness and the tightly pursed mouth reaffirming this impression. The whole body is no longer the symbol of motherly plenitude but is quite masculine, emancipated as we would say, with a powerful neck, very broad almost square shoulders emphasised by inlaid pellets of clay, small breasts, slim waist and narrow hips.

It is very interesting to note that the male figures are similar but the faces of those which are known to us bear a much more benevolent expression, shoulders are even wider than on the females and they hold a sceptre which is clearly an elongated phallus.

Although there is no direct evidence, as we have no clue about their names, at least two pairs of male and female figurines must have represented a king and queen. The similarities between males and females indicate that they both worship or represent the same god, obviously a male, and that the female accepted him as her lord and to some extent even identified with him. However, the ferocious aspect of her face indicates the anger still hidden behind her acceptance of the male rule, whereas the male face expresses satisfaction and pride in his power. His eyes are much larger, more human, and his mouth shows a prim contentment, a faint smile. While their bodies are similar, it cannot be an accident or coincidence that the faces show a distinct difference in expression. However, they both have an imperious and somewhat dangerous aspect, an attitude demanding submission and sacrifices from men.

The king's large phallic sceptre shows his power to enforce those demands.

We must bear in mind the tensions and anxieties experienced by the agriculturalist during the long delay in responses from the earth and the complex interaction of a variety of circumstances upon which the harvest depends. We make offerings to the gods and especially to the male god in order to sustain him in his efforts to fertilise the earth and make her fruitful for us, to give him strength and the reassurance of our love for him, for he is a hungry god who needs to be fed to alleviate his anxiety and he needs to be reassured of his powers of making the earth mother respond to him. So we create ever bigger sanctuaries of his presence, for the very size of sanctuaries and their splendour show the extent of his power. We depend not only on his goodwill but on his strength and potency to fertilise the earth and be a creator of life, and we have to provide dwellings for him to which he can come and be in our midst, a home where he can be fed and celebrated. No dwelling would be too great or too sumptuous to be a fit house of god.

So men built great temples with complex rituals which became a focus for their social activities and drew large communities together in common worship; and in conjunction with these great temples they built large cities whose human resources and skills could fulfil the tasks which religious rituals imposed.

From the foundations laid by the people of Eridu, and other centres in the area which were known as Ubaid culture, the great civilisations of Sumer developed quite rapidly in the south. Several towns have yielded large quantities of valuable finds but none had the renown and prosperity of Uruk, within whose legendary walls the largest complex of sacred architecture so far discovered has been brought to light. Stratigraphical research has uncovered no less than 18 successive levels. Truly coherent and imposing architecture made its appearance from level 5, where limestone blocks (and this in a stoneless country) were employed in its foundations. Several temples are grouped in a part of the city which is described in later inscriptions as E-Anna (house of Annu). Here Imin, the goddess of fertility was worshipped together with Dumuzi, the god adored in all parts of Mesopotamia under various names (Tammuz, Adonis).

If the Sumerians did no more than take over the notions of their predecessors, they gave them a spaciousness and majesty that was wholly new. Architects of genius made plans that skilled workers carried into effect with unremitting care. Since in the absence of written words the names of the temples cannot be determined with certainty, they have kept the names given to them by their discoverers. For instance: the limestone temple, the red temple, etc., or their designation by letters, A, B, C, D.[*]

Temple D., the fourth in the series, is by far the largest: 262 by 98 feet. The central nave, 203 by 37 feet, would contain a very large congregation. Prayers were made to one or more divinities placed at the far end of the edifice, where we have what is either a central chapel flanked by two sacristies, or three adjoining chapels housing a trinity of gods. The outside walls were adorned with columns and niches. The builders often covered walls with white paint, frequently renewed, thus giving a dazzling brilliance to the edifice. Sometimes they added 'cone mosaics', without a doubt a Sumerian invention. They drove into the plaster of walls and massive columns thousands of small pointed cones, black, red and white, in such a way that they formed zig-zags, diamonds and triangles, patterning the surface with a variety of colour.

The culminating temple structure of Uruk was the White Temple which was built on an artificial mountain, some forty feet high, made of rectangular mud bricks. It took its name from the large whitewashed inner shrine, 61 × 16 feet. Here the Sumerians followed the precedent set by Eridu: a large hall, and a series of small rooms with the same ritual ceremonies (offering table and altar on which were traces of burnt offerings and incense) and several entrances for the convenience of the public.

But here we find an important difference from Temple D, described above. For one thing the reduced scale indicates that the builders were already working for the gods rather than for a large concourse of worshippers, and for another, this temple was mounted on a gigantic platform rising high above the ground. It soars up towards a higher region in order to testify to its proximity to the heavenly deities to which men have to lift their eyes. The temple became above all a sacred abode of the gods. We can see here the development of the processes of abstraction by which the divinities become beings which exist independently of man, whose region is in the heavens but have temples provided for them to serve

---

[*] André Parrol: 'Sumer' (Thames & Hudson).

as a temporary home upon the earth. The temple thus becomes not primarily a meeting place for worship but a home for the gods, a place where they can be fed and glorified.

The obsession with god-feeding came to play a large part not only in the religious rituals but also in the economic and social life of the city. The representatives of the gods, the priests and kings, the rulers of church and state, received those gifts on God's behalf, till those feeding rituals became something like a tithe by which the citizens assured themselves of their status in society as the responsible contributors to the establishment, and the establishment was assured of its power and wealth. Men would never have dared to enter the presence of the gods empty-handed.

The theme of gift offering is repeated in a large number of images, on tablets in cylindrical seals where these religious rites are being solemnized. The finest representation of a religious ritual is found in the great alabaster vase of Uruk which depicts a long line of offering bearers carrying baskets of fruit and vegetables and other objects. We can also see a procession of animals moving along a strip of fertile land luxurious with barley and other vegetation. This ritual vase in carved stone has been dated to around 3,200 B.C., and together with many other religious artefacts of the time give us a vivid insight both into their religious imagery as well as ceremonial practices.

It is of particular interest to note that writing first occurred in the form of accountancy to record and classify gift offerings and soon served to facilitate the evermore complicated accounting which had become necessary with the expansion of city and temple economy. Very soon it began to express the emotion which accompanied man's offerings to the gods. A man offering up flour to conciliate an angry deity wrote in the following manner:

> I will send thee to my angry god, my angry goddess, whose heart is filled with furious rage against me. Do thou reconcile my angry god, my angry goddess.

But while the temples became more splendid and the gift offerings more plentiful and elaborate, we notice a change taking place in the psychological nature of worship. More and more we find fear entering into the relationship between man and his gods; the gods become more awesome and threatening and man more self-effacing and frightened. The nature of worship changes; from being pervaded by a spirit of reassuring generosity towards the gods, devoted to the fulfilment of their needs, a sense of fear—even horror—enters into the atmosphere of the great temples. The gods are transformed from being satisfied recipients of man's offerings into frightening monsters. While the temples and cities become evermore grandiose, the hearts of men become fearful and their posture cowed.

In hundreds of statuettes of the late fourth and early third millennium B.C., worshippers gazed at their gods with large eyes expressing fear and submissiveness. The huge eyes staring out from a head sunken between pulled up shoulders seemed focused on a distant object in a kind of hypnotic trance. Lips are shut but from their tense bodies and intense stare enamates a sense of awe and apprehension which obviously indicates the anxiety those people felt in the presence of the gods. An undercurrent of fear is to pervade the great civilisations. Having glorified the gods and made them all-powerful, having given them dominance over the earth and over the mothers, having fed them with the best that the land can produce and having devoted their lives to labour in order to create resplendent temples, men became envious of the gods and began to hate them.

We find here a re-evocation of the Oedipus situation as it occurs in the life of the young man in his family. The boy builds up an image of the omnipotent father by projecting all his own narcissistic as well as phallic fantasies on to him. He wants his father to be strong and powerful in order to master the world and women, to set the boy an example of male power and allow him to participate in it. But having ascribed to his father manic powers, the boy becomes envious of his father, resentful of his sexual dominance over his mother and wants to castrate or kill him. In a similar manner the citizens of the early patriarchal theocracies became envious of their gods and resented their privileges and powers. They wanted to kill them in order to acquire their omnipotence and privileges. But these urges had to be repressed from consciousness for men needed the gods; they also loved them. They had to be propitiated in order to still their rage, but offerings of food no longer sufficed. The gods demanded phallic sacrifices, symbolic acts of self-castration as well as human blood sacrifices to quell their anger.

When we said mythologies are the collective dreams of civilisations then we must bear in mind that, just as in dreams, the actual thoughts and fantasies which produce the dream are subjected to censorship and appear in a distorted and more or less unrecognisable form, so the myths of a culture are expressed in a mysterious and apparently confused manner to hide from the people the true content of the fantasies which they harbour, and particularly, their aggressive, destructive drives. They are hidden behind a screen of displacement and symbolism which, although to some extent understood or rather interpreted by the contemporaries according to custom, nevertheless protects them from being fully conscious of their murderous impulses towards the gods. And we, who encounter those mythological presentations and try to interpret them, experience a reluctance to accept their true meaning.

Indeed, even while I do not have any qualms in acknowledging the sadistic or masochistic nature of patients' fantasies, have felt strangely disturbed by the destructiveness which appears in the religious myths of the foundation culture of our civilisation. The therapist who without hesitation can recognise the dark side of his patients may baulk at accepting the dark and destructive side of his civilisation. And after all, our European civilisation has its roots in the ancient Middle-Eastern civilisations and we not only inherit their achievements but also their bloody, sadistic and sacrificial fantasies.

From the beginning of the third millennium B.C., we find a great number of sculptures and engravings which vividly express the sadistic aspects of the Oedipal conflict. In one scene, depicted on a vase from Mari, we see a man kneeling over a palm-tree while his genitals are being devoured by a snake; on another section of the same vase a mysterious horned animal attacks a snake-like figure, and underneath a similar horned animal grapples with a phallus. The impression we receive from the first figure is that of a god taking possession of the palm-tree whose fruit he contemplates and is about to enjoy while a snake is going to castrate him. Does the snake then symbolise the phallic-aggressive impulses of men intent to castrate the privileged god? From Khafaje come several vases covered in bizarre assortments of animal forms. Here all is blind ferocity—a mental chaos. A monstrous fish attacks a bull lying supine on his back, while another mysterious quadruped attacks the fish. A snake bites phallic images and another animal appears to attack the snake. Most of the figures on these seals and vases are presented in animal form and we can assume that if the Meso-potamians wanted to express elemental drives which are usually repressed from the Ego they would do so by means of animal forms, the animal chosen being associated with the particular emotional primacy which it is meant to express.

However, even animals are insufficient to express the pre-conscious passions of men and have to assume the form of frightening monsters, unreal figures. For it seems that some of men's elemental passions would be too ferocious even for animals to accept as their own.

Half human and half animal figures were mostly chosen to depict the animal strength and power of important gods and their sexual prowess. The bull-man is a favourite image where strength and virility is particularly associated with a god. But nevertheless, the gods frequently were assaulted by mysterious figures, and in this case we can assume that the divinity—the object of worship and identification—is subjected to the attack of the dark side of man's envy and his sadistic impulses. We can be fairly sure that the Sumerians understood what the multitude of such figures and forms signified and in some respects their sculptures and engravings were a kind of religious communication, a form of epic literature.

In the middle of the third millennium B.C., a quite dramatic change appears in the images of men presented by Sumerian artists. While we have noticed the predominance of aggressive-destructive symbolisations in Sumerian art, with the later part of the third millennium more tranquil and dignified images make an appear-ance. Indeed, a new human self-image emerges, that of the proud citizen, the great and respected ruler and king, reminiscent of the eighteenth century picture of the successful bourgeois who also glorifies his king but no longer in superhuman terms but as a successful and powerful individual. In the imagery of Sumerian art from about 2,500 B.C., the human being is freed from sado-masochistic symbolisations and emerges as a real person.

This basic change of attitude is particularly striking if we find it taking place in the same locality among one and the same people. The statues are invariably of worshippers, both men and women, but the faces have now a smiling composure, an amiability and good humour, which prove that the age of abject apprehension of the gods had ended. Ordinary citizens as well as the rich mingled without much distinction. Calm and confident they approached the altar at the foot of which they placed their offerings. We can recognise certain family likenesses among a group of individuals, but the individuals stand out sharply each with his personality clearly indicated.

The women, too, are presented with grace and delicate appeal. The figure of a female worshipper from Ur, now in the British Museum, is full of smiling charm despite the empty eye sockets. Her robe, leaving the right shoulder bare, exemplifies the asymmetrical style of dress so frequently found in statues of young women.

While there is no reason to doubt that sadistic and masochistic fantasies and fears play an important role in the mind of patriarchal man, we can observe that at certain periods they are particularly intense whereas at other periods they are more quiescent producing a state of relative equilibrium both in social relationships as well as in the individual. A factor which significantly contributes towards a sense of social and psychological equilibrium is the discharge of Oedipal aggression upon an external enemy. When the urge to kill God is deflected upon a foreign God, the own God is made to feel safe; every attack on an enemy is, as we have observed in earlier chapters, an attack not carried out on the own God. Moreover, the courage displayed in the battle shows man's readiness to sacrifice himself to his God and king. The citizen who is prepared to protect his God with his life will be protected by the God and assured of his love. Perhaps the most important aspect of warfare is the transference of self-sacrifice onto prisoners taken in battle; they are offered as sacrifices to the god and king. The gathering of prisoners and their ceremonial offering to the Superego is the high point in the celebration of victory.

The displacement of the father-murderer upon a foreign king as well as the sacrificial offering of prisoners are acts of redemption which release men from their guilt and produce a sense of union with the eternal father, king and country. And men become united with each other in their common fatherhood, dignified as the instruments of his will and the agents of his power. In the collective battle against the alien god men identify with each other as defenders of their God, and the common affirmation of his supremacy unites them in an experience of community.

The readiness for self-sacrifice and the ability to defeat the enemy transforms the guilt-ridden sons into proud and dignified citizens.

Are we then justified in tracing the more confident and secure

Ego images of individuals as presented in the statues of the later third millennium to the emergence of warfare, not only as a sporadic activity but as an institutionalised and permanent characteristic of nationhood? There is no doubt that a permanent establishment within the nation devoted to the organisation and pursuit of war, as well as the right of the nation to demand of its citizens to serve as soldiers, and the emergence of the king as war-lord, laid the foundation of what we call the sovereign nation state. The king's power acquired a new dimension: he could command the unquestioned obedience of armies consisting of citizen soldiers or professional soldiers, usually a combination of both, for whatever purposes he deemed fit. And he would provide moral sanction for his wars by the invocation of the gods in whose name he led his men to conquest. It was the time of the creation of empires, of great military conquests and the unification of city states into empires.

It was precisely the right of the king to demand service and sacrifice from his citizens which increased his power and made it absolute, and paradoxically added a new dimension of pride and dignity to the citizens. For with their readiness for self-sacrifice in war their identification with king and country became more complete, and the expansion of the nation, its victories and its transformation into empire, enlarged their Ego, and the king's pride was reflected in the pride of citizens.

On the plaques of Sumer from about 2,600, we see vivid evidence of the organisation of warfare as an established and important aspect of statehood. These plaques, carvings in low relief, depict religious ceremonies as well as scenes of court life and warfare. Real figures also appear in motif plaques—priests and kings who are known to us from other documentation. The famous 'Stele of the Vultures' combines history and religion in its commemoration of a notable feat of arms: the victory won by Eannatum of Lagash over the neighbouring town of Umma. At the same time the two sides of the stele give complementary versions of what happened, on one side the exploits of the warriors and on the other the intervention of the gods.

The men of Lagash advance in close formation, carrying leather shields, ready to attack with their spears. The king stands at the head of this troops. Actually the battle is already won: Eannatum's troops are marching over the prostrate bodies of the enemy, which birds of prey are already beginning to devour. Once victory is theirs the men of Lagash begin to count their dead on the field of battle and provide a decent funeral for them. Their bodies are collected and covered with earth; the customary funeral sacrifices are offered. Next came the important epilogue to all successful wars: a scene of prisoners being led away into captivity. The other side of the stele is devoted to the gods who played an important role in the battle and made victory possible. The mighty figure of Ningirsu, tutelary god of Lagash, dominates the scene. In his right hand he lifts the stone mace with which he is about to bludgeon the luckless warriors trapped in a wide-meshed net held in his left hand which also grabs the symbolic emblem (a lion-headed eagle and two lions), while his huge eye is fixed on an unseen enemy who, we may be sure, is soon to undergo the fate in store for all who will resist the will of Ningirsu.

It is interesting to note here that while his right hand carries the weapon by which the god vanquishes the enemy, his left hand holds the prisoners gathered in a net and also the totem animals, as if he were to feed them with his sacrificial prisoners. There can be little doubt that the prisoners were seen as sacrifices to the totem animal and their helplessness a triumph of the god.

One of the most famous engravings is known as the 'Standard'. Shaped like a lectern it consists of four panels decorated with inlays. The two main panels, longer than the others, are the most characteristic. They illustrate two complementary aspects of existence: on the one war, on the other peace. Only when the former had come to a successful end could the blessings of peace be enjoyed. The theme of war is treated more elaborately than on the Stele of the Vultures. The episodes of war include the earliest known representation of a chariot fight, a type of warfare that must have introduced some sweeping changes into the old infantry tactics. We have already met these war chariots on the Stele of the Vultures. But here for the first time we see them in action. The chariots clear the way and the supporting infantry brings up the rear. Helmeted soldiers advance relentlessly, protected by heavy leather cloaks; all that remains for them to do is round up the miserable herd of captives and drive them to the king, who has alighted from his chariot and is awaiting them, for the fight is over.

After the storm and stress of battle comes the feast to celebrate the victory. Bearers and menials are seen conveying to the palace the spoils of war together with the animals and supplies required for the banquet. Seated, with a cup in his hand, the king takes refreshment with his guests who sit facing their sovereign. While they regale themselves, a woman sings to the accompaniment of a harpist. This banquet is reminiscent of the totem feast in which men are united through the common eating of the totem animal. Only here it is the celebration of victory, the defeat of the aggressive urges represented by the enemy outside which unifies men with each other and with their king. It is the feast to celebrate the good conscience when King and citizens acknowledge and accept each other, and drink to their union, freed from guilt and hostility.

Sargon of Akkad was the first great warrior-king to unite large areas of Mesopotamia into the Akkadian empire, acquiring the title of 'Lord and Master of the Four Quarters of the World'. The bronze head discovered at Nineveh leaves no doubt that it is an actual—if idealised—portrait of the founder of the Akkadian dynasty. The nobility of the face and its beauty continues to leave us spellbound. With his hair bound closely round his forehead, bunched at the nape of his neck in a chignon held by three gold rings, and with his elaborately curled and carefully groomed beard, Sargon takes his place in the line of the great dynasts whose head-dress he has adopted. He showed the same fidelity to tradition in commemorating his victories. A diorite stele has battle scenes carved in the Sumerian manner. The scenes are set forth in rows as in the time of Eannatum, and vultures and a great net holding prisoners figure in them. This arrangement and presentation continues to be orthodox and stylised. But in the reign of Rimush, Sargon's son, who ascended the throne on his father's death, there began a break with the old conventions and the individual aspects both of the soldiers as well as the king are more fully pronounced, their individuality and their movements more freely expressed.

The stele of Naram-Sin, Sargon's grandson, represents the victorious king as the heroic individual. On this stele of pink sandstone fifteen figures are represented, two contending armies, with eight soldiers on one side and seven on the other. The king stands at the front of his troops high above them all. The scene is a wooded mountainous region. The Akkadian soldiers are seen moving up the mountainside in a double column of light infantry with flying colours, while the enemy is in flight before them crying for quarter. The king stands proud and powerful high above them all and tramples upon tangled enemy bodies. With his bow and battleaxe in one hand and his javelin in the other, and wearing a helmet with large horns, he has reached the foot of a boldly stylised mountain, a powerful symbol, and confronts it as an equal. In the sky just above the mountain top shine two stars or, more probably, two suns, whose radiance celebrate the victory of the powerful male over the enemy and his domination over the earth.

Alas, the enemy is perennial and victory has constantly to be achieved in order to assure men's freedom from the threat within and without. But the framework which is to dominate subsequent civilisation has been created, the framework of empire and king by which the Oedipal conflicts of men are to be resolved and constantly re-enacted. However, its symbols are not only embodied by the state and its structure, but also in the imagery of the cosmos. The authority represented by political power is also reflected in the majesty of gods, and the majesty of gods in turn has its representation in the king. So in those persons in whom authority resided—the father in the family, the ruler in the state—the Mesopotamian recognised something of Anu and Anu's essence. As the father of the gods, Anu was the prototype of all fathers, as the king and ruler he was the prototype of all rulers. To him belong the insignia in which the essence of royalty was embodied—the sceptre, the crown, the headband and the shepherd's staff—and from him did they derive. It is Anu's command that issues through the king's mouth, it is Anu's power that immediately makes it efficacious. When in the Babylonian creation story the god Marduk is given absolute authority, and all things and forces in the universe automatically conform themselves to his will so that whatever he orders immediately comes to pass, then his command has become identical in essence with Anu, and the gods exclaim: 'Thy word is Anu.'

We see thus that Anu is the source and active principle of all authority, both in human society and in the larger society which is the universe. When the great gods address Anu, they exclaim:

What thou has ordered (comes) true!
The utterance of prince and lord is (but)
what thou has ordered, (that with which)
thou art in agreement.
O Anu! Thy great command takes precedence,
who could say no (to it)?
O father of the gods, thy command,
the very foundation of heaven and earth,
what god could spurn (it)?

The gods, then represent images of paternal authority projected upon the universe, while their power in turn is represented by the kings. Their universal power is an exaltation of the Ego of the ruler into the image of a god (mythic inflation) and the exaltation of the state to cosmic dimensions.

The great Hammurabi, king of Babylon, linked his destiny to the young and new risen god Marduk, as we can see in the opening lines of his famous code of law:

> When exalted Anu (god of the firmament), king of the angels, and Bel (god of the world mountain), who is the lord of heaven and earth; when these, who determine the destinies of the land, committed the sovereignty over all people to Marduk (patron god of the city of Babylon), who is the first-born of Ea (god of the watery abyss); when they made Marduk great among the great gods; when they proclaimed his exalted name to Babylon, made Babylon unsurpassable in the regions of the world, and established for him in its midst an everlasting kingdom whose foundations are as firm as heaven and earth. At that time Anu and Bel called to me, Hammurabi, the pious prince, worshipper of the gods, summoning me by name, to bring about the rule of righteousness in the land, to wipe out the wicked and evil, to prevent the strong from oppressing the weak, to go forth like the sun over the human race, to illuminate the land, and to further the welfare of mankind.

The rule of the monarch, acquired by human means, is represented as a manifestation of the will and judgment of the creator of the universe, and the celestial orb to which the monarch is now likened is the golden sun whose blaze is eternal and before which shadows, demons, enemies and ambiguities take flight.*

But while the victory of the paternal male is being celebrated and his dominion assured, his powers are, nevertheless, constantly challenged by the older female goddesses and the sons. The Oedipal complex has not been resolved and its continuing conflicts are projected on to the heavens and acted out by the gods. One of the oldest and best known mythic representations of the victory of the sun god over the goddess is the Babylonian epic of Marduk's battle with his great-grandmother, Tiamat. Tiamat here shows her disposition to turn into a monstrous demon when her anger is aroused, but despite her horrific appearance and tremendous power she is defeated by Marduk.

---

* Joseph Campbell: 'The Masks of God' (Souvenir Press, 1974)

Following the accomplishment of this deed of deeds, the gods were assigned to their various cosmic mansions, and they said to their lord Marduk:

'O lord, who has delivered us from the onerous servitude
(to the mother-goddess),
What shall be the sign of our gratitude?
Let us make a sanctuary, a dwelling for our rest;
Let us rest therein; and let there be also a throne,
A seat with back-support for our lord.'
And when Marduk heard this the glory of his countenance
Shone forth and he said: 'So shall Babylon be,
Whose construction you have announced.'

We see here that the great goddess-mother has been reduced to be a monstrous demon, and the city becomes the haven of the victorious god, his citadel whose walls and fortifications continue to protect him. Another well-known epic celebrating the battles of the male god and his victories is that of Gilgamesh, the king of Uruk. While kings acquire a measure of omnipotence through their identification with the gods, they also acquire a sense of the gods' immortality. In this way the nation becomes eternal and its citizens, by submitting to the rule of the king, partake in his immortality.

EGYPT: THE WORSHIP OF IMMORTALITY

Nowhere was the worship of immortality more exalted than in the religious and civic life of Egypt. If there is one aspect of Egyptian culture which can be seen as central to it, it is the unique concern shown by the ancient Egyptians for death and burial. If a culture can be said to have a symbolic speciality then ancient Egypt must be remembered for its elaborate and all-pervasive death rituals. Their burial ritual was one of the key systems through which many of the political, economic and religious aspects of society were unified.

While among the Mesopotamian cultures the worship of their living kings as the supreme moral authority bound the nation together in common obedience, among the Egyptians it was the dead king who became the focus of worship and the symbol of authority.

We have seen that in the earlier cultures of palaeolithic times the spirits of the dead were worshipped both in order to preserve their presence for the protection and security of the living, and also to prevent the dead from returning and taking revenge on the living. The fear of the dead god's revenge would have been enormously intensified in patriarchal societies; but whereas we have found little direct evidence of father-murder rituals in the great patriarchal cultures of the Middle East, we find rich evidence of such myths and rituals in north and east Africa. And there is little doubt that these African mythologies and cultures have played an important part in the development of early Egyptian society.

Around the turn of the century Sir James Frazer and Charles Seligman became fascinated with the custom of the ritual death of kings. Frazer compiled evidence from all over the world in order to study this custom, and he showed that it played a particularly important role in north-east African communities as, for instance, among the Nubians, Abyssinians, the Shilluk, the Dinka and others. Seligman was the first to show the unmistakable similarity between the ritual conceptions of kingship which prevailed among the southern Sudanese tribes and Egyptian concepts of kingship. Indeed, as G. A. Reisner has pointed out, during the early and middle pre-dynastic period (from about 4,000 to 3,400 B.C.,) the cultural development of Egypt was closely linked with the Sudan, and it is only from about 3,400 B.C. onwards that radical changes took place in Egypt, culminating in the establishment of the royal dynasties. While the Sudanese cultures remained more or less static, there emerged a powerful central authority in Egypt which acquired domain over the upper and lower Nile and eventually united the country into one great nation.

An important factor that contributed to the political and economic ascendancy of Egypt was a change in climate which transformed northern Africa from fertile grassland with a rich and varied animal population into what we now call the Sahara desert. From about 7,500 B.C., to 3,500 B.C., the great areas stretching to the west of the Nile, including much of north Africa, were fertile land with plentiful nourishment for the hunting and food-gathering population. From about 3,500 B.C., the climate changed, forcing many communities to move to the Nile regions, to hug the river, so to speak, and populate the fertile pluvial land, regularly nourished by the flooding of the river. Egypt became a strip of green land that cut across brown desert wastes—a veritable oasis in an otherwise barren desert country.

No doubt men quickly found the rich soil on the Nile particularly useful for agriculture. Indeed, agriculture became necessary if the multitude of villages that sprang up along the river were to be nourished and provided with the necessities of life. We can say, therefore, that the Nile encouraged the development of organised agriculture which, in turn, became necessary in order to provide sustenance for a rapidly increasing population. The Nile country, like the rest of north Africa, was and still is essentially rainless; only the waters of the Nile and the rick black soil cultivated by agriculturalists made life possible where otherwise there would be endless waste of sand and rock.

The situation is somewhat different in the Nile delta where irrigable land extended far back from the shores of the canals and rivers, and villages were not confined within a narrow strip clinging to the river. However, this narrow strip was the only means of sustenance that cut across north Africa below the delta.

But the question remains: What enabled the Egyptians to cross the psychological barrier that separates the hunter-gatherer from the organised agriculturalist? While we do not need here to discuss the influence on Egypt of the earlier farming societies of the Middle East, we can say that the people who were forced to cling to the river for sustenance made use of the concepts of divine kingship that prevailed among their ancestral cultures and enabled them to evolve a centralised authority which made the emergence of the nation state and the disciplines of large-scale organisation of agricultural systems possible. Great deities arose, and the powers of their royal representatives far exceeded that which was granted them previously.

We have seen that the power of kings has to be represented by visible symbols, by temples, palaces and large monuments as well as by sculpted and painted symbols. We have observed how these symbolic expressions of kingship emerged in Mesopotamia, but the monuments of kingship in Egypt were typically tombs and burial places, often arranged with the greatest imaginable splendour, and their monumental size depicts the greatness and power of those buried in them, finding their apotheosis in the pyramids—the largest monuments to authority men have ever created.

However, it was not so much in the monuments to the living but to the dead kings which marks off Egyptian culture from all others, and characterises their particular social Superego.

But we must still ask why this worship of the dead, the king's immortalisation in death, has arisen as the central cult of kingship that held together one of the greatest empires of the ancient world. For a clue to this question we must come back to the ancestry of Egyptian kingship.

The concept of the divine king was widespread among African cultures and shared by pre-dynastic Egyptians. The cultures of Nubia, Ethiopia and the Sudan considered the king to be the bearer of the divine spirit, the living representative of the divine ancestor whose offspring they felt themselves to be and from whom they derived their identity. But at the same time they followed the ritual of killing the king. King-murder was common to all these cultures, not merely in myths but in actual ritual and, no doubt, it was also practised by the pre-dynastic Egyptians. Primitive cultures absolved themselves of guilt feelings by ritualising the murder in acts of celebration, which occurred at certain periods and were accompanied by festivals, culminating in the death of the king and his rebirth with the crowning of the young king.

The Oedipal motivations for the ritual killing of the king were rationalised in diverse theories by which these African cultures explained their religious rites to themselves and to the western anthropologists who tried to understand their meaning. The most widespread explanation for these rites were those given by James Frazer, which are still widely accepted: "Primitive peoples believed that their safety and even that of the world is bound up with the life of one of these god-men or human incarnation of the divinity. Naturally, therefore, they take the utmost care of his life out of a regard for their own. But no amount of care and precaution will prevent the man-god, the king, from growing old and feeble and at last dying. His worshippers have to lay their account with this sad necessity and to meet it as best as they can. The danger is a formidable one, for if the course of nature is dependent on the man-god's life, what catastrophes may not be expected from the gradual enfeeblement of his powers and their final extinction in death? There is only one way of averting these dangers: the man-god must be killed as soon as he shows symptoms that his powers are beginning to fail, and his soul must be transferred to a vigorous successor before it has been seriously impaired by the threatened decay. The advantages of thus putting the man-god to death instead of allowing him to die of old age and disease are, to the savage, obvious enough. For if the man-god dies what we call a natural death, it means, according to the savage, that his soul has either voluntarily departed from his body and refuses to return, or, more commonly, that it has been extracted or at least detained in its wanderings by a demon or sorcerer. In any of these cases the soul of the man-god is lost to his worshippers and with it their prosperity has gone and their very existence endangered. By slaying him his worshippers could, in the first place, make sure of catching his soul as it escaped and transferring it to a suitable successor, and, in the second place, by putting him to death before his natural force was abated, they would secure that the world should not fall into decay with the decay of the man-god. Every purpose therefore was answered and all dangers averted by thus killing the man-god and transferring his soul while yet at its prime to a vigorous successor". [*]

We must assume that by means of such rationalisations which take the form of a mythology people not only explain the ritual to themselves but also receive assurance of the continued existence of their father-figure. It is of the utmost importance that the soul of the spirit of the father is protected from suffering, disease or decay as this would leave his people helpless and tormented by guilt feelings. On a pre-conscious level the divine father-figure must be protected from the destructive urges of his sons, and he has to be assured of his continued well-being; his soul is transferred to a young body as soon as he shows signs of old age and weakness, and thus his vitality is assured forever. But the urge to kill him cannot be entirely denied and continues to pose a threat to the father. The impulse therefore has to be discharged in the form of a ritual in which the murder is carried out but given the meaning of ensuring eternal and everlasting life to the father. Through this ritual the father murder is transformed into a declaration of his eternal life; his spirit, his libido, is released from its bondage to the transitory body which is subject to decay and death. In this ceremonial the dreams of the happy and loving father, who does not armour himself against the instincts of love but generously affirms them, find fulfilment, transforming the old king's death into his rebirth

---

[*] Sir James Frazer: 'The Golden Bough'

as a young and vital father-figure. Destruction is thus transformed into an affirmation of life, just as the infant's act of aggression is the means by which the libido previously hidden is enabled to emerge into the open; the annihilation of the individual ensures the emergence of the eternal. The individual and the cosmos, the temporary and eternal become unified through the sacrificial act whereby the permanence and omnipotence of the divine spirit is assured.

Moreover, through the ceremonial killing of the old father, the young man is enabled to take his place and fulfil his wish to become the new king. Every man can, remembering his childhood fantasies, identify with the new king, he sees his fantasies of victory over the old man fulfilled, and takes the old man's place by vicarious identification with the new king. Such enactment of the Oedipal fantasy provides collective gratification to the members of a society.

But cultures based on such rituals are essentially cyclic. The ritual binds groups together in an ever-recurring cycle of the death and rebirth of the father-figure, the collective abreaction of the Oedipal fantasy.

But when people enter into a higher stage of cultural development with the establishment of nationhood, urbanism, organised agriculture and trade, the establishment of a powerful central authority, the rituals of king-killing are no longer tolerated. The Oedipal drive can no longer be discharged by means of rituals of king-murder, on the contrary, such rituals must be repressed and they become memories of an ancient and savage society. But the death of the king continues to be associated with fantasies of having killed him, and those preconscious fantasies have to be compensated for by means of making the dead king not only immortal but also all-powerful. The act of restitution is directed towards the dead king and it is in his death that he becomes glorified and the centre of worship. While his death is inevitable the people must be freed from the guilt feelings of being responsible for it. So, when the king of the nation state dies, his death is interpreted as his entry into the world of eternity from which he reigns forever. The spirit of the 'slain god' is immortalised and he rules from his royal tomb in glory. Indeed, the spirit of the 'slain god' is represented in images of an awesome Superego which in its immobility guarantees continuity to his people and, at the same time, reminds them of their guilt, demands remorse and complete submission to his authority. The process of restitution is here not so much emphasised in grandiose castles and temples to exhibit the king's powers but in the wealth and size of his pyramids and tombs. His death no longer signifies his defeat but his victory as the immortal one.

Besides their importance as spiritual centres the royal tombs performed many political and economic functions: their construction provided occasion to bring together large numbers of people, both specialists and labourers, and organised them to work toward a single tangible goal; they afforded opportunity for the king and his henchmen to demonstrate their leadership ability; they required efficient planning and accumulation of massive food surpluses to feed and house workmen; they required large concentration of wealth, most notably of imported exotic goods which had to be obtained from distant lands; they afforded king, commoner and nobleman with a stage on which to participate in the drama of national unity in the rites of passage of the dead god-king as he joined his fellow gods, and a chance to re-emphasise the continuity of the dynasty through the participation of the heir-apparent in the funeral of his father.[*]

There are many remains of store-rooms and well planned complexes of workshops for metalworking, stone vase manufacture and butchering in the archaic and old kingdom towns from about 3,100 B.C. "It is most probable that from the beginning of the first dynasty the need to give symbolic representation for the power of the king and his noblemen made it necessary to produce artefacts which could be displayed in public, and after the death of the ruler would be buried with him in the subterranean temples of death. Many of these material symbols of power were manufactured in the king's workshop. The commitment of a sizeable proportion of the productive sector to the manufacture of such 'power facts' was an eminently logical activity from an Egyptian point of view, since it was through such goods that eternity was guaranteed".[**]

---

[*] Michael A. Hoffmann: 'Egypt before the Pharaohs' (Routledge & Kegan Paul 1980).
[**] ibid.

The complex of ideas associated with the dead god's sojourn in the realm of eternity did not merely produce a certain type of authority but also a concept of the soul which came to have a decisive impact on the subsequent development of European civilisation.

THE CULT OF THE SOUL

Once the idea of an everlasting life beyond the confines and transitoriness of the body is established in the human imagination, of a living essence that enters the body and gives it life but unlike the body is impervious to decay and destruction, then a concept of duality of soul and body, between essence and substance, between spirit and reality, will emerge as the central and most profound conception of the intellect.

In recent years a considerable number of Egyptian papyri have been translated which show an intense preoccupation with the soul and its central significance in the life of an individual. A man's relationship to his soul, his dependence on it and his dialogue with it, has been the central theme of many poems, some of epic dimensions, whose profundity is bound to astonish the modern reader.

Of the many papyri which have been deciphered in recent years one of the most interesting is the poem entitled 'Rebel in the Soul', which presents a man's dialogue with his soul and, at the same time, with the supreme being Ra with whom his soul is in intimate relationship. The poem has been dated at about 2,000 B.C., and its author is unknown. While it was translated first into German in 1896, it is only recently that a consistent and full presentation of it appeared in English.* The poem deals with a number of themes simultaneously: cosmic existence, the dilemma of the self in relationship to its own essence, the social problem of good and evil.

> To whom shall I speak today?
> Brothers are evil.
> Friends, today, cannot be loved.

---

* 'Rebel in the Soul'. A sacred text of Ancient Egypt. (Translation and commentary by Bika Reed, Wildwood House, 1978).

To whom shall I speak today?
Rapacious are hearts!
Each man takes his neighbour's goods.

(To whom shall I speak today?)
Gentleness is overthrown,
Violence rules all.

To whom shall I speak today?
When dishonour goes unremarked
Honour is debased.

To whom shall I speak today?
He, whose villainy outrages the decent,
is acclaimed by the mob for his evil deed.

To whom shall I speak today?
Men are pirates.
Each man seizes his neighbour's goods.

To whom shall I speak today?
When vice is greeted as a friend
The brother who will remonstrate becomes a foe.

To whom shall I speak today?
Forgotten is the past.
Good deeds go unreturned.

To
whom
shall I
speak today?
For corruption
roams the Earth:
there is no end to it!

In truth, He Who Dwells Within

   will absolve this Crime
   and this Transgressor.

In truth, He Who Dwells Within

   will rise in the Holy Barque of Night
   to consecrate the Supreme
   Offering to the Temples.

In truth, He Who Dwells Within, the Knower,

> will not be denied
> when he holds Ra
> to his word!

When you bring your flesh to rest
And thus reach the Beyond,

In that stillness
shall I alight upon you;

> then united
> we shall form the Abode.

The soul is depicted as the manifestation of a cosmic essence which resides within the self. Just as the citizen relates to the symbols of immortality as represented by the gods and king, so the individual relates to the soul inside himself, the spirit of eternity that lives within. We see here a stage of psycho-cultural evolution where the narcissistic libido demands recognition as the permanent centre co-ordinating the multitude of experiences, the fixed point in the flux of sensations. The soul reminds the Ego that the monuments which man has erected to eternity are but the material embodiment, the outward manifestations of its inner presence; they serve as a reminder of the spiritual entity which resides in man, the externalised essence of the inner self.

As the temples, tombs and palaces remain permanent features of all subsequent civilisations so the concept of soul and its eternal presence continue to dominate the consciousness of man. While the soul no doubt represents the essence and unity of a person's self-awareness, the unifying synthesis of the manifold of perceptions (to use Kant's phrase), it is also the seat of a variety of emotions, each of which it unifies into an image. Thus the soul—the essential self—can be presented in many forms: it can be angry or loving, guilty or confident, dominant or submissive, courageous or cowardly, terrifying or reassuring. Now it is interesting to note that while in subsequent Greek religions these self-images were projected onto the heavens as gods in human form whose emotions were easily recognisable, the Egyptians expressed them largely in the form of animal symbols. The Egyptians called the soul Ba, represented as a stork or a falcon with human head or a human body with falcon's head, a ram or human figure with a ram's head, a scarab, a cat, or a dog-faced ape. The soul is associated with Nut, the soul of the world or goddess of the sky. We see here that the Egyptian mind was still dominated by an animistic view whereby every living phenomenon, every aspect of nature has its own Ba, its soul, and men recognise their state of mind in a certain aspect of nature or in the character of some animal. Thus the various emotional primacies of the human soul are represented by certain animals, plants, by the sun, moon, sky, waters, atmosphere, etc.

The poet, all through the ages, continued to use natural objects as metaphors to express a state of mind. But what the modern poet treats as metaphors, early religions saw as living entities. This is a sophisticated view which, most likely, some intellectual Egyptians would have recognised to be true, but in their mythology they externalised their emotions; they saw their fate determined by symbolic beings which they took to be real and eternal.

Thus, the stork is a manifestation of Osiris, the great god of vegetation and of rebirth, and it is, at the same time, the animating birth-giving symbol. The stork being a migratory bird stands for reincarnation, for birth, death and rebirth. The transcendence of death, the eternal rebirth, is also represented by the phoenix, the Benu.

Simultaneously the soul of Ra, the supreme god of the Egyptians, the sun-god of life and light and fertility also lives in man and is represented frequently by a falcon with human head. When a man reaches maturity and wisdom, the Ba of Osiris unifies with the Ba of Ra, and out of their union emerges the phoenix, transcending the conflict between day and night, life and death.

The soul of the heavens, Nut, represents the birth-giving womb, and is usually shown as the starry heavens of the night. The sky here expresses the mother's all-embracing body. The soul is also represented as an egg, the animating source of life. Like the Ba, the egg can be assessed in a multi-dimensional way. It is totality, potentiality, matrix, and also a synthesis of evolution, the image of genesis.

Commenting upon the papyrus entitled 'The Book of Gates' (also called 'The Book of the Dead'), Bika Reed writes: "The Book of Gates, carved on the alabaster sarcophagus of Seti I (1,400 B.C.), depicts the progression of the sun-god Ra through the night. The twelve hours of the night are presented as the regions of the underworld. Each region is an hour of the night and has its gate. The consciousness of man moves through the underworld from gate to gate in a process of slow animation. For Egypt, life and consciousness are synonymous. 'To be dead' is a state of inanimation preceding consciousness or life. The process of animation presented in the Book of Gates was called 'coming forth into day'. The holy barque of night carries the sun through the underworld (unconsciousness). In this night the hours are stages of transformation towards awakening. Iai, the great ass, rises, symbolised by the sun, circumscribed by the ass' ears. He represents the soul of rebellion tearing itself free from the embrace of the night".

Iai, the ass, symbolises the aspect of rebellion against the embrace of sleep in which men are dominated by the mother goddess. Men must tear themselves free from the goddess of the night in order to arise with the sun to the daylight of new life and consciousness. Here is a mythological story which represents man's gradual awakening into consciousness as a process of maturation.

Like the sun-god, we must traverse through the realm of night, the world of infancy and dependency upon the all-enveloping mother-goddess who holds us in thrall while we are unconscious like children asleep in her arms or as yet unborn in the waters of her womb. The sun-god arises with the dawn of the day and of consciousness to dominate the sky once more, shedding his rays on the land and the minds of men.

In the soul's journey through the night we see the mythological representation of man's submission to the domain of the mother-goddess from which he must free himself in order to awake and enter the realm of daylight, of consciousness and maturity, where the sun-god Ra reigns supreme. This is an admission of the continued power which the goddess exercises over man, but her reign is limited to night when a man's powers are at rest and he is helpless, when the masculine Ego submits to the embrace of sleep, an embrace that re-enacts the mother's embrace of her child. But just as a young man must free himself from the mother's embrace, so a culture must overcome the dominance of the ancient goddess in order to enter into the domain of the male-god who spreads his light across the heavens. He fructifies the land, and it is his possession, his wife, his daughter. And the supreme god entrusts the land to his son, the king, for the specific purpose of ruling and administering it in his name.

As it was written: "As for Egypt men say since the time of the gods she is the only daughter of Ra, and it is his son that is upon the throne". Just as the husband was urged by the books of wisdom to take kindly care of his wife "because she is a field of advantage to her lord",[*] so the king had ownership, authority and responsibility over his land. It was his to control with power but if he were wise he would nurture it with care. For the ancient Egyptians the king was the physical son who issued forth from the sun-god Ra. To be sure, it was recognised that he had been born of woman in this world, but the father who had begotten him was definitely the god Ra who ensured the divine rule of the land of Egypt by making visits upon the earth in order to produce rulers.

For the purposes of actual procreation the supreme god assumed the form of a living king. Thus the queen mother-to-be received the seed of the god and such offspring was the son of god. The god by implanting his seed, which is to become the king, also transfers his immortal soul upon him as well as his omnipotence. And as the king acquires the god's omnipotence his rule is absolute and it encompasses the State of Egypt and by his rule he makes it immortal.

Whereas for the purpose of creation of kings the god has to come down to earth, and in the guise of a spouse has to fertilise the mother-to-be, in the realm of the heavenly gods there is no necessity for such mundane transformation. Ra, as the creator as well as the ruler of the universe, drew from himself and without recourse to women the first divine couple and he was the ancestor of all the gods. It was not until much later that he was given as his spouse Rat, which in any case is only his own name feminised.

As in the fable which Apollo proclaimed in the Oresteia here too the father is the real and only begetter, and while for earthly purposes the male places the life-giving seed into the woman, such expediency is not necessary in the birth of the gods. In the realm of universals the supreme god is the sole creator and all the gods and all of nature are the manifestation of his life-giving powers. Thus, the woman has been displaced as the primary creator and all living beings; male and female carry his seed, his soul, his divine eternity. In so far as men and women, gods and goddesses, kings and queens, are his children, they are brothers and sisters, and brother and sister relationship is strongly emphasised in the marriage of the gods as well as in the marriage of the Pharaohs.

---

[*] Ptah-hotep Papyrus 330.

Perhaps the best known of the brother and sister marriages among the Egyptian gods was that of Isis and Osiris. "According to the priests of Heliopolis, the sun-god Ra reposed in the bosom of Nun, the primordial ocean. There, in order that his lustre should run no risk of being extinguished, he took care to keep his eyes shut. He enclosed himself in the bud of a lotus until the day when, weary of his own impersonality, he rose by an effort of will and appeared in glittering splendour. He then bore Shu and Tefnut, Shu, the male, being the Atlas of the Egyptian mythology as he holds up the sky. And they gave birth to Geb and Nut from whom issued Osiris and Isis. When Osiris was born Ra rejoiced at the news of his birth, and having Osiris brought into his presence he recognised his great-grandson as his heir to the throne.

"Osiris was handsome of countenance and taller than all other men. When Geb, his father, retired to the heavens, Osiris succeeded him as king of Egypt and took Isis, his sister, as queen. The first care of the new sovereign was to abolish cannibalism and to teach his still half-savage subjects the art of fashioning agricultural implements. He taught them how to produce grain and grapes for men's nourishment in the form of bread, wine and beer. The cult of the gods did not yet exist. Osiris instituted it. He built the first temples and sculptured the first divine images. He laid down the rules governing religious practice, and even invented the two kinds of fruit which should accompany ceremonial song. After this, he built towns and gave his people just laws, thus meriting the name Onnophris, 'the good one', by which, as the fourth divine Pharaoh, he was known".

There is no doubt that the king's divinity, combined with the brother-sister marriage, gave the rulers of Egypt absolute power over the land. For in the brother-sister marriage male and female inherit the soul of the universal god and uphold his power. Like Athene among the Greeks who was born from Zeus and, as his daughter, represented his power over the Erinyes, the Egyptian queen was born from Ra—she was his daughter and the soul sister of the king. In this way the Egyptians had finally overcome the claim of the ancient mother-goddess and established the rule of the male god. This does not mean that the mother-goddess was eliminated; her divine functions in the cosmos continued to be acknowledged, but her rule was essentially related to the underworld; she reigned over the child and over men's unconscious; she was the starry heaven of night enveloping men, but in the world of mature consciousness, of reason, law and labour, the spirit of the male, the agriculturalist, the engineer, the administrator, reigned supreme and his rule was unquestioned.

Nevertheless, the rule of rationalism and justice was challenged by rivalry and violence among the brothers, as we find in the story of Set's jealousy of his brother Osiris and his murderous plot against him.

Not satisfied with having civilised Egypt Osiris wanted to spread the benefits of his rule throughout the whole world. He left the government of Egypt to Isis and set forth on the conquest of Asia. As he was the enemy of all violence it was by gentleness alone that he subjected country after country, winning and disarming their inhabitants by songs and by playing various musical instruments. He returned to Egypt only after he had travelled the whole earth and spread civilisation everywhere.

On his return from his journeys, Osiris found his kingdom in perfect order, for Isis had governed wisely in his absence. But it was not long before he became the victim of a plot organised by his brother Set, who was jealous of his power. Osiris, 'the good one', fell under the blows of the conspirators, but his faithful wife found his body and bore it back to· Egypt. Isis, thanks to her power of sorcery and magic, succeeded in restoring her husband's dead body to life. Osiris soon answered Set's accusations and vindicated himself before the tribunal of gods. Resurrected and from thenceforward secure from the threat of death, Osiris could have regained his throne and continued to reign over the living. But he preferred to depart from this earth and retired to the Elysian fields where he warmly welcomes the souls of the just and reigns over the dead.[*]

By his very successes Osiris aroused the enmity of his brothers who resented his powers and conspired against him. We find this theme of brother-murder, the brother's resentment of the favour-ite, as a major theme not only in patriarchal myths but in political history. The brother who has taken the role of liberator from an ancient tyranny is envied by his brothers, and they conspire to slay him: Cain and Abel, Joseph and his brothers, the battle for succession between the sons of David, between Danton and Robes-pierre, and Stalin's usurpation of power from his "older brother Lenin", bear witness to the problem of succession and leadership in

---

[*] Larousse Encyclopedia of Mythology (Paul Hamlyn, 1970).

patriarchal societies. The cyclic transformation of revolution (i.e. the slaying of the tyrant or the overthrow of a tyrannical social structure), the emergence of a democracy to be followed by a new tyranny, has been succinctly stated by Plato.

It was, as we have observed, Freud's fundamental axiom concerning the Oedipus complex that the band of brothers, having killed the father (or saw in his death the fulfilment of their desire to kill him), were overtaken by remorse and a sense of guilt. They resolved to renounce the incestuous wish and to make it taboo. Their shared guilt and their collective submission to the incest taboo bound them together in a primitive democracy where none would claim the mother-sister for himself and all would renounce the primary urge to be the mother's favourite and to have privileges over the others. At the same time they collectively identify with the powers and the skills of the slain father, restore him as their glorious leader and make him into a god to be collectively worshipped. In the totem feast they introject him and, by doing so, acquire his name and his powers. The mother becomes de-sexualised, and sexual gratification must be obtained henceforth from women of other tribes who have not been wives to their father, and their aggression projected outwards towards conquest and the defeat of alien father-figures, foreign gods and kings, and their women become legitimate objects for sexual gratification.

By marrying his sister-mother, the king breaks the incest taboo and sets two opposing processes into motion. On the one hand he fulfils for himself the incestuous desire and, on the other hand, he breaks the bond that held the brothers together and sets himself above them. He gradually assumes the image of the ancient father-tyrant, who denies the sons' incestuous cravings and keeps them in a state of subjugation. While he claims for himself the right to fulfil the Oedipal wish, his brothers must continue to repress it and have to find satisfaction for their sexual needs by means of exogamy. Their marriages reflect the need to repress the primary incestuous urge and to seek secondary gratification with women who are strangers, the women from another tribe.*

---

* While Levi-Strauss recognises the fundamental significance of incest taboo and exogamy as the foundation of society, he has no eye for the psycho-dynamic roots of this process. Instead he takes the rules of exogamy as given and proceeds to construct elaborate schemata which lack an explanatory theory but are made to appear as universal causes for social structures.

The man who takes the mother for wife and, indeed, appears to be chosen by her to be her husband and king inevitably reverts to a role as the father-figure, he becomes the focus of envy and aggression and the cycle of the Oedipus complex is once more set in motion with its perennial ambiguities and its class wars.

The Egyptians did not resolve the Oedipus complex in their socio-cultural system but made use of it by making the slain father into a god-king who, on his death, enters into the realm of immortality and reigns supreme from his tomb. The burial of the dead king becomes a sacrificial rite which transforms the murder into an affirmation of his immortality as the eternal Superego which reigns over men with inexorable inevitability. The soul of the dead king reminds his subjects of their guilt but, at the same time, enables them to overcome it by means of obedience and worship. By the glorification and worship of the king's immortal soul, the Egyptians symbolised and assured their nation's eternity. But the culture which immortalised kingship and nationhood also made them impervious to change. There were some changes of emphasis upon differing godheads, but no striking transformations occurred in their social system once the structure of their culture had been established with the early dynasties.

The centre of new developments in religious and social concepts shifted once more to Palestine and to Greece.

The Jewish concept of monotheism initiated a decisive step forward in theological as well as political thought, while the Greeks' idealisation of the human being, largely freed from the need to identify with a deity, made philosophy, as we know it, possible. The human being, mind and body, became the focus of worship, and their ideals of society reflected their sense of human dignity in community. The Athenians became the inventors of democracy and, however profound their shortcomings in the realisation of their ideals, they remained the model to which subsequent societies aspired. Individualism and democracy, philosophy, drama and poetry emerged during that extraordinary eruption of the human intellect which we call Greek culture.

8 Consolidation of Patriarchy: Athens and Jerusalem

THE INFLUENCE OF MINOAN CULTURE UPON GREECE

It is not possible to understand Greek civilisation and its culture without taking into account the influence which Minoan civilisation had upon it. The importance of the ancient civilisation of Crete can hardly be overrated since it represented the most advanced stage of the Bronze Age cultures of Europe and dominated the Aegean for something like one thousand years. It is, moreover, of particular interest to us as it also represented the last outpost of matriarchy among the ancient civilisations, and developed it to its most exalted and refined form. From its searing, deep-searching confrontations with Cretan matriarchy Greek patriarchy emerged victorious to become a supreme example of patriarchal virtues.

In 1953, a young British architect, the late Michael Ventris, deciphered the Cretan Linear B script—a stupendous intellectual achievement—and found that it was the early Greek language. Furthermore, although the writings proved to be mostly account-ants' recording, among other matters offerings made in temples, the gods to whom the offerings were addressed were those which in classical Greek tradition were associated with Crete. At a site on the Greek mainland, now identified as Pylos, the Mycenaean city of Nestor of the Iliad, a second store of Linear B notations has turned up which tells of a large number of gifts to the sea-god Poseidon. While this linguistic tie-up discloses the Cretan roots of Greek civilisation, it is also of considerable interest to note that Cretan cities and palaces were not protected by defensive walls. Historians emphasise this point as it is almost unique in the early history of towns, and they usually account for it on the grounds that the island as a whole was shielded from piracy by its navy and also that peaceful conditions prevailed within Crete. While it is true also that one can explain the long period of peaceful integration of the Minoan civilisation of Crete by a strong central authority based on the palaces of Knossos, we must still ask what was the nature of their culture which, unlike other agricultural civilisations, made it unnecessary to protect their cities and palaces with elaborate fortifications and in their paintings always showed men unarmed.

Let us recall briefly the historical background. Bronze Age civilisation came to Crete about 2,800 B.C., and for some 800 years ran an approximately parallel course in Crete, the Cyclades, and mainland Greece. About 2,000 B.C., the continuity was broken. In Crete civilisation rose to new heights, and the Cyclades as well as mainland Greece came under Cretan influence.

About 1,400 B.C., the leadership passed from Crete to mainland Greece under the leadership of Mycenae. The fourteenth and thirteenth centuries are known as the Mycenaean Empire. Political power was henceforth vested in the mainland, but the art of the Empire was essentially Cretan. About 1,150 B.C., the palaces of Crete and Mycenae were destroyed. A brief artistic renaissance followed in some areas, particularly in Crete, but the Mycenaean era finally came to a violent end about 1,000 B.C., to be followed by three centuries of poverty and near barbarism.

We have noticed in the previous chapter that navigation in the Aegean goes back to about 6,000 B.C. From that time onwards a movement of trade and population occurred with increased liveliness, mostly from Anatolia and later from Halaf regions and Sumeria, into Europe and the Greek islands (the Cyclades) and Crete.

By its geographical position the island of Crete is easily accessible from Anatolia, from peninsular Greece, and from the Nile. Its fertile lowlands guarantee a living to farmers, its resources of timber, copper and other raw materials can supply the needs of industry. Its natural harbours are not only bases for fishermen but havens for merchants who can transport Cretan produce to urban centres and bring back, in return, the manufactures and know-how of older cities.

By about 2,800 B.C. an increase of trade with Egypt had occurred which began to have a significant influence on the Neolithic population of Crete, transforming it into the Minoan civilisation and initiating its Bronze Age. It is thought that actual immigration of Egyptians during the early dynasties and even during the pre-dynastic periods took place. On the plain of southern Crete, facing Africa, the Egyptian influence upon Minoan Crete can be seen in the most detailed aspects of its cultural remains. At the same time even more explicit and pervading influences from Asia can be detected among the innovations of the Minoan civilisation. Indeed, Minoan metallurgy is largely based on Middle Eastern influences. Its most typical and striking pottery forms have their parallels with Anatolian pottery. The technique of glazed paint that distinguishes Minoan pottery had been earlier employed by the Halaf potters of northern Syria. Equally the cult of the double axe, which came to play an important role in Cretan painting and sculpture, has been foreshadowed by the amulets made by the Halaf craftsmen.

From about 2,800 B.C., Anatolian and Halaf as well as Sumerian colonists, merchants and craftsmen, began to enter Crete, introduced their cultures and their skills and joined with Egyptian immigrants to build the Minoan cities. Minoan civilisation, however, was not brought ready-made from the Middle East or Egypt, but was an original native creation wherein Sumerian and Egyptian techniques and ideas were blended to form a novel and essentially European whole. Indeed, one must not underrate the influences which European craftsmanship of the Bronze Age and, maybe, some aspects of their culture had on the Cretan civilisation, an influence which is exemplified by the Hungarian art of double-edged sword manufacture which was taken up by the Cretans to become one of their outstanding products of craftsmanship.

There is, however, no reason to doubt as Gordon Childe has written: "The admittedly Nilotic and oriental elements that we see superadded to the Cretan Neolithic culture may be treated as concrete expressions of the island economy with the support of capital accumulated by great cities which arose around 3,000 B.C. on the Nile and Euphrates. In supplying their need, the Cretan farmers' sons might find a livelihood in trade and industry; their self-sufficient villages would become commercial cities".*

However, the art and culture that arose out of the stimulus

---

* Gordon Childe: 'The Dawn of European Civilisation' (Granada Publishing Ltd, 1957).

provided by these advanced cultures came to differ quite fundamentally from theirs. The Cretan culture no doubt had its roots in its indigenous native background which had preserved many matriarchal features from a time before the victory of patriarchal rule which we witnessed in the Middle Eastern and Egyptian kingships. We are here forcibly reminded of the Capsians, the north African culture that spread across the continent into Egypt and the Middle East. There is an élan, a liveliness in Cretan art which, besides its handsome acknowledgement of female beauty, evokes memories of vivid and lively scenes painted and engraved by the Capsians some 10,000 B.C. Perhaps the indigenous Cretan culture represented a late survival of Capsian-Natufian races. These are speculations which I do not wish to pursue here, but they may point to some very interesting connections which merit further investigation.

The great majority of their images are of female deities—beautiful and confident goddesses—quite unlike those encountered in the priestly civilisations of the Nile and the Euphrates as well as those from the later patriarchal Greece. Professor Nilsson writes: "Certain characteristics of Minoan religion emerge which are in contrast to the Greek. One is the preponderance of goddesses and female cult officials. Masculine deities are in contrast to feminine very scarce, masculine cult images were lacking altogether. In the cult scenes women appear far more frequently than men, and it is likely that this preponderance of the female sex accounts for the emotional character of the religion... and the observation must be added that all reference to sexual life, all phallic symbols such as abound and are so aggressive in numerous religions, including the historic religion of Greece, are in Minoan art completely missing."[*]

Sir Arthur Evans, to whose labours during the first quarter of this century we owe the discovery of Cretan civilisation, emphasised the connection between their mother goddess and the great mother with her child and consort whom we know from the Middle East. While he was justified in pointing out these connections he underestimated their differences. However, he did point out that from its earliest to its latest phase not a single example has been brought to light of any subject of an 'indecorous' nature.[**]

---

[*] Martin P. Nilsson: 'Geschichte der Griechischen Religion' (Munich, 1955).
[**] Sir Arthur Evans: 'The Palace of Minos' (Macmillan & Co. Vol. 2, 1921—Vol. 4, 1935).

What this means is that there is an absence of the phallic-aggressive aspects typical of the patriarchal foundation cultures.

The grace and elegance of the ladies in their beautifully flounced skirts, generous décolleté, pretty coiffures and gay bandeaux, mixing freely with the men in the courts, in the bullring, lovely, vivid and vivacious, gesticulating, chattering, even donning masculine athletic belts to go somersaulting on the horns and backs of bulls, represent a civilised refinement that has not been often equalled since. As Joseph Campbell has so eloquently put it: "A contrast no less evident sets the Cretan world apart from the kingly states of both Sumer and Egypt. Its mythology and culture appear to represent an earlier stage than theirs of Bronze Age civilisation: a milder, gentler day, antecedent to the opening of the great course of Eurasian world history that is best dated by the wars and victory monuments of its self-interested kings. There were no walled cities in Crete before the coming of the Greeks. There is little evidence of weaponry. Battle scenes of kingly conquest play no role in the setting of the style. The tone is of general luxury and delight, a broad participation by all classes in a genial atmosphere of well-being, and the vast development of a profitable commerce by sea, to every port of the archaic world and even—boldly—to regions beyond".*

The social system which supported the fabric of Minoan civilisation first began with the opening of the Middle Bronze Age at about 2,000 B.C., a period marked in the archaeological record most plainly by the appearance of palatial architecture. There arose an elaborate civilisation based on the royal palaces of Knossos, Phaestos and Mallia. The destruction of these palaces about 1,700 B.C. and their subsequent re-erection scarcely affected the inhabitants. Indeed, the period from 1,700 to 1,500 B.C. is regarded as the apogee of Crete both architecturally as well as politically, and during this period Knossos dominated the whole of the Aegean. However, another destruction of the palaces and widespread disturbances, most probably due to earthquakes and tidal waves which have been linked with the volcanic explosion of Mount Thera, heralded the waning of Cretan power and gave way to the ascendancy of Mycenaean rule, and by 1,400 B.C. Mycenae conquered Crete. However, there is little doubt that from 2,000

---

* Joseph Campbell: 'The Masks of God' (Souvenir Press, 1974).

B.C. onwards, Crete exercised a considerable influence on the Greek mainland and its culture was widely adopted, particularly among the rising towns of Troy and Mycenae. Their palaces were, if not imitations of the great palace of Knossos, largely influenced by it. Mycenae in particular took over political dominance of the Aegean from Crete and by 1,350 B.C. built grandiose new palaces, and under their domination the Cretan cities revived after their catastrophic destruction.

Even while the Minoan influence was unquestioned in the development of Mycenae and Troy it is of considerable interest to note that these cities, and particularly Troy, were elaborately fortified; their culture had taken a new turn—they had moved towards patriarchy. By 1,200 B.C. there was a 'mighty and wonderful city' exactly as in the Iliad, wealthy and powerful and with flourishing trade.

There could hardly be any more impressive representation of the spirit of Cretan society than their sculptures of the snake-goddess, or the goddess of the snake, as she should be more correctly called. A considerable number of them have been found in the palaces of Knossos and Mallia; they show the goddess, impressive not only for her beauty and grace but, above all, for her supreme confidence. Her breasts are proudly exposed, and in each of her hands she holds a snake. She masters the phallic-snake symbol with a show of strength and confidence and it is obedient to her. In some figurines she holds the snake aloft with her arms outstreched by her side. On yet another representation the snake winds around her shoulders and neck and she holds it aloft with her right hand. In these sculptures and paintings her face betrays determination and dominance, while others depict her with ease and grace and feminine satisfaction. She is indeed the lord of the snake, the mother who not only exercises her maternal power over the sons but as a woman perpetuates her power over the grown male.

The numerous paintings and sculptures of the bull-jumpers, athletes, men and women who make somersaults over the backs and horns of the bull obviously symbolise their freedom from fear and their capacity to dominate the bull in the joyful exercise of their vitality, not intimidated by awe of the male god. One of the most famous of Cretan engravings, dating to about 1,500 B.C. and found by Sir Arthur Evans amid the ruins of Knossos, is of particular interest as it represents the high centre of Cretan culture.

The goddess, spear in hand, stands on a mountain flanked by lions who are placed at her feet in a subordinate but, at the same time, protecting and supporting position, and before her, in a posture known from other images to signify adoration, stands a young male, possibly a young Cretan king. This theme of representing the supreme goddess and her consort—a beautiful young man—is repeated in many engravings.

There are many representations of Cretan kings, who are always shown as youths of about twenty. There is never a picture of an old man. This may be due to the fact that none of the young men shown to be kings—consorts of the goddess—would survive beyond the time span of eight years allotted to them, and they would be either killed or replaced by another man. The ritual killing of the king, most probably enacted by means of symbolic rites, ensured not primarily, as among the pre-dynastic Egyptians, that the ruler should retain his health and youthful vigour but that he should be a youthful and vigorous consort for the goddess. The extraordinary beauty of the bull of Knossos, the care and artistry bestowed on him, show him to be a lover of the goddess—not the all-powerful representation of the male god but the consort of the queen. His horns were of gilded wood, the eyes of rock-crystal realistically painted, and the muzzle of shell. That bulls were ritually slain in the ring is shown in many amulets and paintings found in Cretan palaces where a priestly matador, obviously a priest of the goddess, dealt a coup de grâce to the beast coursing in full stadium career.

The word Adon signifies the spirit, the seed that gives life to vegetation and it is frequently depicted by the snake that coils around the sacred tree. Adonis himself is both the god of the tree as well as the fertilising spirit that makes a tree come to life and blossom.

It was the achievement of Cretan culture that the phallic god of the bull and the snake lived in harmony with the goddess, that he served her and she responded to his fertilising power with joy, thus producing the images of graceful vitality which pervaded Minoan culture. On the tree of the Hesperides we see a great snake coiling around the trunk and branches of the tree and three lovely nymphs are in attendance around it. Their movements and expressions manifest pleasure and gratitude as they gather the golden apples, collect water from a spring while yet another caresses the mouth of the snake with easy and natural affection.

It is precisely because Cretan matriarchy had achieved such a high level of civilisation that the battle to overcome its attractions became particularly desperate, involving great psychological conflicts. The worship of the goddesses had to be repressed from consciousness, yet they continued to dominate men's unconscious, constantly threatening the masculine divinities.

We have seen that *Adon* signifies the spirit of fertility, the life-giving energy which, in psychoanalytical terms, can be seen as the libido; we can refer to Reich's concept of the Life Energy—the Orgone—that finds expression in rhythmic pulsations. We know that orgastic energy produces rhythmic movements, narcissistic swaying and dancing and, above all, genital, orgastic pulsations and rhythmic contractions. Thus sensations of aliveness are most often symbolised by the undulations of the snake. However, whenever they are subjected to taboos they arouse anxiety, and their symbolic representations such as the snake become a source of fear.

The tension-discharge-pleasure cycle—the rhythm of the living—if repressed, produces tensions and rigidities. Rigidity becomes the chronic manifestation of inhibited libido. As Reich has put it: "The rigidity of the musculature is the somatic side of the process of repression and the basis of its continued existence". The rigid body, the held-in abdomen, the immobile pelvis and the tense chest, shoulders and neck—all are a defence against sensations of the libido as well as an affirmation of control over them. These defences are not usually conscious to the Ego; they are transformed into symbolic images represented as the Superego.

This duality between the impulses of the male libido and the repressive Superego has come to be clearly represented in the imagery of patriarchal peoples. On one side we find the idealised male as the living joyful Adonis, the agent of erotic stimulation and fertility, while on the other hand he is the lord, the repressive father to whose rules men must submit. These images are exemplified, among others, by the tree and the snake. In Cretan imagery Adonis is the tree surrounded and embraced by the pulsating energy of the snake. Indeed snake and tree, the god of vegetation and the god of Eros, are one. Adonis, the tree-god, is seen in symbiosis with his erotic life-energy, pulsating in snake-like rhythms. In patriarchy, however, Adonis, Adon, Adonai, became the tense, rigid god, the law-giver; the patriarchal tree represents his power while the snake becomes his adversary, the dangerous tempter who seduces men from their submission to his rule.

The snake as the symbol of erotic rhythm is split off from the tree which has become the symbol of the dominant father who has to repress the erotic impulses of men in order to defend his supremacy. Adonis has ceased to be the god of love who relates to the world with openness and joy, but as Adonai he is the god of laws, the lord whose rule dominates all other gods and men.

Among the Greeks Adonis came to be replaced by Zeus as the king of the immortals, the representative and idealisation of the Greek man who combined in himself the erotic powers of the male with the restraints of reason. In order to conquer the old order Zeus had to battle on at least three fronts. First, he had to battle against the old goddess who had turned into a monster in her rage against being subjugated and robbed of her position of dominance; secondly, he had to defend Adonis against her; and thirdly, he had to fight against the murderous impulses of the young gods, jealous of the father and encouraged by the mother-goddess to turn against him and fight him on her behalf—driven by her to become his enemy. The Oedipal passion was repeatedly seen as being instigated by the mother-goddess who drives the young son into an impassioned fight against the father in order to vanquish him. Zeus' battles took place on many levels, but the most enjoyable was his conquest of the female divinities by way of sexual seduction.

The particular problem faced by Zeus when he came to occupy Crete was simply that wherever the Greeks came, in every valley, every isle and every cove, there was a local manifestation of the goddess-mother whom, as the great god of the patriarchal order, he had to master in a patriarchal way. The numerous pretty young goddesses sent him crazy with sexual desire, and there is a large amount of literature describing his sexual conquests and adventures.

But it was not enough for Zeus to enjoy the ladies; he had to show himself to be the true progenitor of a new line of succession. The mythology of Zeus, the birth-giver, is exemplified by the legend of the birth of Pallas-Athene. The name already appears on a Linear B tablet of about 1,400 B.C., from the palace of Knossos, 'Atana Potinija'—'To the Lady of Athana', which is of pre-

Hellenic speech. She represented an important goddess of the palace of Knossos and acted as the personal protectress of the king, and such indeed is the role assumed by Athene. She is the guardian-protectress of heroes and obviously originally a mother of the kingly consort. However, in the classical pantheon of the Greeks Athene is represented as a young and fresh Olympian, born literally from the brain of Zeus.

THE SUPREMACY OF ZEUS

While the Greeks of the classical age had long forgotten the Cretan ancestry of their goddesses,* the battles for supremacy over them continued to be fought in their myths long after they had in fact conquered the civilisation of the Cretans. These battles were remembered not in terms of actual military and political events but chiefly in the myths where gods acted out the psychological conflicts of patriarchy.

Zeus not merely had to establish his primacy and his line of succession as the progenitor of the gods but his own line of succession had to be traced from the beginning of time in order to establish his position as the supreme and pre-ordained ruler of the universe. In his 'Theogony', which has become the source for all subsequent studies of Greek religion, Hesiod traces the history of the world from primeval chaos to the establishment of Zeus as the supreme king of the gods. This epic is of particular interest to us as it projects upon the universe stages in the psychic development of the individual: the primal polymorphous libido in the infant, the emergence of object-related libido and love as well as oral sadistic and aggressive drives not yet co-ordinated by the Ego, the pregenital dependency on the mother and the daimonic battles of the Oedipus complex till the personality of the dominant male emerges bringing law and order into the world and expressing as well as taming the passions of sexuality. Zeus himself is depicted as being at first subjected to the wild passions of the unconscious, only gradually and often painfully emerging to his status of the fully

---

* Plato, however, remembered the Cretan origin of the ideals of justice and civility by placing his 'Laws' in Crete.

grown male when he has to confront and defeat once more the old goddesses and the Oedipal compulsions of his sons.

The 'Theogony' of Hesiod was composed at about the same time as the Epic poems of Homer, probably towards the end of the eighth century B.C., at the beginning of the classical period. The collapse of Mycenaean power at about 1,100 B.C., a period of destruction and turmoil in which palaces were burnt and administration collapsed, was followed by the so-called 'Dark Ages', which lasted until about 800 B.C., when a renaissance took place with the emergence of the classical age of Greece. The great poets, Hesiod, Homer and Theognis, laid the foundations for the stupendous flowering of Greek culture, and they celebrated its emergence with their epics which traced the trials and victories of their gods.

Hesiod's epic, above all others, attempted to provide a cohesive chronicle of the birth and development of the gods and became an 'official' version for the Greek self-image and their pantheon.

> ... Olympian Muses, tell
> From the beginning, which first came to be?,

wrote Hesiod.

> Chaos was first of all, but next appeared
> Broad-bosomed Earth ... and Love, most beautiful
> Of all the deathless gods...
> And Earth bore starry Heavens, first, to be
> An equal to herself, to cover her
> All over, and to be a resting-place,
> Always secure, for all the blessed gods.

The Cretan name Rhea for the earth goddess was transformed into Gaia by the Greeks. Gaia thus gave birth to the heavens, Ouranus, to be her equal and her spouse, and from their union she created the first race, the Titans:

> ... she lay with Heaven, and bore
> Deep-whirling Oceanus and Koios; then
> Kreius, Iapetos, and Hyperion,
> Theia, Rhea, Themis, Mnemosyne,

Lovely Tethys, and Phoebe, golden-crowned.
Last, after these, most terrible of sons,
The crooked-scheming Kronos came to birth
Who was his vigorous father's enemy.

Ouranos and Gaia then gave birth to the Cyclopes, "whose
hearts were insolent", who resembled the other gods but only had
one eye in the middle of the forehead.

Then Ouranos and Gaia bore three sons
Mighty and violent, unspeakable
Kottos and Gyes and Briareus,
Insolent children, each with a hundred arms
On his shoulders, darting about, untouchable,
And each had fifty heads, standing upon
His shoulders, over the crowded mass of arms,
And terrible strength was in their mighty forms.

And these most awful sons of Earth and Heaven
Were hated by their father from the first.
As soon as each was born, Ouranos hid
The child in a secret hiding-place in Earth
And would not let it come to see the light,
And he enjoyed this wickedness. But she,
Vast earth, being strained and stretched inside her, groaned.

From her bosom she drew forth gleaming steel, fashioned a
sharp sickle and addressed her sons, explaining to them the plan she
had made.

My sons, whose father is a reckless fool,
If you will do as I ask, we shall repay
Your father's wicked crime. For it was he
Who first began devising shameful acts.

As she spoke 'fear seized all of them and none replied'. Only
Kronos, her last-born, volunteered to support his mother. As he
spoke the 'giant Earth was glad at heart. She set him in a hiding-
place, and put into his hands the saw-toothed scimitar'.

Great Heaven came, and with him brought the night.
Longing for love, he lay around the Earth,
Spreading out fully. But the hidden boy
Stretched forth his left hand; in his right he took
The great long jagged sickle; eagerly
He harvested his father's genitals
And threw them off behind. They did not fall
From his hands in vain, for all the bloody drops
That leaped out were received by Earth; and when
The year's time was accomplished, she gave birth
To the Furies, and the Giants, strong and huge,
Who fought in shining armour, with long spears,
And the nymphs called Meliae on the broad earth.

  The genitals cut off were carried for a long time on the waves of
the stormy seas:

White foam surrounded the immortal flesh,
And in it grew a girl...

  As goddess she came forth, lovely, much revered,

And grass grew up beneath her delicate feet.
Her name is Aphrodite among men
And gods ... born ... from
The genitals, by which she was conceived.
Eros is her companion; fair Desire
Followed her from the first, both at her birth
And when she joined the company of the gods.
From the beginning, both among gods and men,
She had this honour and received this power:
Fond murmuring of girls, and smiles, and tricks,
And sweet delight, and friendliness, and charm.

But the great father Ouranos reproached
His sons, and called them Titans, for, he said,
They strained in insolence, and did a deed
For which they would be punished afterwards.

And Night bore frightful Doom, the blackness of the Spirit,
And Death, and Sleep, and the whole tribe of Dreams.

In these passages oral-aggressive as well as cannibalistic drives are vividly represented by the fifty heads standing on the shoulders and a hundred arms darting about, in language whose dramatic power of evocation psychoanalytic literature could not match. The Titans symbolise infantile aggressiveness, deflected by the mother from herself towards the father thereby inciting in the male child the desire to castrate him. She thereby not only avoids being the object of the child's aggression but also satisfies her anger against the male who had usurped her powers. The boy becomes her agent of revenge, and the castrated penis a gift offering to her to propitiate her anger, and she is reborn as the beautiful Venus and Eros, and Fair Desire is her companion.

But the father condemns the boys for their insolence and horrid deed, and guilt and the dark spirit of remorse is born to haunt their sleep in dreams. Guilt gives birth to Blame and sad Distress:

> She bore the Destinies and ruthless Fates,
> Goddesses who track down the sins of men
> And gods, and never cease from awful rage
> Until they give the sinner punishment.
> Then deadly night gave birth to Nemesis,
> That pain to gods and men, and then she bore
> Deceit and Love, sad Age, and strong-willed Strife...
> Forgetfulness, and Famine, tearful Pains,
> Battles and Fights, Murders, Killings of men,
> Quarrels and Lies and Stories and Disputes,
> And Lawlessness and Ruin, both allied,
> And Oath, who brings most grief to men on earth
> When anyone swears falsely, knowing it.

Compare this with Freud's passage in 'Totem and Taboo': "After the sons had satisfied their hate towards their father by his removal and had carried out the wish for identification with him, the suppressed tender impulses (towards him) had to assert themselves. This took place in the form of remorse, a sense of guilt was formed which coincided here with the remorse generally felt. The dead now became stronger than the living had been, even as we observe it today in the destinies of men".

The Titans, unlike Freud's young men of the horde, were children, representing the early or first Oedipal period to which I referred in earlier chapters. But their insolence and their crime gave birth to the multi-faceted drama of patriarchy: its madness and its guilt, remorse, paranoid anxieties, mistrust and strife as well as worship and rituals of restitution.

When Ouranos was reduced to impotence, Kronos liberated his brothers, the Titans, and became chief of the new dynasty. Eventually Kronos married his sister Rhea, who gave him three daughters, Hestia, Demeter and Hera, and three sons, Hades, Poseidon and Zeus. But it seems that an oracle had predicted that he would be supplanted by one of his children, or may be that he had agreed with his older brothers, the Titans, to leave no posterity, and Kronos swallowed each of his children as it was born.

The father-gods constantly tried to rid themselves of their aggressive offspring either by burying them in the depths of the earth, i.e. putting them back into the mother's womb, or by swallowing them. By these acts the father intends to deny, or master, the destructive urges which endanger his authority. These acts, above all, dramatically symbolise the process of repression which can also be observed in psychosomatic processes, when people literally swallow their rage, and it goes into their stomach where it produces ulcers or many kinds of digestive disturbances.

Rhea, Kronos' wife, was overwhelmed with boundless grief. She asked herself in despair if she were condemned to see all her progeny thus disappear. When the time approached for her to give birth to Zeus, she beseeched her own parents, Ouranos and Gaia, to help save this child. On their advice she went to Crete and there, in a deep cavern under the thick forests of Mount Aegeum, she brought forth her son. Gaia took the new-born baby and undertook to bring it up. Meanwhile, Rhea wrapped up an enormous stone in swaddling clothes and presented it to the unsuspecting Kronos, who swallowed it at once.

Meanwhile, Gaia had carried her grandson to Mount Ida and given him for safekeeping into the hands of the two nymphs, Adrasteia and Ida, daughters of Melisseus, king of Crete. The two nymphs surrounded the young god with care and attention. They put him in a gold cradle, and to amuse him Adrasteia presented him with a ball composed of hoops of gold. So that Kronos could not hear the baby crying, the Kouretes executed around the cradle warlike dances, bearing their bronze shields with their swords. The Kouretes can be seen as mythological representations of the god-fathers and uncles who since ancient times played the role of the child's protector against the father's wrath. They are also the protectors of the mother, as shown by the fact that the Kouretes were Cretan priests devoted to the cult of the great goddess Rhea. Thus the link with the mother is clearly established and, indeed, the Grecians made the Kouretes protector of Zeus, thereby invoking the great mother-goddess on his side.

Sheltered from his father's cruelty, the young Zeus grew up in the forests of Ida, surrounded by nymphs, wet-nurses and goddesses. The oracle which had predicted to Kronos that he would one day be overthrown by one of his sons had not lied. As soon as Zeus reached manhood he planned to punish his father. He summoned to his aid Metis, daughter of Oceanus. Metis gave Kronos a draught that made him vomit up the stone and with it the gods, his own children, whom he had swallowed. Homer tells how, anguished by the might of Zeus, Kronos was driven from the sky and cast to the very depths of the universe and there enchained in the region which stretches between the earth and fruitless sea.

But the Titans were jealous of the new gods, the children of Rhea and Kronos, and for fully ten years there was a bitter struggle between them. The old gods, the Titans, fought from the summit of Mount Othrys, Zeus and his brothers and sisters from Mount Olympus.

Zeus descended into Tartarus where the 'many-armed' and the Cyclopes were kept prisoners. He set them free and made them his allies. The Cyclopes gave him the thunderbolt and the Hekaton-cheires put their invincible arms at his service. Seizing in their enormous arms great boulders they crushed the Titans. Sea and Earth resounded with a horrifying clamour and the shaken firmament groaned aloud. Zeus, too, was unable to curb his warlike rage and joined in the fray. 'From the heights of Olympus he hurled thunder and lightning. With unwearying hand he flung bolt after bolt, and the air was rent with sound and fury. The earth shuddered and burned; vast forests flamed and all things melted and boiled; the River Ocean, the immense Sea and the entire earth. Around the infernal Titans arose mists and blazing air; their bold glances were blinded by flashes of lightning. The fire even reached Chaos, and from what the eye could behold and the ear distinguish one would have said that sky and earth were confounded, the earth shaken on its very foundations, the sky crashing down from its heights. Such was the mighty uproar of this battle among the gods!'

In spite of their courage and power the Titans were finally defeated and cast into the abysmal depths of the earth—as far below its surface as is the earth itself from the sky.

Zeus had scarcely put down this dangerous revolt when he was forced to undergo a new struggle, this time against the Giants. The Giants had sprung from the blood of the mutilated Ouranos, and were not only distinguished for their size; these monstrous sons of the Earth had legs like serpents and their feet were formed of reptiles' heads. At the instant that they emerged from the ground they appeared in glittering armour, grasping enormous spears. They at once attacked Olympus, which dominated the plain of Phlegra. Islands, rivers, mountains, all gave way before them. Hercules, however, with the help of Zeus, finally defeated them.[*]

And still the forces of destruction were not vanquished; the old goddess could not resign herself to the defeat of her children and raised a final monster against Zeus—Typhoeus, whom she had borne to Tartaros. He surpassed all Gaia's other children in size and strength. Above the hips he was shaped like a man and was so tall that he overtopped the highest mountain and his head often knocked against the stars. He was a terrifying creature whose hands worked ceaselessly and whose feet were never still. From his shoulders sprang a hundred horrible dragon heads, each with a darting black tongue and eyes which spurted searing flame. From his thighs emerged innumerable vipers; his body was covered with feathers, thick bristles sprouted from his head and cheeks. At the sight of Typhoeus, the gods were seized with fear and fled as far as Egypt. Only Zeus stood firm before the monster. He struck him from afar with lightning, and at close range with the steel sickle, and pursued him to Mount Kasion. When he saw that the dragon was wounded, he went to fight him at close quarters. But he was at once caught in the writhing coils of the huge serpent, and the dragon seized the sickle from his hand and cut the sinews from the god's hands and feet. Typhoeus picked Zeus up on his shoulders, carried him through the sea to Cilicia and imprisoned him in his cave. Here too he hid the sinews of Zeus and set Delphyne, a female

---

[*] 'New Larousse Encyclopedia of Mythology' (Paul Hamlyn, 1970).

dragon who was half maiden, half serpent, as guardian over them. But Hermes and Aigipan stole the sinews and secretly gave them back to the god. Zeus became strong again and, appearing from Heaven in a chariot drawn by winged horses, pursued the dragon as far as Sicily where Zeus hurled Mount Etna upon her. This mountain still spits forth the lightnings that fell upon the dragon.

As C. Kerenyi* has pointed out, Hermes is clearly out of place in this story. He was one of the youngest sons of Zeus and brought into the story only because he was a master thief. The real participant in the story was Aigipan—the god Pan. It is very interesting to note that Pan, the goat, the symbol of male libido, allied himself with the god Zeus in his struggle against the forces of destruction.

The defeat of Typhoeus assured the final and lasting supremacy of Zeus. From then on no serious adversary dared to measure his strength with this god who had vanquished all the powers of evil and enabled divine wisdom finally to impose its will on all the aggressive and disorderly elements. The earth became firm, the volcanos subsided, the rivers, well-behaved again, irrigating the plains, and the tumultuous sea no longer tossed its waves beyond the sands of its shores. His reign would never be seriously disturbed, and among the Olympians Zeus maintained his rank of uncontested master of god and man.

It was then that the race of men, of humanity, was born, and it spread over the earth. But while Zeus had finally conquered the forces of destruction among the gods, he still had to encounter rebellious aspirations among the human race, envious of the power and authority of the great god, and still drawn by the lure of the goddess. Prometheus became the representative of humanity. During the revolt of the Titans he had kept a prudent neutrality, and had even made overtures to Zeus when it seemed likely that the war would be won by him. Thus Prometheus had been admitted into Olympus and the circle of the immortals. But he entertained a silent grudge against Zeus and sought to revenge himself by favouring the mortals and inciting them to rebel against the gods.

The task of completing the creation of mankind and of distinguishing men from gods was given to Prometheus. But he began to

---

* C. Kerenyi: 'The Gods of the Greeks' (Thames & Hudson, 1982).

kindle in them a spirit of rebellion against the gods. Zeus, however, crushed the rebellion and withheld from men the gift of fire; Prometheus, however, came to the help of vanquished mankind. He stole the fire from Zeus and brought it to earth; Zeus enraged, bound Prometheus with special chains against a rock at the highest point of the Caucasian mountains and sent an eagle to devour his liver. But what the eagle tore away during daytime grew during night. After 30,000 years or, according to Aeschylus, after thirteen generations, Prometheus was liberated by Heracles, who shot the heavenly bird with his arrow. And the unbound Prometheus thenceforth wore an iron ring as a sign of his subjection to Zeus.

There is no doubt that the story of Prometheus, the originator of mankind, represents yet another rebellion of man against the gods—to rob the gods of their libidinous omnipotence and to acquire it for themselves. "Primitive man", wrote Freud, "could not but regard fire as something analogous to the passion of love or, as we should say, a symbol of the libido. The warmth radiated by fire evokes the same kind of glow as accompanies the state of sexual excitation, and the form and motion of the flame suggests the phallus in action. There can be no doubt about the mythological significance of flames as the phallus. When we ourselves speak of the devouring fire of passion, or describe flames as licking (comparing the flame with a tongue), we have not moved so very far from the thought of our primitive ancestors... It is difficult to resist the notion that if the liver is the seat of passion its symbolic significance is the same as that of fire itself, and thus its daily consumption and renewal is an apt description of the behaviour of the appetite of love which though gratified daily is daily renewed. The bird which sates itself by feeding on the liver would then signify the penis, a meaning which is in any case by no means foreign to it, as we see in legends, dreams, linguistic usage and the plastic representations of antiquity. A step further brings us to the Phoenix, the bird which, as often as it is consumed by fire, emerges again rejuvenated". *

Probably the earliest significance of the Phoenix was that of the revivified penis after its flaccid state when it was consumed by the fire of its own passion and the fiery passion of the female to rise again. If we consider the sun as the male symbol, then its rise in the

---

* Sigmund Freud: 'Acquisition of Power over Fire' (Collected Papers, Vol. 5).

morning is akin to that of the Phoenix. While Freud sees in the
flames of the fire the excited movements of the penis, there is no
doubt that fire can be also the female sexual symbol, as we have
seen in early palaeolithic cultures which referred to the fire goddess
as the protector of men. Fire as the female sexual symbol stands in
a kind of symbiosis with the phallus, and the theft of fire is the theft
of phallic power and therefore also a theft of the female, from
the gods. Prometheus' act, therefore, symbolises both an act of
castration of the gods as well as theft of their women. For this deed
Prometheus had to be punished by being chained on the rock to
remain in a state of bondage to the enraged god, in a state of
paralysis that signifies man's guilt and repression. The iron ring
symbolises his submission to the supreme power of the gods, a kind
of mark of Cain which, as we shall also see, shows men's guilt and
his submission to the will of god. The price of life and of freedom is
man's acceptance of guilt, and the glorification of his gods.

But the victories of the great god did not succeed in establishing
his supremacy once and for all. His adversaries again and again
tried to challenge his power, and he had to use endless stratagems
to overcome them. But out of these conflicts the characteristic and
significance of the Superego as well as man's conception of beauty,
justice and rationality, was ever more clearly defined.

When Zeus gave birth to Athene out of his own head he created
the woman as the equal and true comrade of man, upholding and
defending the supremacy of masculine achievements and aspira-
tion. She was the tomboy beloved by the father, and also the
woman who understands men, thus combining in herself the
attractions of Eros as well as of comradeship. Of all the handicrafts, she most loved and protected the arts of the smith and metal
founders as well as women's crafts like spinning, weaving and wool
work. She was eminently suited to convert the Furies, the representatives of the angry mother-goddess to accept the rule of Zeus.
While Athene represented the woman's acceptance and affirmation
of the patriarchal culture, it was Apollo who, in his person,
represented the resolution of the conflict between sons and fathers.
Not only was he Zeus' most beloved son, he also combined in
himself the qualities of beauty, wisdom and strength. While in
Athene's person the female found acceptance as an equal to the
male, in Apollo the young man found acceptance by the father.
"When Athene was born from the head of Zeus, she sprang forth

with a far-echoing battle-cry, clad in armour of glowing gold. All the immortals were afraid and astounded. Almightily quaked great Mount Olympus, deeply rumbled the earth all round and raging rose the sea in the riot of the purple waves; long did Hyperion's splendid offspring halt the swift horses of the sun until at last Pallas Athene lowered the divine spear from her immortal shoulders. And much rejoiced the god of wise counsel, Zeus".*

In her creation Zeus established his line of succession not only through his sons but also through his daughters, and in the religion of the Greeks Athene took second place to Zeus only. In all these stories told of Athene she was styled Parthenos, 'virgin', but she was also called Meter—mother. There is no doubt that she was the tomboy favourite of her father, and although she rejected her suitors and refused to yield to them, she was sometimes depicted as the mother of Apollo. There is a secret tradition which has preserved the story in which Athene bore to Hephaistos—one of her suitors—a son named Apollo, under whose protection stood the city of Athene. There were also tales in which Athene and Leto—the recognised mother of Apollo—stood in close connection.

When Leto gave birth to Apollo, the earth shook her huge frame with laughter, the young god sprang forth and the goddesses surrounding him cried aloud. Themis gave him nectar and ambrosia, and when he tasted the immortal food, Phoibos Apollo declared to the goddesses: "'Dear to me shall be the lyre and the bow, and in my oracles I shall reveal to man the inexorable will of Zeus'. The goddesses who surrounded him were amazed and Delos, where he was born, shone golden and the whole island blossomed".**

There are many tales of enemies whom Apollo vanquished immediately after his birth. The most formidable of these was the dragon Python. Hera, who was a rival of Zeus and, therefore, also of Leto, and particularly anxious to deny Zeus this glorious offspring, resolved to exterminate Apollo as soon as he was born. She sent the female dragon, Python, against Leto at the moment of Apollo's birth, but mother and child were saved by Poseidon.

---

* Homeric Hymns, 28.5.
** Theognis: 'Elegies'.

Apollo took vengeance four days after he was born and slew the dragon.

Another of his enemies was the giant, Tityos, a phallic monster. Tityos attacked Leto as she was approaching Delphi and, according to many stories, the child Apollo killed him with his arrows. In another version it was Zeus who struck him down.

In the trinity of Zeus, Athene and Apollo, we can see the representation of the supremacy of the patriarchal god unified with the female deity, his offspring, and with his son, thus having overcome the rivalry with the mother-goddess as well as resolving the Oedipal conflict with his son. Sons and mothers are united with the dominant male, they are accepted as his equal as soon as they affirm his rule. But the rule of the great god was not absolute, it remained conditional upon a number of external factors and upon fate.

Above the gods, and above Zeus himself, hovered a supreme power to whom all were subject: Moros or destiny. Son of the night, Moros, invisible and dark like his mother, prepared his decrees in the shadows and extended his inescapable dominion over all. Zeus himself could not set aside his decisions and had to submit to them like the humblest mortal. He had, moreover, no desire to set aside the decisions of destiny, for, being himself supreme wisdom, he was not unaware that, in upsetting the destined course of events, he would introduce confusion into the universe, which it was his mission to govern.

The days of the gods passed in merry-making and laughter. Sometimes, when they intervened in the affairs of men whose quarrels they enthusiastically adopted, the gods would disagree. But these passing storms did not affect the normal serenity of Olympus. Seated around golden tables the gods dined on celestial nectar and ambrosia, and savoured the rising fragrance of fatted cattle which mortals burned in their honour on their altars below. Even when Zeus called them together in counsel on the topmost peak of Olympus, where he resided, the fair Hebe would move among them pouring nectar, and the golden cups would pass from hand to hand. Thus the gods' daily lives resembled that of men in idealised and perfected form because at least in appearance their natures were not dissimilar. Their bodies were like those of mortals, but superior in stature, strength and beauty; their social relationships were dominated by a sense of mutual respect and

harmony even while they quarrelled and sometimes fought especially when they were called upon to represent the conflicting
aspirations and interests of men.

Like mortals the gods were subjected to human passions. They
were susceptible to love, hate, anger, even to envy. They cruelly
punished all who aroused their enmity, but showered favours and
gifts on those who revered and honoured them.

It has been said that the Olympian gods represented the religion
of the aristocratic ruling class which replaced the kingship systems
of the older Aegean civilisations. During the Mycenaean age, and
even during the Dark Ages, the system of kingship had prevailed.
The king's authority was sanctioned by tradition and by religion
which made him divine, and the king's son had the right to
succession. Towards the end of the Dark Ages and particularly with
the emergence of the classical period, kingship disappeared and
became replaced by the next layer of authority, the aristocracy, the
aristocracy of the clan leaders who had long formed the king's
council and his court. Even while the title of king was preserved,
the king became a magistrate at Argos, Athens and Corinth and a
priest at Ephesus, Miletus and Naxos, but the council of elders was
now in control of the king who became one of several magistrates.*

The power of the aristocratic council was more decisive and more
deeply entrenched than that of the kings in the social structure of
the city state. The reign of the aristocracy as the chief governing
and co-ordinating body of Greek society which emerged out of the
chaos of the migrations and the Dark Ages could thus have found
its imaginative representation in the reign of the Olympic gods.

As Gilbert Murray wrote: "When the Olympians conquered their
kingdoms, what do they do? Do they attend to the government? Do
they promote agriculture? Do they practice trades and industries?
Not a bit of it. Why should they do any honest work? They find it
easier to live on the revenues and blast with thunderbolts the people
who do not pay. They are conquering chieftains, royal buccaneers.
They fight, and feast, and play and make music; they drink deep
and roar with laughter at the lame smith who waits on them. They
are never afraid, except of their own king. They never tell lies,
except in love and war".**

---

* N. G. L. Hammond: 'The History of Greece to 332 B.C.' (Oxford Univ. Press).
** Gilbert Murray: 'Five Stages of Greek Religion'.

It must be admitted that the gods were creatures made in the human mould and subject to human passions, and even the all-powerful Zeus was only a partial exception. Though there was a wide and unbridgeable gap between man and god, the gap consisted entirely of the god's superior power and his immortality.

FROM GODS TO PHILOSOPHERS

While the gods presented much more than the image of the ruling class nevertheless the humanisation of the gods had made great strides. It established a significant step forward in the development of Ego-consciousness among the Greeks; instead of seeing their gods as representations of the Superego in the form of animals and monsters dominated by oral-sadistic and phallic-aggressive primacies, they assumed the image of mature persons confident of their personal power and freedom. They saw their idealised self-images reflected in the Olympians, a kind of heavenly fulfilment of their desire for power, luxury and enjoyment as members of a privileged class. Even their occasional shortcomings and crudities reflected a sophisticated awareness that gods, like men, cannot always be expected to be entirely rational and behave according to the laws which they upheld.

But there came a moment in the history of the Greeks when they felt capable of realising some of the qualities of human perfection which they had previously only seen manifest in their divinities. Men began to rival the gods by demanding for themselves the right to exercise their human potential to the fullest extent. There is no doubt that a society which permits men and even demands of them to take an active part in the shaping of social events will encourage them to exercise their intellectual faculties to the full and give them a consciousness of personal power.

It was the polis, the democratic council of citizens which encouraged men to apply their intelligence and responsibility to public affairs, and the Greeks responded with vigour to this challenge; the polis enabled the Greek to live the full, intelligent and responsible life that he wished and marked in his mind the difference between Greek and barbarian.

For the Roman, 'civitas' was only a machine of government; so long as it protected the citizen he did not much mind who worked it. The Athenian of the fifth and fourth centuries B.C. did not think that way, for if the Greek was not in direct contact with his decision-making council, and did not feel himself an active member of it, if he were not within a day's walk of his political centre, then his life was something less than the life of a true man.

The energy shown by the Athenians in this period is almost incredible; they aimed at, and for a short time held an empire which comprised or controlled not only the whole Aegean, but also the Corinthian Gulf and Boeotia. The debates, theatres and law-courts and processions must not obscure the fact that the fifth century Athenian is first and foremost a man of action. A vivid description of democratic institutions was provided by a sketch of the Athenian character in Thucydides' 'History of the Peloponnesian War'. He describes the report of a Corinthian delegation which came to Sparta: "You have no idea (say the Corinthians) what sort of people these Athenians are. They are always thinking of new schemes, and are quick to make their plans and to carry them out: you are content with what you have, and are reluctant to do even what is necessary. They are bold, adventurous, sanguine: you are cautious and trust neither to your power nor to your judgment".

It was a common assumption among the Greeks that the polis had its origin in the desire for justice. Demosthenes, the orator, talks of a man 'who avoids the city', which as H. D. F. Kitto remarked, might lead the unwary to suppose that he lived in something corresponding to the Lake District, or Purley. But the phrase 'avoids the polis' tells us nothing about his domicile; it means that he took no part in public life, and was therefore something of an oddity. The affairs of the community did not interest him.*

Pericles in his Funeral Oration, recorded by Thucydides, compares the Athenian polis with Sparta and makes the point that Spartans admit foreigners only grudgingly and from time to time expel all strangers 'while we make our polis common to all, nor do we deny them any instruction or spectacle', words which are almost meaningless until we realise that the drama, tragic and comic, the performance of choral hymns, public recitals of Homer and games were all a necessary and normal part of public life. These are the sort of things Pericles had in mind when he speaks of institution

---

* H. D. F. Kitto: 'The Greeks' (Penguin Books, 1972).

and spectacle. Pericles praises the liberality of Athens: 'The law is impartial, public distinction is given to merit, not to party or class; in social matters toleration reigns and in public matters there is self-restraint and an absence of violence. Athens too is rich in the spiritual, intellectual and material things of civilisation... In Athens wealth gives opportunity for action, not reason for boasting, and it is idleness, not poverty, which is disgraceful. A man has time both for his private affairs and for the affairs of the city, and those engaged in business are yet quite competent to judge political matters. A man who takes no part in public business some call a quiet man: we Athenians call him useless. Speech we do not regard as a hindrance to action but as a necessary preliminary; other people are made bold by ignorance, timid by calculation; we can calculate and still be audacious. Also, we are generous, not out of expediency, but from confidence. In fact, our polis is an education to all Greece."

To the Athenian, self-rule by discussion, self-discipline, personal responsibility, direct participation in the life of the polis at all points, were the breath of life. The savage, living for himself alone, could not have it, nor the 'civilised barbarian' living in a vast empire ruled by a king and his servants and administrators. It is true to say that the Athenian polis became an inheritance of European consciousness, an expression of political and personal maturity that served as a model for civilisation and all too often has remained an unattainable ideal during the subsequent history of Europe.*

But even surpassing the political significance of the polis was the culture it produced within a short span of some two hundred years, an upsurge of cultural achievements that was without compare in

---

* I cannot here enter into a discussion on the vexed question of slavery which as many critics have pointed out made the free life of Athenian citizens possible and, at the same time, contradicted their idea of freedom. But let me just say that while the custom of taking prisoners of war as slaves was prevalent in all patriarchal societies since their inception, the Greeks had many laws and rules to humanise the life of slaves, to a point when a Spartan visitor to Athens ridiculed its citizens by pointing out that on walking through the streets of Athens one could not recognise the difference between citizen and slave; that furthermore their lives were very little different from that of the European working-class up to recent times and, in some respects, more secure. And also that the killing of slaves as sacrifice to the gods or king, generally practiced by the kingdoms of the Middle East, was abandoned by the Greeks.

the ancient world, and its sheer concentration of genius has not been equalled since. The Athenians occupied a territory—Attica—about the size of Gloucestershire, and in its greatest period had about two hundred thousand inhabitants. This was the size of the state that gave birth to Solon, Pisistratus, Themistocles, Aristides and Pericles among statesmen, to Aeschylus, Sophocles, Euripides, Aristophanes and Menander among dramatists, to Thucydides, the most impressive of all historians, and to Demosthenes, the most impressive of orators, to Mnesicles and Ictinus, architects of the Acropolis, and to Phidias and Praxiteles the sculptors, to Phormio, one of the most brilliant of naval commanders, to Socrates, Plato and Aristotle—and this list takes no account of mere men of talent. "During the same period she beat off Persia, with the sole aid of 1,000 Plataeans, at Marathon, did more than the rest of Greece together to win the still more critical victory of Salamis, and built up the only truly Greek empire that ever existed. For a considerable part of this period the exquisitely designed and painted Athenian vases were sought and prized all over the Mediterranean and in Central Europe, and perhaps the most remarkable thing of all, the popular entertainment—that which corresponds to our cinema—was the loftiest and most uncompromising drama which has ever existed".*

Athens from about 480 to 380 B.C. was clearly the most civilised society that had yet existed, and came to exercise a commanding influence on the consciousness of the western world, a permanent inspiration for intellectual and moral excellence. It became a kind of collective Ego ideal of western civilisation that strove to replace the older religious Superego.

As we have seen, the epic poems of Homer and Hesiod were created during the periods of aristocratic rule and to some extent can be said to reflect it. (I do not wish, however, to exaggerate the impact of political reality upon the concept of heavenly processes). But when these regimes gave way to the rule of the polis, and individuals took full responsibility for the running of their society, the gods lost their power. Men took it upon themselves to be the originators of events. But the intelligence that went into political decision-making also had to apply itself to an understanding of the

---

* H. D. F. Kitto: 'The Greeks' (Penguin Paperbacks, 1972).

world which was no longer symbolised and determined by the gods. (It is true that even during the high period of Athenian culture the Olympic myths were kept alive, but the intellectuals considered worship of the gods as a kind of religious custom which did not influence their rational judgment. The gods were regarded with scepticism, their motivations and behaviour considered rather uncouth and not taken very seriously by the sophisticated).

The phenomena of nature upon which men depended, the ocean, thunder, earthquakes, winds, rains and eclipses, the earth and heavens and transformations of seasons, ceased to be seen in the form of personalised deities; their causes had to be discovered in order to make them comprehensible as well as predictable. As it was men's minds and their rational faculties that determined both their social conditions and their ability to gain understanding of natural processes, they began to investigate the nature of mind. Furthermore, men had to learn to express themselves in a manner that would carry weight in debates which decided on political issues. Thus a philosophy of nature, an enquiry into the working of the mind, epistemology, and dialectics, the art of debate and oratory was born.

When the gods faded, reason had to take their place—when religion ended, philosophy began. Men had to strain their capacity of understanding and wisdom to the full; they had to observe nature, analyse their minds and their motivations, investigate the nature of reality and the role of perception, clarify the paradoxes of freedom and discipline and formulate purposes, in order to comprehend the duty and destiny of mankind. Their self-image and sense of identity had to be reappraised from scratch so to speak once the divinities which had explained everything and carried full responsibility had disappeared from the heavens. But this straining of the rational faculties became a new way of life, a new culture that was conscious of its superiority over everything that had gone before; a culture which once established could no longer entirely disappear from the memory of western civilisation.

It was the first great experiment in maturity, when the Ego dared to affirm its supremacy, its authenticity over the divine Superego. 'Cogito ergo sum', said a much later representative of the philosophical god-killers, but while Descartes, still under the influence of Christianity, seemed to consider the body irrelevant in the process of knowing, no Greek would have contemplated such a duality. The unity of body and mind, the glory of the whole person, became his chief credo.

After millennia when men projected their narcissistic fantasies upon the gods, the Greeks redirected the narcissistic libido upon the self in the image of the free and perfectable human being. The body was just as glorious and beautiful and worthy of worship as the mind, and they created a religion of reason which in no way denied the worship of the body. Indeed, the Athenian Narcissus, excelling in sport and articulate in debate, in poetry and song, became a focus of worship, an aesthetic ideal that claimed by far to surpass the attractions of the woman. Men came to respect and to acknowledge the self and its perfectability as a living, knowing and deciding person, the causative agent and creator of his reality. And here the male achieved his highest accolade: the sons took over the powers previously vested in the father. It was they who had all the best arguments, and they claimed the right of free thought and free speech.

The polis were of course not restricted to Athens. By about 600 B.C. we find them playing an important part in Greek society—Ionia, the islands, the Peloponnese except Arcadia, central Greece except the western parts, and south Italy and Sicily when they became Greek. All these were divided into an enormous number of quite independent and autonomous political units. One may say that the earliest conscious and deliberate attempt to arrive at an understanding of the characteristics and processes of nature developed during the sixth century B.C. among the Ionian philosophers who came to be called philosophers of Nature: Thales, Anaxagoras, Anaximander and Anaximenes. Their writings are widely known and need not be discussed here. It is interesting however that their works would hardly have become known to us if it had not been for Aristotle's great interest in them as precursors of his scientific speculations.

As we move to Athens of the fifth and fourth centuries B.C., the emphasis shifts towards the enquiry into the mind. 'Man is the measure of all things', proclaimed Protagoras, and 'Man know thyself' became possibly the most important motto of Greek philosophy. A theory of knowledge was born devoted to the rational investigation of reason itself. As the intellectuals became increasingly sceptical towards traditional ways of thinking, they attempted to arrive at secure foundations for the correct use of cognitive processes. A science of logic, first as an instrument of debate and oratory and then as an independent sovereign science, emerged with Plato and Aristotle. Already the Sophists had spread new schools for the improvement of understanding and the correct operation of the reasoning faculties. On a lower level they taught the art of arguing and the acquisition of as much knowledge as would help in this art; they were prepared to show how to argue for or against any opinion, and to follow an argument wherever it might lead them. Their principal values were a kind of erudition which puts man in possession of all knowledge useful for his purpose and virtuosity which enabled him to choose his topics expediently and to present them in a captivating manner. Probably one of the greatest of the Sophists, Protagoras, the humanist, expected everything of art and culture. In the opening of his treatise, he wrote:

> Man is the measure of all things, of what is,
> what it is, and of what is not that it is not.
> Moreover, men should only concern themselves
> with human things.
> As to the gods, I can neither know that they exist or that they do not
> exist.

However, out of this pursuit of the logic of an argument or a proposition they gradually emphasised the sheer virtuosity in debate associated with political and moral cynicism. This resulted —in spite of the great talents of the Sophists—in a conception of the intellectual life guided solely by success. They were prepared to show how to argue for or against any opinion and were not concerned to advocate conclusions of their own. They pursued the truth of logical propositions and ignored any moral considerations, and often it led them to scepticism and a readiness to exploit their knowledge for whatever advantage it might provide. This aroused odium not only among large sections of the population but also among many philosophers, with Plato in the vanguard. Bertrand Russell however sides with the Sophists against Plato, and his successors; he upholds the notion that the pursuit of truth must ignore moral considerations, and accuses him of always being concerned to advocate views that will make people, what he thinks, virtuous. He prefers the intellectual honesty of the Sophists because they refuse in any way to prejudge the process of logic by its moral consequences.*

However, it is precisely the increasing cynicism and even frivolity of the Sophists, who would nowadays call themselves hard-nosed rationalists, and their readiness to support any cause or interest irrespective of its moral aims, that evoked the strong condemnation of Socrates and Plato. It was the absence of any kind of moral conviction, or even their deliberate denial of such, which led Plato to consider the importance and significance of moral concepts in rational thought. For him the concept of the true and the good became intertwined into an indivisible whole, the dual representatives of reason. It was the good thought and the virtuous behaviour which, together with the investigation into the nature of truth, became the focal point of Platonic philosophy.

After Pericles, the leaders of the Assembly were mostly drawn from successful men of trade, men sometimes of great ability but opportunists; men who, by nature and training, took partial views dictated by self-interest and they welcomed sophistry as an expedient instrument to serve their ambitions. By the end of the fifth century B.C., nobody was sure about eternal verities: the clever were turning everything upside down, and the simple felt they had become out of date. To speak of virtue was to provoke this response: 'It all depends upon what you mean by virtue', and nobody knew. While the Athenians found great delight in a well argued and well turned speech, and were fascinated by the elaborate style and subtle arguments invented by the Sophists, they became, as Ceon told them, experts and connoisseurs rather than citizens, while the plain man, worsted in debate or cast aside in his lawsuit, grumbled at the way in which justice was being perverted.

Plato was concerned to establish rational principles at a time when traditional values of religion or sophistry no longer commanded respect. He set out to find universal criteria for truth and morality which would successfully replace the lost certainties. Philosophy for him was the discovery of a new form of intellectual life, the search for truth arising out of disciplined application of reason, but related and applied to society. He was twice called by Dionysius to be his counsellor in matters of social organisation, and twice he failed. When he was asked why he made the long and

---

* Bertrand Russell: 'History of Philosophy'.

arduous second journey as an old man, he replied that if he had not made the attempt he would have been considered merely a man of words.

Plato, the philosopher, lived on many different dimensions which appear to be in conflict with each other and at the same time give expression to the manifold aspects of the search for truth. On the one hand, the philosopher is the man withdrawn from the world who has purified himself from the limitations of the senses and transcended the boundaries set to the mind tied to appearances, and at the same time, he is the true lawgiver and politician who, on returning from his excursion into the transcendental realm, offers society his wisdom and becomes its leader. While he is the discoverer and advocate of a rigorous logic, he is also the man of enthusiasm inspired by Eros, the begetter of the beautiful. To rational discussion Plato added the dialectic of love, expressed with lyrical effusion and mystical contemplation. He proclaims a method of philosophy which represents the fundamental forms of the human understanding: the process of synthesis and of analysis. While the analytic process specifies given concepts of phenomena into their constituent parts, the synthesising process connects the parts into a homogeneous correlation till the mind arrives at the concept of the whole. It is the pursuit of both methods of thought, separation and connection, that philosophy can be assured to arrive at true concepts regarding the nature of the world, and at moral certainties. It is particularly by means of the synthesising process that we are enabled to arrive at universals.

However, Plato's concept of the universal is itself an intuitive statement which arrives out of inner necessity whose origin can only be found in the erotic impulse, the impulse to unite and harmonise what was prevously separate. This core of existence, the One or the Absolute, the permanent point in the flood of appearances, is not merely an hypothesis that springs out of the very structure of the mind but comes down to men by Eros, that mainspring of life itself.

There is, according to Plato, an eternal essence which cannot be apprehended by sensory perception.

In the 'Phaedo', Socrates approves of Anaxagoras' statement that 'intelligence is the order and cause of all things'. But on continuing with the examination of the methods of enquiry adopted by Anaxagoras, Socrates finds that his chief concern is air, water, ether and other physical aspects of nature. He complains that Anaxagoras would explain that he, Socrates, was in prison not because he refused to escape but because his physical organism had such and such a property, an explanation that leaves out the factor of Socrates' will, and his ideas. Everything that happens, however, presupposes a purpose which constitutes the ultimate cause and explanation. For instance, the behaviour of the stars cannot be explained by mathematical relations or geometrical forms; these only describe their positions; they can only be explained by the fact that the behaviour of the stars realises a plan or purpose behind them, and this purpose is the Good. The good or goodness is what everything presupposes, without presupposing anything at all. (Shades of Einstein's declaration that if a scientific formula is not elegant or beautiful it cannot be true). Even justice and beauty are worth nothing if they do not derive from the good. The good is like the sun in whose light other things are known for their reason of being, and by whose warmth they exist. 'The good then is not a being, it is beyond being in dignity and power'.

While Socrates, in contradistinction to the Sophists, employs dialogue not merely to apply logical processes in order to persuade or defeat an opponent but, above all, to liberate him, so to speak, from the prejudices and false certainties which cloud his thoughts, Plato goes a significant step further. And it is this step which established an important break-through in philosophy, namely, the discovery of universal concepts from which men have hitherto been estranged.

Whereas all previous thinking had projected the qualities of eternity and absolute reality upon the gods, Plato gave those qualities back to men. It is man's mind, his eternal Idea which is in possession of the true nature of things. But this innate Idea has become obscured by the illusions of sensory reality and forgotten —lost to his consciousness. The eternal Idea is represented by Plato not by a divinity but in human terms, such as goodness and universal purpose and truth, which the human intellect, if properly employed, can re-discover. There are, however, a number of contradictions in Plato's teaching regarding the manner by which this forgotten knowledge can be recalled—remembered.

We find a major dichotomy in his exposition between the knowledge that comes from the analytical mode of enquiry, the rigorous pursuit of logic, which can be taught and perfected by means of rational discipline, and the knowledge that comes to man in a state of passion inspired by love. This dichotomy has continued all through the ages. On the one hand, as Leonardo da Vinci has said: 'We cannot understand a thing unless we love it', and on the other hand, reason claims that we cannot comprehend unless we subject our mind to rigorous study, experience and rational discipline.

Are beauty and justice innate to the soul and revealed to men spontaneously by intuition or must they be learned? Can the just society be established through love for mankind or by submission to rationally established rules? The paradox of these polarities has continued to puzzle mankind. At best it is understood that the two must go together, but in practice they are divided; the just society of the poet, its appeal to the child's innocence, unaffected by manipulative logic, and the just society of the lawyer, the maker of rules that acquire authority over the minds of men. And Plato himself in his later years turned against the inspiration of love and put his trust in the order imposed by reason. His 'Republic' and his 'Laws', while being the most exalted manifestation of human rationality, nevertheless became symbols of coercion to later centuries. And the Dionysian cult of passion and love which had inspired Plato in his youth and early maturity, and which he came to abandon later in a sense of despair, lived on in Greece as an underground culture.

Men have learned to dispense with the gods to discover the essence of truth and beauty, in themselves. But when they tried to comprehend it by reason and give it expression through laws they once again subjected it to repressive controls, betraying their innate potential for beauty, truth and goodness.

After Plato we find a decline in the level of rational speculation. However, there was still the great, the phenomenal figure of Aristotle, Plato's disciple, who upheld the pride in men's reason. But he no longer had Plato's trust in pure speculation. It was, however, precisely for his reliance on the application of reason to experience mediated by sensory perception that he came to be the founder of the scientific method of enquiry. The difference between the two was said by Schopenhauer to consist in the fact that Plato was a philosopher of depth whereas Aristotle was a philosopher of width. 'Give me the findings gathered by the scientist, the observers of nature, and I shall co-ordinate them into a theoretical edifice that will reveal the truth about the world', proclaimed Aristotle. But the seeds of Aristotle's genius had to wait two thousand years to ripen; they began to blossom with the genius of Newton, whereas it can be said that it was Kant who first brought Plato's genius to fruition and laid the foundations of modern philosophy.

In the meanwhile, however, Athens was defeated by the Persians and the Greek genius was overwhelmed by the gods of Persia.

Late Hellenism became an amalgam of Platonic essentialism that adopted world-denying forms and Zoroastrian dualism. The truth could no longer be found to reside in men to be revealed by reason or love but in a heavenly realm, whereas the world of man was suffused by evil. The yearning for truth and beauty was once more projected on to the supernatural, and men had to wait for a heavenly messenger to fight the realm of evil. The conflict between the world of light and the world of darkness was no longer entrusted to men but to a cosmic duality. Men once more became subject to gods and kings. But while this domination of divine and kingly rule was to last far into the future, a religion arose in the Middle East long before Plato, at a time when the great epics of Hesiod and Homer were written. Another masterpiece of the intellect emerged that gave men a completely new concept of truth and justice in the form of God. A God who resolved in Himself and promised to resolve in mankind the conflicts which the Athenians so courageously confronted but were unable to resolve in their time.

MONOTHEISM AND THE CULT OF THE SACRIFICED SON

The Athenians replaced the gods by the affirmation of reason. In the tradition of the Greek philosophers we restitute god in ourselves—through the affirmation of reason he is reborn in our soul.

The Jews conceived another form by which the male of patriarchy came to be presented. They proclaimed the ultimate supremacy of the mature male and his omnipotence by his idealised projection upon the one God, who alone made the world and who reigns supreme over everything He created. He has eliminated all the other gods and goddesses from the heavens; He is the sole creator, the causa prima, the agent of life, the embodiment of purpose and reason, of fate and eternity. His will and his purpose gives meaning to all that exists, and the lives of men reflect His intentions. Through His purpose men's history emerges as a movement towards the goal that God has set before them.

Through Him men expected to acquire great powers, the knowledge of the essence and purpose of life; through Him they hoped to be the masters of fate, the initiates of justice and the creators of laws. The soul of men would not be confined to an individual, with an isolated, and limited existence but become unified with eternal life through Him; by accepting His laws men would be freed from guilt and assured of His protection and His love.

The Jews' image of themselves is fundamentally interwoven with the image of their God; they see themselves entirely as His children, and their historic chronicle is really a reflection of God's view of them. It is how God sees them, His experience of them that is revealed in their great writings, and their relationship to Him and their shortcomings, their agonies, trials and triumphs before His gaze.

The Jewish concept of God represents a remarkably high level of abstract thought. While the Hebrews invented the idea of monotheism, their God does not appear in terms of an anthropomorphic image. He is not presented in a perceptual, bodily form, but as a cosmic spirit, endowed with will, purpose and intelligence, and revealed to man by His words and His commandments. His eternity and omnipotence transcend the limitations of time and space to which human perception and understanding are bound. In Kantian terms we could say He is unaffected by the human categories of the understanding, i.e. time, space, substance and causality. He is the cause of all things, but He is not caused by anything and thus not subject to causality. He is the beginning of time but not limited to time because He is eternal. He exists but He is not perceptible, and unlike Zeus He is not subject to any other power such as fate for He is fate. He is both existence and essence, He is the One and the many, for all that exists is His emanation. The world of existence is a manifestation of His will and His thought. He is not a phenomenon but a noumenon, and all phenomena, all existing and perceptible things including man are the expression, the embodiment of His mind. But He reveals himself to his highest and latest creation, mankind, by the laws inscribed on the tablets of stone and by the words which He speaks to the prophets. Indeed, man's existence in history reveals His purpose, and the holy script, the Bible, shows man's struggle towards fulfilment of the purpose He has in mind for them; and it shows the divine mission of the Jewish people to be an example to mankind, and their failures, their agonies and their successes.

Being timeless, this God has no history; He is not born, He had no parents, He has no love affairs, does not get married, nor does He die. But His creations, and in particular His most interesting and rather special creation—mankind—has a history. He gave birth to mankind and assigned to it a purpose, and in pursuit of this purpose it acquires a history. He implanted a soul and a rational faculty in men to enable them to comprehend the meaning of the words which He spoke, but He has also given them freedom, a capacity for choice by which they can transcend their natural limitations and reach out towards an understanding of His vision. He gave them the ability to grow, to learn, and to perfect themselves, the potential for knowledge or ignorance, good or evil, and to fulfil His purpose by their efforts.

Why, it can be asked, and it is often asked in desperation, has God not given mankind perfection in order to accomplish His aims? Why has He given them the freedom to be evil and ignorant when He could easily have made them wise and good? The answer must be that men could not have comprehended a God who ignores their manifold destructive, aggressive, narcissistic, egocentric, greedy and selfish impulses. As men are only too aware of their destructive and anti-social drives as well as their desire for love and friendship, they need a God who understands their conflicts; who furthermore responds to them emotionally with love or anger, for otherwise He would appear distant and indifferent and His expectations would become a burden rather than guidance. The sons need their father's human proximity, his emotional involvement in order to feel accepted and assured of his love. But, nevertheless, being a father his love is not unconditional: he expects his sons to improve themselves and to learn, for otherwise there would be no progress, no growth, and men would remain bound to their limitations. He is teacher as well as supporter. It is his duty to ensure that his sons acquire knowledge and skills, and he has to threaten and punish them sometimes as well as showing his love.

The God conceived by the Jews is the first truly universal God, the omnipotent father who gives birth to all life, who creates and destroys universes at his will. All human beings are His children, brothers and sisters under His divinity. His purposes and His laws permeate the universe, but humanity is endowed by Him with intelligence and will, enabling it to understand and make choices, to learn to perfect itself.

The history of mankind is the period of struggle to fulfil God's expectations, and while men cannot, as yet, perceive his true nature, God has given them texts to guide them and prophets to inspire them. And at the end of history, when mankind has achieved a measure of perfection which satisfies God, He will reveal Himself and the Messianic Age will be initiated. It will be the time when man has achieved his maturity—the capacity to unfold his true potential. It will also herald the resolution of the Oedipus conflict, when "Elijah will turn the hearts of the fathers to their children, and the hearts of children to their fathers", as it is written in the last sentence of the Old Testament.

The people who have conceived this vision of God and of history regarded themselves as His first-born, chosen to proclaim His existence and His glory and to reveal His purpose to humanity. They consider themselves as a nation of priests and teachers charged with the awesome responsibility of setting an example to the nations in righteousness, to guide and educate them in the ways of God. But they were fully aware of the difficulties of their task and the burden imposed on them. They had experienced in their souls the fateful ambivalence towards the father, and they knew that others would resent their efforts to teach them. They repeatedly found the task laid on them too burdensome, but when they wanted to escape their God-given responsibility, their divine Superego, the voice of God within would not release them. Their ambiguity towards God, their love for Him as well as their rebelliousness, their aspirations to greatness as well as their obstinacy, are recorded in their scriptures.

By claiming to be the representatives of the omnipotent father, His Chosen People, His favourites, they arouse envy and hatred among those with whom they get into contact. In a kind of sibling rivalry, the people who feel themselves upstaged by the arrogant Jews, project their anger and aggression as well as their repressed sexual, sadistic, anal and manic fantasies upon the 'people of God', so that they acquire the image both as the strict and meticulous guardians of the law and, at the same time, the embodiment of the 'evil one', of everything that is impure, despicable and dangerous. This process of projection became sharply intensified with the advent of Christianity, where it acquired a cosmic dimension.

When the Romans conquered Israel and demanded that the Jews deny their God and worship Caesar, desecrated the Temple and the Holy of Holies, when those amongst the Jews who rose up against the oppressors were crucified by the Romans and their crosses lined the highway out of Jerusalem, when their rabbis were persecuted and the High Priests forced to co-operate with the conqueror, many Jews felt that God had forsaken them. Some, such as the Zealots, resolved to fight Rome by the sword, hoping to invoke God's help and to initiate His kingdom on earth; others prayed for the miraculous intervention of God to show His power not only to the Jews but to the world.

It was a time of desperation not untouched by hysteria. People hoped for a miracle and they looked for signs of it happening. It was in this situation that many listened eagerly to a young rabbi from Nazareth and wanted to believe his announcement that a divine victory over the forces of evil was imminent, a fundamental world renewal where God's glory is at last revealed. His charismatic personality, his impassioned advocacy of rabbinic convictions, his remorseless attack on the priests and Sadducees, and his powers as a healer, which may have appeared miraculous, no doubt made a deep impression on those who heard him. Although he was a Pharisee, probably an accredited rabbi, his charisma and passionate conviction of being inspired by God lent him some of the qualities of the prophets of old.

But if we study the development of his short ministry we cannot fail to recognise a transformation both in style and content. He began to preach in typical Pharisee language, announcing in his parables the ideas set out by the School of Hillel—the liberal faction of the rabbinic movement—using well-known passages from scriptures to make his point. But as he gained influence among the people, he became more and more absorbed in a mystical vision which stressed the supremacy of unconditional surrender to God's love and His mercy, transforming the male divinity into a maternal symbol which dispenses with the need for study, discipline and observance of ritual, preferring the childhood characteristics of innocence and trust. Indeed, the return to childhood became a major theme in his oratory. While his God is still the Jewish God, His love is that of the mother for her children. His God not only loves His children but prefers them to remain children. "The disciples came to Jesus, asking: 'Who is the greatest in the kingdom of heaven?' And he said: 'Truly I say to you unless you turn and become like children you will never enter the kingdom of heaven. Whoever humbles himself like a child is the greatest in the kingdom of heaven'." (Matthew 18)

The 'good news' announced by the rabbi from Nazareth spread to Rome and to the Hellenised people of Southern Turkey and Greece, where Orphic mystery cults were widespread. To the slaves of Rome as well as to many of the Hellenised intellectuals he appeared as the reincarnation of Dionysus, the young and beautiful son, beloved by the mothers on whose behalf he set out to smite the powerful father figures and reinstate the kingdom of childhood, where mother's love reigns supreme. He became associated with the image of the lamb who leads the people into battle but is eaten at the totem feast, where his followers partake of his flesh and drink his blood and its sweetness enters into them. On his death he rises into the kingdom of heaven, and all those who have eaten his flesh and drunk his blood and believe in him unconditionally, as he believes in them, are liberated from the reign of the earthly fathers, the perennial authority figures of this world, and take their seat with him beside the true and everlasting father in heaven, the androgynous God of love and mercy.

Coupled with this Orphic vision we find the imagery of Zoroastrian gnosticism, namely the descent of the Son of Light, the 'soter' from heaven onto the darkness of a corrupted earth, till the Pharisaic tradition is hardly recognisable. While the Orphic and gnostic mystery cults came to exercise a powerful influence upon the Christian imagination, Jesus was a Jew and in his address to his people he referred to the scriptures in order to validate his claims. He could only pronounce himself the Messiah if he was seen to fulfil the prediction of the prophets. But he presented himself personally as the incarnation of the Jewish people, the favourite sons of God, chosen by Him to set an example to the world: in his person he claimed to be the embodiment and realisation of the role which the Jews claimed for themselves collectively as a people. He was the beloved son "who came in the name of the Lord" to announce the coming of His kingdom. While to his own people he spoke as a Jew, he treated them as being estranged from God, for they had forsaken Him. It was not God, he declared, who has forsaken His people but it was they who had forsaken Him: it was only through their belief in him—Jesus—that they would be reunited with God. And those among his people who denied him, the priests and the lawyers, the rich and the arrogant, the stiff-necked and obstinate who refused to yield to his message would be unable to enter the new world order, they would remain cast out from God's kingdom.

While Jesus himself never condemned the Jewish people as a whole but came to drive a wedge between the people and their leaders, it was not long before the Jews were collectively cast in the role of the unredeemed sinners: they were pronounced "the sons of the devil and the Law a curse upon men". Under the growing influence of the Orphic mythology, the followers of Jesus transformed his message into a cosmic confrontation between the world of light and the world of darkness, making the Jews into representatives of the world of darkness, the eternal protagonists of the forces of evil.

The Orphic myths and their worship of Dionysus gave public expression to man's yearning for a return to the world of childhood, where he was enveloped by mother's love and the supreme object of her affection and admiration. There is in every male a memory of the boy's desire to be his mother's hero who vanquishes the big male who intrudes into the son's special relationship with his mother and liberates her from his unwelcome domination.

In the Zoroastrian gnostic myths the son is already victorious. He represents the world of light and love and descends onto the corrupted world ruled by men who are empty of libido and do not know love. All those who have become powerful and rich in this world, the priests who justify the rule of the old men with their sermons and their rituals and the lawyers who fabricate rules by which they keep the sons in a state of fear and oppression, they are all in bondage to the world of darkness. And on the Day of Judgment the Son of Light will cast down the stiff-necked and the stubborn, the hard-hearted and loveless to the hell of unremitting guilt, to be forever tortured by their bad consciences, and make the world free from their reign forever.

These mythological fantasies, normally repressed in patriarchal cultures, tend to erupt to the surface and take possession of man's mind whenever the fathers lose their power and appear impotent and the sons can no longer see them as models and guides for their masculine aspirations. In times of crisis of patriarchy, the unconscious conflict erupts into the religious and political consciousness and a battle ensues between the romantic images of the mother goddess, the symbol of freedom and love, and the harsh disciplines and laws of the male god. It was inevitable that this battle became particularly intense in a culture where the male god had claimed for himself absolute powers to be the sole begetter of life and guide for humanity and appeared to have become helpless in face of his enemies and unable to protect his people. But we must not forget that beside the yearning for a return to the world of childhood, the resurrection of an idealised world where mother's love reigned supreme, there is in every man an equally strong urge to leave her world, to turn to the world of men to develop and fulfil his masculine urges for sexual pleasure, to acquire the skills and knowledge necessary to become a fully approved member of male society, to acquire possessions and power and prove himself as a man.

The followers of Jesus, however, came to consider these drives as sinful, as manifestations of an unrepentant adherence to a world of perdition. The Christian was called upon to deny these urges and guard against them at all times. But while these drives in men can be repressed they do not disappear but constantly strive for expression and demand to be given satisfaction. In order to defend himself from these urges, a Christian has to split himself off from them and project them outwards onto the enemies of the Son of Light and especially onto the Jews—Christ's own people who refused to follow him. And in the same way as in the infantile, unconscious mind a refusal to accept (introject) an important person means not merely to reject him but to kill him, the Jews became the killers of the Saviour of the world. And as Jesus came to be seen not only as the child-hero, the messenger from heaven, as the son of God but as God himself, God's incarnation on earth, the Jews acquired the image of the God-killers. They became the adversaries of the world of light and love which Christ had initiated, perennial representatives of the world of darkness and of everything that is unclean, greedy, lustful and dangerous. Not only were they seen as the eternal enemies of Christ but as a danger within the soul of every Christian, for there is 'a Jew' in every

Christian and he has to be constantly guarded against and vanquished. The soul of man is split once more and the world becomes a battlefield between the forces of good and the forces of evil. The Ego and the whole world is balanced precariously between the kingdom of hell and the kingdom of heaven. Thus monotheism has failed to resolve the Oedipal conflict.

But who were the Jews who initiated the stupendous concept of monotheism, the notion of one law that governs all natural phenomena and one morality that applies to all men? Who were the early Christians and who, in particular, was Jesus? How did a Jewish rabbi, a charismatic teacher in the Pharisaic tradition, come to be transformed into an Orphic deity?

While a psycho-cultural and historical analysis of these questions certainly falls within the scope of this book, I cannot include it here for it would take several hundred pages to do it some justice. I have, therefore, decided to deal with this theme in a separate book entitled 'Judaism and Christianity'. However, I want to consider here one of the most important concepts of Christianity, which had a fateful and profound influence on our civilisation, namely the dogma of original sin.

9 Original Sin and the Battle between Heaven and Hell

The Early Church Fathers universalised the sinfulness of man and traced it to his very nature. Through his bondage to nature, manifest in his body and his desires, man is condemned to be sinful and belongs to an order of existence which is antagonistic to the spirit, unholy and profane. He is born in sin and is subject to the temptations of sex, greed, avarice and cruelty. 'Original sin is the fault and corruption of the nature of every man that is engendered of the offspring of Adam, whereby man is very far gone from original righteousness and is of his own nature inclined to evil, so that the flesh lusteth always contrary to the spirit; and therefore in every person born into this world, it deserveth God's wrath and damnation'.* To be sinful is the consequence of being natural; man's existence represents a battle between the kingdom of sin, i.e. his natural being, and the kingdom of heaven which is supernatural or unnatural existence. The split between the kingdom of sin and the kingdom of heaven, between the call of nature and the call of the spirit obliges men to purify themselves from the demands of nature, to repress their urges and to sacrifice them in the image of Christ's own sacrifice.

The condition of man after the fall of Adam is such that he cannot turn and prepare himself, by his own natural strength and good works, to faith and calling upon God: "Wherefore we have no power to do good works pleasant and acceptable to God, without the grace of God by Christ preventing us, that we may have a good will, and working with us when we have that good will. We are accounted righteous before God, only for the merit of our Lord

---

* The Book of Common Prayer: 'Articles of Religion'.

and Saviour Jesus Christ by faith, and not for our own works or deservings... Christ who truly suffered, was crucified, dead, and buried, to reconcile his father to us, and to be a sacrifice, not only for original guilt, but also for all the actual sins of man".*

When the Jews abolished human sacrifices, they extended the autonomy of the Ego to choose between good and evil, to curb its passions and to sublimate them with the help of the divine Superego. As a moral being man is given the responsibility to choose whether God's expectations are to be fulfilled, whether God's purpose on earth is to find its realisation or whether His purpose is to come to naught. In the very last words of the Hebrew Bible it says:

> Behold, I will send Elijah the prophet... and he will turn the hearts of the fathers to their children and the hearts of the children to their fathers, lest I come and smite the land with a curse.
>
> Malachi, 4.

The punishment threatened is not due to the sin inherent in man but to his incapacity to fulfil his god-given potential, his capability of living a life of love and of understanding. This Jewish concept of human self-perfection is admirably expressed by Blake: 'Men are admitted into heaven not because they have curbed their passions or have no passions, but because they have cultivated their understanding'.

While Christianity inherited the monotheistic concept of the whole man, his mind, his body, his sexuality and his creativity conceived by the mind of God and created in His image, it transformed man into a being that was half beast and half angel, as Feuerbach has remarked. The natural half of man came to be identified with the ancient pagan symbol of sexuality—the goat— and assumed the form of the devil, whereas the divine part became denaturalised spirit, pure and untainted by man's inclinations. This split image of man, driven by two opposing forces which were considered to be in a state of war with each other, pervaded not only the imagination and thinking of the Christian Church but also its laws and its politics. The battle between heaven and hell, between God and the devil, took place not only in the individual but also in the political universe of Christianity.

---

* The Book of Common Prayer: 'Articles of Religion'.

This doctrine of man's fundamental sinfulness and his guilt from which only the Church could release him became a most powerful tool in the propaganda of Christianity and its claim to rule not only over the mind of men but over the world. The promise of salvation became a political weapon which gave total power to kings or bandits who managed to gain the sanction of the Church and could claim to be its representative. Secular rule would claim to be of divine origin, the king the vicar of God, and those who resisted him considered subjects of the devil and enemies of God.

Indeed, it came to pass that all law was held to be eternally valid and in some degree sacred, as the providence of God was conceived to be a universally present force which touched men's lives even in their most trifling details. Whether the king succeeded to office by election or heredity or by usurpation of power, he still ruled by the grace of God. That secular rule was of divine origin and those who resisted it were subjects of the devil was doubted by no one. The obligations of Christians to respect constituted authority came to be deeply embedded in Christianity.

Already Paul in his 'Letter to the Romans' wrote the pronouncement which was to be fundamental to the politics of Christianity:

> Let every person be subject to the governing authorities. For there is no authority except from God, and those that exist have been instituted by God. Therefore he who resists the authorities resists what God has appointed, and those who resist will incur judgment. For rulers are not a terror to good conduct, but to bad. Would you have no fear of him who is in authority? Then do what is good, and you will receive his approval, for he is God's servant for your good. But if you do wrong, be afraid, for he does not bear the sword in vain; he is the servant of God to execute his wrath on the wrongdoer. Therefore one must be subject, not only to avoid God's wrath but also for the sake of conscience. For the same reason you also pay taxes, for the authorities are ministers of God, attending to this very thing. Pay all of them their dues, taxes to whom taxes are due, revenue to whom revenue is due, respect to whom respect is due, honour to whom honour is due.
>
> Romans XIII, 1–7

For Paul, and for all important theologians after him, it was the office rather than its holder to which respect was due; the personal virtues or vices of a ruler had nothing to do with the matter. A bad ruler was a punishment for the sins of the people and must still be obeyed.

Such injunctions were to have a powerful influence on the political developments of Christian Europe. The cosmic conflict which is constantly enacted in the individual and in society is clearly expressed by St. Augustine in his book 'The City of God'. Augustine was the genius of imperial Christianity, the ideologue of the Church-State alliance and fabricator of medieval mentality. Next to Paul, who supplied the basic theology, Augustine did more to shape Christianity than any other human being. 'The history of the Church', he writes, 'is the march of God in the world, and human life is the theatre of a cosmic struggle between the goodness of God and the evil of rebellious spirits. Man's nature is twofold: he is spirit and body and therefore at once a citizen of this world and of the heavenly city. On the one side stands the earthly city, the society that is founded on the earthly appetites and possessive impulses of human nature; on the other stands the city of God. The first is the kingdom of Satan, beginning its history with the fall of Adam and the disobedience of the angels and embodied in the pagan empires of Assyria and Rome. The other is the kingdom of Christ which embodied itself first in the Hebrew nation and later in the Church and the Christianised empire'. Augustine maintained that the powers that be in the Christian empire are ordained by God and that the use of force in government was made necessary by sin and as the divinely appointed remedy for sin. He regarded the appearance of the Christian Church as the turning-point of history; it marked a new era in the struggle between the powers of good and the powers of evil. Henceforth human salvation is bound up with the interests of the Church, represented by the kings appointed by it as the vicars of God, and these interests are in consequence paramount over all other interests whatsoever.

Augustine not only gave theological justification for the establishment of the Church in society as the centre of state authority, but he provided the ideological foundation for the Christianisation of the Roman Empire. He ascribed total power to the Church as the embodiment of Christ on earth and to the rulers of nations who were appointed by the Church, and any opposition was not only futile, it was a betrayal of Christ's mission. Human ideas of equity were, according to him, like 'dew in the desert'. 'Human suffering, deserved or not, occurred because God was angry. This life for mortals is the wrath of God. The world is a small scale hell'. Man must simply learn to accept suffering and injustice. There was nothing he could do about either. Augustine saw the human race as helpless children. He constantly used the image of the suckling baby. Humanity was utterly dependent on God, the race was prostrate, and there was no possibility that it might raise itself by its own merits. That was the sin of pride—Satan's sin.

Mankind's posture must be that of total humility. Its only hope lay in God's grace.

Augustine thus represents the radical transformation from the human optimism of the classical world to the despondent passivity of the Middle Ages. The mentality he expressed was to become the dominant outlook of Christianity and to encompass the whole of European society for many centuries. Christianity gave Europe some essential fragments of Jewish law, a thing which the Jews with their appeal to moral discipline would not have been able to do, but the cost of the success of Christianity was not only a paganisation of Jewish morality, it was the universalisation of a split mind. By introducing the concept of original sin, Christianity intensified men's guilt about his natural self to a degree unknown in any other religion. Nature became evil and had to be conquered both within man and around him. But as the nature which exists in man does not cease to function, indeed, cannot cease to function, it becomes split off from the self, unacceptable to the moral Ego and projected outwards where it operates as a constant threat.

God Himself became an enemy of the natural man, of man's nature, and He became ever more frightening so that man could only relate to Him through the mediation of Jesus. Without His mediation man was doomed, the inevitable victim of God's wrath. Thus, the Church as the representative of Jesus could present itself as the only source of man's salvation and its claims of total power as unquestionable.

An atmosphere of fear and absolute dependency on the Church and its secular representatives dominated the Middle Ages. Never before in history had authority acquired such awe in the eyes of the people, as a constant reminder of man's sin and his innate wretchedness; it became the all-seeing eye of the Superego which constantly watches the individual, sees not only his action but his very thoughts and desires.

The Church survived when Rome had fallen and with it survived Roman organisation. The Church inherited and took over the organisational structures of Rome and acquired a prominence without parallel. The Church alone remained as a cohesive force amid the welter of tribes and kingdoms which followed the break up of the Roman Empire. Its bishops became the most important men in the cities, now bereft of imperial officers, and in the dioceses. Towns, for so long the centre of wealth and power, lost their pre-eminence and declined. Though they continued to exist they were no longer the foci of power which they had been in the Roman Empire. Wealth and authority shifted to the country and was bound up with landholding. The unit of society was the estate, with the lord at the head of a descending hierarchy of tenants. The tenant peasant, or serf, held his land and implements from his lord in return for rents, in labour, kind or money, and was subject to his jurisdiction. While the protection offered by the lord was often the peasant's only chance of survival in a world of famine and war, it was the Church which maintained social cohesion and unity, and it was indispensable for law and order. Moreover, from the fourth century the Church became a landed proprietor. All over the West, bishops ran large estates and provided an element of continuity between the best kind of Roman imperial estate management and the most advanced farming of the Middle Ages. In the eyes of the medieval peasant churchmen were 'modern' farmers who kept accounts, planned ahead, invested. The Church also had a key legal instrument, the Roman-style land deed which embodied the concept of freehold. Land actually farmed by the Church grew enormously in extent; throughout Western and Central Europe the Church established itself as the largest landowner.

This development could not have taken place, or certainly it could not have endured, as Paul Johnson observes, if clerics had not proved themselves to be better than average farmers and land administrators. For this the development of monasticism was largely responsible and monasteries played a key role in the development of modern agricultural estates owned by the Church. Thus the Church created a continuity between estate and state management and it became an indispensable force in the running of the state. It held the monopoly of learning and literacy, and without clerics to help, even the simplest tasks of government—writing commands or making charters—could not be carried out. The monasteries were the only centres of organised education from the sixth century onwards and dominated intellectual life. However, it was in the interest of the Church to have strong kings to govern nations and it gave the status of the king a new dimension of authority.

Kingship came to be regarded as a sacred office with the king more a priest than a tribal ruler. He was God's representative, and his supernatural character was symbolised in the ceremony of anointing, marking him off from other men. This transformation is most clearly epitomised in Charlemagne, an outstanding personality who, in addition to being king of the Franks, became at the hands of the pope the king of the Holy Roman Empire in 800. This revival of the imperial idea shows not only the medieval belief that Christendom was the heir to Rome but the central place that papacy occupied in Western Europe. The creation of an emperor was an attempt to give the pope a protector and partner in directing Christendom; it put imperial power under papal auspices. In government and prestige alike Charlemagne relied upon the Church. It provided the surest means for strengthening and maintaining his empire; its baptism and its bishoprics were the best guarantee of co-ordinating his own tribes into the unit of nationhood and of assimilating his enemies.

It is hardly surprising that education and Christian propaganda occupied a leading place in the Carolingian empire. Only through a literate and trained clergy could the empire endure and its objects succeed. Thus for the first time we see a conscious educational policy designed to stimulate learning. From the first however its end was a Christian one, and it was concerned not with reviving the philosophical speculation of classical times but to train ecclesiastics in knowledge of the Scriptures. Its chief object was an understanding of the established truths found in the Christian Bible and in the writings of the Church Fathers. With the Carolingian empire—the Holy Roman Empire—we have the first great victory and consolidation of the Christian religion in Europe.

*THE MIDDLE AGES: CHRISTUS VINCIT, CHRISTUS REGNAT**

With the crowning of Charlemagne by Pope Leo III on Christmas Day of the year 800, the papacy asserted its right to make and

---

* The last verse of the 'Laudes' or liturgical acclamation with which a new emperor was consecrated.

unmake emperors, and Christendom became the unity behind the separate Christian states. Thus the figure of Christ, the Saviour of the world, majestically enthroned at the centre of the Cross, flanked by the symbols of the evangelists and surrounded by the twelve Apostles, is an image that came to dominate the whole of the Middle Ages, conditioning the world-view of contemporaries as well as their attitude to society and public duty. The search for ultimate truth, like the search for ultimate authority, led back to a single source—the teaching and agony of Christ. It united countless tribes and kingdoms into a community of guilt, with the Church holding the key for redemption. The Cross became a symbol of magic that not only reminded people of their sinful nature but also of their salvation through Christ. It became a shield against innumerable fears and terrors, both psychological as well as concrete, which had beset men since time immemorial. With the political as well as spiritual victory of the Church, the dogma of man's original sin became firmly established in the consciousness of European man.

By declaring men's sexual urges to be evil, the devil's doing which had to be conquered, the Church not only gave sexual repression a new urgency but it also set in motion large-scale regression to pre-genital, infantile primacies. Symbolic representations of archaic fantasies poured into the consciousness of medieval men and populated their universe. Devils, witches, gnomes and monsters, demons of all kinds crowded the imagination of medieval men and found expression in their art and cosmology. A mass of facile beliefs and childish fantasies degraded the ideas of God and reduced even the concept of Christ to primitive magic. According to Gerson, writing in the fourteenth century: 'The world is exposed to all sorts of fancies, dreams and illusions, and mysticism is brought into the streets. Many people take to it without suitable direction, indulging in too rigid feasts, too protracted vigils and too abundant tears, all of which disturbs their brains. There is a disorder of the imagination which in its turn is due to diabolical illusion'.*

Oral-aggressive, sado-masochistic and anal fantasies played a major role in the hysterias of the Middle Ages. 'Thus, many saints were conspicuous for their fanatical reverence for virginity, taking

---

* Gerson: 'Contra vanum curiositatem'.

the form of a horror of all that relates to sex. St. Colette is an instance of this. She is a typical representative of what has been called by William James the theopathic condition. Her super-sensibility is extreme. She can endure neither the light nor the heat of fire, only the light of candles. She has an immoderate horror of flies, ants and slugs, and of all dirt and stenches of all kinds. Her abomination of sexual functions inspires her with repugnance for those saints who have passed through the matrimonial state, and leads her to oppose the admission of non-virginal persons to her congregation. The Church has ever praised such a disposition, judging it to be edifying and meritorious'.*

Oral-aggressive characteristics found expression in the large number of demons and devils who were projected upon God and Christ. The image of the devouring Christ is vividly described by Ruysbroeck in 'The Mirror of Eternal Salvation': 'His hunger is immensely great; he consumes us entirely to the bottom, for he is a greedy glutton with a voracious hunger; he devours even the marrow of our bones... First he prepares his repast and in his love he burns up all our sins and our faults. Next when we are purified and roasted by the fire of love, he opens his mouth like a voracious being who wishes to swallow all'.**

The pious man, in his oral-devouring cannibalistic fantasies, imagined that by eating up the body of Christ he entered into a holy communion with him: 'You will eat Christ, roasted by the fire, well-baked, not at all overdone or burnt. For just as the Easter lamb was properly baked and roasted between two fires of wood or of charcoal, thus was gentle Jesus on Good Friday placed on the spit of the worthy cross and tied between the two fires of his very fearful death and passion and of the very ardent charity and love which he felt for our souls and salvation; he was, as it were, roasted and slowly baked to save us'. On the other hand a nun feels quite deluged in the blood of Christ and faints. All the red and warm blood of the five wounds flowed through the mouth of blessed Henry Suso into his heart. Catherine of Siena drank from the wound in his side. It is no wonder that the medieval religion denigrated man's nature, made man ashamed of it and, at the same time, kept the degrading and painful aspects of it always in view.

---

* J. Huizinga: 'The Waning of the Middle Ages'.
** Ruysbroeck: 'The Mirror of Eternal Salvation'.

At times sado-masochistic fantasies engendered by Christianity acquired the dimension of an epidemic. We hear of flagellation breaking out in eleventh century Italy and then on a huge scale in the thirteenth century, after which it spread all over Europe becoming endemic.

The flagellants marched in procession led by priests with banners and candles and moved from town to town, parading before the parish church and lashing themselves for hours on end. The German flagellants with their rituals, hymns and uniforms were particularly ferocious; they used leather scourges with iron spikes; if a woman or a priest appeared, the ritual was spoiled and had to be started again; it culminated in the reading of a 'heavenly letter', after which spectators dipped pieces of cloth in the blood and treasured them as relics. Pope Clement VI encouraged public flagellation in Avignon. Hundreds of both sexes took part. And the pillar of Spanish orthodoxy, the Dominican anti-Semite and rabble rouser, St. Vincent Ferrier led a party of flagellants through Spain, France and Italy. There was orthodox flagellation, heretical flagellation and apparently secret flagellation too.

During those centuries, the Christian hostility towards the Jews emerged with especial ferocity. Sadistic fantasies of the most primitive kind were projected onto them and repeatedly culminated in violence and large-scale massacres. The ancient fantasies adumbrated by Paul and Augustine of the Jews as the sons of the devil, the Anti-Christ, the children of perdition, etc., were revived and integrated into a whole new demonology.

From the First Crusade onwards, Jews were presented as children of the devil, agents employed by Satan for the express purpose of combating Christianity and harming Christians. It was in the twelfth century that they were first accused of murdering Christian children, of torturing the consecrated wafer and of poisoning the wells. But above all it was said that Jews worshipped the devil who rewarded them collectively by making them masters of black magic, so that however helpless individual Jews might seem, Jewry possessed limitless powers of evil.

The rage against the God for imposing strict taboos on sexual gratification was displaced and projected onto the Jews. They were seen as the representation of all the aggressive-sadistic-destructive urges, of all kinds of perverse and filthy pursuits of which the Christian mind had been purified by the sacrifice of Jesus. It was the Jews who were the God killers, the devils and, at the same time, representatives of the angry God who sought vengeance onto the sons, while the Christians saw themselves as innocent children. While the Christians were beset by fantasies of receiving God's blood as their food of salvation, they accused the Jews of drinking the blood of Jesus and of Christian children, of desecrating the water causing it to bleed. We see here a combination of sadistic fantasies split off from the Christian Ego and projected onto the Jews, with a paranoiac delusion which maintained that there was a world-wide conspiracy by Jews to overthrow Christendom, to murder Christian children, to profane the host and to commit other fantastic acts.

With victory of the Christian Church and its domination over Europe during the eleventh and twelfth centuries, the hostility towards the Jews erupted into organised persecution and mass murder. The Jew, who in the theological delusions of Christianity was seen as the persecutor and murderer of Christ, became the object of the most horrifying vengeance. The Christians discharged the full rage of their libidinous frustrations upon him. Let us look at some examples.

In 1285, one hundred and eighty Jews were burnt to death in Munich for allegedly having bled to death a Christian child in the synagogue. In 1298, a priest was responsible for spreading the rumour that Jews were driving nails through holy wafers, thereby crucifying Christ again. Among those murdered that year, because of the fantasy of a maddened cleric, were six hundred and twenty-eight Jews in Nuremberg. (Mordecai ben Hillel, the famous scholar was one of the victims). In 1370, five hundred Jews were dragged through the streets of Brussels and without distinction of sex or age mutilated until dead. Eighteen tableaux showing Jews driving nails through holy wafers and blood flowing from the host were painted in the cathedral, still to be seen.

On January 9, 1349, all the apprehended Jews of the Swiss city of Basel were burned by a mob, infuriated by church sermons which accused the Jews of deliberately giving the current plague known as 'the Black Death' to Christians. The Jewish cemetery was destroyed and the old tombstones with their Hebrew inscriptions used for building fortifications. In the German town, Erfurt, on June 26, 1221, a band of pilgrims from Friesland bound for the Holy Land stormed the Jewish quarter and killed twenty-six Hebrews. In the same town three thousand Jews were murdered in August 1348, accused of poisoning the wells. The accusation was spread by Dominican monks of that city.

In 1262 in the city of London, fifteen hundred Jews were butchered. In 1279, two hundred and eighty more were executed, and the rest driven from the city. Their possessions fell to the Crown. In 1290, King Edward I, on All Saints Day ordered that all Jews be shipped out of his kingdom on hired boats. Many captains drowned their Jewish passengers for their remaining belongings. The early kings of England played a sinister game of collaboration with the bishops: the bishops got the Jews killed or exiled, the kings got their property.*

These are just a few examples—a minute part—of the massacres of Jews during the Middle Ages, and they continued right through the centuries from generation to generation up to our own times. "They constitute the most abhorrent chapter in the whole bloodstained history of Christianity and are the most discreditable feature in a religion notable for the grotesque and horrifying forms of its pathology".**

Another feature of the feverish imagery of the Middle Ages is worth mentioning, namely the epidemics of witch-hunt. They represent the deep ambiguity towards the women endemic in Christianity. On the one hand the woman is seen as the de-sexualised, pious, God-fearing, Jesus-loving, submissive and virtu-ous lady. She is depicted in thousands of medieval paintings and sculptures as the adoring madonna, worshipping the Jesus child or mourning his death at the foot of the cross, always with an expression of utter innocence, her eyes turned towards heaven in a gesture of faith and submission. On the other hand she is the rampaging, sex-hungry temptress, mistress of the snake and the devil, the witch. The woman is seen in medieval imagination as a profoundly split personality, representing the split personality of Christendom.

She is either the good, sexually repressed, Christian woman or the utterly uninhibited lover of Satan, flaunting all kinds of sexual perversions and, as such, it is interesting that witches began to

---

* Dagobert D. Runes: 'The War against the Jew' (Philosophical Library, N.Y., 1968).
** C. R. Badcock: 'The Psychoanalysis of Culture' (Basil Blackwell, Oxford, 1980).

obsess the popular imagination not long after the appearance of Mariolatry, the worship of Mary, during the thirteenth century. In the fourteenth century epidemics of witch-hunt and large-scale trials and executions of witches took place all over Europe. Every woman became suspect of having links with the forces of darkness and of plotting against the Church. Conversely, every Christian woman was in danger of being seduced by the evil one, or of seeing him appear in her looking-glass. These anxious preoccupations with the possibility of their women being tempted and seduced by the devil are the consequence of the repressed male's fear of sexuality. While the libido is split off from the Ego of the good Christian and projected onto the devil, the woman would be attracted to him (the devil) and he would play a lively and dangerous role in her erotic fantasies; she would rebel against the God who denies her natural instincts and ally herself to His enemy.

The ancient images of the angry goddess who rebels against the male re-emerged in the mind of medieval man. She would be a major threat to the bond between father and son from which she is excluded and she would seek vengeance against them and the civilisation which uphold man's love for his God as the supreme virtue. In her fury she threatens to bring 'a sterile blight upon the earth and pock its surface with infections'.

The medieval vision of the universe represents man's precarious balance between the underworld, which is a morass populated by dragons, snakes, toads, spiders, witches and devils stoking the fires of hell where the souls of men are heard to scream in anguish, and the world above, where everything is bright, calm, peaceful and harmonious, where love reigns and no evil is ever thought. The earth and all human existence is seen to be in a state of suspension between the two eternal realms, and the demons and devils of the underworld constantly clamour to take possession of the minds and bodies of men and can only be warded off by Christ on the cross, the symbol and weapon of the heavenly powers. The images created by theologians, poets and painters represent the cognate universe, they are the cosmology of the time. Art is not experienced as an aesthetic representation of states of mind which have little or nothing to do with the empirical world, but it is the presentation of the world as it is thought to exist in reality. The Holy Trinity of theology has its existential representation in the trinity of heaven, earth and hell, with earth and man in a delicate balance between the two. Earthly existence thus has no autonomous or independent existence but is essentially a temporary battleground of two cosmic powers—heaven and hell—the state of beatitude and the state of sin.

A sombre melancholy weighed upon people's souls: whether we read a chronicle, a poem, a sermon, a legal document even, the same impression of man's sadness is produced by them all. In the literature of the time but above all in the paintings, we see an image of man which we would now describe as strangulated by an overwhelming sense of guilt; this state however also evokes profound yearnings for release from the sin that holds people in bondage, a release into a world of light, of sweet reconciliation and forgiveness. The bitter-sweet melancholia of 'dolce Deo' was considered by Huizinga to have been one of the most active elements of religious life of the Middle Ages. We can surely diagnose this melancholy as a mourning for a state of perfection which a loving God had intended for man but which men were unable to achieve. Prayers for forgiveness and for divine compassion with human frailty outweighed by far the determination to study God's laws and uphold man's responsibility for living in accordance with them. A deep sense of having failed God, of having disappointed Him pervaded the consciousness of the time and aroused a feeling of God's anguish for the incapability of His children to fulfil the tasks He had given them. Having lost contact with the purpose which God had in mind for them men became helpless playthings of evil forces utterly dependent upon divine intervention and grace. Man had lost the image of the human being that unites in himself both the divine spirit as well as the forces of nature and encompasses the manifold of desires and aspirations into an overriding purpose of life.

The fourteenth century was ruled by a preoccupation with death. Villon and his contemporaries were obsessed with it. Because so many men's thoughts were set on death, the doctrine of purgatory and the possibility of buying indulgences to shorten its duration gained a new importance at a time when wars made the old way of saving one's soul by repentance and pilgrimage impossible; and such abuses profoundly undermined the faith. England and France wore themselves out in the Hundred Years War and the Wars of the Roses; the employment of mercenaries changed the basis of feudalism. Everywhere, but especially in France and England, plague, pestilence and famine followed and accompanied war. There was a decadence, and that decadence made it possible for a new civilisation that was essentially Italian to spread over the rest of Europe.

Part 3

10   The Renaissance: The Ego Rebels against the Oppressive Superego

THE REDISCOVERY OF NATURE AND HUMANITY

The drive towards maturity, for freedom and self-respect could not be denied forever. The forgotten doctrine of man's holiness as a creation of God, as propounded by Jewish monotheism, and the Platonic theory of man's innate capability to comprehend the truth were brought back to Southern Europe by Jewish and Arab scholars, and they contributed greatly towards the reawakening of the concept of humanity and of the universal man. Men strove to rehabilitate the body, the senses, the heart and the intelligence, and they rekindled the fascination for nature. The Renaissance rediscovered the unity of man and nature and man's nature as the being chosen by God to fulfil His purpose. In these aspirations we can recognise the powerful drives of the human Ego for self-expression after a 'latency period' of over a thousand years.

The conception of man's humanity was proclaimed by Pico della Mirandola in his essay 'On the Dignity of Man', which Burckhardt declared to be one of the loftiest of that great age. God, he tells us, made man at the close of the creation to know the laws of the universe, to love its beauty, to admire its greatness. He bound him to no fixed place, to no prescribed form of work, and by no iron necessity, but gave him freedom to will and to love. 'I have set thee', says the Creator to Adam, 'in the midst of the world, that thou mayest the more easily behold and see all that is therein. I created thee a being neither heavenly nor earthly, neither mortal nor immortal only, that thou mightest be free to shape and to overcome thyself. Thou mayest sink into a beast, and be born anew to the divine likeness. The brutes bring from their mother's body what they will carry with them as long as they live; the higher spirits are from the beginning, or soon after, what they will be forever. To thee alone is given a growth and a development depending on thine own free will. Thou bearest in thee the germs of a universal life'.

Pico della Mirandola (1463–1494) read Plato in Greek and Moses in Hebrew. When the sacred writings from Jerusalem mingled with the philosophy of the Greeks and were transplanted together upon the soil of fifteenth century Italy, a new flower grew from it unlike any flower man had seen before.

The rediscovery of Greek philosophy and art is generally known to be the basis upon which the Renaissance of Italy developed. The fallow soil of Christian Europe readily and enthusiastically responded to the seeds of Greek aesthetics and its passionate admiration for the intellect. Starved of the love for the human body and the free exercise of the mind by centuries of Christian denial, fifteenth century Italy absorbed the culture of antiquity and brought forth not only a few very exceptional individuals but in its popular culture a new blossoming of human creativity which was to become the example for the liberal civilisation of Europe. It is, however, not sufficiently realised that the rediscovery of Greek philosophy, literature, drama and art was accompanied by a rediscovery of the Old Testament and the philosophy of monotheism.

In his book, 'Heptaplus' or 'Discourse on the Sevenfold Narration of the Six Days of Genesis', Pico della Mirandola endeavours to reconcile the 'Timaeus' of Plato with the Book of Genesis. He dedicated his book to Lorenzo the Magnificent, whose interest in the wisdom of Moses was well known.* In proclaiming the harmony between Plato and Moses, Pico imbues every natural object with a higher meaning as an analogue to a divine purpose. The Jewish cosmology, governed by a moral purpose, and the Platonic concept of human reason combined to produce an image of humanity which is not a helpless victim of the cosmic conflict between good and evil but a being who, in his freedom to exercise his innate potentialities, is capable of fulfilling God's aim in the world.

In the full exercise of his reason and his will-power the man of the Renaissance not merely attains a sense of his own achievement but through his achievement he also fulfils the design of God. The

---

* Walter Pater: 'The Renaissance'.

idea that the full exercise of men's abilities pleases God was perhaps the most significant factor in the maturation of European man. Men ceased to be afraid of their own individuality, of being and seeming unlike their neighbours. The poet of the Renaissance, in setting forth and relating the depth, wealth and variety of individuality, became the most celebrated herald of his time.

The quest for an ideal human image also found expression in the art of biography which began to flourish in the fifteenth century. Whereas in the Middle Ages biographies were meant to serve for pious contemplation or as narratives without any sense of what was individual or unique in them, among the Italians of the Renaissance on the contrary the search for the characteristic features of highly accomplished individuals predominated.

Autobiographies also began to appear which no longer emphasised the renunciation of worldly pursuits and the salvation of the soul through the Church but a man's unremitting fight for the affirmation of his talent and ability. The autobiography of Benvenuto Cellini describes the whole man with marvellous truth and completeness. While most of his other works remain uncompleted and many have been surpassed by his famous contemporaries, Benvenuto Cellini, as a man, will interest mankind till the end of time. He was one who dared to do all; he could do many things to a high degree of excellence and he considered himself the sole judge of his activities.

The liberation from the dogma of human guilt opened many eyes to the enjoyment of nature and the cultivation of the environment for the pleasure it afforded. The comical and satirical literature of the Middle Ages could not dispense with pictures of everyday events. But it is another thing when the Italians of the Renaissance dwelt on this picture for its own sake, for its inherent interest, and because it forms part of the great universal life of the world. In his treatise, 'On the Sober Life', Luigi Cornaro describes the way of life which he leads at his advanced age of 83: "My friends are wise and learned people of good position, and when they are not with me I read and write, and try thereby, as by all other means, to be useful to others. Each of these things I do at the proper time and at my ease in my dwelling, which is beautiful and lies in the best part of Padua and is arranged both for summer and winter with all the resources of architecture and provided with a garden by the running water. In the spring and autumn I go for a while to my hill in the most beautiful part of the Euganean mountains, where I have fountains and gardens and a comfortable dwelling; and there I amuse myself with some easy and pleasant chase which is suitable to my years. At other times I go to my villa on the plain; there all the paths lead to an open space in the middle of which stands a pretty church; an arm of the Brenta flows through the plantations, fruitful, well cultivated fields, now fully peopled, which the marshes and foul air once made fitter for snakes than for man. It was I who drained the country; then the air became good and people settled there and multiplied, and the land became cultivated as it now is, so that I can truly say: 'On this spot I gave to God an altar and a temple and souls to worship Him'. This is my happiness whenever I come here. In the spring and autumn I also visit the neighbouring towns to see and converse with my friends, through whom I make the acquaintance of other distinguished men, architects, painters, sculptors, musicians and cultivators of the soil... but what most of all delights me when I travel is the beauty of the country and the places, lying now on the plain, now on the slopes of the hills, or on the banks or rivers and streams, surrounded by gardens and villas".

The fifteenth century is, above all, writes Burckhardt*, that of the many-sided man. There is no biography which does not, besides the chief work of its hero, speak of other pursuits all passing beyond the limits of dilettantism. The Florentine merchants and statesmen were often learned in both the classical languages; humanists read the 'Ethics' and 'Politics' of Aristotle to themselves and their sons; the daughters of the house were highly educated. It is in these circles that private education was first treated seriously. Leon Battiste Alberti declared that men can do all things if they will, and Ghiberti writes in his autobiography: 'He who learned everything is nowhere a stranger; even if he be robbed of his fortune and without friends he is yet the citizen of every country and can fearlessly despise the changes of fortune. Wherever a learned man fixes his seat, there is home'.

Emancipation from the authority of the Church and liberation from its mental shackles led to an astonishing display of genius in the arts and in literature and in the unfolding of the multiplicity of human sensibilities. There is no need here to write the names of the

---

* Jacob Burckhardt: 'The Civilisation of the Renaissance in Italy' (Phaidon Press).

men of genius and wonderful talent who arose in Italy and made its towns fountainheads of high civilisation, the like of which had not been seen since the flourishing of Athens—from Petrarch and Dante, Leonardo da Vinci, Michelangelo and Raphael, to Botticelli and many, many others—unforgettable wherever civilisation reigns. But it also led to determined individualism and the cult of personality. While the individual was free to explore nature and the human being, both in its intellectual as well as aesthetic aspects, while the universe became the roving ground of the mind, this did not lead to the establishment of universalistic doctrines or dogmas. While this can be taken both as a result of the political and economic circumstances in Italy as well as a deliberate rejection of doctrine and dogma of which there had been a surfeit during the Middle Ages, it produced in Italy an individualism that degenerated into the rule of condottiere, petty rulers and princes.

The concentrations of power in the Italian Renaissance were the city-states. The most important of these were Milan and Venice in the north, Florence, Rome and Naples towards the south. As Burckhardt put it, in these cities the state became a work of art. It ceased to be dominated by the authority of the Church. Indeed, in the struggle between the city-states, the papacy itself became transformed into a secular power.

The new state was no longer guided and moulded by custom and dogma but by men. Therefore, the state as a work of art created a new art—the art of statesmanship.* The dealings of states with one another were no longer regulated by Church and feudal authority. From the intrigues and alliances by which the city-states tried to outwit one another grew a second art—the art of diplomacy. In these struggles for power, the concept of the balance of power was evolved, and with it the modern notion of a community of states.

Of the population of one of the city-states, perhaps one to two thousand called themselves noble. Leonardo and other artists may have been leaders of the Renaissance, but it was the small aristocracy for whom they worked. It was not, however, a permanent aristocracy of birth, for it was constantly entered by the more successful merchants and bankers. This rising class of traders lay just below the aristocracy and formed the reservoir for it and for

---

* J. Bronowski & Bruce Mazlish: 'The Western Intellectual Tradition'. (Hutchinson, 1960).

the councils of government. Below this lay the larger classes of artisans and then of labourers.

The city-states had prospered from a combination of causes. But one cause was central to the rest: they traded. Italy lay at the hub of trade; one could travel east to Asia Minor and the Far East, and west to Spain, south to Africa and north to Europe. Above all, the rising trade between the East and Europe made her rich. Money made in trade became the new backbone of power in Italy. It provided the material conditions for the Renaissance and the psychological climate as well. Making money was no longer regarded as somewhat disgraceful. The Medici in Florence carried proudly in their crest the golden balls which now hang on pawn-brokers' shops.

The Renaissance was also the beginning of modern capitalism. Capitalism can be defined as a system in which the individual seeks, consciously and rationally, by economic means to attain financial profit as its end. Thus on the scale of individual business activity, rational methods of bookkeeping were introduced and involved banking operations were carried out. On the scale of the city-state, calculated economic imperialism marked the new age.*

When the Renaissance movement spread north across the Alps, it encountered different social-economic conditions and acquired a different character. The Church there still held sway and feudalism was still the dominant order of society. A late medieval annalist wrote that in the Church of Germany a man like Cesare Borgia would not be permitted to rise above the lowest ranks of the clergy.

The Renaissance and the Reformation are usually considered to be only vaguely connected and distinct in character. However, there is a most significant link between them to which I would like to draw attention. It is the friendship between Pico della Mirandola and Johannes Reuchlin. The young Italian philosopher became the teacher of the German scholar, his inspiration and model, and it was largely through Reuchlin that the great ideas of the Renaiss-ance spread into Germany and eventually developed into the ideas of the Enlightenment.

Encouraged by Pico della Mirandola, Reuchlin entered into a systematic study of Hebrew and the original texts; in particular, it was the Kabbala that aroused his interest. On his return to

---

* Ibid.

Germany he began to advocate the introduction of Hebraic studies in German universities as well as the study of the Greek language and Greek literature. While he managed to establish courses in Hellenistic studies in the universities of Stuttgart and Heidelberg, his efforts on behalf of Hebrew aroused furious opposition from the Church. However, his 'Rudimenta Linguae Hebraicae', which was published in 1506, was used by all who sought to add to their knowledge of Greek and Latin a knowledge of the sacred language. His 'De verbo mirifico' (1496), an introduction to the Kabbala, also excited wide interest. It was, however, not merely the new ideas which he had propagated but the fanatical opposition of the Church and his persecution by the Inquisition which created a stir among German scholars and for a time made him the rallying point of the new movement.

The attacks on Reuchlin were stirred up by a theologian called Pfefferkorn and backed by the Dominicans of Cologne, who obtained from the Emperor Maximilian an edict for the surrender of all Jewish books suspected of containing anti-Christian interpretations of the Bible. The polemic between Pfefferkorn, who aimed at getting all Jewish books burnt, and Reuchlin, who declared Jewish exegesis to be indispensable for the understanding of the Bible and called for the introduction of Hebrew teaching in all the universities, became very acute. Reuchlin, having been accused of plagiarism and condemned by the Dominican theologians of Cologne, appealed against this treatment to all his learned friends, denounced the low tricks of his opponents and the ignorance of the university teachers and, when eventually summoned to appear before the inquisitor in Mainz in 1513, appealed to Rome. Reuchlin's condemnation by the Mainz tribunal, though suspended by the Curia on Leo X's order, shook all Europe, dividing opinion in the universities; this happened all the sooner because the Cologne Dominicans decided to submit the case to the faculties of Erfurt, Louvain and Paris. This was a fine opportunity for the traditionalists to attack the 'friend of the Jews', and with him the modernists in general.

Scholars at Erfurt and Paris pleaded Reuchlin's cause in vain. All the same, he went on with his teaching and his work of publishing. The Reuchlin affair forced out into the open the resentment felt by the established theologians against the innovators, providing the occasion for a clash which rallied many scholars to his side.

In 1511 he wrote a book entitled 'Augenspiegel' to defend the Talmud which the Dominicans of Cologne were proposing to burn. His book was condemned by the inquisitors at Mainz and solemnly burnt at Cologne. Both sides appealed to the pope who finally upheld the condemnation in 1520. The efforts of the inquisitors to secure Reuchlin's fall appeared to be so fanatical and ignorant as to drive most of the German humanists into sympathy with Reuchlin and contempt for his opponents. Not only the reactionary theologians of Cologne but traditional theology in general was now violently attacked by the supporters of Reuchlin. They considered the ban on Hebrew books a threat against the basic values of humanism. By the second decade of the sixteenth century German secular culture had reached such a stage in its development that no compromise with the traditional learning of the scholastic school-men was any longer possible.[*]

Reuchlin was not the first of the scholars of northern Europe to arouse a permanent interest in the Italian Renaissance, but his fight against the Church dogmatists united the humanistic scholars in their support at a crucial moment of European history.[**] From 1500 onwards Italy had become an object of incessant attention, not only from travelling clerics and scholars but also from diplomats and courtiers of all European countries. The meeting of northern scholarship with the Italian humanistic Renaissance was bound to have a powerful impact upon a development of European culture. Although the new learning which arose in many parts of Europe was at first meant to give new direction to religious studies, its actual effect was like opening a window and looking out onto the wider, new world that had emerged in Italy in the previous two centuries. "Thenceforth, the assimilation and adaptation of the Italian achievements in education and politico-historical thought, in literature and art, in social intercourse and the philosophy of man became a basic task of all cultural life".[***]

Everywhere minds turned towards Italy. Citizens and scholars in the northern countries began to free themselves from the tradition of scholastic culture and searched for a new type of education that

---

[*] Robert Mandrou: 'From Humanism to Science 1480–1700' (Pelican, 1978).
[**] Owen Chadwick: 'The Reformation' (Pelican History of the Church, 1968).
[***] The New Cambridge Modern History, Vol. 1: 'The Renaissance' (C.U.P., 1971).

was at once humanistic and religious; they wanted to replace the guilt-laden dogmas which the Church had imposed on the European mind for centuries past by a devotion which gave much wider recognition to the freedom of the intellect and a greater degree of respect to the humanity of man. They searched for a Superego that accepted and loved the Ego and allowed it a much greater degree of freedom to exercise its intellectual and emotional faculties. Florentine neo-Platonism as developed by Ficino and Pico della Mirandola became the source and inspiration of the humanistic culture that spread across Europe. The Hebrew doctrine of the holiness of man both as an individual as well as a species, his spirit as well as his body being the creation of God and therefore sanctified, lent powerful support to the humanists. By condemning Hebrew books the Church sparked off a crisis that created an unbridgeable division between the old theology and the new humanism and made compromise impossible.

If there was one person who may be said to have personified the various trends and ideals of north European humanism it was Erasmus of Rotterdam. He voiced the discontent of the powerful minds of the age; princes and even popes heard him with pleasure and were his friends. The popular masses of that age felt the same discontent but for them it was voiced more dramatically by Martin Luther.

THE REFORMATION: WORLDLINESS BECOMES GODLINESS

Martin Luther nailed his 95 theses on indulgences to the door of the Church at Wittenberg on 31st October 1517—the eve of All Saints' Day. With that gesture he turned discontent into action. The Church could no longer smile at its own weaknesses, as the popes who befriended Erasmus had done. Luther had studied the works of Erasmus and had been guided by them but he sensed that Erasmus was not either in temperament or by opinion prepared to go far enough. Luther wanted to bring about a final break with Rome and provide an alternative Church of Christ, a step which Erasmus would not have countenanced, as he was unwilling to push the criticism of the established Church to a point where those who were committed to it would be forced to take up an inflexible position against the reformers. Erasmus wrote: "I see that the monarchy of the pope at Rome, as it is now, is a pestilence to Christendom, but I do not know if it is expedient to touch that sore openly. That would be a matter for princes, but I fear that these will act in concert with the pope to secure part of the spoils". In short, he was afraid that the Church Establishment, together with the secular princes, would counter-attack and destroy the humanist movement if it were imprudent enough openly to challenge Rome and declare war on it.

Luther was not prepared to submit to the restraints of sophisticated expediency. He was a revolutionary, a zealot determined to carry the widespread antagonism towards the Roman dictatorship to its logical and practical conclusion. He wanted to give concrete expression to the spiritual discontent which he knew to be a new force in Europe, and he felt that the secular rulers would eventually support him. His instinct turned out to be correct. The time was ripe for radical change on the theological as well as political front. The princes welcomed his boldness and used it to throw off their dependence on Roman authority. But Erasmus was right when he foresaw that in this battle for power the spirit of the humanist reform movement would be severely damaged. He was convinced that while Luther's criticism of the Church was just, it would entrench in the Church the uncompromising men, the bigots whom the humanists had worked so hard to replace. He was afraid that if Luther was defeated then the reactionaries would sweep away all that the humanists had gained. As it turned out however Luther was not defeated by Rome but in his victory he betrayed the humanists.

It was not only Luther's unbridled temperament which made Erasmus retreat from his side. He found Luther's opinions more and more distasteful. He did not care for his German nationalism, for his fanaticism, his intolerance and, above all, for his belief in the essential hopelessness of man under the divine will, which left no room for the humanist belief in the essential goodness of man.

When Catholic hotheads insisted that he was the man who laid the eggs which Luther had hatched, Erasmus protested: "I laid a hen's egg, Luther hatched an egg of a different kind". But the eggs were all broken together. His books were put on the Index or expurgated and Erasmus himself was condemned by the Council of Trent as an impious heretic. He had given his life to the belief that virtue can be based on humanity and that tolerance would replace fanaticism in the new image of man which he hoped to establish. In his good years he had travelled Europe as if this empire of the mind, this 'free Christian community' had already been created. For a time the courts of Italy and England, the universities of France and Spain, the houses of cardinals and reformers were open to him. But his longing for universal good could not survive the violence on both sides of the coming struggle.

What was Luther actually attacking, and who supported him? Martin Luther had started out just like the rest of the clerics who were inspired by the humanists to bring about a reform within the Church. The Augustinian monk who went to Rome at the beginning of the century and who gave most of his time to reading the Scriptures was not—before 1517—a man whose career was out of the ordinary. He was deeply shocked by the trivialities of the Roman Curia and by the irreverent atmosphere of the city, as were many other visitors taken aback by this capital of the western Christian world. But when he returned to Germany he did not at once give outward expression to the exceptional indignation he felt. As a great reader of the sacred texts, which he annotated line by line, and anxious to find through his readings the answer to his misgivings about salvation—one of the principal features of religious sensibility both in Germany and elsewhere—the young monk was in no way unusual, but shared with many clerics throughout the empire that disquiet which moved the world of scholars at the opening of the century. A hard worker, he applied himself to the most difficult passages, striving to interpret them. At Wittenberg in 1515 and 1516, he gave a noted series of lectures on 'The Epistle to the Romans'. Though a scholar of high quality, as he proved while a member of the Augustinian community and still more impressively later on when he translated the entire Bible into German, Luther was hardly exceptional in a country where biblical researchers and studies were further developed than anywhere else in the West.

On the very eve of his public outburst in October 1517, he was stirred and scandalised by the campaign for the sale of indulgences organised by the pope's commissioner in Germany, the Dominican Johann Tetzel, in order to provide Rome with the funds needed for the construction of the basilica of St. Peter, and for the new archbishop of Mainz, who had borrowed money from the Fugger bankers in order to pay the papacy for his confirmation and was now being pressed by the Fuggers to pay back the loan. A visionary endowed with a powerful imagination like so many men of his time, there emerged from the depths of his personality that bold reaction of revolt which decided him to draw up at the end of October 1517 the 95 Theses in which he attacked the practices of the Roman Church. According to the Church, indulgences, which had behind them a long tradition, took their efficacy from the surplus grace that had accumulated through the lives of Christ and the saints. The purchase of an indulgence put the purchaser in touch with this surplus grace and freed him from the earthly penance attached to a particular sin, but not from the sin itself.

Tetzel, however, led his listeners to believe that an indulgence purchased for a relative in purgatory released that relative's soul so that it might forthwith fly to heaven. Tetzel's little ditty was as follows:

> As soon as pennies in the money-chest ring,
> the souls out of their purgatory spring.

Luther's comment on this was short and to the point: "It is certain that when the money rattles in the chest avarice and gain may be increased, but the suffrage of the Church depends on the will of God alone". (Thesis 28). Luther claimed that it was not only Tetzel but the papacy itself which had spread the false doctrine of the indulgence.

The protest represented by the 95 Theses—a public appeal for a thoroughgoing reform of the Church—was heard more widely than all the learned works that were being published at the same time ornamented with cordial dedications and aimed at the restricted public of readers familiar with 'good letters' and the subtleties of translations full of cross-references and notes giving all known versions of the correct text. Within a few months the 95 Theses—first transcribed, then printed—had spread all over Germany, becoming a matter for discussion among advocates of reform and even for comment by the common folk, the craftsmen, printers and others in the great cities of that country.

All through 1518, the monk of Wittenberg received proofs of the interest aroused by his initiative. From the summer of 1518 onward preachers who had hitherto lacked a guide set out to meet Luther in his Saxon monastery, while others sent him their approval and encouragement in writing or asked for his advice. By the autumn of 1518, Luther himself was able to measure the actual consequences of his deed. His appeal to the ecclesiastical authorities had become a political act no less than a religious one for he had stirred the consciences of the German princes, and not only the pope but the emperor too were paying attention to him. Throughout the empire an extensive public made up of humanists, students and burghers had long been made aware of this problem of Church reform, of clerical life and of the role to be played by the laity in Church affairs, problems on which so many writings had already long since been put into circulation. Luther brought an answer to a widespread uneasiness which had never before been expressed with such clarity and vehemence. With the support of such scholars as Karlstadt, Thomas Münzer and Melanchthon (Reuchlin's great-nephew), Luther had within a few months become the leader of the reform movement among the Germans.

By attacking indulgences, Luther moreover attacked the entire theology and Church structure. It was a short step from saying that without contrition the indulgence was invalid to saying that contrition alone, without any papal paraphernalia, was sufficient. Thus, by making salvation dependent on the individual's own faith and contrition, Luther abolished the need for sacraments and a hierarchy to administer them. At first Luther thought he might reform the Church from within, but by around 1520, three years after the posting of the 95 Theses, his break with the Church became evident and acknowledged. After that date reconciliation was no longer possible. Luther became the founder of a new Church and created a new set of institutions with all the consequences that the establishment of a Church entailed by way of definitions of discipline and orthodoxy, not to speak of the inescapable struggles that had to be waged on the borders, geographical and spiritual, of adherence to this Church.

The new faith and worship were defined explicitly: simplification of ritual; participation of the laity in services; reduction of the number of sacraments; proclamation of justification by faith (the famous 'Crede fortius'); suppression of the cult of saints and restriction of the cult of the Virgin Mary. Luther's associate, Karlstadt, introduced many liturgical innovations after 1520, such as reading and singing in German, abolition of images among others, which quickly formed into a coherent doctrine.

We have seen that originally Luther relied on the support of the humanists in his attempt to reform the existing Church. They agreed with his denunciation of the abuses of the Church and like him wished to put the emphasis on piety and Christian virtue rather than on dogma underpinned by scholastic authority. But when it became clear that Luther was attacking not only the abuses of the Church but the Church itself, most of the humanists turned their backs on him. However, the princes, knights, merchants and peasants of Germany increasingly gave him their support. Their grievances against Rome were as much political and economic as religious. Already in 1508, the German Diet resolved not to let money raised by indulgences leave Germany. And in 1518, the Diet of Augsburg stated that the real enemy of Christendom was not the Turk but the 'Hound of Hell' in Rome.

Luther, who had begun with a universal Christian idea, ended as a German nationalist; he turned from reforming a world Church to erecting a German Church. Born by the wave of national sentiment he carried the fight against Rome. He exhorted Germany to seize the lands of churchmen, and his message fell on ready ears; knights and princes joined in grasping at the lands of the Church. Luther would never have succeeded as a religious reformer without political support, and this he often purchased at the price of his original beliefs. While he originally believed in the efficacy of the word alone and maintained that what did not come from a man's conscience ought not to be forced by coercion, he soon justified the use of the sword in support of the word. Moreover, he reconciled himself to the fact that the princes who had rallied to his cause were secularising for their own benefit the property of the Catholic clergy which they had seized. Indeed, he became largely dependent on the support of the princes and was perfectly conscious that his church could only succeed as a major force in Germany by aligning itself with the political interests of the ruling strata. In its final form, Luther's doctrine was well calculated to appeal to the existing political authorities: he advocated the doctrine of passive obedience; thus, he did not approve of a social revolution which would correspond to the revolution in religious life he had initiated and would provide the latter with different social foundations.

In the midst of the peasant revolution in Germany, in a frenzied pamphlet which he called 'Wider die räuberischen und mörderischen Bauern' ('Against the thievish, murderous peasants'), he allowed full authority to the princes to crush these revolts in blood so as to restore the "order established by God". He advised the princes to "ruthlessly exterminate" the peasants. The princes hardly needed this injunction; by 1526 the revolt was crushed with over 100,000 peasants dead.

While a young man Luther struck a truly liberal note in his revolt against Rome when he declared: "I wish to be free. I do not wish to become the slave of any authority, whether that of a council or any other power, or of the university or the pope. For I shall proclaim with confidence what I believe to be true, whether it is advanced by a Catholic or an heretic, whether it is authorised or not by I care not what authority". In this declaration that it was neither safe nor honest to act against one's conscience, Luther sounded the really important note of protestantism, one in accord with much of the intellectual movement of the sixteenth century, whether in the field of the humanities or of science. However, by 1530, when he had secured the support of the princes, Luther declared that: "Therefore stern, hard civil rule is necessary in the world, lest the world become wild, peace vanish, and commerce and common interests be destroyed... No one need think that the world can be ruled without blood. The civil world shall and must be red and bloody".

Turning completely to the princes, Luther confirmed them in the righteousness of their power. The result was an alliance of Church and State, in which the former was subservient to the latter. In effect, therefore, Lutheranism made a total surrender of the individual to state control.

The transformation of doctrine finds its corollary in the transformation of Luther as a person. The young Luther who boldly called upon men to allow only their conscience to guide belief and actions soon became a rabid opponent of personal freedom, preaching men's duty to submit to authority. It was not merely a question of political expediency: we notice a profound change in his personality. Max Brod, the friend of Franz Kafka and biographer of Reuchlin, maintained that this change (which had important consequences for the development of Protestantism) calls for an investigation by psychologists or even psychiatrists. Luther's transformation of character was particularly evident in his attitude to the Jews.

As a young man Luther wrote (and I am translating from the Old

German vernacular which Luther used): "Our fools, the popes, bishops, sophists and monks, have up till now treated the Jews in a manner which would make anyone who considered himself a good Christian wish to become a Jew. And if I had been a Jew and saw how such fools and knaves govern Christendom and are acclaimed as its teachers, I would prefer to be a pig rather than a Christian; for they treated the Jews as if they were dogs instead of human beings".

It appears incomprehensible how a man who in his early writings repeatedly declared his friendship for the Jews as the people of Christ, and pronounced his indebtedness to them, became their violent antagonist and expressed his hatred in most brutal and virulent attacks on them, both in speech and in writing. Max Brod, like many other modern students of Luther, was appalled by the brutality of his late writings, especially by his book 'Wider die Juden und ihre Lügen' ('Against the Jews and their Lies'), and considered them to be amongst the most disgusting expressions of anti-Semitism in the history of mankind.

We get a glimpse of the psychological roots of this transformation in Luther if we take account of the paranoid fantasies which he came to entertain about the magic powers of the Jews. In a letter to his wife, he wrote: "I felt a great dizziness and weakness come over me on my journey as I came near to the town of Eisleben. If you had been with me you would have declared it to be the fault of the Jews or their God. For there are many Jews in Eisleben, and it is quite possible that they blew upon me. There are at present about fifty Jews in this town. And the truth is that when I came close to the town I distinctly felt a cold wind coming upon me from the back of my carriage going through my hat into my head as if it was trying to turn my brain into ice... Once I finish my business at hand I must make every effort to get rid of the Jews".

In his book, "Against the Jews and their Lies", Luther declares that apart from the devil there is no more embittered poisonous, violent enemy than the Jews, 'those bloodthirsty dogs and murderers of Christendom'.

I shall quote some points from the instructions Luther gave to the German people 'in order to atone for their guilt of not having properly avenged the blood and agony of Christ':

1 Burn down synagogues; throw sulphur and tar upon them as

they burn, and what is not consumed by fire should be covered by earth so that no stone should remain visible for all times.

2   Destroy their homes, herd them together in stables to make the Jews realise that they are not the lords of the land but prisoners in exile.

3   Take away from the Jews their prayer books, the Talmud and the Bible, so that they no longer have the power to curse God and Christ.

4   Forbid their rabbis under sentence of death to teach, to praise their God in public and to pray to him, so that they can no longer carry out their divine service.

5   Deny them the right to travel upon the highways of the German empire.

6   Prohibit them from pursuing usury; take from them their money and their gold and silver and other property, because everything they possess they acquired and stole through usury.

7   The young and healthy amongst the Jews should be given spades, axes, shovels and other tools of labour, so that in the sweat of their brows they earn their daily bread, although it would be best if they would be expelled from Germany as well as from Spain, France, Bohemia and other countries.

Max Brod points out that this previously almost unknown book was published by the Nazis in popular mass editions complete with 'expert professorial commentaries'. The Nazis used it as a ready-made programme for their persecution of the Jews. So the man who was determined to arouse the conscience of the German people to protest against the hypocrisy and superstition of the Church of Rome fell himself victim to pernicious superstitions which clouded his judgment and made him forget the most fundamental tenets of the humanists. It was Luther's reliance on conscience alone as the supreme judge of man's beliefs and actions that in the end defeated his humanistic morality and perhaps sheds a light on the problems of humanism in general.

While in the traditional Christian cosmology it is accepted that man is a congenital sinner by his very nature and could rely on Christ and the redemptive paraphernalia of the Church to mediate for him—he could go on pilgrimages, flagellate himself or persecute Jews, he could buy indulgences to pay off his sins—the conscience is a much more relentless and uncompromising judge, whose condemnation it is far more difficult to escape. The humanists aspired towards a harmonious collaboration between Ego and Superego in a new morality that would not depend on external coercion or dogma. The conscience as the internalised father would respect the Ego, his son, and encourage him to cultivate and trust his rational and moral faculties and take full responsibility for his judgments. But the patriarchal individual who takes upon himself the responsibility to control his instinctual drives—the urges of the Id—still needs to split them off from his Ego and project them outwards. Thus, even the humanist needs an enemy to allay his conscience. In particular, aggressive urges which continue to linger in the unconscious need an external enemy upon whom they can be discharged. People like Erasmus sublimated their aggression by rational attacks against the authoritarian dogmas of the Church and its oppressive authority. They expressed contempt, impatience and anger with prevailing superstitions—the magic of graven images, the worship of the bleeding host and other symbols of salvation, and the whole gamut of superstitions exploited in the paraphernalia of Church worship. They wanted to free people from their puerile credulities, their mindless adoration, from superstitious fears and show them the potentialities of reason and rational morality towards a genuine change of heart and life. It was Erasmus' concern for true religion which turned his satire into the severest form of condemnation: 'Perhaps thou believest that all thy sins are washed away with a little paper, with a gift of a little money or some waxen images or with a little pilgrimage. Thou art utterly deceived'. He directed his shafts of anger and ridicule against the Church which had usurped Christianity and made it into a ritual of superstitions.

For Luther such declarations were not enough. He had to fight the authority of the Church on all fronts—spiritual as well as political—to break its established powers. In order to succeed he appealed to the ordinary people in language they could understand, and he appealed to the princes in a manner that responded to their political interests. Soon secular authority and many representatives of the Church Establishment rallied to his side. They befriended him and he had to befriend them, they became his necessary allies. He had to make compromises, the clear-cut convictions became confused and he became corrupted. He entered into allegiance with evil and betrayed his God. He swallowed—internalised—his erstwhile enemies and their dirt was inside him, and he deserved to be punished.

Masochism, of course, has played a prominent part in the preaching of Jesus and, in particular, of Paul, and it remained a fundamental aspect of Christianity. It became a moral injunction to suffer punishment or to exalt one's own worthlessness as a miserable sinner, to attain a measure of release by penance and by submission to divine punishment. However, Luther's intensification of guilt and need for self-punishment recreated the deep sense of his worthlessness from which he had suffered as a youth, producing constipation, painful spasms of bowel and stomach, and paranoid fantasies. He felt that the devil was inside him, the dirty, smelly, obscene being that dwells in the stomach and threatens to take possession of brain and soul.

'The painters paint the devil black and filthy', said Luther, and indeed his colour has always been black because of the association between black and filth and also with the bad conscience. Hieronymus Bosch painted the devil on the latrine where damned souls fall out of his anus. Luther experienced the devil with greater immediacy, horror and persuasiveness than any other great figure in his time. In his 'Table Talks' he repeatedly described his encounters with the devil—never as encounters with a symbol but always with a living being which stank and farted. The ink Luther hurled at him is anality thinly disguised. He repeatedly enjoined the devil to kiss his arse, to shit into his pants and to wear them around his neck; he threatened that he would empty his bowels into the devil's face or put him inside, that is, Luther's arse, where he belonged; and finally he drove the devil away by farting. It is obvious that Luther recognised the devil as incarnation of his own anality, of his dirty inside, but in order to purify himself he projected the filth and everything that was disgusting in him upon the Jews and became a virulent anti-Semite. The more his conscience troubled him the more he hated the Jews.

The conflict between the devilish drives, which were associated with preoccupation of material things, and the need for repentance, the fascination with filth and yearning for purity, obsessed not only Luther but the Christian mind in centuries to come; the condemnation of money as the devil's realm on the one hand and the organised pursuit of wealth and profit on the other hand came to be the heritage of the Protestant mind.

Just as Baudelaire and Blake stressed the essentially satanic character of trade, Luther had already identified the devil with both merchant and death. Luther's most important statement on capitalism is the sentence that money is the word of the devil through which he creates all things, the way God created through the true word. The structure of Luther's kingdom of Satan is essentially capitalistic: "We are the devil's property, he is the lord of this world. The world cannot get along without him, it cannot do without usury, avarice, miserliness, the desire to amass wealth or theft. The world is the devil's hostelry and we are his bondsmen. Whoever wants to walk peacefully in this world must be money's guest. But while our flesh is in bondage to the devil, our spirit is not". Consequently, the spirit remains free, while the flesh pays homage to the devil. Luther's critique of monasticism, as an escape from reality, pointed to this world as the only place where salvation can be won. As Christ surrendered to the Cross, so the Protestant surrenders to life in this world and to acquisition of money. To take up the Cross does not mean doing penitence as Catholics think, but to assume the sin and burden of earning money. Once, however, the world of material things does not have to be denied and becomes an area of legitimate activity, then it gradually acquires the image not only of the bad and dirty devil but also of the good and productive devil. The colour of the devil changes from being black; it becomes lighter, many-coloured and particularly it reverts back to its original colour before it was smitten with guilt and disgust, namely, gold.*

PROTESTANTISM AND THE THEOLOGY OF CAPITALISM

Encouraged by the Italian Renaissance and the Old Testament (translated by Luther and made widely available through the printing press) with its sanctification of life on earth as the creation of God, men began to feel free to turn their curiosity to the material world and to the shaping, handling and manipulating of their material environment. Men acquired the right to manipulate coarse reality and to make it give forth wealth and to reveal its secrets. The fascination with material things broke loose from its long inhibi-

---

* See: 'The Unknown Self'. Anal libido and projection.

tions; the world responded to men's productive activity, it allowed itself to be moulded and manipulated to produce wealth, to reveal its magic and its secrets and to hold up a mirror to men's Ego. Work became a redeeming activity, a form of salvation; it became a virtue and the wealth produced a symbol of men's self-realisation.

There is no doubt that through the Reformation men came to feel that by their productive labours they glorified God and the world. This new attitude was to some extent a revival of the Judaic concept in which God sent man out from the Eden of childhood to transform the world in order to create the new paradise of maturity. Just as God created man in His image out of matter, so man must transform matter in his own image so that in his products he realises his own true self; it is man's greatest gift to God to exercise his skills and his intelligence to this purpose, not merely for the enjoyment which wealth affords, but as an offering to God for his pleasure and approval.

The spirit of Protestantism does not encourage conspicuous consumption or the impulsive enjoyment of riches, it is the creation of surplus value, the saving and accumulation of profit for new investment in further productive capacity that pleases the Protestant God. In this way it is the spiritual foundation of capitalism. While in the ancient religions surplus products are offered to the gods on altars and burnt and cooked for their consumption, while even in the temple of the Jews animals were offered in sacrifice and gold and precious stones adorned God's habitation to signify his glory, while the churches of Christianity had great wealth, ornaments and wonderful works of art bestowed on them and the Vatican amassed untold wealth (while holding the half-starved Christ in his agony on the cross up to the world as the symbol of worship), the wealth of the Protestant was given over to making better machines, bigger workshops and factories, new inventions and the organisations of accounting houses and banks: these were the altars of God.

Marx came close to an understanding of the spirit of capitalism as a ritual of sacrifice, but then he made the crucial mistake in thinking that it was the capitalist himself who assumed God's role, to whom the workers were made to sacrifice their labour and an essential part of their humanity. We shall return to the problem of the sacrifice of the worker in capitalism, but it must be understood that in the foundation ethics of capitalism it is the entrepreneur who sacrifices the product of his ingenuity and enterprise and his surplus value to the god of industry and, at the same time, to the God in heaven. He himself is a worshipper and the wealth he creates is a gift to the greater glory of God and a step towards the new Eden.

The moralisation of work, its sanctification as a religious act of worship, produces a variety of problems. First, there is the paradox regarding the question as to who should receive the narcissistic reward from labour—God or man. Is it God's narcissism which is to be satisfied in the creation of wealth, is it He who is to be glorified and exalted, or is it the entrepreneur. In other words, should the entrepreneur enjoy his wealth or should he live a frugal life, devoting himself single-mindedly to his task as a form of repentance to secure his salvation in the eyes of God. There is no doubt where Luther and Calvin stood in regard to this question. But there is also no doubt that the personal prestige, the pleasure and enhancement of power that comes from the possession of wealth, was and continues to be an important incentive for the capitalist.

The importance given by Luther and Calvin to repentance and faith emphasise the sacrificial aspect of work and profit—the pursuit of wealth as a kind of asceticism. This sense of frugality, self-discipline, hard work and horror of ostentation which goes by the name of Puritanism, no doubt provided the impetus and motivation of capitalist systems. This cult of abstinence and restraint of impulsive enjoyments moreover satisfies the anal-retentive character, his disposition for hoarding, saving and amassing, and his utter fascination with money. Material riches retained and prevented from being discharged, i.e. spent, creates a sense of gratification typical of anal-retentive individuals and also the obsessive weighing, measuring, calculating and pedantry that goes with it. Puritanism, which we can define as the ascetic pursuit of profit, thus responds to the anal-retentive primacy and upholds it as the most virtuous of all human dispositions. It produces an attitude of obsessiveness which no doubt encourages exactitude, logical reasoning, the hard-headed attitude to facts and impersonal relationships. These qualities were clearly manifest in the thinking and character of Calvin who more than Luther provided the Reformation with a clear-cut dogmatic creed and fixed laws. The emphasis he gave to the sacrificial aspects of work is exemplified by the regime which he imposed on the citizens of Geneva when he became not only their moral leader but also exercised legislative powers in that city. It was a regimen that demanded that people get up very early, work very hard and uphold the virtues of thrift and abstinence. He constantly warned against self-indulgence and luxury and also demanded that the New Church avoids the luxuries, greed and pomp which so outraged him in the Church of Rome. Calvin enforced his rules with vigour and ferocity. One of his citizens was beheaded for writing a set of what Calvin called obscene verses. A player of cards was pilloried and an adulteress whipped through the streets and then banished. Many other individuals who broke the rules of puritanic asceticism by pursuing their pleasure were killed or tortured, insulted and expelled from the community under Calvin's rule.

In fact the summum bonum of the puritanical ethics, the earning of more and more money combined with the strict avoidance of all spontaneous enjoyment of life, is completely devoid of any hedonistic admixture. As Max Weber has pointed out: 'This reversal of what we should call the natural relationship is definitely a leading principle of capitalism as it is foreign to all peoples not under capitalistic influence'.

Benjamin Franklin based his puritan work ethic upon Old Testament writing, and in particular on a passage which his Calvinist father drummed into him again and again as a youth: 'Seest thou a man diligent in his business? He shall stand before kings'. (Proverbs 22, 29).

However, we see here a significant difference between the puritan denial of pleasure and the Jew's right to enjoy the fruits of his labours so long as he shares them with his God. For the former, the very exertions of the worldly calling, which may be devoted to the creation of wealth, were a form of asceticism.

We find Luther and Calvin as well as their successors engaged in a constant effort to uphold the difference between the oral-receptive and anal-retentive motivations of wealth creation and, equally, to separate the gratification of the Ego's narcissistic urges from the need to satisfy God's narcissism. As the oral-receptive as well as the narcissistic motivations of the entrepreneur could hardly be denied, he had constantly to be reminded that it was his thrift and frugality that pleased God and that it was his duty to save and invest rather than consume his profit. Accordingly, the Puritans preached that the only way of living acceptable to God was not to suppress or deny worldly activities in monastic asceticism but solely through the fulfilment of the obligations imposed on the individual by his position in the world. The 'calling' of a man ('Beruf'—profession—which literally means 'calling') expresses his devotion to God. This conception of a man's calling and discipline and sense of duty which goes with it, gave everyday worldly activity a religious significance and it provided capitalist pursuit with an ethical content.

Luther developed this concept of a man's 'calling' in the course of the first decade of his activity as a reformer. At first quite in harmony with the prevailing tradition of the Middle Ages, he thought of activity in the world as a thing of the flesh, as the indispensable condition of a life of faith, but in itself, like eating and drinking, morally indifferent. But after his break with the Catholic tradition he declared the monkish life to be a dictate of evil, not only quite devoid of value before God but he also considered its renunciation of the duties of this world to be a form of selfishness, an escape from worldly obligations.

This, let me point out again, did not mean the pursuit of labour devoted to profit as a form of self-aggrandisement or self-indulgence. Hence, Luther's sharp condemnation of usury which he saw not as a moral obligation imposed by one's calling but an exploitation of it for selfish purposes. In this way he condemned the Fuggers and the large corporations and bankers of his time, who, in his eyes, misused their powers to the detriment of others and were an insult to God's intentions.

Calvin, in even more clear-cut terms than Luther, accepted the new economic order. He assumed the existence of a capitalistic economic system for society and set up his ethics on that basis. Calvin openly accepted the main features of a commercial civilisation and broke with the tradition which regarded preoccupation with economic interests beyond what is necessary for subsistence as reprehensible and had stigmatized the middle man and merchant as a parasite.*

But while Calvin condemned the excessive exaction of usury from the poor he accepted the fact that a merchant ought to pay interest on the borrowed capital which made his profits possible.

---

* R. H. Tawney: 'Religion and the Rise of Capitalism'.

However, we find a constant conflict between the Puritan-Protestant concept of worship by means of accumulation of wealth and the opportunity for ostentation and exercise of power which it provided. Indeed, many observers have pointed out that the Calvinistic discipline so restricted capitalism in Geneva as to keep it in a primitive form. Nevertheless, the Reformation gave moral justification and encouragement to the rising bourgeoisie and allowed its members to uphold a conviction that in their activities they served God and, moreover, it is quite true that the great entrepreneurs and capitalists frequently preserved a frugal life-style, avoided ostentation and found spiritual fulfilment in the creation of riches.

Besides the spiritual justification and encouragement which Protestantism has provided to the new capitalist class, they derived, as we have said, deep psychological gratifications in their pursuit of profit. The satisfaction in the making of wealth, money and gold, the manipulation, calculation, hoarding, saving, the holding back and letting out in investment, the power to control and to give, the satisfaction of being mean, stubborn or generous at other times, of making others dependent on one's powers which riches provide, all these play an important part in the life of the capitalist. But the pleasure of gold and money, the handling and manipulating, still encounter a lingering taboo on anal activities imbibed in childhood and which continue to put an imprint of dirt and filth on the money so lovingly amassed. The Puritan money-maker, who is deeply concerned with cleanliness and purity and virtue, thus had to split the dirty and forbidden aspects of his activities from himself and project them onto others. He will separate his riches which he considers to be clean and moral from the riches of others which he will consider to be dirty and immoral. In particular, he will project the dirty aspect of it, the mean, selfish, exploitive aspects of usury upon the Jews, the primeval enemies of the good Christian. And indeed, it is interesting to note that it was precisely during the late sixteenth and early seventeenth centuries when the rising bour-geoisie still had to justify their preoccupation with wealth that the Jews were attacked as the dark devils of usury, and all aspects of capitalist activity which still carried the stigma of guilt were transferred onto them.

So we find the extraordinary situation that not only the victims of the capitalist system but also its protagonists blamed the Jews for making money, exploiting the Christian poor, amassing riches and plotting for power.

Despite the conflicts and paradoxes which the Renaissance and Reformation evoked in the religious and political landscape of Europe, the mould of the Christian dogma that had dominated the Middle Ages was broken. Its heavy and oppressive Superego lifted from the minds of men and they could look at the world once more with fascination and curiosity. Not only the instinct to handle the material environment and making it respond to the human will and cause it to bring forth wealth and fruitfulness but also intellectual inquiry received a powerful impetus. Men could look at the world with a new freedom, as interest in nature was now permissible and had acquired a sense of virtue. The fascination with material things and the Renaissance ideal of the universal man reflected a new vision of men's capabilities to discern the universal laws which lay behind the manifold of appearances. Matter became interesting, nature an object of passionate investigation.

11 The Authority of Reason

The new sciences were governed by the belief that the study of phenomena can lead to an understanding of universal laws and theories concerning those general laws; that theories, in turn, can be tested by observation in order to show whether the theories are congruent with the observed data. Jacopo Sabarella (1533–1589) explained how theories are formed by investigating phenomena: "When we form some theory about the matter, we are able to search out and discover something else in it; where we form no theory at all, we shall never discover anything".

Whereas the Christian Middle Ages had split the world into a number of separate compartments and was concerned with the process of separation and the fixation of separates into isolated units, the new approach also used the method of classification and separation but merely as a first step in the process of unification. The natural order was seen by medieval philosophers as God's museum of things and creatures, eternally divided into their kinds and alienated from the creative process insofar as they were finished products. By searching for the unifying principle behind the phenomena, the Renaissance philosopher attempted to get nearer to the Creator and understand his mind and purpose which gave form to his products.

Previously, theologians had avoided investigation by means of induction to arrive at general or universal principles, as this would have asserted the primacy of human reason over the dogmas of the Church. Pope Innocent III in 1219 and Gregory IX in 1228 declared that theology must exert its power over each separate faculty as the mind over the flesh, and it must be explained solely according to the traditions tested by the saints and not through the use of the 'carnal arms' (i.e. observation by the senses). Statements of authority, or reasons deduced from authority, are advanced for each topic. Thus the Creator is separated from his creation, and all the things that exist remain static and isolated from each other forever. As man is isolated from God's reasoning, he is denied the use of his own reasoning.

The Renaissance transformed the static universe of the Middle Ages into a developing universe, the tyrannical God into a reasoning and creative being, whose intentions and activities became intelligible to man. Man's emerging powers of self-determination were reflected and encouraged by the image of a rational deity who created man and intended him to become rational also. The movement of the Renaissance was inspired by the re-emergence of an intellectual optimism which had flourished in ancient Greece and also among the Jews but had lain barren through the intervening centuries. Karl Popper called it the most optimistic view of man's power to discern truth and to gain knowledge.* The birth of modern science and the whole movement of European rationalism had its foundation in this optimistic epistemology, whose main spokesmen were Francis Bacon and Descartes. They taught that there was no need for any man to appeal to authority in matters of truth because each man carried the sources of knowledge within himself, either in his powers of sense-perception which he may use for the careful observation of nature, or in his powers of intellectual intuition which he may use to distinguish truth from falsehood, by refusing to accept any idea which is not clearly and distinctly perceived by the intellect. This belief in the power of human reason is linked with a doctrine of human dignity and the belief in a God who is near to man and wants man to learn to be a rational, responsible and creative being. Conversely, the denial of this belief in the power of human reason is almost invariably linked with distrust in man.

Thus epistemological pessimism is associated historically with the doctrine of human depravity, the indignity and sinfulness of his nature, and produces a demand for an authority which would think on his behalf and save him from folly.

---

* Karl Popper: 'Conjectures and Refutations'.

If God deems us to be sinful and degraded then he does not expect us to understand Him, and we shall lack the instruments of knowledge and remain dependent on dogma; but if God wants us to know and understand then He equips us with the instruments for knowledge, with the senses to study his creations, and with an intellect by which we can comprehend their meaning.

Roger Bacon (c. 1215–1294), the 'Doctor Mirabilis', was the foremost among the early champions of the unity of wisdom, and his works struck at the very roots of Thomism and its careful partitioning that prescribes for each thinker the limits beyond which he must not venture. He assumed that intellectual knowledge contains an 'agent intellect' that encompasses all forms and, in this respect, shows an affinity with God's intellect.

The new intellectuals who were encouraged by the Renaissance assumed that there is harmony and unity behind the manifold of appearances and they devoted themselves to the search for the unifying principle through the observation of phenomena. Thus classification of phenomena and their separation was no longer an end in itself but a first step in the process of unification, i.e. induction, in order to arrive at the general principle that lies behind things. 'The true way of philosophy', writes Francis Bacon, 'is to derive axioms from the sense and particulars, rising by a gradual and unbroken ascent so that it arrives at the most general axiom last of all.' Induction, which became the paramount rule for scientific activity, could only have become generally accepted when the universe of sensory objects was seen to be the manifestation of God's activity.

Copernicus, like many of his contemporaries, was guided by a vision of a world that was both monotheistic and Platonic, a world order expressing a universal purpose, characterised by harmony and founded on orderly, rational, mathematical relationships. Medieval astronomers had been content with any astronomical model that would 'save the phenomena', that is, 'grind out' models roughly in accord with observation. Copernicus maintained that all such models were inadequate and that the true geometry of the heavens would be known by the 'unalterable symmetry of its parts' and by the contrast between the evident necessity of its relationships and the arbitrary character of false systems.

Copernicus had two outstanding merits which are not necessarily or even rarely found together: immense patience of observation and great boldness in framing hypotheses. These two qualities were much encouraged by the renewed influence of monotheistic theology and Platonic philosophy. Few among the ancients possessed both merits together and no one in the Middle Ages possessed either: Copernicus possessed both.

The extent to which the new intellect had outpaced the founding fathers of the Reformation, like Luther or Calvin, can be seen by their reaction to Copernicus' work. Copernicus communicated his theories to German Lutherans among others, but when Luther came to know of them he was profoundly shocked: 'People give ear,' he said, 'to an upstart astrologer who strove to show that the earth revolves, not the heavens or the firmament, the sun and the moon. Whoever wishes to appear clever must devise some new system, which of all systems is of course the very best. This fool wishes to reverse the entire science of astronomy; but sacred Scripture tells us that Joshua commanded the sun to stand still, and not the earth'. Calvin, similarly, demolished Copernicus with the text: 'The world also is established, that it cannot be moved' (Ps. xciii,1), and exclaimed: 'Who will venture to place the authority of Copernicus above that of the Holy Spirit?' Protestant clergy were at least as bigoted as Catholic ecclesiastics; nevertheless there soon came to be much more liberty of speculation in Protestant than in Catholic countries, because in Protestant countries the clergy had less power. The important aspect of Protestantism was schism, not heresy, for schism led to national Churches, and national Churches were not strong enough to control the lay government. "This was wholly a gain, for the Churches everywhere opposed as long as they could practically every innovation that made for an increase of happiness of knowledge here on earth".*

Descartes based his optimistic epistemology on the theory of 'veracitas dei': what we clearly and distinctly see and know must be true, for otherwise God would be deceiving us. We can find the roots of this theory in Plato's theory of anamnesis which grants to each man in some measure the possession of the sources of knowledge. For Descartes, it is, to be sure, the sensible world about which philosophising goes on, but the method of correct procedure must not rest on sense experience. In truth, we perceive no object as it is by sense alone but only by our reason exercised upon sensible

---

* Bertrand Russell: 'History of Philosophy' (Allen & Unwin).

objects: "We must seek the 'certain principles' of material things not by the prejudices of the senses but by the light of reason, and which thus possess so great evidence that we cannot doubt of their truth".

The mind that thinks is for Descartes the very source of human experience and the core of his existence. "The truth, 'I think, therefore I am', is so solid and so certain that all the most extravagant suppositions of the mystics are incapable of upsetting it. I judged that I could receive it without scruple as the first principle of the philosophy that I sought".*

This passage is the kernel of Descartes' philosophy of knowledge and contained what is most important in his philosophy. Most philosophers since Descartes have attached importance to the theory of knowledge and their doing so is largely due to him. 'I think, therefore I am', makes mind more certain than matter and gives the Ego's intellect a supremacy that goes beyond anything earlier thinkers have dared to do.

Spinoza, perhaps the most lovable and most noble of all great philosophers, upheld that the wise man, so far as human finiteness allows, endeavours to see the world as God sees it, under the aspect of eternity. Love for God, he said, must hold the chief place in the mind. Every increase in the understanding of what happens to us consists in referring events to the ideas of God since, in truth, everything is part of God. This understanding of everything as part of God *is* love of God. When all objects are referred to God, the idea of God will fully occupy the mind.

We can recognise two fundamental propositions in Spinoza's work. Firstly, he identified nature with God, the natural world being His body, an extension and manifestation of His Being; while the second proposition maintains that God loves Himself and His Creation with an infinite intellectual love. The first proposition overcomes the separation between world and nature from God, and the second, which has caused much puzzlement and controversy, completely projects men's narcissism onto God. Nature and all aspects of this world and all that happens in it is sanctified as the necessary emanation of God's Will and existence. "We are part of the universal nature and we follow her order. If we have a clear and distinct understanding of this, that part of our nature which is

---

* René Descartes: 'Discourse on Method' (1637) and 'Meditations' (1642).

defined by intelligence, in other words, the better part of ourselves, will assuredly acquiesce in what befalls us". This sounds very much like passive submissiveness to fate; it implies complete acceptance of God's Will in the world. However, it is the intellect which is the agent by which we find the way to God. In so far as man has grasped the sole reality of the whole, by means of his intellect, he is free. In this sense Spinoza attempted to unify his pantheistic cosmology with an ethic that is based on love for God who is in the universe and not outside it and manifest in our reality.

The intellectual devotion to an understanding of God, underpinned and motivated by love, has given an important impetus to the study of nature as a means to the understanding of God's mind.

We shall see that, by drawing God from His heavenly existence and bringing Him into the world, Spinoza paved the way to a deification of nature; it was not long before nature herself became the object of worship as well as enquiry, as the philosophy of nature and as science, and God disappeared into the world.

Newton was perhaps the last of the great scientists who had not forgotten God in his worship of nature, indeed, his scientific activity was a worship of God who made everything and created the laws which Newton endeavoured to observe and reveal. Like Descartes, he intended to discover the logic and mathematical laws which guide the mechanics of nature by means of reason and scientific experiment as substantial proof for the existence of God.

In the second edition of his 'Principia' (1713) Newton writes: 'From His true dominion it follows that the true God is a living, intelligent and powerful being; and from His other perfections, that He is supreme, or most perfect. He is eternal and infinite, omnipotent and omniscient; that is, His duration reaches from eternity to eternity; His presence from infinity to infinity; He governs all things, and knows all things that are or can be done. He is not eternity or infinity, but eternal and infinite; He is not duration or space, but He endures and is present. He endures forever and is everywhere present; and by existing always and everywhere He constitutes duration and space".

Elsewhere Newton speaks of God as 'containing in Himself all things as their principle and place'. Newton specifically insists on the active divine control of the world. 'God, being in all places, is more able by His Will to move the bodies within His boundless uniform sensorium, and thereby to form and re-form the parts of the universe, than we are by our will to move the parts of our own bodies'. As absolute space is the divine sensorium, everything that happens in it, being present to the divine knowledge, must be immediately perceived and immediately understood by Him. 'The divine consciousness furnishes the ultimate centre of reference for absolute motion'. God for him is not only infinite knowledge but also all-mighty Will. He is the ultimate originator of motion and is able at any time to add motion to bodies within His boundless sensorium. Thus all real or absolute motion in the last analysis is the resultant of an expenditure of the divine energy, and whenever the divine intelligence is cognisant of such an expenditure the motion so added to the system of the world must be absolute.

Newton was confident that empirical facts open to anybody's observation implied unqualifiedly the existence of a God of a certain definite nature and function. God was not detached from the world that science seeks to know: 'Indeed, every true step in natural philosophy brings us nearer to a knowledge of the First Cause, and is for this reason to be highly valued'. It will enlarge the boundaries of moral philosophy also, inasmuch as, 'so far as we can know by natural philosophy what is the First Cause, what power He has over us and what benefits we receive from him, so far our duty towards him as well as towards one another will appear to us by the light of nature.'* So, although religion and science are fundamentally different ways of approaching the universe, each valid in its own way, yet for Newton, in the last analysis, the realm of science was dependent on God and led the reverent mind to a fuller assurance of His reality and a readier obedience to His commands. 'The main business of natural philosophy', Newton maintains, 'is to argue from phenomena without feigning hypotheses, and to deduce causes from effects, till we come to the very First Cause, which certainly is not mechanical... Does it not appear from phenomena that there is a being incorporeal, living, intelligent, omnipresent, who in infinite space, as it were, in his sensory, sees the things themselves intimately and thoroughly perceives them, and comprehends them wholly by their immediate presence to Himself?'**

We witness here a transformation of men's relationship to God:

---

* Sir Isaac Newton: 'Optics'.
** ibid.

the Superego authority which had previously been perceived as forbidding and aloof, unfathomable and awesome, changes into a friendly god, who loves man and is pleased with the universe he has created. He wants men to understand him and is close to them as a guide and teacher. Secure in the thought that they are acknowledged and protected by the omnipotent father, his sons feel free to develop their intellectual and moral faculties.

THE DEATH OF GOD AND THE DEMYSTIFICATION OF THE UNIVERSE: THE ENLIGHTENMENT

The reconciliation between God's omnipotence and the confident expression of man's ego faculties eventually led to the expansion of the ego into the universe, and men began to take over from God.

With Spinoza and Newton God was expanded throughout all space and time and there was still something spiritual in the world; the Superego was still present and all-powerful and recognisable. However, Newton's conception of the world was gradually shorn of its divine foundation. The categories of rational thought invaded the universe till it was conceived in terms of mathematics and geometry and experimentally proven causal relationships. Space, time, motion and causality needed no further explanation through the existence of God and seemed capable of exact and final formulation by the laws of mechanics, geometry and mathematics. The process of eliminating the providential elements in the world-order reached its climax in the work of Laplace, who believed himself to have demonstrated the inherent stability of the universe by showing that all its irregularities are periodical and subject to an eternal law which prevents them from ever exceeding a stated amount.

While God was thus being deprived of his duties by the further advancement of mechanical science and men were beginning to wonder whether the self-perpetuating machine thus left stood in need of any supernatural beginning, Hume questioned whether the concept of a First Cause was as necessary an idea or reason as it appeared, and Kant was preparing the penetrating analysis which removed God from the realm of knowledge altogether.

Thus, some time during the eighteenth century God disappeared from men's view; he got lost in the mechanistic universe. What then happened to the Superego? What happened to its image that had for millennia been projected from its habitation in the mind upon the heavens in the same way as a projector throws the pictures inside it on to the cinema screen and men watch the shadowy reflections, pretending them to be reality. Two things happened: one was that with the advance of science the material universe assumed the dynamics, the reverence and awe previously vested in God; secondly men began to recognise that the seat of reason and the images of power are located inside the brain. God, the ancient projection, was returned to where He came from—to men's mind.

These two types of perception came to represent the two cultures which have not ceased since to be in a state of conflict with each other: the world of science and the world of the humanities. At first, however, the conflict was not evident. The humanists of the Enlightenment were, above all, concerned with freeing the human Ego and its rationality from dependence upon the divine Superego, and they declared men to be the measure of all things, the source of knowledge, the causa prima, the creative agent.

The idea of the Enlightenment was beautifully described by Kant: 'Enlightenment is the emancipation of man from a state of self-imposed tutelage... of incapacity to use his own intelligence without external guidance. Such a state of tutelage I call self-imposed if it is due not so much to lack of intelligence but to lack of courage or determination to use man's own intelligence without the help of a leader. Dare to use your own intelligence! This is the battle-cry of the Enlightenment'.* The struggle for spiritual freedom represents the quest for man's maturation, his emancipation from childish dependency upon an omnipotent and omniscient father-figure. In order, however, to achieve maturity and the capacity to make rational and correct judgements, he must be equipped with the necessary tools and skills to use them. On the intellectual level this means that man is equipped with reason and that he can acquire the skills of rational thought to obtain knowledge. Bacon and Descartes upheld this optimistic view, the one emphasising the capacity to arrive at the intuition of the truth by means of empirical observation, the other emphasising the primacy of the intellect in the process of cognition. 'Cogito ergo

---

* Immanuel Kant: 'What is Enlightenment' (1785).

sum', said Descartes, but equally, 'Cogito ergo est', meaning, 'I think, therefore I create the truth about the universe'.

While Bacon did not rely upon the senses alone for obtaining knowledge of general laws, and Descartes was not merely an idealist or rationalist but also a very considerable mathematician and scientist, Kant connected the concept of the centrality of the human mind in the processes of cognition with the activity of the senses, and showed that they do not only interact in practice, but must *necessarily* interact in rational thinking. Although confirmed by observation, scientific theories are the result not of these observations merely, but of our own ways of thinking, of our attempts to order our sense data and understand them. It is not these sense data but our own intellect which is responsible for our theories. Nature as we know it, with its order and with its laws, is largely a product of the assimilating and ordering activities of our mind. 'Our intellect does not draw its laws from nature, but imposes its laws upon nature'.*

Men's independence from a divine authority placed a new obligation on men, which the great minds of the time grasped with alacrity. In the same way as in the great period of Greek culture men had to discover how the mind works, both in order to acquire knowledge and also to formulate the principles of right conduct in order to create an ideal society, so the men of the Enlightenment had to discover the principles by which they themselves, without reliance on God, could create a society that reflected the principles of reason and morality.

Newton believed that 'every true step in natural philosophy brings us nearer to a knowledge of the First Cause, and will therefore enlarge the bounds of moral philosophy also, inasmuch as, so far as we can know by natural philosophy what is the First Cause, what power he has over us, and what benefits we receive from him, so far our duty towards him, as well as towards one another, will appear to us by the light of nature'. The new intellect which took over from Newton found this path barred. In their enthusiasm for the new found freedom men had lost their eternal ruler; they became fatherless in the universe and had to brace themselves to acquire for themselves the powers and wisdom previously ascribed to God. Pascal, Bayle, Voltaire, Rousseau,

---

*Kant: 'Critique of Pure Reason'.

Hobbes, Locke, Hume and Kant, among others, saw new gates of knowledge and freedom opening up before mankind and they announced their visions to a fascinated public. New scientific academies were set up all over Europe. And yet this new view of things should not give rise to the illusion of a linear progress. The maturation of the European Ego and its struggle for independence was beset by many conflicts and complexities which characterise cultural and personal development. Old primacies, fixations and traditions, and vested interests in the preservation of an ancient establishment, the defenders of orthodoxy and dogma, continued to defend their positions against the innovators.

However, nothing could for long stifle the development of the new spirit that spread over the intellectual landscape. The controversies, the exchanges of information, the borrowings and recoveries, only served to uphold the new sciences as an example to intellectual life as a whole. They all contributed from different angles to lay down the co-ordinates of a new society and a new world that was going to be built. Many dreamt of a changed mankind and even of a changed world of nature created by experiment and calculation. They won the attention of their contemporaries because they fulfilled deeply held desires for a better knowledge of nature which would enable men to dominate it more fully, and for a better understanding of themselves.

Man no longer faced God primarily but nature herself, and he approached nature with that sense of awe and wonder previously reserved for God. His prayers were transformed into study and experiment and the answers to those prayers were to be attained by his control over nature. At the same time man faced himself; his reason had to direct itself to an investigation of the capabilities, conditions and limitations of his rationality. Epistemology (the theory of knowledge) became the focus of philosophical enquiry, with Locke, Hume and Kant as its most profound exponents.

At the same time man took a new interest in the world of political and economic reality, and above all that supreme organisation of society, the state. Institutions of state, no longer accepted as an expression of God's Will and thus permanent for all time, became the object of rational investigation. The intellectuals responded to the challenge of the new found freedom to decide what kind of world men want to live in.

Rousseau wished to provide a rational sanction for society and called on men to rebuild the state anew by choosing their form of society freely and rationally. He wanted to free men's communal relationship from its anchorage on authority and overthrow established systems in order to enjoy the model society he encouraged men to visualise. In this way he was a revolutionary. He upheld the total legislative powers of the people expressing the general will. The voice of the people, he said, is in fact the voice of God. It is not difficult, however, to see how out of this deification of the just state he provided philosophical justification for the totalitarian state. But one must recognise the duality of his achievement: the paradox of the dictatorship of the will of the people which allows the state to claim to be its unquestioned representative, thus acquiring total authority, and his great attempt to define the 'Republic of Virtue'.

We can see the consequences of this paradox in the epochal confrontation between Robespierre and Danton, the prototype for many other such confrontations between the aspirations for freedom and their transformation into dictatorship.

But Rousseau was only one of the great minds who addressed themselves in the eighteenth century to the construction of a free and just society when the old certainties and dogmas ceased to be acceptable.

As men applied their new understanding and ability to manipulate natural forces, and the science of mechanics and mathematics to the improvement of tools, they also employed the authority of reason for the justification of power. The ruling classes, particularly the emergent bourgeoisie employed science and its philosophic advocates both for the improvement of the means of production as well as their pursuit for power.

It was Francis Bacon (1561–1626) who more clearly than anyone else captured the spirit of science, and was probably the first to advocate its application to industry. Some people called him the philosopher of industrial science. He upheld that 'science must be known by its works; it is by the witness of works rather than by logic or even observation that truth is revealed and established. It follows from this that the improvement of man's lot and the improvement of man's mind are one and the same thing'. In his 'Thoughts and Conclusions' he wrote: 'The mechanical arts grow towards perfection every day as if endowed with the spirit of life. Philosophy is like a statue. It draws crowds of admirers, but it cannot move. With their first authors, the mechanical arts are crude, clumsy and cumbersome, but they go on to acquire new strength and capacities. Philosophy is most vigorous with its earliest author and exhibits a subsequent decline. The best explanation for these opposite fortunes is that in the mechanical arts the talents of many individuals combine to produce a single result, but in philosophy one individual talent destroys many. The many surrender themselves to the leadership of one, devote themselves to the slavish office of forming a bodyguard in his honour and become incapable of adding anything new'. And he continues this argument in his book 'Novum Organum': 'Such has been the course of philosophy. It cannot do without natural history, but in fact nothing has been duly investigated, nothing verified, nothing counted, weighed or measured. The reason is that natural history has never hitherto been regarded as the necessary foundation of a philosophy of works. As soon as one attempts to use it for this purpose, its hopeless inadequacy is revealed. But the remedy is easy. It is to collect a natural history which includes, as a major part, the history of the mechanical arts. The secret workings of nature do not reveal themselves to one who simply contemplates the natural flow of events. It is when man interferes with nature, vexes nature, tries to make her do what he wants, not what she wants, that he begins to understand how she works and may hope to learn how to control her'.*

In this statement, which can be considered at the heart of his thoughts, Bacon reveals the Ego of the free and active man who employs his reason in order to take possession of nature, to explore her and make her submit to his will. He epitomises the young patriarchal male, who has overcome the restraints of parental taboos and whose intellect has vanquished superstition and dogma. But like many other prophets of the new science, he could not have foreseen the consequence of the industrial revolution which he helped to inaugurate.

------

* Francis Bacon: 'Novum Organum, Thoughts and Conclusions'.

12 The Rise of the Bourgeoisie and the Industrial Revolution

SCIENCE ENTERS THE WORKSHOP

When the new intellectuals proclaimed science to be the correct approach towards an understanding of nature, the capitalist entrepreneur turned to the scientist to increase production and enhance his profit. The application of science to the process of production and to the organisation of business provided the impetus for a tremendous expansion of industry and its large-scale mechanisation. The mechanisation of production, involving ever larger numbers of workers and greater quantities of commodities, necessitated mathematical, statistical control of business and commerce. The productive processes, which previously depended on human skill and human use of man-made tools located in the traditional workshop, were invaded by scientifically constructed mechanical tools which controlled the labour of masses of workers in factories, organised on mechanical and mathematical principles.

The engineers who were employed by the entrepreneur were not so much concerned with the application of the laws of mechanics to an understanding of the universe but with the invention and improvements of machines

The steam-engine, to take perhaps the most important innovation responsible for the mechanisation of industry, had begun as a machine to pump water from mines. However, in 1781, on a tour of Cornwall, Boulton wrote home to his friend Watt, who had invented the steam-engine: 'There is no other Cornwall to be found, and the most likely line for increasing the consumption of our engines is the application of them to mills, which is certainly an extensive field. The people in London, Manchester and Birmingham are steam-mill mad. I don't mean to hurry you, but I think that in the course of a month or two we should determine to take out a patent for certain methods of producing rotative motion'. The steam-engine had so far only pumped up and down. Urged by Boulton, Watt had no difficulty in inventing several ways to make it turn a machine. In this form it became the new source of power for the factories.

The mechanical inventions which necessitated a new organisation of production caused a traumatic disturbance of man's relationship to his tools. Whereas tools represent an externalisation and extension of the individual, activated and controlled by the rhythms, the skills and intelligence of his craftsmanship, machines almost suddenly invaded the traditional workplace and made his tools irrelevant. The machines became increasingly specialised, production of a commodity was broken up into the manifold isolated part performances carried out repetitively, while the worker ceased to be responsible for making the whole product. Division of labour was enormously enhanced, the human image of the product was broken, the worker no longer saw his skill and personality reflected in what he produced. Craftsmanship was replaced by mindless and unimaginative labour. The mechanical logic which governs the functions of machines dominated the organisations of factory production; the conveyor belt replaced the work-bench, mass-production replaced the craftsman's workshop. While traditionally a man's tools were his property, inherited from his father or made by himself, or sometimes bought with his savings, the machine was owned by the capitalist entrepreneur. It was an extension of the capitalist, the embodiment of his power.

The workers receive a wage for their labour, they serve the machine but the machine is not an extension of themselves, it is an alien power that dictates their work activity and, above all, it has robbed them of their traditional skills; it is their adversary and their conqueror.

One can say that the rule of mechanics which dominated machine production diminished man's power as a craftsman and producer, whereas it enhanced the power of the bourgeoisie.

It is generally accepted that the transformation and the structure of industry, to which the title of industrial revolution has been given, was the harnessing of machines to the productive process, driven by non-human and non-animal power, i.e. power derived from coal, steam and later oil, and electricity. Marx asserted that 'the crucial change was, in fact, the fitting of a tool wielded by human hand into a machine. The important thing is that a mechanism, after being set in motion, performs the same operations that were formerly done by the workman with his tools... The machine which is the starting-point of the industrial revolution supersedes the workman who handles a single tool, by a mechanism operating with a number of similar tools and set in motion by an extra human motive power, whatever the form of that power may be'.* This crucial change from men's handling of a tool to having to serve a machine radically transformed the process of production.

The activities of the human producer had to conform to the rhythms and demands of the machine process; this transformation from the producer being the master of his tools to becoming dependent and subservient to the machine had its socio-economic reflection in the growing dependency of labour on capital, and in the growing role played by the capitalist as a coercive and disciplinary force over the human producer in his detailed operations. It was the main object of the new machinery that it led to the "equalisation of labour, dispensing with the special aptitudes of the 'self-willed skilled workman' and reducing the task of work-people to the exercise of vigilance and dexterity".**

In the old days production had been essentially a human activity, generally individual in character in the sense that a producer worked in his own time and in his own fashion more or less independently of others, while the tools or implements he used were little more than extension of his own hands. His muscular strength, his skills and his intelligence determined production down to the smallest detail. In the old situation, the independent small master embodying the unit of human and non-human instruments of production had been able to survive because the latter remained an appendage of the human hand and skill, but in the new situation he could no longer retain a foothold, both because the minimum size of a unit production process had grown too large for him to control and because the relationship between the human and mechanical instruments of production had been transformed.

----

* Karl Marx: 'Das Kapital' (Vol. 1).
** Andrew Ure: 'The Philosophy of Manufacture' (1835).

The merchant in his role of the man who 'removes' the goods produced by the guilds, or peasants, and sells them for his profit, had an external relationship to the mode of production. The goods he bought from the workers were produced by traditional craftsmanship and protected by the guilds. He was an outsider who did not interfere with the way things were produced—he only bought and sold the products. Gradually a section of the merchant class, as well as landowners, took direct possession of the production process, breaking the handicraft restrictions of the guilds. In some cases traders associated themselves into organisations such as drapers or haberdashers which monopolised the wholesale trade in these commodities, and brought the organisation of the craftsmen under their own control. Having absorbed the guilds into their own organisation, they felt free to put out work to craftsmen into areas which were free from the regulation of the Town Crafts Guilds.

Thus the early capitalists were merchants, and the most significant among them came to use mechanical innovations; they began to see the importance of the machine in the mode of production for the increase of profit and enlargement of their enterprises. The essence of the early entrepreneur was that he was an organiser, a man capable of imposing rational principles of efficiency upon his production methods. He transformed early capitalism into industrial capitalism by harnessing machines in the productive process and use of non-human, i.e. steam-power, instead of human power.

Large amounts of capital were now needed to finance the complex equipment required by the new type of production unit; and a role was created for a new type of capitalist, no longer simply as usurer or trader in his counting-house or warehouse, but as captain of industry, organiser and planner of the operations of the production unit, the embodiment of an authoritarian discipline, of a labour army which, robbed of economic citizenship, had to be coerced into the fulfilment of its onerous duties in another's service by the whip, alternatively of hunger and of the master's overseer.*

The earliest industrialists were 'putters-out'. The clothier, a type of entrepreneur who, it has been claimed, was the first of the industrial capitalists, was a man who owned the wool from the time it left the sheep's back until the time it went to a tailor. The

---

* Maurice Dobb: 'Studies in the Development of Capitalism' (Routledge & Kegan Paul, 1963).

specialisation of labour usually entailed at least a dozen stages between shearing the sheep and selling the cloth, each performed by a different group. The clothier organised the whole process. To do so, he needed organising, 'entrepreneurial' skill, capital and good business contacts. Efficiency eventually dictated that some of the stages at least should be performed under one roof. That roof was owned by the capitalist, and the machinery that came to be invented was installed and owned by him as well. The industrial capitalists, therefore, became owners of fixed capital who employed workers by the hour, or day, or week, on their premises. The capitalists owned not merely the materials used in production, but the tools and buildings. The fixed capital (as opposed to the 'circulating capital' represented by the raw materials being processed and the wages advanced to the workers before the goods were sold) embodied the technological progress known as the industrial revolution. The fixed equipment, which used energy in the eighteenth and nineteenth centuries derived ultimately from coal, was extremely expensive, and the industrial capitalists often therefore became big capitalists. By the mid-nineteenth century the term 'capitalist' came to be applied mostly to industrial manufacturers. As a result of this change the old mode of production, based on small-scale production of individual craftsmen, was destined to be uprooted; the factory proletariat was largely taken from the ranks of that class of small producers who could no longer compete with the mass production methods of the industrialist and were, therefore, robbed of their livelihood. The economic gulf between the master class and the employed, between owners and ownerless, was significantly widened by the new economic barrier which the initial outlay now involved in starting a production unit imposed. Very few craftsmen could afford to buy the new machinery and make the investment necessary to acquire an industrial enterprise; they had to leave their old workshops and old homes and enter the factories as labourers.

An ever greater number of people was needed to supply the labour force for the new industrial enterprises, a proletariat willing to hire itself to the new factory kings. The commodity 'labour power' had not merely to exist, it had to be available in adequate quantities in the place where it was most needed, and here mobility of the labouring population was an essential condition. The immense impetus to capital investment provided by industrial enterprises promoted a considerable net increase in the demand for labour, and it required that the supply be not merely sufficient to fill a given number of available jobs but in sufficient superabundance to cause labourers to compete against one another for employment in order to ensure that the price of the labour community would not rise with its increased demand.

The new industries of the north-west factory towns of England were able at this time to draw on a plentiful supply of starving immigrants from Ireland, an important labour reserve which fed alike the need for unskilled building labour in the middle eighteenth century, the expanding factory towns of the industrial revolution, and navvy labour for railway constructions in the 1840s and 1850s.

In the heyday of the industrial revolution natural increase of population powerfully reinforced the proletarianising of those who had previously been engaged on the land or in handicrafts. The masses of farm labourers and craftsmen who had been deprived of their livelihood by the competition of fast expanding industries had to seek employment in those very factories which robbed them of a livelihood, and they became the chief source of supply of labour power. With starvation as a relentless goad to employment, economists were able to argue that a rising demand for labour, wherever it arose, would generally cause the supply to be satisfied within a reasonably short interval of time.

By the time Marx came to write 'Das Kapital', it was a generally held assumption, expressed in the practice of economic management, that the responsibility of industry to its labour force only extended to providing it with a means for subsistence; this was considered sufficient to guarantee an adequate inflow of workers to the factories.

The skilled craftsmen, who struggled against the falling costs of factory competition, fell into pauperdom and misery. Some of the agricultural workers similarly lost their status in pre-capitalist agriculture and did not find a new place in capitalist agriculture. They lost rights which they had taken for granted, to graze their animals, to glean, to collect firewood, and there was no work for them.

Pre-capitalist societies had a rhythm of work and social behaviour which were dictated by the seasons and weather, which reflected a ritual interpretation of life with fiestas and fasts, high days and low days. Productivity was low, but people were not conscious of this because there was no other kind of productivity with which to compare it; the regularity of life was governed by the unconscious rhythms of a traditional society. The industrial society is different. The pattern and rhythm of life is set by machinery and team-work. Everybody in a working group has to start together and stop together. If the machine speeds up, the worker speeds up; if it stops, he stops. The shift from one mode of working to the other is traumatic. Discipline in the early factories was harsh, dismissal was instantaneous and the atmosphere was tyrannical.

The early workers in industry had few rights. Ignorant, desperately poor and frightened, they depended on the factory masters for the bare conditions of life. Wages were at a minimum, and if they sought more there were others to take their place. If men were expensive, women could be used. Children of five or six were drafted into the factories. Hours were extremely long. Accidents were frequent. Life was cheap. In some barracks or cheap lodging houses, successive shifts of workers shared beds; as one shift went on duty, their beds were taken by those coming off duty. Conditions in early industrialisation always seemed to have been terrible; first in England (on the basis of which Marx and Engels wrote their reports), then on the Continent of Europe and in America; then in Russia and Asia the same experience of oppression and exploitation was undergone. There is a literature, from British official publications to Maxim Gorky, from Charles Dickens, Jack London to Upton Sinclair, describing the horrors of early industrialism.

These conditions lasted for several generations before some amelioration set in. England in the nineteenth century began to develop a group of labour managers, industrialists who were interested in labour conditions, who realised that shorter hours and more sympathetic treatment might raise productivity and so reduce costs, increase output and not lower it. In this respect they were soon overtaken by the Americans, where the supply of cheap labour was continually replenished by immigration but frequently depleted by movement to the west. Labour prices were forced up, and so it was essential to deal with labour as a scarce factor of production and not as an abundant one, as it was in Europe.* This factor in turn encouraged increased mechanisation of industry, the

---

* John Vaizey: 'Capitalism and Socialism' (Weidenfeld & Nicholson, 1980).

introduction of more and more efficient machinery to counter the cost of wages.

Thus in the space of a few generations the bourgeoisie acquired the role of sole provider, the only source of income for the masses of working people; machine production became the rule and the model for work activity. Labour as such was a commodity, an element of investment to keep the machines turning and to churn out the product. One no longer spoke of a worker as a carpenter, blacksmith, weaver, metal-worker, builder, etc., but as a labourer in general terms; his skill no longer characterised him as a person, he became an abstraction in the statistic of industrial production. The term 'worker' became depersonalised, abstracted from the actual individual, as a generic term for masses of people—the proletariat.

Marx's brutal exposé of the capitalist system, or rather his exposé of its brutalities, found their accompaniment in the dramatic descriptions provided by Charles Dickens in England and Upton Sinclair in America. Marx's stinging attack on capitalism had its core in the alienation and dehumanisation of the worker and his transformation into an abstract, statistical entity in capitalist economy.

The concept of abstract labour, represented in the value of commodities, has an important place in Marx's thinking. To many people the expression 'abstract labour' suggested something slightly mysterious, somewhat metaphysical and unreal. However, nothing of the sort was intended by Marx. Abstract labour is abstract only in the quite straightforward sense that all special characteristics which differentiate one kind of labour from another, and one kind of worker from another kind of worker, are ignored. 'Abstract labour', in short, is, as Marx's own usage clearly attests, equivalent to 'labour in general', it is what is common to all productive human activity. Marx points to Benjamin Franklin as one of the first economists who understood the nature of labour value, and commented in this way: "Franklin is unconscious that by estimating the value of everything in labour, he makes abstraction from any difference in the sorts of labour exchanged, and thus reduces them all to equal human labour. But although ignorant of this, yet he says it. He speaks first of 'the *one* labour', then of 'the *other* labour', and finally 'labour' without further qualification, as the substance of the value of everything".

In another connection he remarks that, "It was a tremendous advance on the part of Adam Smith to throw aside all limitations which mark wealth-producing activity and to define it as labour in general, neither industrial, nor commercial, nor agricultural, or one as much as the other". ('Das Kapital').

Marx was well aware that Ricardo adopted the same point of view and followed it with greater consistency than Adam Smith. It is important to realise that the reduction of all labour to a common denominator, so that units of labour can be compared with and substituted for one another, added and subtracted and finally totalled up to form a social aggregate, is not an arbitrary abstraction dictated in some way by the whim of the investigator. It is rather an abstraction which belongs to the essence of capitalism.[*]

With the disruption of man's relationship to his tools, a fundamental disturbance of the processes of self-externalisation and identification with his externalised self and his products occurred; the worker could no longer project himself into the world outside and recognise himself in the things he had produced and acquire a sense of identity from them. It was not just that society had undergone a fundamental change; man's psycho-biological pattern as a human being, his very humanness came under question, and he suffered a profound narcissistic injury. As the industrial revolution developed, penetrating into all aspects of society, this injury did not remain confined to the working-class—it spread to all classes and to all mankind subject to the domination of industrial machine production. Men's narcissistic need to see themselves reflected in the things they produce, is being increasingly denied, they become anonymous parts of the machine system, its dispensable and interchangeable appendages. Instead of the product being a mirror in which a man can see his self-image and his abilities reflected, a source for his self-esteem and affirmation of his identity in the world, it became an alien thing ignoring the person who created it. The human skills have been taken over by the machine, it has devoured man's creativity; it acquires the human characteristics denied to the worker. The machine becomes increasingly human as the worker is dehumanised, it acquires a will and an intelligence while the worker becomes helpless and ignorant. But that is not all. The machine reproduces its identity in its products, and they

---

[*] Paul M. Sweezy: 'The Theory of Capitalist Development' (New York, 1970).

become more and more machine-like, till in our time the buildings, articles of use and of entertainment, the images presented in cinema, television and even the theatre have acquired machine-like qualities. The machine becomes an object of fascination and magic; the chief playthings are video machines and computers, and architects want nothing better than to conceive of homes as machines for living. Nature herself has come to be regarded as a bio-chemical machine, subject to the laws and logic of mechanics. Under the influence of a machine-made environment and a mechanical concept of the world, men have begun to see themselves as machines; both their productive as well as their mental processes are conceived in terms of a machine.

REASON BECOMES A MACHINE: MAN LOSES HIS MIND. 'THE SECOND INDUSTRIAL REVOLUTION'

We do not need to go into further detail to describe the development of the process of industrialisation and mechanisation during the nineteenth and twentieth centuries. A voluminous library has been written on this subject and there is no need for us to enlarge on it. Suffice it to say that the process of mechanisation has developed apace over the last one hundred and fifty years, dominating more and more aspects of human existence.

A whole new world has developed, marked by machines, instruments, experiments, measurability, functionality and abstraction. This world is dominated by technology, science and industry, and imposes its stamp upon the structures of society and upon man's sense of his own identity.

Whereas for millennia men have projected their self-image, which they derived from their parents, from the father's role in the world, his purposes and his activities, and from their own idealised, narcissistic fantasies of power and grandeur, into the heavens as an omnipotent God, and then derived their own sense of identity from him, men have now lost their God, he disappeared from the heavens, and a new mechanical system, a machine-like apparatus is seen to govern the world and men's fate.

The God of the Jews, the first monotheistic God, was an idealisation of the agriculturalist. He represented the creator and producer of sustenance, He made the earth give forth plenitude by imposing His skill and will-power upon her, and she responded to His labours. The monotheistic God is the sole creator and maker of *all* things, he is the omnipotent farmer-craftsman, the child's image of the father who dominates the world and makes things according to his purpose. So, God laboured for six days and made everything there is, brought forth life, made order out of chaos and tried to instruct His children in His wisdom and skill. The human being, on the other hand, who invented machines and computers and then found himself dependent on them, sees them in his pre-conscious mind as all-powerful beings, he projects them on to the canvas of his imagery as omnipotent rulers of the world and then attempts to identify with them. And the philosophers and scientists become the theologians of the new deity, the priests and prophets of its glory and power, and they enjoin men to walk with their new God, so that He will bestow His blessings upon them.

This priestly establishment of scientist and 'scientific' philosophers preach the machine-like nature of man, and they fill our intellectual horizon with imaginings of our perfectability as machines. But they not only show us how to fulfil our mechanical potentials (through behavioural engineering, genetic engineering, brain engineering), but also how to reproduce the human intelligence in artificial thinking machines which would be a great improvement over the human machine.

'Man is a machine', declares B. F. Skinner, Professor of Psychology at Harvard, 'but he is a very complex one. At present he is far beyond the powers of man to construct, except of course in the usual biological way'. But he points out that the problems of simulation are strictly 'technical'. It is accepted for the time being that man as a machine still reigns supreme. When one examines the balance sheet, it is apparent that man's advantages still outweigh his disadvantages, but there are important entries on both sides of the ledger. Among the pluses, as delineated by General Electric's G. L. Haller, we find that:

1   Man can repair himself, physically and mentally, consciously and unconsciously.
2   He can programme himself.
3   He can adapt his programme to unexpected information.
4   His memory capacity is many orders of magnitude greater than that of other computers.

5 His logical sophistication is many orders of magnitude greater than that of other computers.

However, there are a good many scientists who believe it is only a matter of time until man is eclipsed in each of these five areas. Meanwhile, Dr. Haller points out, man is already at a disadvantage (when compared to electronic computers) in the following respects:

1 Man is subject to fatigue and distraction.
2 He requires motivation.
3 His access to his memory is unreliable.
4 His logical processes are slow and notoriously unreliable.
5 He is unable to reproduce on demand most of the logical steps in his processing of information, because he is unaware of them.
6 His read-in/read-out processes are several orders of magnitude slower than his logical processes.
7 His input and output devices (specifically language, the most important) are inexact, and therefore subject to misinterpretation.

During the next forty years or so, Dr. Haller expects to see computers evolve through the following succession of capabilities:

1 Produce readable translations of technical literature.
2 Translate ordinary newspaper prose into colloquial prose of the target language.
3 Translate literature of a high aesthetic content, with a skill comparable to that of a competent linguist.
4 Manipulate logical concepts, using symbolic logic.

Beyond the next forty years, maintains Dr. Haller, computing machines may advance to two further stages of development: learning to investigate properties of alternative logics, such as Aristotelian logic, many-valued logic, probabilistic logic and Hegelian logic, and to carry on a conversation with a human being (perhaps through neuron taps or analysis of brain waves) and analyse his conceptual framework and his method of thought.

In the process of all this, man the machine may learn to improve his own effectiveness, learning to 'talk like machines quite as much as machines learn to talk like people'. Thus, says Dr. Haller, in forty or fifty years Juliet may say of Romeo, 'Delta symbol not imply delta referent attribute end'. By the time this occurs there will exist an increasingly close relationship between man and other intelligent machines. The distinction between 'me' and 'my computer', will be difficult to make, but the scientist will then think more precisely and be much more aware of this thought process, because by then his computer will have begun to analyse his thinking for him.*

In the view of some of these scientists man will submit and accommodate himself to the intelligent machine almost as an act of love. Man will abandon part of his old identity so that he can be forged anew, fashioned in such a way that he can be welded to machines that amplify his senses, extend his grasp, deepen his understanding of himself and his world. *Together* man and machine become something more than either could ever have been alone, an entirely new order of life, a cybernetic organism.**

While many of the pronouncements made during the 1960s and 1970s regarding the potentials of the computer had a somewhat hysterical quality, a mixture of religious vision and the advertiser's exaggeration, such declarations have become more measured in tone, more restrained and sophisticated. To some extent this is due to the very successes of the new technology. Some of the prognostications of the 1960s have indeed been fulfilled; the new computer technology is taking possession of industry, commerce and finance, and is beginning to invade people's homes. People, and in particular, young people, are increasingly familiar with its technological terms, its language, and its capabilities; it is accepted as a commonplace phenomenon in practical life.

We are beginning to take this thinking machine for granted. Indeed, the advertisers already emphasise that the human being *also* has a role to play in production and in entertainment. A recent advertisement for a hi-fi system complains that "their machinery does everything to bring perfect music into the home but cannot actually choose the music" (not yet, we presume).

One cannot but feel a sense of astonishment at the speed in which this transformation of industry and life in general, the transform-

---

* David Rorvik: 'As Man becomes Machine' (Souvenir Press, 1973).
** Ibid.

ation from a civilisation based on farmer and craftsman to large-scale mechanisation and computerisation of society, has taken place. The suddenness of this transformation and its traumatic impact on civilisation can perhaps be compared to the emergence of Cro-Magnon man in Europe and the agricultural revolution at the end of the ice-ages. However, we must see this current revolution of technology, and its profound impact on human life, as merely the most advanced and most recent manifestation of a process that has occurred over the last two centuries and was, indeed, foreshadowed by Descartes.

The idea that life has the attributes of a machine reflects man's desire to understand, manipulate and control and ultimately to create his environment. Man, the creator cannot rest until he feels he can acquire for himself the capabilities of the supreme creator, and this means in the long run that he can by his own knowledge and power create himself. To understand a system as a machine is to be able to create it. Having dispensed with the image of God as the supreme creator, man wants to take his place.

However, conceiving the mind as a machine, i.e. as a system of material substances governed by the laws which operate in the physical world, primarily the laws of mechanics, has encountered formidable difficulties. Descartes made a fundamental distinction between mind and matter when he stated that mind is characterised essentially by thought but lacking extension, while the physical world is characterised by extension. This distinction made the two domains conceptually incommensurable, with no common ground for explaining their mutual influence. This impasse led Descartes to postulate two separate existences: body and mind. It is said that he spent some seven years at Leyden dissecting brains and eyes. He was convinced that the human body was a machine and could be understood completely through physical laws. This applied also to the brain, except that it was inhabited by a non-material entity, the soul.

The materialist school which succeeded Descartes, particularly in France during the eighteenth century, but continued to develop right through to the present, came to reject this dualism and any need for a spiritual entity, considering it as mere metaphysical fantasy. Gilbert Ryle, the late Oxford philosopher, called Descartes' concept of the soul derisively 'the ghost in the machine' or 'the horse in the locomotive'. According to the materialist-mechanistic school, all phenomena such as sensations, emotions, volitions, imagination and valuation will in time be identified with specific physical processes in the brain. This school is best characterised by the following statement by the neuro-physiologist, J. Z. Young: 'Consider that without leaving the topic of the brain, we can at least begin to discuss many, perhaps all, human activities. The method I am going to suggest as a working basis is to organise all our talk about human powers and capacities around knowledge of what the brain does. When the philosopher studies the way in which people think, let him consider what activity this represents in the brain. For certainly there is some. When the theologian studies the fact that human beings tend to organise their activities around statements about gods, let him consider the activity that this involves in the brain...'*

The structure of the brain and the physical processes we can observe in it are the subject matter of neuro-anatomy and neuro-physiology. These studies have been immensely successful in recent years but they have been very slow in shedding light on the question of the brain's relationship to the mind. The problem cannot even be discussed without using words or phrases that offend one school of thought or another. This has led the mechanistic-empirical school to proclaim that the problem does not even exist, and that the mind is a concept which has no room in scientific thought.

The brain is generally viewed by neuro-physiologists as a very complicated and delicate machine whose functioning they are trying to understand. The human brain is approximately three pounds in weight of living tissue (anything between 1,100–1,600 grammes), consisting of blood vessels, some membranous linings, some fluid-filled cavities, and many billions of specialised cells, the most important of which are about ten thousand million neurons. These form a communication network of unmatched complexity. Apart from overseeing and controlling all vital processes in our bodies, the brain is the unique organiser that imposes a *oneness* on the various parts of the body. It is the originator and the repository of *selfhood*. It alone can make the distinction between that which is part of *me* and the rest of the world. Curiously, "it has no sensation of its own existence. I never see my own brain, it makes no noises

---

* J. Z. Young: 'Doubt and Certainty in Science: A Biologist's Reflection on the Brain' (Oxford, 1960).

like my stomach, I can't feel its functioning like the pulse beat of my heart, I can't even squeeze it, pinch it, palpate it. It is the most hidden and unobtrusive part of my body. It never hurts; a surgeon's knife could slice through it without causing any discomfort. Yet it is fiercely protective of that which it defines as its own".*

Is mind then an aspect, a function of the physical brain, even while no person can feel or investigate his own brain? Erich Harth concedes that this seems almost to be an inevitable conclusion but that it does not fully satisfy our intellect. Mind is like no other property of physical systems. It is not only that we do not know enough about the mechanism that creates and produces mind, we have difficulty in seeing how *any* mechanism can give rise to it. This is in short the problem Schopenhauer has called 'the world knot'.

This does not, however, deter many empiricists from continuing to uphold their conviction that the material structure of the brain is responsible for the attributes and qualities which are collectively called the mind.

In the middle of the nineteenth century the Austrian physicist Boltzmann expressed his conviction in the following way: 'Only when one admits that spirit and will are not something over and above the body, but rather complicated sections of material parts whose ability so to act becomes increasingly perfected by development, only when one admits that intuition, will and self-consciousness are merely the highest stages of development of these physical-chemical forces of matter by which primeval protoplasmic bubbles were able to seek regions that were more, and avoid those that were less favourable for them, only then does everything become clear in psychology'. This became something of a credo for the materialistic approach to the mind, and a century later Jacques Monod stated it simply and categorically: 'The cell is a machine, the animal is a machine, man is a machine'.

Let me quote from an exposition of the brain as a machine, typical of the brash self-confidence of the 1960s. I take the following extract from an essay by Percival Bailey, published in 1962: 'If we look at the cerebral cortex as a machine, the apparent conflict between psyche and soma begins to evaporate. A machine may function badly because it was constructed from inferior

---

* Erich Harth: 'Windows on the Mind: Reflections on the Physical Basis of Consciousness' (The Harvester Press, 1982).

materials, because of water in the gasoline, because of rusting from being left out in the weather, because of long, hard usage or merely from over-loading. In the same way a nervous system may function badly because of hereditary or congenital defect, because of improper food supply, because of being soaked in alcohol, because of constant wear from interminable conflict, or because of a single overwhelming crisis. It is futile to talk of the effect of the mind on the body. 'Thought' is a name we give to the functioning of our thinking-machine (cortex), just as 'flight' is a name we give to the functioning of flying machines (airplanes); the plane is worn out during flight, but not by flight; it is worn out by friction of the air, of the crankshafts, by buffeting from wind and weather. Our cerebral cortex is worn out also by the buffeting of the environment, both internal and external that gives rise to thought and, if too severe, causes it to knock or chatter in its functioning, which we call the mind.

'It is conceivable that it might be possible to build a machine that would have insight, or could be given insight, into its own malfunctioning and take certain measures to correct it. Perhaps this will have to wait until our insight into our own difficulties is less rudimentary. Even so, the machine would have to find ways that avoid the necessity to replace a defective part, just as we are unable to replace cortical neurons destroyed by toxins or senile decay; no psychotherapist can do it for us, and God will not. But the machine can be built to recognise obstacles and avoid them instead of wearing itself out against them. And the mechanic can, by increasing the gain, make it see obstacles that it previously did not recognise'.*

Just what is meant by machine is not always clear, but reference is usually made to whatever man-made contraption is the most sophisticated of its time, embodying the latest advances in science and technology. Today this honour must go to the electronic computer. The mathematician, Norbert Wiener, who was very much involved in the computer revolution, defined a machine as 'a device for converting incoming messages into outgoing messages'. He pioneered cybernetics, conceived as a symbiosis between man and machine in an integrated information system.

---

* Percival Bailey: 'Cortex and Mind', from 'Theories of the Mind'. (The Free Press, New York, 1962).

Information is the speciality of our age. It saturates the air. It bounces back from the most distant planets. It is stored in memory banks just in case some of it may be needed some day, when it can be retrieved with the push of a button and spelt out on a fast printer. Micro-electronic information systems provide employee data, consumer data, sales data; they serve pay-rolls, job costs, time billing, inventory and many other types of ready information for business, offices and factories, as well as for homes and for amusement. It may be said that all this is very useful, but it is a different matter when its advocates claim to have reproduced, and in many instances, improved on the human brain with these machine operations. It is a disturbing state of affairs if the very core of one's being, one's intellect and one's mind parades as a separate entity outside one's self as a machine that claims to do one's thinking for one, making one's own thought inferior or even irrelevant.

There is already a widespread fear that man's reasoning powers and his judgements, being made redundant, would atrophy and we would be reduced to being mindless robots, slaves to the superior brain machines which would then rule the world.

Unlike the advocates of the materialistic-mechanistic concepts of intelligence, scientists engaged in cybernetic and computer systems are more clearly aware of the limitations of a purely materialistic approach to the mind and tend to ridicule the claims that the subjective factor plays no part in human behaviour.

In his book on cybernetics Professor Kenneth M. Sayre writes: 'We have to choose between the materialists' thesis that subjective states are inessential to our understanding of human behaviour and the opposing thesis that subjectivity properly understood is essential to any adequate amount of human activity. Our evidence for the latter is surely more impressive. Arguments for the materialists' position are generally limited to rebuttals of opposing viewpoints, for the position enjoys little evidence of an empirical nature. In favour of the claim that subjective awareness plays a major role in guiding human behaviour, on the other hand, we have not only the emphatic testimony of commonsense but also evidence in the biological origins of human consciousness. If subjective awareness plays no part in the guidance of human behaviour, it would secure no advantages for organisms possessing it and hence find no favour in natural selection. To the contrary, however, the emergence of subjective awareness in the form of perception, and thought especially, surely was a major juncture in the development of the human species and the major factor in its achievement of biological dominance. Hence it is a reasonable supposition that factors are present in the guidance of human behaviour which we can understand only with reference to subjective states'.*

Cyberneticists believe that a communication technology can be constructed which would greatly improve man's productive capacity and his absorption of knowledge. 'In the cybernetic theory of man, the procedures by which the human organism operates may be understood as a set of statistical structures. Consciousness in particular is a mode of information processing and as such is describable in terms of communication theory. However formidable the task might be in practice, the informational structure of consciousness might be exhibited as notations on paper, as functions across a transmitting line or in any other fashion available for the representation of mathematical relationships. There is no necessity that this means of representation is dependent upon material structures'.**

There is no doubting the success of this concept in its own terms as we can see in the explosive proliferation of computerised information and programming systems and their application to an ever wider field. However, while the theory and practice of artificial information systems does not depend on the limitations of a materialistic concept of intelligence, and indeed comes closer to a correct replication of brain functions, it is nevertheless highly reductionistic and a gross simplification of mental and intellectual processes. While information technology can send out agreed symbols of information by means of electronic circuitry, these signals have to be processed into words and numbers which again have to be processed by the human mind into percepts, concepts and ideas. And these in turn serve to provide the information which men find useful within a collectively held consensus regarding a certain interest or purpose, be it an intellectual enquiry, a business interest or any other purpose of practical or amusement value. These frameworks of purpose are established by human minds and

---

* Kenneth M. Sayre: 'Cybernetics and the Philosophy of Mind' (Routledge & Kegan Paul, London, 1976).
** Ibid.

the symbols provided by the computer are interpreted according to their agreed meanings. Thus it is the human mind which programmes the computer input according to preconceived interests and agreed symbols, whose meanings in turn have to be reinterpreted in the output process and converted into meaningful information.

Besides, we are beginning to find that the rather grandiose expectations of computerised information for business, industry, for health programmes and education, show profound limitations and are often counter-productive, i.e. they frequently defeat the very purpose which they set out to serve. But above all what interests us here is the impact of all these artificial systems of intelligence and information upon the psyche of man and his social relationships. For there is no doubt that 'thinking' machines masquerade as an embodiment of the human intellect, an externalisation of his invisible brain, and perform at least some of the functions which man has always considered to be the most intimate and subjective of all, namely, those of his own mind.

The core of the narcissistic Ego is made into an object that confronts man as an external power. This is not an entirely new event. We have seen that man has always had the capacity and disposition to externalise his motor organs into tools, his images into objects, to the point where he projected his narcissistic self, his ideal personality, into an external object and made it omnipotent as a God. Man has placed his most intimate desires and fantasies upon heavenly beings and then attempted by means of ritual and prayer to regain the powers of these externalised beings. The prophets and priests who serve this process of projection and introjection have now become engineers, neuro-physicists, behavioural engineers and computer technologists; they are serving a new god.

We are now in the process of projecting our humanity, our narcissistic self-image, our dreams for power, our fantasies of omnipotence and omniscience upon this new technology. But as we project our aspirations onto these machines and dream of their omnipotence we become dependent on them. We allow them to absorb and devour our faculties in a new form of worship, so that we may partake in their magic. Already children are being made to rely on calculators to do their sums, to depend on the word-processors for writing, and are increasingly prevented from developing their own numeracy and literacy. Shopkeepers are becoming lost without a calculator, designers have to handle computers in order to carry out design-projects, workers depend on automated transfer-machines and computerised robots which dictate their work activity and take from them the skills of the craftsman.

It is hardly an exaggeration to say that computer-orientated education systems deprive children of a wide range of intellectual stimulations, reduce their effort-making ability and curiosity outside the limited range of automated learning processes. Mature people are reduced to having to imitate robots who control their work and to become themselves robots. The stimulation and excitement of work which comes from the exercise of skill, involving a measure of risk and uncertainty in every act of production and thus provides the stimulus of a sense of adventure, is lost in the necessity and determination of computerised command. The sheer monotony and pressure of the modern assembly line creates not only considerable boredom but often acute mental stress. Employees in business, bank and civil service offices are subjected to the same regimentation, and while a few computer engineers and designers find all this very interesting as well as profitable, employees who can no longer exercise their initiative and skills, which often involve personal relationships with other staff, with partners and directors, find the new system dehumanising and often difficult to bear.

While however the life of working people becomes monotonous and meaningless, the life of the machine becomes increasingly exciting. It lives our lives and has the world for its stage on which it can enact all the adventures denied to men.

Besides the benign purposes which the computerised machines are meant to serve with more or less success, as in education, medicine, psychology, public administration and a whole host of public services apart from industry and commerce, they also serve destructive purposes.

Already nations measure their power by the machines of destruction they possess: computer controlled aeroplanes with nuclear capability, ballistic missiles with independently controlled multiple nuclear warheads and missile defence systems, computerised target finding systems of mass-destruction, continental and intercontinental rockets—land based, submarine based, aircraft based— and a vast range of computer guided weaponry dominate the arsenals of nations. It is the possession of such machines which determines the standing and self-confidence of nation states in the planetary battle for supremacy.

The aeroplanes and satellites traverse countries in minutes, and continents in half-an-hour, they span the planet and it lies prostrate before them. The awesome and terrible power of these machines, those mad and unrestrained external organs of men, can tear continents apart, destroy the planet and its biosphere, making it into a graveyard to satisfy the destructive fury which resides not in the machines but in man's mind. The machine is but an instrument of the human neurosis, it enhances man's destructive obsession a millionfold, till it seems to have no limit, reaching out to the universe. Men have split their madness off from themselves and projected it onto the machine and see themselves merely as its innocent victims. It is of course true that men are victims of their unconscious, which is the secret stage manager of reality and determines our destiny, and it is equally true that these machines represent our unconscious fantasies of power and grandeur and increasingly dominate our lives.

We face these machines with a fearful ambiguity: on the one hand they provide us with a sense of great satisfaction and on the other hand they confront us with a danger that has no parallel in the history of mankind. It is not merely their unbounded destructive capability but their capacity to make their own decisions that gives them their awesome power. We are trapped by their logic; they follow their own rules and we seem obliged to submit to them.

The human person, the representative of the gods, endowed with intelligence, foresight, purpose-direction and imagination, the king of creation, the consort and protector of the earth, is abdicating and is about to relinquish his power and his mind to the machines he has made.

The new machines' claim to intellectual superiority further undermines patriarchal man's self-confidence, already shattered by two world wars of unprecedented bestiality, traumatic betrayals of social ideals, continued wars, tyranny and injustice in many parts of the world and unredeemable poverty among the majority of the world's population. Modern man's sense of helplessness in face of perpetual crises inclines him to glorify the machine as a harbinger of a new civilisation. Where men have failed to fulfil the obligations of civilisation they are disposed to let the machine take over. But we must remind ourselves that on the intellectual level the new gods represent a throw-back to the levels of reasoning that are analogous to that of a small child. Both intellectually as well as spiritually they are a regression to infantilism.

It would indeed be generous to accredit to computers a level of reasoning that corresponds to a child of about three or four years of age, although on that level they can think extremely quickly and their memory is prodigious. They can remember information fed into them with quite phenomenal speed, but their logic and their 'thought' processes are strictly limited. Alan Cohen, a computer consultant and systems designer, puts it this way: 'The computer:

* 'reads' input data from the outside world
* 'stores' and 'manipulates' data
* 'writes' output data to the outside world
* makes use of reference or permanent data

All data used, and the rules for manipulating it, are described to the computer in a machine-understandable form known as a program. The rules must always be complete and unambiguous. The range of computer-based applications is restricted as follows:

* all quantitative data read and written must be calibrated
* the manipulative rules must be expressible as arithmetic operations and/or binary (yes or no) decisions
* information stored must be classified and filed in a form known to the computer

Modern systems can be very powerful. As a consequence:

* numeric quantities can be held to great degrees of accuracy
* the manipulative rules can become long and complex
* new filing and different access methods can be devised

The quantity of data used and speed of manipulation lead to talk of computers 'thinking'. By varying the type of data used and the nature of the manipulations computers can be applied to new and varied tasks such as:

* colour and three-dimensional graphics, where the gradations of information processed become very fine

* education, where a discursive subject is codified so that the computer can treat it as data
* medical diagnosis, where the diagnostic rules become data itself subject to other manipulative rules

If we recall the basics noted above then even in these new areas it remains true that:

* the computer models some aspect of natural human endeavour
* all data used is codified and measured
* all rules used are deductive and logical in a mathematical sense

Correspondingly there is no room for

* judgment and opinion
* inductive or intuitive reasoning
* abstractions

except insofar as even these have been codified and measured. There is apparently no foreseeable limit to these developments. We can even make computers learn provided we give them the rules of learning. We can always find new applications by codifying more aspects of human activity. But the 'thinking' is always in terms of fixed mathematical-type rules using quantifiable and codified data".* To this we may add that their thinking lacks the psycho-biological motivations, the libidinous drives and conflicts which in human beings generate myths, ideas, beliefs and purposes, the metaphysical foundations of rationality.

The view therefore that the computing machine replicates human reasoning processes is not only misleading but it narrows man's intellectual self-image, squeezes it so to speak into the confines and limitations which characterise even the most advanced computer technology. It sets up the machine, the logic of the engineer and the logic of computer information systems as the supreme judge, the critical standard by which the reasoning of man is to be evaluated. If we allow ourselves to be persuaded—and the high priests of technology are pressuring us to do so—that the computer is a valid

---

* From a private communication to the author.
Also: Alan Cohen: 'Structure, Logic and Program Design' (John Wiley & Sons, 1983).

and superior model of reasoning, then we shall be inclined to imitate its functions and to apply them to all kinds of human activities, and without quite realising what is happening we shall regard those aspects of the human mind, which the computer does not and cannot replicate, as irrelevant; indeed, we shall feel obliged to repress our awareness of the mind and to deny its existence. Wherever we look nowadays, in education, medicine, psychology and social studies, even in philosophy, scientific sounding, statistical-mathematical-quantitative methods are being upheld.

In an age obsessed with machine and cybernetic communication theory it is not surprising that words are proclaimed as being nothing more than signs and symbols and philosophers are determined to strip language of its traditional meaning. Having dispensed with the concept of mind, considering it as a kind of antiquated myth of a pre-scientific age, the modernists had to find new ways of explaining thought, language and communication. Semiotics, semiology, hermeneutics and structuralist theory parade as the new sciences of communication, agonisingly shedding the 'antiquated' notions of mind, ideas and cultural imagery from human discourse.

Students of the psycho-social sciences, philosophy and literature have to perceive them through the mist of this new scholasticism, their observations muddled by technicalities which attempt to eliminate the innate understanding and feeling for language. However, human discourse cannot be reduced to a system of information by means of notation or signs, for communication embraces mental activity on a much wider scale. Communication always involves values and value judgments, religious concepts, ideals and beliefs as well as philosophical and social ideas; it includes feelings, a groping for things not yet understood and ideas for which we have not yet found words, and a thousand notions upheld by a culture, the conflicts within a culture and between cultures. Even theories which are the product of our rationality are outcrops of a culture myth and, in turn, frequently express a critique of that myth.

It is surprising that these things have to be said nowadays, for they ought to be tacitly understood and taken for granted. But our priests preach the gospel of reductionism in order to convert us to the religion of the machine and to forget our minds; they are concerned with exactitude and predictability, and they view the thoughts of men, swayed as they are by all kinds of emotions, prejudices and uncertain gropings, with grave misgivings. They want to impose the parameters of engineering and industrial efficiency upon the relationships of men, they see society as a machine and men as an integral part of it, subject to its rules. As Jacques Ellul has written:

> Technique requires predictability and, no less, exactness of prediction. It is necessary, then, that technique prevail over the human being. For technique this is a matter of life and death. Technique must reduce man to a technical animal, the king of the slaves of technique. Human caprice crumbles before this necessity; there can be no human autonomy in the face of technical autonomy. The individual must be fashioned by techniques, either negatively (by the techniques of understanding man), or positively (by the adaptation of man to the technical framework), in order to wipe out the blots his personal determination introduces into the perfect design of the organisation.*

The direction of human activities, whether they be political, economic or cultural, can no longer be left to the intuition or feelings of individuals but demand the attention of specially trained experts. Around this central core of experts who deal with large-scale social requirements, there grows up a circle of subsidiary experts who, battening on the general social prestige of technical skill, assume authoritative influence over even the most personal aspects of life such as sexual behaviour, child rearing, mental health, nutrition as well as caring for the handicapped and deprived. The parameters of engineering govern all these fields of human activity as in technocratic society everything aspires to become purely technical, the subject of expert attention.**

I have called the technocrats high priests of the machine culture of technocracy. We can define technocracy as that society in which those who govern justify themselves by appeal to technical experts who in turn justify themselves by appeal to scientific forms of knowledge. And beyond the authority of science, there is no appeal.

The technocrats are then the representatives of the new Super-ego, represented as a machine, and its rules and its logic are

---

* Jacques Ellul: 'The Technological Society' (A. A. Knopf, 1964).
** Theodore Roszak: 'The Making of a Counter Culture' (Faber & Faber, 1970).

perceived as the supreme guide for correct reasoning and behaviour.

We may say to an individual or to a culture: "Tell me who your God is and I will tell you who you are". From the nature of its God we can discern the character of a culture, but what are we to make of a culture whose God is the machine?

The 'new intellectuals' of the seventeenth and eighteenth centuries were fired by the ideals of the Enlightenment and being liberated at last from the 'ancient repressor' felt free to expand their rational faculties and to explore the universe. The age of science was born and its protagonists were determined to enhance the status of humanity and free it from its traditions of subservience to authority and the weight of poverty. The notions of democracy and man's right to self-determination encouraged the intellectuals to explore to the full the spiritual and material potentials of humanity. Having rid themselves (though not humanity) from the rule of the father-God, the brotherhood felt free at last to relate to mother nature, to explore and worship her and to make her fruitful.

But soon the democratic ideals upheld by this band of brothers, the inheritors of the Enlightenment, were made to serve the interests of the rising elite, the industrial barons and capitalists and, more recently, the centralised bureaucracies of the state. While they jealously guarded the principles of the Enlightenment and their freedom of thought and exploration, they were compelled to serve those who employed them and could not afford to take too much notice for what purposes their activities were used. Occasionally they protested against the misuse of their ideas and achievements—they protested against the iniquities and cruelties of the capitalist as well as communist systems—they protested against the use of science for the purposes of mass destruction in war and they raised their voices against the horrors of nuclear holocaust. But these protests were of little avail. The exploitation of science and technology by capitalists and state bureaucrats continues. They serve increasingly primitive and irrational goals, and the machine itself, despite its ever growing powers, has become a symbol of primitive, infantile satisfactions, the embodiment of man's retreat from reason and from the ideals of freedom. Guilt made its appearance and a remorse for the murder of God. The God had to be worshipped anew, and he returned as the machine.

The Ego of man has once again lost its nerve and no longer trusts its rational and moral faculties. But when the Ego feels discouraged and is unsure of itself it regresses to obsessive rituals and to pre-rational attitudes of mind. We may say that the collective Ego of Western civilisation has become unsure of itself since the defeat of the Enlightenment; Scientific activities have become increasingly obsessional; they are preoccupied with efficiency, quantitative exactitude and correctness. There is preoccupation with means rather than ends, refusal to think an idea through to its conclusion. The predominance of instrumental reasoning that regards itself as a means only for a purpose imposed from outside has become the hallmark of Western science. In personal and particularly political communication slogans take the place of ideas and reasoning is devoted to tactical manipulation whose purposes are left unexamined. Indeed, such human activities as purpose conceptions are lost behind the authority of facts and the dominance of given conditions (states of affairs) which the contemporary intellectual has to follow without too much questioning.

The capacity of the mind to extend itself in time and space, by which it sees the present in relationship to the past and judges it from the point of view of the future, has succumbed to an obsession with the immediately given. The time-space of consciousness is confined to a narrow circle of immediate preoccupations coupled with an inability to see their wider meanings or consequences.

If we enquire into the psycho-biological roots of these phenomena of modernism then we find that they are due to a predominance of tensions, a narcissistic tightening of the periphery in order to compensate for a sense of isolation and estrangement. Thus a culture which has lost the love and protection of its divine parent surrogates, its God or its ideals, will adopt tight, pedantic, narrow types of thinking. It will be mistrustful and closed to a factual, delibinised, unfeeling world, and avoid intuitive or spontaneous ideas; it will not trust its impulses as it does not trust the responses from a world which is bereft of a loving and responsive spirit. The world of facts has no feelings towards the modern intellectual, so he must be careful in his dealings with the universe and not manifest any emotions towards it. (This does not apply to the greatest scientists, who have retained their love for nature and trust their feelings and hunches to guide them in their quest for discovery. Einstein never tired of saying that in order to make real

discoveries one must have a feeling for the truth and an apprecia-
tion of its aesthetic qualities).

The dominance of 'the hard-nosed' among the psychologists has
had most unfortunate consequences on their science. Their discipline has failed to produce a coherent body of laws, and their fruits
are as trivial and dry as the scientists who have grown them. Their
attempts to justify psychological research in terms of its social
utility have an air of bathos and appear increasingly pathetic in
view of the triviality of its contributions: eleven-plus examination,
I.Q. tests, motivational research for advertising, statistical evaluation of opinion polls, etc. One might as well, as Liam Hudson has
remarked, try to justify space exploration in terms of its technological spin-off, the non-stick frying pan!

This pedantic and churlish attitude towards scientific enquiry has
been particularly noticeable among philosophers of recent times.
Individuals like Wittgenstein, Gilbert Ryle, Feigl, Reichenbach and
J. L. Austin among others have imposed a narrow and pedantic
attitude upon the whole philosophical enterprise. J. L. Austin has
exemplified this tendency very clearly. To quote from one of his
lectures: "What we have above all to do is, negatively, to rid
ourselves of such illusions as 'the argument from illusion', an
argument which those (e.g. Berkeley, Hume, Ayer) who have been
most adept at working at it, most fully masters of certain special,
happy style of blinkering philosophical English, have all themselves
felt to be somehow spurious. There is no simple way of doing
this—partly because, as we shall see, there is no simple 'argument'.
It is a matter of unpicking one by one a mass of seductive (mainly
verbal) fallacies, of exposing a wide variety of concealed
motives—an operation which leaves us, in a sense, just where we
began".*

Although I do not wish to elaborate on this here, Wittgenstein is
also a case in point. He had become estranged from his father and
his background, isolated himself and developed a sense of acute
mistrust towards the world at large to the point of paranoid
tendencies. He had strong homosexual leanings, suffered acutely
from this 'horrid pathology' and was very ashamed of it. He
mistrusted his emotions as he mistrusted the world; he was highly

---

* J. L. Austin: 'Sense and Sensibilia' (Reconstructed from the Manuscript Notes by
G. J. Warnock, O.U.P, 1962).

repressive towards himself. He sublimated his acute repressions in an unceasing effort to cut out emotivistic values from cognition and to create a philosophical framework which would guarantee their exclusions from rational thought.

I shall give more space to illustrate the tight pedantry which dominates much of contemporary philosophy in my book 'The Crisis of Morality'. Let it just be said here that the results of the philosophy are even less productive than those of the hard-nosed psychologists in their respective fields, and the public has long ago become disenchanted and bored by philosophy as a whole. Generous young minds, who had turned to the psychologists or philosophers to find new insights and an enlargement of their understanding, had their hopes mutilated by these intellectual negators with their mean and destructive type of reasoning.

But when people are made to doubt the validity of their rational and moral faculties and their exercise is inhibited by the all too narrow criteria of what modernism regards as permissible forms of cognition, when thinkers are made to mistrust their own minds and can no longer take pleasure in its activities, then the libido is withdrawn from it and regresses to more primitive primacies. But as the intellectual faculties, are a manifestation of the Ego functions, their inhibition is felt as an inhibition, as a negation of the Ego. The personality as a whole, and man's self-image, will feel under attack, and it will not only submit helplessly to external conditions but it will also succumb to primitive impulses from within.

Thus when cultural influences reduce the power and integrity of the Ego, when a cultural Superego denies and represses the free experience of the Ego functions and generates a feeling of mistrust for them, then a spiritual and psychological process of disintegration occurs leading to regressive developments.

We have seen how the Ego depends upon the Superego for guidance and for a sense of identity. For millennia and, indeed, all through history, human beings have produced cults and religions to acquire a sense of identity which instinct does not provide. This spiritual need in man, unique among animals, is now in danger of being denied, and men have difficulty in perceiving the world around them in a co-ordinated and meaningful image. Under such conditions the process of regression to primitive primacies develops apace, a psychic disintegration, which shows signs of acquiring the characteristics of a collective psychosis. There are many signs that the perceptions of our culture are swamped by infantile modes of thought, and there are few signposts of sanity by which we can judge them. Reason has great difficulty in differentiating between what is infantile and what is mature, what is rational and what is irrational, what is true and what is false, or what is good and what is bad. These developments of disintegration of the perceptual universe and loss of the human self-image are most clearly reflected in the arts.

13 Aspects of Cultural Regression

It might be presumptuous of a psychoanalyst to think that he can capture the meaning of art in the net of his rational categories and explain it either to himself or anyone else, for does not the artistic act of creation represent the deepest and most perplexing aspects of what is indefinable in the mind and what is concrete at the same time, its never-ending quest to give concrete expression to the mysterious? Yet we might think that art cannot be much more puzzling than dreams, and these have yielded at least something to our enquiries. We analysed dreams, the language of psychotics which is the language of dreams, and a wide variety of bizarre symptoms of mind and body. Moreover, in our journey through the landscape of the mind, as it has unfolded through man's evolution, we have constantly encountered works of art, we have studied them as signposts in the evolution of cultures and gained some insight into the mind of our ancestors. And indeed art has been and continues to be the chief cult of cultures, the outer reflection of man's inner imagery, of his desires and fears, his dreams and nightmares, the dream world of man become manifest in material form.

Through art we recreate the image of the ancestor with whom we need to identify in order to gain his strength and protection, we restore the spirit of the slain god and make him eternal in stone or paint. But the art object is also the externalised self-image, the pre-conscious perception of the self projected upon a canvas or stone, the mirror of Narcissus, the act of self-recognition, a statement of a person's perception of the world, of his judgments and values.

But now we are in the world of machines, the scientist's concept of reality, a world of microwaves, molecules, elementary particles and wave particles, quantum mechanics and relativity physics.

The High Priests of telescopes and cyclotrons
keep making pronouncements about happenings
on scales too gigantic or dwarfish
to be noticed by our native senses.

discoveries which, couched in the elegant
euphemisms of algebra, look innocent,
harmless enough but, when translated
into the vulgar anthropomorphic

tongue, will give no cause for hilarity
to gardeners or house-wives: if galaxies
bolt like panicking mobs, if mesons
riot like fish in a feeding frenzy,

it sounds too like Political History
to boost civil morale, too symbolic of
the crimes and strikes and demonstrations
we are supposed to gloat on at breakfast.

How trite, though, our fears beside the miracle
that we're here to shiver, that a Thingummy
so addicted to lethal violence
should have somehow secreted a placid

tump with exactly the right ingredients
to start and cocker Life, that heavenly
freak for whose manage we shall have to
give account at the Judgment, our Middle-

Earth, where Sun-Father to all appearances
moves by day from orient to occident
and his light is felt as a friendly
presence not a photonic bombardment...

                          W. H. Auden: 'Ode to Terminus'

Just as the machines of the nineteenth century and factory mass production had undermined the native rhythms of work and blurred man's self-image as a producer, so the new concepts of physics have undermined the native perceptions of reality. When the scientists began to discover that matter is not what it appears to be, that the seemingly solid forms we have perceived as reality had to be interpreted in terms of waves, particles and energy fields, then our very perception of reality came under question.

In Renaissance painting objects are solid entities immersed in a neutral Newtonian space. The individuality of things is respected even when misgivings and apparent blurrings are resorted to. Indeed, as Professor Gombrich remarks: 'Leonardo achieved his most remarkable feats of life-likeness by blurring just those which are most obviously life-like and so forcing us to notice them. Drawing becomes the most supreme means of material delineation and emphasis and the world-view of an entire age is shown in the emphasis placed on its importance. In painting, the step by step build up, the juxtaposition of paint, the enhancement of natural structure and the texture of brushwork induce a strong feeling of externality'.

However, the solid entities which dominate our perceptual reality and which therefore have been the subject matter of art can no longer be taken for granted and they have lost their place in artistic enterprises. Moreover, while natural and human images were traditionally used to illustrate mythological and religious themes, they can no longer serve in this way; the anthropomorphic representations of the world are being destroyed by the concepts of modern science, and they have disappeared from the images of art. As Alain Jouffroy has stated: 'We are no longer concerned with a myth or with an idealistic conception of man and the universe but with a materialisation of the presence of invisible energy'.

Wassily Kandinsky, the founder of abstract painting, expressed his views about the role of art in the modern world not only in his paintings but also in his writings: 'New images have to be found, a new kind of language of artistic communication, which reflect a radical break with tradition'. 'Many abstract painters presented a reality in which object form was seen in its atomic particles, vectors and trajectories, lines of tension and strain. Form in the sense of solid substance has melted away and resolved itself in its elemental forces'.* Others saw in the anonymous beauty of technological structures a new model for art.

We might ask whether the artists of the turn of the century

---

* Kenneth Coutts-Smith: 'The Dream of Icarus, Art and Society in the 20th Century' (Hutchinson, 1970).

anticipated a conceptual revolution of modern science or whether they reacted to it. There can be no doubt that the disintegration of the Superego images of Western civilisation provided an important emotional and intellectual impetus for the development of the new sciences and that the most sensitive artists both anticipated and responded to it. We could say that the response to the new conceptual universe took three main forms:

1 The artist reflects the scientific concepts and imitates the imagery of modern physics.
2 He protests against the new world of physics and technology, seeing man as its victim.
3 He gives expression to a regressive process, to the disintegration of a culture and of human personality. He is both victim and representative of regression.

While the abstract painters, cubists, futurists, constructivists and other schools of modernism reflected the impact of the physical sciences, there was another science, namely, psychoanalysis, which revolutionised our view of the world and of man.

The discovery of the fourth dimension of the mind, the unconscious, paralleled the discoveries of the fourth dimension of the physical world, of relativity theory and quantum mechanics. The world of the unconscious, which has its existence in the hidden and unknown regions of the mind below the level of consciousness but emerges in our dreams, became the chief subject of surrealist painting.

André Breton worked in the Psychiatric Institute of Saint Dizier near Paris and made drawings of the fantasies and dreams of schizophrenics and analysed them. He also analysed and drew dreams of children, whose mental processes he recognised to be closer to the deep layers of the mind than normal adults. He wanted to discover an inner world which is usually hidden and repressed from consciousness but determines a man's life without him having any knowledge of it. In his 'Manifesto of Surrealism' he wrote: 'Surrealism is based upon the belief in a higher actuality, in forms of association which have up till now been largely neglected, in the importance of dreams as the aimless game of thought. It is the aim of surrealism to dissolve or destroy all those psychological mechanisms which have hitherto hidden from us our unconscious processes in order to arrive at the solution of the fundamental problems of human existence'. *

In other parts of his 'Manifesto', Breton declares that the domination of rationalism, civilisation and progress have thwarted man's imaginative capabilities and that it is therefore the task of surrealism to mobilise the powers of the unconscious in order to re-establish an equilibrium of all human faculties.

Chirico, Miro, Max Ernst, Yves Tanguy, Dali and Man Ray presented a dream world where the categories of time and space, of form and substance are in abeyance: a juxtaposition of object relationships, of memories of things past appearing in things present, of undefinable tranquillity and undefinable terror in a general breakdown of organised perceptions. Images of childhood or schizophrenia characterise their paintings. However, by penetrating through the veils of repression they challenged the dominance of the Ego, they allowed the world of the Id to appear on the stage of their paintings. To some extent we may say that they were willing servants of the Id clamouring to find expression in the real world and in consciousness; they opened gates which had been kept locked and well guarded by the Ego's defences. In Salvador Dali's brilliant presentation of unconscious and dreamlike images we encounter many aspects of sado-masochism, anal-eroticism and paranoia in a clarity and sharpness unparalleled since.

Surrealism and abstract art in general—and they have both interacted and dominated modern art—created a new dynamism and excitement, an eruption of colours and sensations, a degree of self-expression on a depth and scale never before attempted. These movements occurred not only in painting but also in music and architecture, in literature and drama; they had an impact on human relationships and behaviour. Everywhere old boundaries were broken, traditions were rejected and modernism meant informality in manners, in conversation and in thought: the hidden was to be revealed!

The friendship between Kandinsky and Schoenberg provides us with an insight into the aims and ideas of the innovators of modernism. The founders of abstract painting and of atonal music held a lively and intensive correspondence between 1911 and 1914

---

* André Breton: 'Manifesto of Surrealism' (1924)

when Kandinsky finally abandoned figurative painting and Schoenberg gave up traditional tonality in his compositions. To quote a few extracts from their correspondence.

Kandinsky to Schoenberg, January 1911: 'I find that our 'new harmony' cannot be found in the traditional geometric manner but, on the contrary, in the anti-geometric, anti-logical forms. This is the way of dissonance in art, in painting as well as music, and the present musical and artistic dissonance is the consonance of the future'.

Schoenberg's reply contains these sentences: 'What you call the anti-logical I call the exclusion of the conscious will in art. Art belongs to the unconscious. One must express oneself! Express oneself spontaneously and directly, not one's taste or one's education, or one's reason, one's knowledge or one's skill! One should not bother with characteristics which are not inborn but with those that are innate, instinctual. All form, all conscious form plays with mathematics or geometry, with the golden mean and such like. Unconscious creativity alone produces genuine art, it alone brings out those archetypal images which are then imitated by those lacking originality and in whose hands they become formulas'.

Kandinsky to Schoenberg: 'In one's work one should have no conscious considerations but only one's inner voice should be heard and be in command'.

Alban Berg, Stravinsky, Picasso, Strindberg, Wedekind, the second generation of pioneers, continued and consolidated the spirit of modernism, a celebration of the libido set free. 'The morning sun of a new freedom', a discovery of new worlds of the mind and an exposition of its oppression flurried the artistic consciousness of Europe before and after the First World War.

But just as Einstein, having discovered the stupendous energies locked up in matter, could not have foreseen the consequences of his discovery and came to regret it when he saw that these cosmic energies were used for nuclear bombs, so the originators of modernism could not foresee the consequences of their art.

A curious thing happened. The vision of a free and expansive humanity, liberated from the strait-jacket of convention, gave way to the vision of a world in which the human being had disappeared; the individual dissolved into a world of random particles and chance eruptions of energy in a cauldron of dissociated sensations and impulses. In other words, the discovery of primeval forces in nature and the energy of the Id had not led to an expansion and enrichment of the human self-image but to a loss of identity. The integrative functions of the Ego succumbed to the onslaught of Id forces and gave way to dissociation, purpose-direction to confusion.

Instead of the 'new equilibrium' we find images of disintegration and dissonance on a scale undreamt of by the founders of modernism. It appears, in retrospect, that in their attack on the Superego they had forgotten or underestimated man's ambiguous relationship with it. On the one hand, men need the Superego in order to draw strength from it and acquire a sense of identity and, on the other hand, they feel oppressed by it and wish to destroy it in order to be free. But by destroying it, they destroy the models for the Ego, the father-killers are overtaken by fear and guilt unless they can effectively transform the rule of authority by the joyful experience of brotherly co-operation.

But the ideas of modernism, although they fascinated people and gained many adherents, did not penetrate into the structure of society. The revolutions which were inspired by the new intellectuals and by a deep revulsion among the masses against the wars and injustices of the old establishment showed themselves to be ephemeral. Hardly had the sons overthrown the old power structure than a new one arose, in many ways more brutal and oppressive than the old one. Freedom was short-lived. The deep structures of the Superego gained their revenge by imposing a reign of terror, first in Russia and then in Germany. Stalinism and Naziism made a terrible mockery of men's aspirations for freedom; they were unable to realise their primordial desire to share the earth-mother with each other in mutual respect and co-operation, to treat her with love and admiration and to gain her favours. They showed themselves to be incapable of taking over from the old man and they did not know how to treat the mother and she rejected them. Far from proudly bearing a new sense of identity they hid their faces in shame and lost their self-image in a world that appeared to be too complex and hostile to control. If they showed their faces at all it was only in mockery, in a sense of self-disgust and confusion.

Already in the early part of this century, the Expressionists gave warning of the threat to the human personality. They saw the danger in the growing regimentation, the cold mechanisation of life imposed by the authority of the state and industrial mass-production. Expressionism was the outrage of the artist against the

cold logic of machine technology and the mathematical calculations of the profit motive which take no account of native skills and
intuitive responses of the human being. In their work they aligned
themselves with the socially deprived, with the masses who became
victims, outcasts of industrial society. They propagated an intensification of human self-expression with all means available to
them. Their forms were exaggerated, sharp and sudden, decidedly
aggressive, not by any means realistic or natural but still very much
presentations of the human image. Many among them showed
humanity squashed, distorted, horror-struck and confused by the
modern world. They aimed for unrestrained self-expression and
impulsiveness, and empathy was their most widely used word and
could be taken as their slogan. Empathy was considered to be of
a higher order than knowledge or accuracy. For only through
empathy and exaggeration could the deeper feelings be expressed,
the vibrancy and excitement of nature and of man find adequate
presentation.

Ludwig Kirchner, Erich Haeckel, Munch, Gauguin, Otto Müller,
August Macke, Egon Schiele and Kokoschka were just a few of the
artists who followed this school. But their humanistic endeavours
to reaffirm the human self-image in an increasingly alien and
threatening environment were swamped by the very forces which
prevailed in that environment. The world which no longer sees the
human being as its central and meaningful figure, either in the
affairs of nature or in the affairs of society, found reflection in an
art which would not perceive the human being. (Franz Marc, one of
the most sensitive of the early modernists, never painted human
beings, giving as his reason that men impose themselves on nature
as alien beings and disturb its equilibrium). The schools which had
dominated during the first forty years of this century more or less
merged and succumbed to a common imagery of chaotic dissociation of emptiness. After the traumas of the Second World War,
Abstract Expressionism became the overall name for the prevailing
forms of painting. This movement was not circumscribed by a
definite style or direction but served as a platform for all possible
forms of expression which did not follow figurative or concrete art.
It upholds the conviction that creative communication cannot be
based upon rationality or logic but upon spontaneity, impulsiveness
and feelings. Their slogan is: 'Liberation from all rules, order and
formality'.

The only difference from the earlier movements is that the new practitioners have given up or forgotten the ideals of a new equilibrium between man and the forces that operate in nature and between the Ego and the unconscious to create a new image of man more powerful and more free than ever before. They are now united in their annihilation of the human image and the disintegration of native modes of perception.

If we look at contemporary paintings we behold a thundering emptiness, an overwhelming confusion of aggressive forces, or a brutal negation. Hope has given way to dark forebodings, to images of explosive powers, of spooky apprehension of doom, to a cult of dissociation.

It is here that regressive processes make their real impact, for if the Ego finds that the most recent development of its libido and the highest functions of the psyche, its most important emotional and cognitive processes, are not accepted by the world and cannot find expression, then it will retreat to more primitive stages in development. It will vacate its most advanced outposts and retreat to its bases, to use Freud's military metaphor. While we cannot bear to be fully conscious of the disappointments and tragedies, the injuries to our narcissism which reality causes us to suffer and keep hidden in the preconscious areas of the mind, they are revealed to us by the artist. His sensitivity reflects experiences of which we have only been dimly aware and he makes us face them. In our time he shows us not only the images of a machine-dominated world which pervades our existence and confronts us with unimaginable dangers, but above all the world's rejection of our humanity—our impotence and sense of futility in a world which happens without us and takes no notice of our judgments and aspirations. He shows to us just how dispensable we have become. But the psyche does not give up that easily; it will attempt to find new ways, new forms of projection and self-externalisation; and if our higher faculties are rejected and cannot find expression, then the Ego will retreat to more primitive stages of the libido and of psychic functioning in order to gain gratification.

So we move backwards, and early primacies emerge from the unconscious and dominate our minds.

We could, in such conditions, predict a predominance of dissociation and disruptivism, visions of chaos and paranoid anxieties, an epidemic of tensions, a perception of barriers and hostile forces, a cult of anxiety, confusion and disintegrated aggressiveness. Indeed, the artists have obliged us by showing precisely such forms of regression.

While the early modernists as well as the more recent abstract expressionists and tachists gave visual expression to Ego disintegration, retreat from reality and chaotic aggressiveness, the process of regression goes further.

As the Ego finds it increasingly difficult to integrate the manifold drives from the unconscious, the repressed breaks through its old boundaries and begins to dominate consciousness. We can in this way speak of the normalcy of madness. We must expect an eruption of anal defiance, sadistic, masochistic and destructive drives. They do not merely declare war on the norms and values of our culture, they glory in images of self-destruction. And the artists give public expression to these fantasies: bodies are torn apart, revealing visions of blood, skeletons, pieces of skin and intestines, excreta paraded defiantly, human beings presented in grotesque forms of catatonia, pain and terror—all our defences are deliberately shocked and our senses outraged.

Oral-sadistic images, skulls with threatening teeth, claws ripping at bodies, bodies torn open, drenched in blood, figure prominently; skeletal, emaciated bodies, lobsters with fangs intermingled with human figures, huge bloody vaginas with teeth, self-portraits with horrifying aggressive skulls symbolising the dominion of sadism superimposed upon the conscious Ego, can be found in a multitude of themes in very many paintings. Jannis Kounellis shows very large canvasses, ten of them covering the walls of an exhibition hall, with entirely identical paintings of numberless skulls executed in primitive style; and Francis Bacon has become an expert exponent of human horror and despair shown in a sadistic manner. There is little compassion to be found in these paintings, rather an exploitation of human tragedy and suffering for the sadistic pleasure they provide to the artist and, presumably, to the onlooker.

Where artists of earlier decades painstakingly calculated hairbreadth geometry, semiotic theories and various visual and intellectual concepts, the artistic scene has been invaded by an international army of new artists who want to shake up everything with their self-consciously bad manners, a kindergarten world of frightened or angry children intent on destroying what they consider to be restraint and order. Such outbursts of destructive and regressive images tend to dominate the exhibitions of contemporary paintings.

The ancient mythological figures are recreated once more but are invariably presented as monsters, bestial, frightening and spooky, distorted apparitions of primitive cultures. In the 'Berlin Exhibition of Contemporary Art 1982', cryptically entitled 'Zeitgeist', the human figure re-emerges but only to be savagely attacked, mauled, torn to pieces, dismembered in an orgy of sado-masochism which in its horrific violence is without precedents. The examples of human figures torn to pieces are too many to name here, but just to mention a few: 'Angel of Death', 'Headhunter' by Siegfried Anzinger; 'Untitled', 'Away from the Window', 'Eagle in the Window', by Georg Baselitz; 'Meeting', 'The River', by Erwin Bohatsch; 'Dangerous Surroundings of Thought' by Peter Bömmels; and 'Chi-Tong'—Evocations of Primitive, Mythological Savagery by A. R. Penck.

An introductory essay in a lavishly produced book to the 'Zeitgeist' Exhibition is of particular interest here. It vividly describes an extreme sense of estrangement between parents and sons and the latters' hostility towards established authority and all its values. By giving this essay a prominent place, the organisers of the exhibition obviously assume that it catches the mood and spirit of modernism. I would like to quote a part of this essay:

'My parents lived well', I said, 'but they existed only by annihilating me. And your parents lived reasonably well in their house by gradually annihilating you, though for you it was a prison which you never left all your life, for unlike me, who escaped, you never escaped, because you always lacked the strength'. 'Then they would fill their rucksacks', I said, 'and as they did so they would gloat over the contempt I felt for them on such occasions. I hated everything they packed into those rucksacks—the reserve stockings and reserve caps—as they called them—the sausages, the bread, the butter, the cheese, the muslin bandages, etc. Finally my father would pack the bible, from which he would read to us in the alpine hut. Always the same passages and always in the same voice, you remember? And we had to listen and mustn't say anything. If we did say something it was regarded as impudence and brought inevitable punishment. And then we had to walk more quickly uphill or faster downhill, as the case might be, and at times we got nothing to drink when we were thirsty and nothing to eat when we were hungry, because the offence, indeed, the crime we had committed by speaking was so great, for to contradict was a heinous transgression. My mother's callousness was always borne in on me during these alpine excursions, and so was her ruthlessness. My father was simply the observer of this callousness and ruthlessness. Not once, as far as I remember, did my father interrupt his observation to intervene with a comment for or against her, let alone to contradict her. My mother was the cruel one, my father the observer of her cruelty. Your father didn't say anything either when your mother tormented you with her hectoring or took her stick to you and nearly killed you. Fathers let mothers have their way in their destructive madness and don't lift a finger. We were destroyed by our parents', I said. 'But it was all much worse for you than it was for me, because I escaped, I freed myself, whereas you never freed yourself. Of course you did leave your parents, your begetters, whelpers and tormentors, but you didn't free yourself from them. At sixteen, however, it's almost too late', I said. 'By then you can only go through the world as someone who has been destroyed, and the world points its finger at you, because it can recognise someone who has been destroyed, even from afar. The world is ruthless when it catches sight of someone destroyed by his parents', I said.

The distant or denying primary object, the indifferent or hostile mother evokes aggressive urges leading to a cult of violence which dominates contemporary paintings. We also find many versions of anal defiance, the urge to exhibit excrement and to flaunt it before the eyes of the world. In some exhibitions in London there was a great show of 'dirty knickers', underpants with faeces, piles of excrement on the floor made to look very life-like. We can take this to be a defiant gesture of the self which has been made to feel dirty and bad by parents and by the 'clean and ordered' world at large. The narcissistic self that wants to be admired and loved but encountered rejection or disgust is hitting back at its tormentors, gaining revenge by outraging them with obscenities and by breaking their rules.

There was recently a 'sculpture' of a vast pile of old motor car tyres in a prominent position on London's South Bank, causing affront to inhabitants and visitors to that area. One outraged person set fire to this pile and in doing so suffered severe burns of which he died soon afterwards. Even more disturbingly, perhaps, there is now in the same place a 'sculpture' which consists of a huge pile of books, many thousands in fact. What is the meaning of such 'sculptures'? Indeed, what is the meaning of old bits of iron,

broken chimney pots, old bicycles, fragments of machinery, un-
wanted sewing-machines and such like exhibited as sculptures?

They obviously serve to disturb and outrage the onlooker by
claiming artistic significance for what most people regard as
discards.

We see here a declaration of war against the cultural Superego, a
demand for a right to express any impulse previously considered
taboo. Sublimation itself, the very foundation of culture is declared
as a barrier to freedom, an instrument of repression. This new kind
of libertarianism is not at all what the founders of modern art had
intended. Now we find that the gratification of aggressive urges
in the fight against repression has become an end in itself, while
the expression of anal impulses are meant to humiliate and vilify
everything that is considered normal or decent.

I remember an unpleasant experience at the studio of a prominent Austrian artist who, among many other contemporary types
of sculpture and tracts against capitalism, had a number of plastic
cushions with portraits of Mozart, Beethoven and Schubert painted
on them. For an Austrian these are obviously establishment figures,
and when I asked her what these cushions are supposed to signify,
she told me to sit on one and find out. On sitting on it the cushion
emitted a loud noise whose intended meaning was unmistakable.
When I again asked her in considerable bafflement what on earth
this is supposed to mean, or some such words probably less polite,
she said, with some impatience at my naivety, that it means that we
now shit on everything that is considered admirable by bourgeois
society.

Other 'artists' exhibit piles of bricks or enormous heaps of sand
and even fairly fresh manure (apparently to provide viewers not
only with a visual but also a smell experience), and progressive
museums pay large sums of money for these 'sculptures'. The
moderns thus have forced the establishment into swallowing their
insult and make rubbish respectable. As almost all children find
satisfaction in the thought that even grown-ups have bottoms and
defecate, and gleefully proclaim that mummy and daddy and
indeed everybody has a bottom, so the modernists defy the taboos
of respectability and show that we all have bottoms and defecate,
and that faeces, symbolised by refuse, must receive proper attention. One might say they show their bottoms and excrement to the
world. Moreover, there is no doubt that the modernist identifies

with those people who have, through the ages, suffered the opprobrium of belonging to a lower order, the 'common' people, the unclean ones, who work with their hands and soil themselves with dirt in the course of their labour, literally, the 'lower' order, the working-class, the lumpenproletariat, the outcasts and refuse of society. They consider themselves to be fighters against the bourgeoisie and refined people who have projected their anal fantasies on to the lower order and made them bear the stigma of dirtiness. Under the impact of taboos imposed by civilisation, the child's urge to play with faeces is condemned as a nasty and dirty activity, and those who have to labour with their hands are identified as the dirty people. We have seen that the separation between the clean and the dirty, between those who have freed themselves from anal fixations and avoid contact with dirty matter, the clean and superior people, and those who make themselves dirty—soiled themselves in the course of their labours—plays an important role in the class structure of society.

While the working class has fought for its dignity and rehabilitation in society, their spokesmen, the intellectuals, advocated their cause in clever phrases and books but have not touched on their real feelings nor did they have any fundamental impact on the old taboos. The academics, the professors, politicians and party leaders mouth clever phrases like 'freedom and equality', 'democracy or socialism', 'anomie and alienation', and use the troubles of ordinary people in order to promote their own status in the world and to gain attention for themselves.

And it is almost understandable that the artists who regard themselves as active fighters against social injustice are impatient with civilised refinements and want to throw dirt into the face of the world so that it experiences that insult which ordinary people have to live with.

THE SOUNDS OF INFANTILE RAGE

It is, however, in music, or what goes by the name of music, where the process of 'regressive desublimation', the cult of infantilism and violence has had a particularly far-reaching influence. Its sounds invade homes, shops, workplaces, entertainment centres and urban streets; they are practically inescapable in contemporary life due to their mass communication by radio, gramophone and television.

We have pointed to the meeting of minds between the innovators of modern painting and music, and since then the two arts have undergone an almost parallel development—from atonality to the growing influence of 'scientific' concepts of musical structure, the disintegration of melodic themes, sounds intended to imitate machinery and, more recently, computer music culminating in an unrestrained display of primitive emotions in pop, beat, rock and punk noises. The traditional perceptions of Western music, representing a wide range of emotions integrated into melodic themes and harmony, are under attack by the infantilistic noise-makers, promoted and exploited by profit-seeking entrepreneurs and the vested interest of the electronic industry and communication media.

It is not the place here to discuss the movements in music which followed the innovations of Schoenberg, composers like Bartok, Berg, Webern, Hindemith, Henze and Stockhausen, the music 'scientists' like Schillinger or the computer music of Cage and Xenakis. For an excellent review of these composers, their works and their theories, I would refer the interested reader to the books of H. H. Stuckenschmidt.[*] I want here only to draw attention to the spirit which motivated the popular pop, beat, rock and punk musicians.

From its beginnings in the early nineteen-fifties, rock music was par excellence the medium through which young people explored and expressed their emotions in dancing and sensory stimulation. Theodor Adorno considered American jazz of the thirties and forties—by which he seems to mean everything from delta blues to tin-pan alley—as a product of modern technology and the capitalist market masquerading as uninhibited primitivism, 'jungle music'—a commercial confidence trick. His contempt for what one might call 'ersatz' self-expression is echoed many times by the more serious and committed pop journalists. They saw pop as a mission and wanted its star performers to be prophets of pure expressiveness and not priests of a routinised variant.

---

[*] H. H. Stuckenschmidt: 'Twentieth Century Music' (Weidenfeld & Nicholson, 1966) and: 'Die Musik eines Halben Jahrhunderts' (Piper & Co 1976).

The same dualism between a genuine movement of protest and its exploitation by commercial interest which aroused Adorno's despair also impressed itself upon John Cage, musician and doyen of the avant-garde. In an interview for the 'Village Voice' in 1966, Cage was asked his opinion about jazz, the old symbolic protest music of negroes and white radicals. He replied that he didn't much like jazz, principally because he found the beat oppressive; it reminded him of all the boring and only marginally useful things in life, like the ticking of a clock. "I myself revolt against the notion of measurement". He did not even think much of the freedom to improvise in jazz, since the so-called freedom of the soloist was dependent on the constriction of the rhythm section which had to keep the beat. (The development of free jazz by the avant-garde of that movement was precisely a response to this contradiction in a 'free' medium). Cage found rock and roll more interesting; at least everyone was in agreement there. He noted: "This business of one thing being free while something else is not being free bothers me. Everyone seems to be together in rock and roll music. With it! Another thing which is quite fascinating is its use of electronics. This makes it extremely pertinent to our daily experience... It's a curious thing, but the reason the beat does not oppress me as much in rock and roll as it does in jazz, I think, is because the volume is so high. In other words, one's attention is taken away from the beat by the amplitude. The volume of sound is so great that it blurs, as it were, the fact of the beat". Beat here is considered as a restraint, as still a remnant of the classical measure of rhythm which in rock is obliterated by the sheer power of noise.

The breaking down of all boundaries and restraints has been the preoccupation of composers like Cage and Rauschenberg who used all black as well as all white pictures to dissolve all boundaries and say everything. Cage believed that the results would be even better if, say, three or more rock groups played at once in different tempi and with different starting and stopping times. This would complete the logic of electronics because "nowadays everything happens at once and our souls are conveniently electronic (omniattentive)". Something of this kind did happen at the avant-garde end of pop. Groups like 'The Who' and 'The Rolling Stones' used phenomenal noise levels to blur not only beat but lyric, melody and rhythm alike and achieve anarchic, contourless but all-engulfing noise: freedom and instant belonging at the same time. Nik Cohn, the rock journalist, writes of the 'Stones': "All that counted was sound and the murderous mood it made. All din and mad atmosphere. Really it was nothing but beat, smashed and crunched and hammered home like some amazing stampede. The words were lost and the song was lost. You were only left with chaos, beautiful anarchy. You drowned in noise".

This is what Paul Goodman calls the "sacramental use of noise" in youth culture. On the one hand there is the noise, the endless and changeless beat, and on the other hand an overlay of musical or lyrical anarchy, usually accented by antics, appearance and body movements to emphasise the aggressive convention-smashing elements.*

How are we to understand the "sacramental use of noise and beat"? It certainly represents a ritual of sacrifice, the ecstasy of killing the totem of convention and Superego and, at the same time, the obliteration of Ego restraints, a collective hysteria induced by the hypnotic influence of the beat and the noise, that obliterates the restraints and fears of the Ego and allows the ancient Oedipal murder to be acted out, at least in a simulated act of ecstasy. We witness here an encounter with intimations of catastrophe, but catastrophe which is at the same time liberation, self-expression. Through the experience of unrestrained destructiveness youth experiences liberation and self-realisation. But is it any different from the grown-ups who organise catastrophe in a rational manner? Are they not both in their different ways—one through infantile spasms of orgastic sadism, and the other in cold calculation—devoted to the same purpose? "What is this apocalyptic catastrophe we are heading for?" asks Eugene Enesco. "Neither politicians, nor philosophers, Marxists or non-Marxists can explain it".

We have seen that the philosophers, the rationalists and the scientists have long ago lost their nerve. Their deliberations move very firmly in a self-ordained groove, and they disclaim any responsibility for saving the world from a course of events which they no longer claim to comprehend or explain. And the rock addicts are fully aware of this failure of nerve and of articulation on the part of the 'grown-ups'. Indeed, they declare war on

---

* Bernice Martin: 'A Sociology of Contemporary Cultural Change' (Basil Blackwell, 1981).

articulate language and retreat to a pre-verbal babble which by its very incomprehensibility claims to reveal a mystery beyond understanding; and it is in this mystery of pre-verbal communication, the realm of unrestrained self-expression that salvation is to be found. Abandonment to the infantile, submission to the uncontrolled reflexes of sexuality and aggression, of defiance and destruction, opens for them the gates of vitality and a sense of aliveness otherwise locked.

"Rock reaches its supreme aesthetic achievement when it 'speaks in the unknown tongue', when it obliquely and fugitively expresses the inexpressible. Some place between the incapturably transitory and the imperceptibly infinite is the stage upon which something is acted out between the ungraspably holy and forgettably profane... This is the realm of the unknown tongue.

The greatest and most familiar analogue to the unknown tongue in mere human experience is the orgasm. An orgasm, as we all know, arises slowly as it builds up and suddenly strikes, leaving one back on earth but perceptibly richer".*

Mysticism and death are Meltzer's most persistent metaphors mingling with the impressions of sex and violence. The process of regression towards the most primitive stages of the libido, oral aggression and sadism, are shown in the undisguised symbols of the punk cult. A great parade of pins stuck in the sides of faces, hairpins embedded in cheeks and earlobes, zips symbolising rows of teeth in a menacing manner proliferating on garments, hobnailed boots and the menace of razor blades and flick-knives, heavy chains and whips combined with postures of sadistic hysteria, produce an image of youth culture entirely devoted to aggression, to smashing and destroying. The names of their groups are intended to capture this image: 'Sex Pistols', 'Blockheads', 'The Master Bashers', 'Blazing Metal', and so on. A recent number of a rock journal, 'Metal Mania', announces a new group: "'Motor Head' are unquestionably Britain's leading metal merchants. Indeed, for skull-cracking, brain damaging, mayhem inducing rock and roll, they cannot be topped. Your mother definitely would not like them; one blast of their music would probably produce a cardiac arrest to anyone over fifty".

---

* R. Meltzer: 'The Aesthetics of Rock' (Something Else Press, N.Y., 1970).

Being curious about the possible attractions of this pandemonium of noise and violence, I enquired of a rock enthusiast what on earth he finds attractive about it. He told me, after serious reflection, that what he likes above all is the "noise grinding into his brain"—a remark I found more revealing than the rationalisations produced by the journalists and philosophers of the rock world. Sadism and masochism, the destruction of external as well as internal inhibitions, have become the driving forces of an important subculture, with which a large segment of young people identify.

One might be inclined to dismiss this movement as a manifestation of the perennial hysteria of adolescents, or as a displacement of revolutionary ardour into an harmless art form, a fashion encouraged and exploited by commerce, but this would be wrong. Even if fashions change with great rapidity and give way to different forms of self-expression, there can be no doubt that the spirit which has motivated modern brutalism has taken deep roots. The movement of protest, the attack on sublimation and gratification delay continue to challenge the very foundations on which Western patriarchal civilisation rests. The modernists have loosened the structures of inhibition, they have powerfully challenged the Superego and enjoined the youngsters to express their rage and their long pent up sadistic fury towards the authority of the fathers. The 'propagandists of the Id' have proclaimed our right to destroy the old oppressor and his social establishments, the rules of order and authority. While the modernists have removed the ancient inhibitions against perverse and sadistic impulses and demanded their right to be shown openly in public, this right to attack and destroy has spilt over into the real world, to give it expression not only in the artistic imagination or in symbolic forms of entertainment but in the actuality of social behaviour and action.

THE DELINQUENT AND THE REVOLUTIONARY

We had to make the discovery that liberation from the traditional restraints have not led to an enrichment of the human personality and its creative potentialities, to a liberation from guilt, anxiety and mistrust, but on the contrary to a release, an outburst of aggressive-destructive urges previously held in check.

The cult of unrestrained self-expression which Kandinsky and Schoenberg initiated in their respective art, which Freud encouraged in psychotherapy and Reich elevated into a principle of healthy existence, did not lead to a life-affirming enrichment of our culture, but paradoxically to a worship of violence and necrophilia. And this phenomenon is not restricted to the arts. It is invading all aspects of social life.

> it is 1968
> i am a magic realist
> i see the adorers of che
>
> i see the black man
> forced to accept violence
>
> i see the pacifists
> despair
> and accept violence
>
> i see all all all
> corrupted
> by the vibrations
>
> vibrations of violence of civilisation
> that are shattering
> our only world[*]

The impact of modernism not only in the arts of painting and music but also in philosophy and social sciences, with their ethical relativism and avoidance of value judgment, can be compared to a kind of social therapy which has gone wrong. We find here a corollary in the psychoanalytic treatment of individuals when they begin to be less afraid of the Superego and their guilt feelings are reduced.

In his book 'The Sexual Revolution' Wilhelm Reich describes the initial stage in the treatment of neurosis: "Character analytic treatment releases the vegetative energies from their fixations and their armour. The immediate result of this is an intensification of the anti-social and perverse impulses and of social anxiety". In my own work I also find that the liberation of libido energy initially releases aggressive urges of which the patient has not been con-

---

[*] Julian Beck: 'Paradise Now' (International Times, London, 1968).

scious previously. Reich explains the next stage of therapy. 'While previously the whole thinking and acting was determined by unconscious, irrational motives, the patient now becomes increasingly capable of acting and reacting rationally. While previously the patient was completely armoured, incapable of contact with himself and his environment, capable only of unnatural pseudo-contacts, he now develops an increasing capacity for immediate, natural contact with his impulses as well as his environment. The result of this is a visible development of natural, spontaneous behaviour instead of the previous unnatural, artificial behaviour.'

However, while these developments occur in the successful treatment of individuals, on the social level we have remained fixated upon the first stage: an almost indiscriminate release of aggressiveness not only in the arts but also in civic behaviour and in politics which defies the restraints of civilised morality. Paradoxically, it seems that the more tolerant it appears on the surface, the more fear and insecurity the Superego arouses in the deeper layers of the psyche. It no longer imposes its taboos in the form of authoritarian demands but has adopted a posture of tolerance and even encourages us to express our emotions. But this modern posture of tolerance appears, particularly to young people, as indifference. The fathers appear tolerant because they no longer seem to care for their sons. The big world of the fathers show no understanding for young people's deeper emotional needs; it only understands substitute gratifications of greed and wealth, material possessions and the relentless pursuit of status and power. These secondary drives are given priority in modern society and regarded as the true characteristics of 'human nature' and there is nothing beyond. In other words, society's tolerance extends only to the substitute drives, while the primary needs for love, cooperation and friendship continue to be repressed and we dare not express them for fear of being ridiculed; the cynical world of the 'grown ups' regards them as utopian and politically unrealistic.

We witness a phenomenal growth in delinquency, lawlessness, the cult of violence in civic behaviour as well as in political activity. The rise in youthful lawlessness expressed by mob hooliganism and the rise in juvenile crime figures has been seen in many countries since the 1950s. But it is in the last ten years that it has acquired proportions of an epidemic. If we look at statistics of total indictable offences among males in Great Britain between the ages of 17 and 21, we find the following:

1938	1956	1961	1980	1981
21,800	24,700	52,800	200,000	206,000

These figures of actual law-breaking are only part of the story. What is even more noticeable is the appearance of an unrestrained hostility towards authority in every form which could flare up into violence through a trivial cause.

Perhaps most startling of all are figures of those convicted for offences of violence against the person. In the age group 14 to 21 we find:

1938	1956	1961	1980
243	1,700	4,420	9,000

In crimes among all age groups, we find:

Violence against the person:	1971	1982	1983	1987	1988
	47,000	100,200	108,700	130,000	151,000
Muggings:				10,500	11,800
Robbery:	7,500	20,300	22,000	27,000	30,000

While the increase in delinquency and violence of the young surprised and startled the public and the social workers during the 1950s, these were only the first ominous signs of a breakdown of civilised life in many urban areas during the 1970s and 1980s. What is particularly disturbing is the absence of inner restraints among young offenders; they appear to be utterly unconcerned about breaking the law and lack any sense of regret or sympathy for their victims. There is not only a dramatic increase in the amount of delinquency but in its degree of violence and cruelty in many instances.

I cannot here give detailed statistics about types of violence perpetrated, but let us just consider the ruthless attacks on old people, often causing severe injury or even death, which are a daily occurrence in large towns in America and England and, to a lesser degree, in Europe. Mugging has become so frequent and almost commonplace that women in many areas are frightened to go out into the streets after dark. Gangs of boys attack individuals, sometimes children, entirely unknown to them; old people are savaged in their homes, either by individual youngsters or by gangs 'just out for the thrill'.

These meaningless and random attacks on innocent and uninvolved people, often entirely unknown to the attackers, are reminiscent of the bands of young men roaming the territory outside their tribe in primeval times, looking for human or animal prey and declaring war on the territory where the inhibitions of tribal morality do not apply and they are free to vent their aggressiveness. Their modern counterparts see the wilderness of the urban landscape as alien territory where taboos and jurisdiction of civilisation are suspended. The defiance of taboos and breaking of laws, coupled with the excitement of the hunt and savagery inflicted on the prey, provide satisfaction which they consider to be self-evident and do not need any further motive or justification.

Whether these hunting gangs of youths, who feel themselves to be outside the law and, therefore, free to satisfy their destructive urges, call themselves mods or rockers, punks or blacks, makes little difference. However, there is no doubt that the 'black power movement' has provided an important impetus to the declaration of war by youthful rebels against the 'establishment'. Leaders of this movement have given encouragement to black youngsters to attack the rule of 'white oppressors', not any longer by means of clever words pleading for justice but by violent activism and destructiveness. Their marauding gangs see themselves as glorious representatives of the ancient tribal warriors and scalp-hunters, considering the country of their residence as an enemy tribe on which vengeance can be meted out without inhibition. Indeed, they are quite surprised and indignant if they are restrained by the police and arrested; they even claim in most vehement terms that the police should not 'invade' urban areas which have a large black population. The police are seen as the representatives of the 'enemy' and therefore have no right to be there. The black parents, who are distressed by the violence of their youngsters, often declare they have lost control over them largely due to interference by left-wing social workers and community leaders who seem to encourage young blacks in their 'revolutionary activities'. In fact, there is a vested interest among certain political movements which regard crime and violence among black and white youths, the 'victims of capitalist oppression', as a way of promoting a revolutionary situation.

Any form of resistance to the established order and its disruption is regarded by them as a step towards the overthrow of capitalism and, therefore, must be given the greatest encouragement. For instance James Forman, the black power leader, wrote in his 'Manifesto' (adopted by the 'National Black Economic Development of America'): "There are reparations due to us as people who have been exploited and degraded, brutalised, killed and persecuted... It follows from the laws of revolution that the most oppressed will make the revolution, whose ultimate goal is that we must assume leadership, total control... inside of the United States of everything that exists. The time has passed when we are second in command and the white boy stands on top. In order to achieve this reversal, it will be necessary to use whatever means necessary, including the use of force and power of the gun to bring down the colonizer".

A considerable number of such declarations not only on behalf of the blacks but also the 'white victims of capitalism' have provided a significant impetus to the youth rebellion. They have largely contributed to the 'liberation' of young people from their internal inhibitions against violence and law-breaking. This 'liberation', the new 'freedom' to attack and defy the established norms of discipline or respect for authority, can be seen to have had a devastating effect on young people's behaviour, in public places, in schools, in the relationship between parents and children.

Groups of youths frequently enter department stores and steal articles in full view of shop assistants and managers, defiantly daring them to remonstrate while they nonchalantly complete their theft. Indeed, assistants and managers are usually too frightened to challenge the thieves and they get away triumphantly with their hoard. Violent attacks by young hooligans on bus conductors and drivers, often for no other reason than being asked for their fare, are evermore frequent occurrences, often causing severe injuries. There have been a number of strikes by bus crews in protest against the dangers of being attacked and abused by uncontrollable youngsters, demanding trade union support in order to gain protection.

Another feature of unrestrained hooliganism is the disruption and violence in schools, particularly in working class areas of big cities. Any teacher will testify to the difficulty, or even impossibility, of keeping a semblance of order in the classroom or gain their pupils' attention. Many teachers have been subjected to attacks and harassment from schoolchildren, both boys and girls. Indeed, it is commonplace to hear teachers exclaim that it is not so much a question of what they can teach in their schools but how to survive the day.

However, this dramatic lessening of internal restraints upon aggressive-destructive behaviour, this uninhibited attack on the social representatives of the Superego, whether they be old people, department stores, public transport, police, or schoolteachers, has a psychological effect not merely upon the public, but on the young people who feel free to commit such acts. By rejecting all kinds of discipline and refusing to accept internal inhibitions against aggression and violence, by dismissing the directions and models of the Superego, they deprive their Ego system of goal direction and diminish its ability to integrate impulses into coherent and purpose-directed activity. They suffer from difficulty in concentrating upon any given task, their attention span and learning ability are greatly reduced. Diffused behaviour patterns and disintegration of mental processes prevail and neurasthenic restlessness characterises their behaviour. They are unable to tolerate gratification delay which is fundamental to acquisition of skill and knowledge.

By maintaining a show of indifference to expected standards, their actions are diffused, disintegrated, dominated by impulse, and can change abruptly without any apparent connection. There seems to be no continuity in behaviour, no discernible purpose, no apparent meaning to it.

T. R. Fyvel, in his book 'The Insecure Offenders' wrote: 'Their state of mind is one where it simply does not occur to them that an impulse, a desire which seizes them should not at once be gratified. The gangs in which they gather sanction this behaviour to follow impulses and hence its attractions. The gang is a protection against the outside world dominated by father-figures, authorities and their values, and a mutual protection in their quest for 'valueless' activity. Any attempt to guide them, to interfere, is therefore like an attack on their security and as such opposed or evaded at once".* This is what makes these young men so intractable and so difficult to deal with.

As an illustration of this non-integrated, shiftless, impulse domi-nated personality type among a great number of young people, Fyvel quotes a youth leader from a notorious London area:

> Perhaps this latest generation is even more delinquent than the last in pinching motor-bikes and cars, but what strikes me is the way they do it—the growth of sheer irresponsibility. The other day some of our boys went to the market and simply began to throw goods from stalls all over the place, and so they came up before the court. But for them it was just having fun. They would pinch a car in the same way. You saw what an impressive new club building we have; for a good 25% of the 14–16 age group it makes no difference. They will never be constructive. They just come for a game of darts, a coffee; they flit in and out, nothing else. We thought: 'We must give them easy things to do'. Right! We organised badminton groups, judo groups, a snooker tournament, but they never stuck at anything more than half an hour. Then suddenly one of them would say: 'Comin' out...?', and they'd all flock after him like sheep. If you ask where to, they'd say, 'To the chip shop' or 'Sit in the cafe'. It's just to be somewhere different, to move about with no objective.
>
> But when they've got no objective, they've got no faith, no religion, they don't see why they're in this world. Basically, it's a matter of seeing how selfish you can be. They're not interested in their jobs—money is the only thing that counts.*

Since then we have witnessed an intensification of defiant-disintegrated behaviour, an inability or refusal to submit to the educational and learning processes in the home and in school. The degree of aggressiveness and sense of irresponsibility for the consequences of their actions acquired a new proportion. Destruct-iveness towards the environment spread into the open, into the streets of cities, football grounds and other places where young people gather, and violent attacks upon people become more frequent as the statistics show, and as we witness in our daily experience.

This increase in destructiveness is reflected in the pronounce-ments of many left-wing philosophers who not only tolerate such behaviour, blaming not the perpetrators but bourgeois society and

---

* T, R. Fyvel: 'The Insecure Offenders' (Pelican Books, 1964).

actively encourage it. Not only the artists but also the philosophers preach the ultimate meaninglessness of innate concepts of good and bad, of ugliness and beauty, from their academic rostrums, their books and in newspaper articles. The philosophers of the left, in tacit alliance with academic psychologists of the right, are engaged in a major campaign of intellectual destructiveness aimed at moral values. They maintain that it is fallacious to ascribe general validity or truth value to moral standards, proclaiming that they are merely manifestations of particular cultures, or fashions, emotional attitudes without any rational significance. These critiques of ethical concepts are not presented as speculations but as irrefutable dogma given the name of ethical relativism, which has spread to the educated members of society and from them to the masses, until it has become an important aspect of our 'Zeitgeist'. Its main effect has been to spread the impression that one cannot rationally condemn people for defying the rules of behaviour prevalent in our civilisation, and that it is rather our duty to understand and sympathise with the delinquent. Indeed, if anyone is to blame for their defiant and aggressive actions, it must be society in general, and the capitalist system in particular, for it deprives them of their material and emotional needs, so making them feel outcasts of society.

The simplistic concept of 'deprivation' has become a facile explanation and, by implication, justification for youthful delinquency and antisocial behaviour. Social workers, psychologists and sociologists have conspired to create the impression that it is the delinquent who is the victim of society, and the public, and even those who suffer from such violence, are to blame. We, who are not delinquents, who uphold the laws of the state, are the guilty ones and fully deserve to suffer from the rebellion and violence of the deprived and oppressed. These attitudes are particularly prominent in psychological theories which uphold the virtues of emotional self-expression including aggression as a kind of therapy.

Cathartic therapies which put particular emphasis upon the expression of aggressive urges, encounter groups, transactional group therapies, therapies of the primeval scream, over-simplified Reichian vegetotherapy and such like flourished in the 1960s and 1970s, popularising the impression that restraint and gratification delay are harmful. It was but a short step to the idea that discharge and aggression in public, a show of rage against the repressive

Superego not only benefits the individual but is a significant aspect of revolutionary activity. The theatre of revolution or the 'third theatre' adopting Camus' slogan 'I rebel therefore I am' aroused sexual and sadistic passions in the audience, and invited them, upon leaving the theatre, to attack the police and cause an affray in the streets; the worship of raw emotionalism and naked slogans, the encouragement of all kinds of protest movements, from the squatters' movement to the radical student movement, the politicising of pensioners' rights and children's rights, the acceptance of graffiti as an 'art form'—all became part of the counter-culture which became increasingly politicised. Thus law-breaking and aggression, hooliganism and delinquency—all came to be seen as an attack upon the capitalist order and needed to be channelled into political action.

LIBERATION THROUGH VIOLENCE: THE BRUTALISATION OF THE LEFT

There were many nineteenth century writers and propagandists of socialism who upheld that the unrestrained expression of aggressive urges constitute a revolutionary act or, to put it the other way round, that revolutionary acts involve unrestrained aggression against the environment.

Mikhail Bakunin was a distinguished representative of this school of thought, and although he personally did not commit any acts of terrorism or violence he saw himself as a destroyer of established society. As a young man he wrote: "The people... because of their origin and position have been deprived of property, condemned to ignorance and in practice, therefore, to slavery. Now they grow menacing... the air is sultry with storms... let us then put our trust in the eternal spirit which destroys and annihilates only because...it is the eternally creative source of all life. The urge to destroy is also the creative urge". Destruction, root and branch, of established society, including its culture, became Bakunin's object. In a pamphlet which he wrote later in life, while he was under the influence of the terrorist Nechaev, he declared: "The brigand is always the hero, the defender, the avenger of the people, the irreconcilable enemy of the whole state regime, both in its civil and its social aspects... The brigand is the revolutionary without phrase-making and bookish rhetoric... and the world of brigands alone has been in harmony with the revolution". It was typical of him to write that everything which stands in the way of freeing the people must be destroyed without sparing lives or shrinking from the commission of crimes. However, as Edward Hyams[*] observes: 'What is absurd and distasteful in Bakunin is the difference between theory and practice: he frequently engaged in open insurrection, but never in the kind of terrorism which he licensed in his writing. He was a bit of a fraud. Nevertheless, he was at the origin of the great anarchist movements in Italy and Spain and later of the libertarian movements in many parts of the world.'

We might also recall Georges Sorel who, at the beginning of the century, tried to combine Marxism with Bergson's philosophy of life, and thought of the class struggle in military terms; yet he ended up by proposing nothing more violent than the famous myth of the general strike. He approved of the general strike and of the Marxist class war on the ground that only in acts of violent strife does a man encounter those moments of truth which liberate his true character and, therefore, as society is composed of individuals, liberate and advance it. Notwithstanding his enthusiastic approval of Lenin and the Russian Revolution, he turned towards the right in his later life, and although he was unimportant as a socialist thinker, his advocacy of violence provided Mussolini with an ideology for fascism.

The plentiful evidence provided in this century that the exploitation of violent emotions for revolutionary purposes can and frequently does transform the revolutionary into a fascist however did not prevent Sartre from declaring (in his preface to Frantz Fanon's book 'The Wretched of the Earth') that 'irrepressible violence is man recreating himself', and that 'it is through mad fury that the wretched of the earth can become men'.

The philosophy of the destruction of capitalism by violent means has a long history but it must be remembered that it was repudiated as a primary form of socialist struggle by such protagonists of socialism as Proudhon and Marx and such anarchists as Malatesta and Kropotkin. They did not entirely preclude the possibility of violence in the transformation of society from capitalism to socialism but they maintained that it has to be subordinate to

---

[*] Edward Hyams: 'The Millennium Postponed' (Secker & Warburg, 1974).

strategic considerations and carefully controlled. It is only when the socio-economic situation and the consciousness of the masses were ripe for a socialist transformation of society tactics required a certain degree of violence.

Marx waged a constant war against terrorists such as Nechaev and Jacob Most, denouncing them as enemies of the socialist movement. While according to Hegel man 'produces himself through thought', for Marx, who turned Hegel's idealism upside down, it was labour, the human form of metabolism with nature, that fulfilled this function. It was thus for Marx the transformation of human conditions of labour and the resulting changes of man's relationship to each other which would transform society.

However, it is perhaps no coincidence that the terrorist movements in Germany, the Baader Meinhof gang and the Red Army Faction, had their beginnings in a psychiatric clinic. One of the psychiatrists working there became convinced that his patients' needs would be best served if they would express their aggressive urges by attacking police stations and public offices, and he strongly encouraged them to do precisely that. He organised a 'revolutionary patients commune' which began to engage in acts of terrorism and soon attracted considerable following from revolutionary-minded young people who felt that we all are diseased victims of capitalist oppression and that the only way to regain our psychological as well as our social freedom was to discharge our repressed rage by means of political terrorism.

While our latter day revolutionaries have succeeded in disturbing the innate restraints which govern human relationships in civilised societies, they have failed to inspire the population with a vision of "the humanisation of man" (of which the young Marx had spoken), in a society where men's full potentials can at last unfold.

The protest movements, the outbursts of violence and defiance have not liberated us from the ancient authority structures, both psychologically as well as socially, and we remain dependent on them. Indeed, our revolutionaries need the father-figures as objects onto whom they can vent their rage but are unable to take their place. Their battles are mock battles; their revolutionary activities are the posturising of children who know that they are incapable of accepting full responsibility for the creation of an alternative society; their dream of replacing 'the old oppressor' and establishing the kingdom of man's maturity has remained a dream, and their dreams have all too frequently turned into nightmares. Humanity is still divided against itself, both in the conflicts within the nations and between the nations.

And here we confront a dimension in the crisis of patriarchy which looks like being the ultimate crisis of humanity. It looms before us as a spectre from which there seems to be no escape, the spectre of our destructive fantasies acted out on the planetary level. Assurances that we shall be defended from the enemy only intensify our fears, for our defences themselves are the agents of destruction committing us still further to our nightmare.

THE ULTIMATE STAGE OF PATRIARCHAL PARANOIA: THE POLITICS OF GLOBAL DESTRUCTION

I have dealt at some length with the brutalising and regressive manifestations of the conflict between freedom and authority in modern society because the inability of civilisation to overcome these conflicts is paralleled by its inability to overcome the compulsions for warfare. The battle within the psyche of patriarchal man which is acted out in his society, the Oedipal conflict between the sons and fathers, kings and subjects, capitalists and workers, dictators and the people, the quest for freedom and the compulsion to submit to the Superego, the drive for maturity and the pull of the infantile, has its inevitable counterpart in the battle against the alien gods, the enemy tribe, the enemy nation. As long as men are unable to come to terms with the internal Superego they will continue to project a large part of their aggression against 'the own God' outwards upon 'the other God' and are compelled to make wars; the patriarchal compulsion for tribal warfare, the patriarchal paranoia, persists. As the very last paragraph of the Old Testament proclaims:

> Behold, I will send you
> Elijah the prophet
> Before the coming
> Of the great and terrible
>   day of the lord.

And he shall turn the heart of the
   fathers to the children,
And the heart of the children to
   their fathers;
Lest I come and smite the land
   with utter destruction

And 'utter destruction' obviously means the internal disintegration of nations as well as their destruction through war.

Indeed, in our time we face the ultimate test—ultimate because the tribal system has reached the last stage of its development. The thousands of tribes, and nations, religions and ideologies, which have during man's history populated the earth have now become fused into the two remaining tribal systems, and there are, in effect, only two tribes left: the two superpowers and their respective client nations. There are still many nations on this earth but they have come under the domination of one or other of the superpowers and are used and manipulated by them for the global confrontation. America and Russia not only dominate all other nations economically and militarily but they also consider themselves to be the embodiment of the last two effective religions or ideologies left in this world, capitalism and communism—the ideology of market economy and personal freedom confronting a centrally planned economy and totalitarianism. Of course, as there are many other nations so there are other religions and cultures, but while they still show some obstinate independence and resistance to the super-religions they are nevertheless in effect absorbed by them and do not make much difference in the overall global scenario. It is furthermore true that while America poses as the universal protector of the bourgeois ideals of freedom, and Russia as the universal protector of the socialist ideals of equality, we find on closer inspection that America's capitalism is not very democratic nor does it provide real freedom for many of its citizens, and Russian communism is not very equal, nor does it protect the human rights of its workers. The one, in practice, upholds the virtues of ruthless competition, showing little respect for those who do not emerge successful from it, and in the other a tyrannical state bureaucracy ruthlessly oppresses and manipulates the masses.

In fact, these two superpowers are becoming increasingly alike, twins united in rivalry with each other, without quite realising that this rivalry binds them together in mutual fear. They both only respect power, economic and military, while, at the same time, claim to be the sole representatives of European culture. But while they claim to be the ultimate representatives of the highest ideals of European civilisation, one cannot help considering them as parvenus, as outsiders, who are determined to take over the mantle of civilisation when Europe itself has become decadent and weak. They both claim to defend Europe, while making it hostage to their megalomania.

So the people of the world are expected to divide into two camps, each ready to submit to their respective deity and, if necessary, sacrifice themselves to it. And the people of the world are aghast and incredulous at the presumption of the superpowers to speak for them and their demand for the ultimate sacrifice. But the people of the world cannot find a way to unleash themselves from this bondage and find all kinds of rationalisations for it, whereas, in effect, the bondage is within, the old tribal and patriarchal compulsions anchored in the very structure of society. Of course the superpowers feed these compulsions. Armies of propagandists, agitators, informers and secret agents, in fact the whole apparatus of the nation state, see to it that people remain bound to their respective tribe and their loyalty assured. The military preparations for war are accompanied by psychological and spiritual preparations, by a propaganda war, a war for people's minds.

The most simple of these propaganda efforts is to feed the paranoid fears of the 'Other'. It is one of the attractions of tribal paranoia that a community can deflect its aggressive urges upon other communities and see its own unconscious and unacceptable characteristics reflected in the enemy. One's own community then can regard and proclaim itself to be peace-loving and the innocent victim of aggression by the 'Other' and, at the same time, adopt the most aggressive attitudes for the sake of legitimate self-defence. It is worth while to remember that the Nazis tortured and killed over six million Jews in order to defend Germany from their 'poisonous machinations'.

It is truly amazing how nations can perpetrate the most dreadful acts of murder and destruction in order 'only' to defend themselves. They all find some plausible reasons for their aggression and, what is more, come to believe in them. So we see the superpowers amassing the most barbarous weapons of destruction, only defending themselves against the enemy.

Besides tribal paranoia we find phallic aggressiveness to be the most potent driving force in the competition between tribes and nations. The paranoia provides the excuse, while the phallic-aggressive urges provide the sense of satisfaction in the possession of the weapons of war. The phallic symbolism of spears, arrows, guns, rockets and bombs are obvious, as a show of virility in the competition between males and sexual superiority. Although it is true that even in the hunt, and in the production process, there is a measure of competition and assertion of virility, it is nevertheless subsidiary to the fight for sustenance and survival, a symbol of the male's prowess as a provider. All tools and machines have that dual aspect, but in a war between tribes, the weapons are phallic-destructive symbols of aggression. The urge to attack and castrate the father, or the own God, is projected onto the foreign God, the deities and rulers of *other* nations who are perceived as the castrators wishing to claim for themselves phallic omnipotence, and then there is no question but that we have to defend ourselves against them and do everything to assert our prowess and the nation's pride. For what would our people and our women and children think of us if we succumbed to the other male? We must make sure to protect our virility and to show it to be greater, more potent and powerful than that of the other fellow.

There is no gainsaying that these things provide a distinct excitement and satisfaction. We identify ourselves gladly with the great achievements of our nation, especially in the field of warfare. Each one of us vicariously experiences the power and virility of our weaponry and our armies.

So the propaganda of nations, today the superpowers, play upon these drives (which have almost acquired the quality of instinct) and engage in phallic boasting and competition in order to defend our nation's pride and security.

The employment of the atomic bomb to destroy Hiroshima and Nagasaki was based on the calculation that it would save the lives of some 40,000 American soldiers, and put an early end to the war. In a message to the American people on the same day, August 6, 1945, the American President, Harry Truman, radiated the pride of the nation: "What has been done is the greatest achievement of organised science in history, thanks to the capacity of industry to design, and of labour to operate the machines and methods to do things never done before". He boasted that there was no other

country where such a combination could be got together. Address-
ing the enemy he warned that the United States was "now prepared
to obliterate more rapidly and completely every productive enterprise the Japanese have above ground in any city. We shall destroy
their docks, their factories and their communications". With these
remarks Harry Truman, in effect, christened the nuclear age and set
up the stage for America's role in it. That role in 1945 seemed
awesome and unassailable, "the greatest" in terms of military
technology; it represented a quantum jump in the art of warfare
that was indescribable. Until then the most devastating bomb
dropped from the air had been the block-buster about nine tons of
T.N.T., but by applying the principle of fission to uranium, an
explosion had been produced equal to 13,000 tons of T.N.T.
Human ingenuity had devised a means of killing human beings far
beyond anything known before, and it seemed to Truman, and
most of his inner circle, that the nation which had a monopoly of
this instrument had the wherewithal to impose its will on world
affairs for a long time to come. The peaceful potential of fission,
moreover, offered prospects in the near future of cheap and limitless supplies of electricity, again giving the nation an impressive
advantage.

However, the scientists, having successfully dealt with the scientific challenge of a nuclear bomb, "a challenge that had to
be conquered because it was there", as Robert Oppenheimer
explained (but also, let us admit in fairness, in order to forestall
a possible development of nuclear weaponry by the Nazis), were
troubled by their humanitarian scruples when they succeeded in
making the bomb. Some scientists, including Robert Oppenheimer,
became worried how the chain reaction, released in the explosion,
would affect "the hydrogen in sea water. Might not the explosion of
the atomic bomb set off an explosion of the ocean itself?" Nor was
this all that Oppenheimer feared. The nitrogen in the air is also
unstable, though to a lesser degree. Might not it too be set off by an
atomic explosion in the atmosphere? The planet, in other words,
could be 'vaporised'.

On the Monday morning that the test was made, Enrico Fermi,
the physicist who had effected the first chain reaction, was making
bets with his colleagues on whether the bomb would ignite the
atmosphere and, if so, whether it would destroy only New Mexico
or the entire world.

A listener on August 6, 1945, hearing Truman's paeons of national self-congratulations on radio, could not have guessed that scores of scientists, who had produced the bomb, had pleaded with their government not to use it; that such generals as Eisenhower and Henry H. Arnold had grave misgivings about it; that the man most responsible for initiating the atomic programme in 1939, Leo Szilard, and others who had made decisive contributions to fission science, most notably Niels Bohr, had warned, correctly as it turned out, of an impending nuclear arms race. But popular acceptance of the bomb was achieved in 1945 and by subsequent governments playing on the pride of the American people and— their fears. Nuclear weapons were presented as a necessary 'deterrent', as being essential for maintaining 'stability', for their tremendous powers of destruction would prevent any world leader to use their weapons against America. This was buttressed by statements such as made by Eisenhower that "war has become not just tragic but preposterous. With modern weapons there can be no victory for anyone!"; or even more explicit remarks of General Douglas McArthur that "war has become a Frankenstein to destroy both sides... No longer does it possess the chance of the winner of the duel, it contains rather the germs of double suicide". And the picturesque comment by John F. Kennedy after the 1962 Cuban missile crisis that "the fruits of victory will be ashes in our mouth".

And with these melancholy thoughts we are coming to the end of our story. This can be taken as a double entendre, for we have reached the end in terms of having arrived at the present; whether the end of our reflections on man's history coincide with the end of history, the end of mankind, is a question which no writer ever had to contemplate in previous times. But we are bound to ask this apparently unthinkable question. The fact is that at this point of time man stands at a crossroad, more dramatic and final than any he has confronted during his whole evolution. Is he able to choose the correct path for his continued survival and development, or is he compelled to take the path which leads to destruction? There have been many other species who in the course of their evolution have been in a similar situation, and thousands of species have perished, for survival is not guaranteed to any. But there is this difference: no other species could ever ask this question consciously, nor did it have the power to make a conscious choice in those decisive moments of its history. We are the first species, so far as we know, which can consciously contemplate the end of its existence and speculate about possible ways of survival. (The unique human ability of mental experimentation with a great multitude of possible events before they occur may possibly serve us in good stead). There is also this difference: we are the first species with the power to destroy life itself.

Whether the evolution of life on this planet continues depends on our ability to make the right decision now. For if we fail to do so we are likely to destroy not only ourselves but the biosphere, the life-supporting system of this planet. This is not a fanciful exaggeration of the problem in order to give it dramatic impact but a fact upon which there is wide agreement among scientists who have studied the effects of large-scale nuclear explosions. But here comes the crucial question: Can reason respond to this challenge in view of its proven inability to stem the onslaught of the deep-rooted and mostly unconscious drives of destruction?

14 Diagnostic Summary

We may say that of course we want to avoid the dangers of self-destruction confronting us and that of course it is important to know something about the causes of our irrationality but can we really expect a resolution to be more rational in our social conduct to be any more successful than such resolutions have been in the past? Has not the study of human behaviour shown us again and again that the conscious mind has very limited powers to stem the onslaught of unconscious drives—just as well tell an obsessive individual to give up his obsessions because they are irrational or an alcoholic to give up drink, or an addict to stop taking drugs, or a maniac to stop having ideas of grandeur, or a sadist to find other, less harmful means of gratification! So what good does it do to tell us that we are being irrational and are likely to do ourselves and the world irreparable harm? And do we not also know that if we tell a psychotic that he is being unrealistic, he will, as likely as not, give us perfectly rational sounding reasons why he is in fact right and that it is we who are mistaken; and humanity, being in a state of cultural psychosis, will find endless rationalisations to justify its course.

How then can we find a cure for man's destructive compulsions, for his collective psychosis, and how can one change society to become the embodiment of sanity? For as Einstein has put it: "The first atomic bomb destroyed more than the city of Hiroshima. It also exploded our inherited outdated political ideas".

Before one can possibly decide upon the kind of therapy one ought to adopt or whether a therapy is indeed feasible, one has to diagnose the disease. In view of the long history of humanity, the immense variety of races, cultures, religions and beliefs, and the complex history of civilisations, one may consider it foolhardy to attempt such a diagnosis. Yet it may be worthwhile to try as it may help us to become aware of our common humanity and to appreciate the deep-seated psychological problems which we all share and which are at the root of our apparently insoluble socio-cultural conflicts. Indeed, at a time when science does not shrink from investigating the most intractable mysteries of the cosmos, the nature of life and its origins, the human psyche and its socio-cultural manifestations should not be considered outside the scope of scientific inquiry.

The diagnostic summary which I present in the following pages does not claim to be comprehensive in the sense of taking into account the enormous number of factors involved, but I shall concentrate upon those factors which I consider to be the most important.

THE INSTINCTUAL VOID AND MAN'S FUNDAMENTAL INSECURITY

Our prehuman ancestors were biologically ill-equipped to survive the ice ages; they lacked strength and speed, their natural organs of aggression were woefully inadequate for the ferocious battle for survival in a barren and hostile world. The vegetarian hominid had to become a carnivore, he had to kill animals more powerful than himself as vegetation, his accustomed source of sustenance, had all but disappeared in the arctic world around him. He had to become a hunter, but more often than not he was hunted by his prey, the killer hominid was in constant danger of being killed. So he had to equip himself with artificial organs of aggression in order to survive, and his brain enabled him to do so. He externalised his inadequate biological organs of aggression into artificial weapons and tools and his brain expanded dramatically during the process of self-externalisation. The 'brain explosion' transformed the hominid into Homo erectus able to cope with the extremely hostile conditions of the Late Palaeozoicum.

The expansion of the brain and especially of the prefrontal areas of the cortex, moreover, freed our early ancestors from the constraints of instinctual determinants and enabled them to choose between a wide range of possible responses before committing themselves to action. The advantages of this capability are quite obvious in the struggle for survival and have made it possible for them to acquire supremacy over animals much more powerful and biologically better equipped. However, the capacity to dominate all other animals and eventually much of nature was acquired at the cost of a deep-seated sense of insecurity.

It is in the nature of the 'new brain' that it provides us with internal presentations of events and situations, images of the past and the possible future, and enables us to see ourselves acting and doing things even if we are not engaged in any activity. Thus we can experiment with activities in our minds and choose those which seem most likely to promote our interests and fulfil our needs. This ability of our minds, which has made us supreme amongst animals, has the drawback that we can never be quite sure whether our image of reality, our judgments of reality and our choices are correct. While animals are trapped in the inevitability of their instinctual responses and within the certainty of their reactions, humans are compelled to choose and are free to make mistakes. We are frequently apprehensive of dangers even when they do not occur in reality, and we are never quite sure which particular response is correct or whether our judgment of reality is valid. Thus a wide range of activities, which in animals are determined by genetic programming as instincts, are in our species determined by complex psychological processes, memories, images, valuations, judgments and ideas. Even the eye-blink reflex, for instance, which has always been considered a true instinct, can be altered by hypnotic suggestion, and it is well known that the sexual instinct does not entirely determine our sexual behaviour, for it is subject to very considerable modifications by psychological influences. This not only applies to human beings but also to the higher Primates. Gorillas in zoos, who have never seen or experienced their parents having sexual relations, are frequently unable to perform the sexual act.

ANXIETY HYSTERIA

Past experiences are not only stored in the brain, producing reflexes which have proven advantageous in the course of natural selection, but are retained in the human mind in the form of images and fantasies which can arouse emotional reactions just as intense as those produced by actual events in the world outside. Images or mental representations of past dangers and traumas as well as anticipations of possible future dangers carry an emotional charge which transforms instinctual fear reactions, common amongst animals, into anxiety states. Anxiety, in turn produces physiological disturbances and motor responses long after actual situations of danger have disappeared and we have ceased to be conscious of them.

The extremely dangerous environment which our ancestor had to confront during the ice ages, his relentless battles with fierce animals much more powerful than himself continued to engage his imagination even when he was safe in his cave. His battles were not confined to the actual confrontation with the prey during the hunt but were elaborated in his mind; he constantly relived dangers and catastrophes, refought old battles and imagined himself victorious in new battles by employing new and better techniques and experimenting with new skills. But his monstrous adversaries and the freezing, barren world surrounding him lived on his imagination and produced states of anxiety which Freud was right to diagnose as anxiety hysteria. However, man's mind was not only filled with images of danger, terror, hunger and cold, but also with images of pleasure and security, of the warmth and love of his cave, and these images sustained him.

Thus man carries a dramatised version of reality in his mind, and there is no end to the battles, victories and defeats, happiness and sorrow which he enacts in the theatre of his imagination.

PRIMARY PARANOIA: THE SPLIT BETWEEN THE WORLD INSIDE AND THE WORLD OUTSIDE

I differentiate here between a paranoid state which is fundamental to mankind's condition since its very beginnings and paranoia proper which evolved at a later stage and has its origin with the onset of the Oedipus complex.

In view of the fact that early man had to fight incessantly against the dangers surrounding him, a great part of his libido was transformed into aggression. Indeed, he needed every bit of aggressiveness to survive, both psychologically as well as biologically; but the man of the ice ages also needed warmth, love and security to sustain him. And he found it in the warmth of his hearth inside the cave, and above all in the warmth of the woman-mother and the members of his family group. Without the image of a safe and warm place to return to, the welcome of his loved ones, he could not have survived the rigours of the hunt and the dangers of the world outside. Just as the infant needs the constant reminder of his mother's love and the warmth of her embrace in order to still its terrors, so the man of the ice ages needed the awareness of the warmth and embrace of his cave. Thus early man's libido was not only transformed into aggressiveness but also split in a dualism of outside—danger, anxiety and aggressiveness, and inside—security and warmth. As a large part of his libido is deflected to aggressiveness, to the skills of killing, and flows into the externalised organs of aggression, he attains a degree of pleasure in the killing and in victory as well as in the welcome he will receive in bringing home the prey. It is true to say that this process represents a successful adaptation to the environmental condition prevailing during the ice ages.

But the anxiety continues even when there is no actual danger. Man is obsessed with dangers and the aggressive urge continues to demand expression. He forever populates the world with prehistoric beasts of his imagination, his fears are constantly aroused by them, and he has the urge to fight and protect his family, his troop, his tribe, his nation.

We can see these paranoid obsessions operating all through history in the religions and politics of all civilisations, we can observe them in neurotic individuals and in little children. By a process of psycho-genetic inheritance, the nature of which we barely understand, the child of our time experiences the fears and aggressiveness of our ancestors. It constantly clamours for reassurance from its mother and her protection against the monsters lurking in the world of its dreamlike consciousness, not yet fully awake to the actual world in which it lives.

MANIC COMPENSATION AND THE BIRTH OF GODS

When the young men of primitive societies had to leave the primary bonds of their mother-dominated world and venture out into the strange and dangerous world outside, they developed manic fantasies—reflected in the ancient images of Adom, the gigantic man who spreads from one end of the world to the other—to compensate for their anxieties and insecurities.

We know from the observation of children that with the emergence of narcissistic self-awareness they are not at first aware of the differences between their fantasies and objective reality, being dominated by the omnipotence of thought. It is a world where wishes and images acquire primacy over the reality principle. Manic self-images are usually emphasised when the child feels that its narcissistic needs are not responded to by its environment and it is made to feel unacknowledged and helpless in an alien world.

The young men and boys of the ice ages needed the father—just as the child does in our time—for his guidance; they needed his strength to reassure them and his skills to inspire and lead them, and they needed him for his judgment and knowledge. And they projected upon him their fantasies of omnipotence and omniscience, and when he died they ate his brain, either directly or in symbolic acts of ritual, in order to receive his powers. The cult of introjection of the parental presence is indeed the basis of cultures. The father thus became an imaginative presence, an immortal ghost, a guide and judge, and they came to call him god. He not only led the sons into the hunt but he was the fount of correct thought and judgment, of all knowledge in man's quest to understand and master the universe. The more complex human societies became, the more complex their relationships with each other and with other tribes, the more they needed their god to be all powerful in order to guide them through the contradictions and complexities of their lives. The gods not only allowed them to partake in their powers but also gave them a sense of their own identity. Thus they projected their manic fantasies upon the fathers and made them into gods.

OEDIPUS COMPLEX: THE PSYCHO-SOCIAL CONFLICTS OF PATRIARCHY

In the culture of patriarchy the bond which united the members of the family or group is profoundly disturbed by the rivalry between fathers and sons. A part of the aggressive drive, which previously was directed outwards, now enters the home and its social extensions. While previously fathers and sons, gods and men were allies in the struggle for survival against the hostile and dangerous world, there is now conflict between the father who has become an all-powerful ruler and the community of men upon whom he imposes his authority. Having projected their manic fantasies upon him, the sons resent the father's powers over them and are driven by a desire to kill and devour him in order to regain his powers for themselves. But the murderous fantasies are followed by remorse and contrition; the sons become afraid of the ghost of the murdered father, of his revenge and punishment, and they have to declare themselves helpless before him and restore to him his role of omnipotence in order to propitiate his anger. Conscience demands that he is glorified and his will reigns supreme over them and over the universe. Thus worship and awe is born and men's submission to the supreme authority of the father-figures.

SEXUAL REPRESSION AND PLEASURE ANXIETY

Besides the manic component of the Oedipal rivalry, the sexual rivalry between fathers and sons plays an important role in the dynamics of the Oedipus complex. While Freud did not sufficiently emphasise the former, he was surely right to draw attention to the latter and show its importance in the formation of patriarchal civilisations. The sons, who saw the father as a major obstacle to their sexual gratification, wanted to kill him and developed patricidal fantasies. But remorse, guilt and the fear of losing the goodwill and protection of their father made them turn against their sexual desires, which had led them to commit this hideous crime (in fantasy and maybe sometimes in fact), and they came to consider the sexual drive as evil and sinful. This, in the first place, applied to their desire for the mother and made her taboo as a sexual object. The fear of incest may be considered the main motivation for exogamy, the displacement of the sexual urge outwards towards women of other families and tribes, as this would have been approved by the father. But it had the effect that sexuality as a whole became circumscribed by taboos and acquired a stigma of sinfulness. It became subject to repressions, causing pleasure anxiety, mistrust of erotic urges, inhibitions, blocks and a wide range of somatic rigidities.

THE PATRIARCHAL SUPEREGO

And men came to be mistrustful of themselves and of each other; they handed over judgment of right and wrong to their divine, appointed kings, his judges and priests, to depend upon their higher wisdom and their authority as they can no longer trust their own desires and impulses. But they can regain the knowledge of right and wrong by submission to the authorities who judge and decide for them; and their will be done in thought and reality. The perfect citizen is he who introjects their authority into his own ego and sees himself judged by their all-seeing eye and relates his thoughts and his behaviour to their internal commandments. But he is also aware of his own constant shortcomings and his temptations to defy their commandments, and will turn to his external authorities for correction and guidance and forgiveness.

Thus the superego of patriarchal man exercises its internal as well as external powers in society as it does in the family, and men need it as a model for their personality. The manic fantasies which men have to repress in themselves are projected upon god and his authorities, and the restraints which apply to human beings do not apply to the state and its rulers. Indeed, the more manic the state, the more grandiose its aspirations for power and glory, the more satisfaction it gives to its citizens. By identifying with his nation and his king the citizen can enjoy the manic satisfactions which he had to deny in himself. But the father still has to guard against the Oedipal wish, which is reinforced by the sons' anger against his new powers over them and his constant demands for their sacrifices. But as they depend upon him both psychologically as well as practically their aggression towards him must at all cost be repressed and projected outwards. Other gods and tribes or nations became imbued with the hostility which the sons themselves feel unconsciously towards their god. Thus the unconscious drives of aggression, which the sons experience towards their own father, are acted out by other tribes. And the father has to be protected against the enemy, who represents the dark, hidden fantasies of the sons.

The enemy within has to be transformed into an enemy without, and the gods have to be defended by their subjects.

THE DIVINITY OF KINGS: WORSHIP OF AUTHORITY

And in every patriarchal city there is an altar where the god resides and is worshipped, and the city takes its name from him. Men had to make sacrifices to their gods, feed them and satisfy their needs, and devote themselves to lifelong labours to build temples for them, and walls and towers for their defence. There emerged an elite who organised the sacrifices and conducted the rituals of worship. They also enforced payment of taxes and other material contributions for the maintenance of the temples and their administration, and they appointed an individual to be the supreme representative of the gods—the divine king—and became his priests, clerks, governors and courtiers. They controlled the instruments of education, whereby they ensured that the community accepts their rule as divinely ordained and natural, and they acquired means of coercion to ensure their rule. And the state as we know it was born.

COMPULSION AND RITUAL

Despite all the taboos imposed upon it by the authorities, external and internal, the sexual drive constantly demands gratification, and threatens to break through the inhibitions set up against it, becoming a source of fear. Its renunciation has to be constantly repeated and reinforced in ritual. The act of undoing the sinful urge becomes an obsessional neurosis in individuals and, in its communal manifestations, religious ritual. Rituals and incantation play a major part in religious ceremonies. Orthodoxy represents a rigid system of defences against the fobidden impulses, a denial of spontaneity manifested in mental as well as somatic rigidities.

Insofar as the sexual drive occupies the dominant part of the libido, its denial as sinful influences all other libidinous drives. The most important of these is probably the anal libido with its association with uncleanliness and dirt. The taboo-ridden sexual drives become associated with the anal libido, and are then stigmatised as unclean and dirty. Purification from sexual guilt takes the form of cleansing rituals, ceremonial washing in holy rivers and sprinkling with holy waters. These purification rites signify the cleansing of the members from the dirt of the anal libido, from the impurities of their minds and bodies. Uncleanliness is identical with bad conscience, being dirty means to be a companion of the devil, and inability to be cleansed means to be condemned to hell—the bad conscience of dirty minds where the devil rules. This means to be outcast from god, from the membership of the clean ones.

DEATH AND REBIRTH OF GOD

Just as much as there is an urge for dependency upon authority figures, there is an instinct to grow up and affirm the freedom to exercise one's innate potentialities, both in individuals and in cultures. All through history men have aspired towards independence from the coercive powers of the superego; by the full exercise of their skills, wisdom and knowledge men strove to emancipate themselves from the tutelage of their gods and to assert their maturity.

We can recognise three high points of European civilisation when it celebrated its potentialities for maturity and, by doing so, left an indelible imprint upon its character, making it unique amongst civilisations: the culture of Athens of 500 B.C., the Renaissance of 1500 A.D., and the Enlightenment of 1800 A.D. They can all be considered Enlightenment movements, declarations of freedom from the shackles of infantile submission to superhuman powers. They were great moments of maturity to test man's innate creative and intellectual capabilities: I rebel against authority, I think, I perceive the beauty and order of life, I choose freedom and justice, and therefore I am. Men aspired to face the world without the old gods and without the guilt and fears which had informed earlier cultures.

But after these heroic declarations of independence, men began to feel anxious again, and the gods began to assert themselves in the mind of man, and overwhelmed the freedom movements, the progressive, revolutionary nations and transformed them once more into authoritarian systems. Men find it very difficult to dispense with the old superego, and they feel insecure and lonely without a god. They hand over their intellectual and moral aspirations to the old father-figure and ask him to reign in a new guise acceptable to the pretensions of rationality. Even while rationalism and science have forced God to retreat beyond the galaxies, and the heavens are no more than oxygen and ozone lit up by the sunlight—an unfit habitation for gods—He still reigns in the regions not accessible to reason and He inhabits the unconscious regions of the mind. While men can no longer perceive Him rationally, they feel insecure and anxious and guilty without a secure point of reference provided by the heavenly father. The ideals of the Enlightenment have failed to provide the certainties of purpose which they had promised.

GOD BECOMES A MACHINE

Reason, which was the vehicle for the creation of 'humanity', has now become the servant of the machine-system, and men have to serve the machine and model themselves upon it. As God had become depersonalised and turned into a machine, men can only see himself as a physical entity like a machine. God has lost His personality and His soul and men are no longer conscious of their own soul. The problem is no longer whether we can be free or not but whether we are to become robots. But robotism means the denial of personality, of the narcissistic libido, the erosion of the sense of self.

THE ATROPHY OF REASON

At a time when we are increasingly clever in manipulating the machines that manipulate the environment, when the art of calcula-tion, the preoccupation with numbers, statistics and quantitative values has reached the highest level achieved by any civilisation, our rational faculties have atrophied. For the manipulative and calculating modes relate to the world and to people as soulless objects with whom we have no personal relationship or sense of community. Instead of seeing human affairs in terms of subjective interactions and personal relationships, they are depersonalised as external, objective events, which we have to manipulate. As we do not recognise the subjectivity of others, and do not recognise them as persons, we lose our own sense of subjectivity, the inner world of our personalities is diminished. We become strangers to ourselves, objects in a world of things and objects.

Scientific fact worship has not only destroyed the gods and deprived the universe of its soul, its purpose and meaning, but it has also denied the soul, the subjectivity of man. We can no longer feel the heavenly father's concern and his expectations of us; we no longer perceive his mind and we do not know what he wants from us and what he thinks. Instead, we are left with thousands of experts and specialists dividing the universe among themselves, handing us disconnected and frequently discordant bits of knowledge and leaving us disorientated. We know thousands of things but despair of understanding anything. Understanding means the ability to relate to the purpose, the will, the mind of phenomena, which makes them behave the way they do, or to the mind of God when he created the universe, as Einstein as well as Newton have put it. We now only see the outside manifestations of things and have lost empathy with them. For science has shown us that nature has no soul, no purpose, and it is we who have projected human values upon it; and that is strictly against the rules of science. Only a value-free, impersonal, objective approach to things is considered cognitively valid, and this also applies to ourselves and to our fellow men. Psychologists have denied the psyche and only study behaviour, philosophers have denied mind and only study language. Even Wittgenstein, however, had to admit that: "There are indeed things that cannot be put into words. They are what is mystical". But what he calls 'mystical', being beyond reason and therefore non-sense, what cannot be put into words and therefore cannot be spoken of, is none else but the mind that in the first place produces words and the vast region of pre-verbal and pre-conscious mentation.

Man's need to have an internal presentation, an image of the world which enables him to understand the causes and aims of events around him is replaced by a mass of information which he cannot absorb and connect into a unified concept. We are bombarded by an information explosion, transmitted, by the media, from all corners of the world; our intellect is swamped by bits of information which it cannot connect into a coherent whole, and at the same time we are told by the experts that it would be presumptuous and irresponsible to try to do so, as no one person could possibly coordinate the vast amount of information available. Thus the intellect is intimidated, debarred from trying to understand the world and to form a coherent image of it. The most important part of our intellect, namely, its synthesising faculty, is stifled and disillusioned.

As we cannot perceive a purpose in the world, we are losing a sense of purpose in our lives. We are surrounded by a random universe of inexplicable, disconnected events, happenings without overall meaning, and moments without much sense of a past or future. In an impulse-dominated universe we are, as persons, dominated by impulses, and the ego, whose task it is to coordinate the thousands of stimuli from within and without into a coherent and permanent sense of self, atrophies and leaves us insecure without a purpose-directed will, without much sense of identity, dissociated in our thoughts and actions. While there is no doubt that an increasing number of people are becoming aware of a cultural crisis, no one knows what to do about it.

An international survey conducted by the National Geographic Society revealed a stunning ignorance about the world among young American adults; 5% could not name their nation's capital, half of college students could not find Vietnam on the map. The continuing slide in intelligence and literacy has encouraged the view that something more profound than poor teaching is taking place. Just as the printing-press and the industrial revolution have transformed language, so the electronic age is reshaping twentieth century society. Video and computers are breaking down human communication and the passing on of human values. For Professor Blum the future is a teenage boy tapping silently to the beat of headphones who has never heard of Shakespeare or Plato. Neil Postman declares: "America is amusing itself to death. With his or her mind numbed with video pulp and the new electronic folklore, the average citizen is becoming detached from reality".

REGRESSIVE DE-SUBLIMATION AND THE CULT OF INFANTILISM

Postman has invented a name for the New American—the 'kidult'. He argues that childhood in America is fast becoming obsolete. As a result of the non-stop flow of information from television in easy-to-digest little chunks, there are no secrets left to children. Thinking they know it all by eleven, they have little patience for formal education and fail to learn to read or reason productively. The child then turns into the unthinking adult philistine, materialistic and devoted to technology and gadgetry.*

The shortened attention span among the new child-orientated adult, epitomised by the arrival of 10 second sound bytes on the television news and the flicker of short shots on films, reflects the mind's inability to co-ordinate perceptions into a coherent, unified image. The satisfactions which the ego experiences in its synthesising processes of understanding are thus sharply reduced and leave a narcissistic void, a neurasthenic restlessness which demand constant stimulation and excitements of an increasingly aggressive and primitive nature.

NARCISSISTIC VOID AND THE HUNGER FOR INSTANT GRATIFICATION

The restlessness of the kidult is accompanied by a craving for commodities and possessions of all kinds. We demand more and more of the commodities which the machine can produce, and need more and more machines to produce the commodities. We can agree with Marx when he said that the more powerful machines are, the more dehumanised we become. We have observed earlier that our species suffers from an instinctual void, but now we have developed a narcissistic void which we are trying to compensate by a constant craving for stimulations and possessions, and expect machines to provide them. As Fromm has observed: "We see machines as mechanical cows"; but being mechanical they provide goods without warmth and love and we remain unsatisfied. We feel isolated, without a sense of personal I–Thou relationships, unable to share our minds and our feelings. Thus we are preoccupied with the self and its satisfactions. We know from the observation of children that if their narcissistic needs are not acknowledged and they cannot share them with the world around them, they will develop an intense narcissistic hunger, withdraw libido from

---

* Charles Bremner: 'Is this, like, cultural decline' (The Times, 9.9.1988).

objects and vest it in the self. Being unable to share our needs and not being allowed to understand the world or to trust it, we will demand instant gratification, leading to an expectation explosion, an unlimited desire not only for commodities and possessions of all kinds but also a cure for all ailments and anxieties. When technology has adopted the image of omnipotence then we want it to cure all our problems—instantly. Medicine is expected to release us of all diseases which befall our bodies, and all the disturbances of our minds and emotions. As we no longer feel the power to act as causative agents in the world and to have an influence upon it, we no longer trust our bodies to repair themselves or our minds to restore a measure of equilibrium. The medical body engineers claim to understand and to be able to repair the human machine, and the medical mind engineers, the neuroanatomists and neurochemists to repair the brain and provide a drug for every disorder of the emotions, and we demand that they fulfil their promise.

The preoccupation with personal well-being, the cult of narcissism has produced an increasingly obsessive preoccupation with health food, healthy exercise and a cultivation of the body beautiful. On the other hand there is an epidemic of drug-addiction, an anxious dependency upon the curative magic of drugs provided by the pharmaceutical industry, not only to restore a sense of well-being to the body but also to the mind. But people are still restless, anxious and neurotic, and one can indeed speak of an epidemic of emotional disturbances. Neither the medical establishment with the huge industrial complex to back it nor the proliferation of so-called alternative medicines can relieve us of our narcissistic deprivation. For we need the world to relate to us, whether we call it nature or God or society, to acknowledge us as persons and as creators. The symbiotic relationship between the self and the world, the subject and the world of objects, remains broken. We have no feeling for the trees we cut down, the animals we kill for food or torture for medical experiments, for the air, the waters and the earth which we pollute with our industrial excrement.

CONCLUSION

Reason tells us that the planet is now our home, our only home in a vast, empty universe, that we live our lives in a planetary spaceship and depend upon each other for our safety and our sustenance. But our emotions are still split between the world inside and the world outside, our primal fantasies are still governed by the paranoid anxieties and Oedipal conflicts; they continue to make a mockery of our moral and rational aspirations. Thus we divide our spaceship earth into enemy territories and competing tribes and arm ourselves with all the destructive weapons which now have cosmic forces available to them. We still regard the planet as the hunting ground on which to discharge our aggressive drives, if not with the weapons of war then with the weapons of industry and commerce. The natural environment is still regarded as prey, raw material for the production of an ever greater mass of commodities to satisfy our insatiable hunger for possessions and wealth. We devour the planet with our technological claws and teeth and despoil it with our industrial excrement, and there is still not much empathy with it as our home. Nor have we arrived emotionally at a sense of community with our fellow-humans, the concept of humanity is still an abstract notion without much reality.

How long it will take till we explode our planetary spaceship or destroy its life-support system is anybody's guess.

Mankind has acquired the skills necessary to transform the earth into a new Eden; we have eaten of the Tree of Knowledge and, after our long journey through history, have acquired mastery over the earth; but in our mastery we have also eaten of the Tree of Life and become like gods. However, we find it hard to admit that the fate of the world depends on us alone; we hide behind infantile images of the Superego, superhuman authorities that guide our destiny.

Still, man must learn to face the truth of his maturity: there is no superior power above him on whom he can depend for salvation, no power outside him whom he can blame and whose support he can invoke. It is man's will that will be done for good or for evil, there is no other god now.

It is we who determine whether the planet will live or die, whether the life out of which we have evolved will continue to unfold or whether it will be destroyed. The consciousness of this awesome responsibility may shake mankind out of its schizophrenic dream-state and unite it in a resolve to protect life and participate in its further evolution.

Bibliography

Abraham, Karl: Selected Papers on Psychoanalysis (Hogarth Press 1955)

Adorno, T. H. et al: The Authoritarian Family (Norton 1969)

Altman, J: 'Effects of Early Experience on Brain Morphology' in Malnutrition, Learning and Behaviour ed. N.S. Scrimshaw and J. E. Gordon (M.I.T. Press 1967)

Andrews, Antony: Greek Society (Pelican Books 1981)

Bachofen, J. J: Myth, Religion and Mother Right (Routledge and Kegan Paul 1968)

Bailey, Percival: Cortex and Mind (New York 1962)

Baldwin, J. M: Mental Development in the Child and the Race (N.Y. 1895)

Bell, Daniel: The Coming of Post-Industrial Society (Heinemann 1974)

Benedict, Ruth: Patterns of Culture (New American Library 1959)

Bernfeld, Sigfried: Sigmund Freud (International Journal of Psychoanalysis 1951)

Bertalanffy, L. von: General Systems Theory (Braziller 1968)

Bowra, C. M: Ancient Greek Literature (Butterworth 1933)

Brace, Loring C: A Consideration of Hominid Catastrophism (Current Anthropology 1964)

Brehier, Emile: The Hellenic Age (University of Chicago Press)

Briffault, Robert: The Mothers (Macmillan 1927)

Brod, Max: Johannes Reuchlin und Sein Kampf (W. Kohlhammer Verlag 1965)

Bronowski, J. and Marlish, B: The Western Intellectual Tradition (Hutchinson 1960)

Buber, Martin: Between Man and Man (Fontana Library 1961)

Burckhardt, J: The Civilisation of the Renaissance in Italy (Phaidon Press)

Campbell, B. C: Human Evolution (Chicago, Aldine 1966)

Campbell, Joseph: The Hero with a Thousand Faces (Princeton University Press 1968)

Cambridge Ancient History, The, Volumes 1 and 2 (Cambridge University Press 1980)

Chadwick, Owen: The Reformation (Pelican History of the Church 1970)

Child, V. G: Man Makes Himself (Watts 1936)

Claparède, Edouard: La Genèse de l'Hypothèse (Archives de Psychologie 1933)

Clark, W. E. le Gros, and Leakey, L. S. B: The Miocene Hominids of East Africa (British Museum, London 1951)

Clark, W. E. le Gros: The Antecedents of Man (Edinburgh University Press 1962)

Clarke, G: World Prehistory (Cambridge University Press 1969)

Cohen, Alan: Structure, Logic, and Program Design (John Wiley & Sons 1983)

Cohn, Norman: Warrant for Genocide (London 1967)

Cole, S: The Prehistory of East Africa (N.Y. 1963)

Couts Smith, K: The Dream of Ikarus, Art and Society in the 20th Century (Hutchinson 1970)

Crook, J. H: Gelada Baboon, Herd Structure and Movement (Zoological Society, London 1966)

Dart, R. A: Australopithecus Africanus (Nature, London 1925)

—— Adventures with the Missing Link (Viking 1961)

Darwin, C: The Descent of Man (Watts, First Ed 1872)

—— A Biographical Sketch of an Infant (Mind 1877)

Descartes, René: Discourse on Method (1637)

—— Meditations (1642)

Dobb, Maurice: Studies in the Development of Capitalism (Routledge 1963)

Doblhofer, Ernst: Voices in Stone (Souvenir Press 1961)

Dobzhanski, T: Mankind Evolving (Yale University Press 1968)

—— Cultural Direction of Human Evolution (Human Biology 1963)

Dubos, René: So Human an Animal (Rupert Hart-Davis 1970)

—— The Torch of Life (Simon & Schuster 1962)

Ellenberger, H. F: The Discovery of the Unconscious (Allan Lane 1970)

Ellul, Jacques: The Technological Society (A. A. Knopf 1964)

Engels, F: The Origin of the Family, Private Property and the State (New York 1942)

Erikson, E. H: Childhood and Society (Hogarth Press 1965)

—— Young Man Luther (1958)

Evans, Sir Arthur: The Palace of Minos (Macmillan; Volume 2 1921, Volume 4 1935)

Farrington, Benjamin: Francis Bacon, Philosopher of Industrial Science (Macmillan 1973)

Fenichel, O: A Critique of the Death Instinct, in Collected Papers (Norton 1953)

Ferenczi, S: Contributions to Psychoanalysis (Hogarth Press, 1926, 1952, 1955)

Finley, M. J: Early Greece (Chatto & Windus 1981)

Foucault, M: The History of Sexuality, Vol. 1 (Pantheon Books 1978)

Fox, R: In the Beginning: Aspects of Hominid Behavioural Evolution (London 1967)

Frankfort, Henry: Kingship and the Gods (Chicago 1948)

Frankl, George: The End of War or the End of Mankind (Globe Publications 1955)

—— The Failure of the Sexual Revolution (Kahn & Averill 1974)

Frankl, Viktor: The Will to Meaning (Souvenir Press 1970)

Freud, Sigmund: Introductory Lectures on Psychoanalysis (Hogarth Press 1929)

—— New Introductory Lecture on Psychoanalysis (Hogarth Press 1931)

—— Three Essays on the Theory of Sexuality (Hogarth Press 1962)

—— The Future of an Illusion (Hogarth Press 1973)

—— Civilisation and its Discontents (Hogarth Press 1957)

—— Group Psychology (Hogarth Press 1967)

Fromm, Erich: The Sane Society (Reinhardt 1955)

—— Psychoanalysis and Religion (Yale University Press 1950)

—— The Crisis of Psychoanalysis (Cape 1971)

—— The Anatomy of Human Destructiveness (Cape 1974)

Friedenthal, R: Luther (London 1970)

Gay, Peter: Freud for Historians (O.U.P. 1985)

Gedo, J. and Pollock, G. H: The Fusion of Science and Humanism (Psychological Issues 1975)

Gellner, E: Words and Things (Gollancz 1959)

Gimbutas, Marija: The Gods and Goddesses of Old Europe (Thames and Hudson 1974)

Goldman, Lucien: The Human Sciences and Psychology (Cape 1969)

Gould, Stephen: Ontogeny and Phylogeny (Harvard University Press 1977)

Graves, Robert: The White Goddess (London 1948)

Hall, Stanley: A Synthetic Genetic Study of Fear (The American Journal of Psychology 1914)

Hammond, N. G. I: The History of Greece to 332 B.C. (O.U.P. 1959)

Harrison, J. E: Prolegomena to the Study of Greek Religion (C.U.P. 1903)

Harth, Erich: Windows on the Mind: Reflections on the Physical Basis of Consciousness (Harvester Press 1982)

Hartmann, E: Philosophy of the Unconscious (Trueber & Co. 1884)

Hartmann, E. and Kris: The Genetic Approach in Psychoanalysis (The Psychoanalytic Study of the Child 1945)

Helbaek, J: First Impressions of the Çatal Hüyük Husbandry (Anotalian Studies XIV 1964)

Howell, F. Clark: Early Man (Time Life Books 1965)

Howells, William: Mankind in the Making (Secker & Warburg 1961)

Hudson, Liam: The Cult of the Fact (Cape 1972)
Jahoda, Marie: Freud and the Dilemmas of Psychology (Hogarth Press 1970)
James, E. O: The Cult of the Mother Goddess (London 1959)
Johnson, Paul: A History of Christianity (Weidenfeld 1976)
Jolly, C: The Seed Eaters (Man 5 (1) 1970)
Kerenyi, C: The Gods of the Greeks (Thames & Hudson 1982)
Kitto, H. D. F: The Greeks (Pelican Books 1972)
Koestler, Arthur: The Ghost in the Machine (Hutchinson 1967)
Lasch, Christoper: The Culture of Narcissism (Warner Books 1979)
Leakey, L. S. B: Adam's Ancestors (Harper and Row 1960)
Leroi-Gourhan, A: The Art of Prehistoric Man in Western Europe (Thames and Hudson 1968)
Lichtenstein, Heinz: The Dilemma of Human Identity (Jason Aronson 1977)
Maccoby, Hyam: Revolution in Judaea (Orbach & Chambers 1973)
—— The Sacred Executioner (Thames & Hudson 1982)
Malinowski, B: Sex and Repression in Savage Society (Routledge 1960)
—— Sex, Culture and Myth (Mayflower-Dell 1967)
Mandrou, R: From Humanism to Science (Pelican Books 1978)
Marcuse, Herbert: One-Dimensional Man (Sphere Books 1968)
—— Eros and Civilisation (Sphere Books 1969)
Martin, Bernice: A Sociology of Contemporary Cultural Change (Basil Blackwell 1981)
Mead, Margaret: Coming of Age in Samoa (Pelican Books 1950)
—— Cooperation and Competition Among Primitive Peoples (Beacon Press 1961)
Mellaart, J: The Neolithic of the Near East (Thames & Hudson 1975)
—— Earliest Civilisations of the Near East (Thames & Hudson 1978)
—— Çatal Hüyük; A Neolithic Town in Anatolia (Thames & Hudson 1967)
Mumford, Lewis: The Myth of the Machine (Harcourt-Brace 1967)
Nageran, H. et. al: Basic Psychoanalytic Concepts of the Libido Theory (Allen & Unwin 1969)
Napier, J: The Roots of Mankind (Smithsonian Inst. 1970)
Nilsson, Martin: Geschichte der Griechischen Religion (Munich 1955)
Oakley, K. P: Man the Toolmaker (Chicago 1961)
Oparin, A. I: Life: Its Nature, Origin and Development (Oliver & Boyd 1961)
Pallantino, M: The Etruscans (Allan Lane 1974)
Pfeiffer, John E: The Emergence of Man (Nelson 1970)
—— When Man First Stood Up (N.Y. Times Mag. 1965)
Piaget, J: The Origin of Intelligence in Children (Routledge 1953)

Pilbeam, D: The Evolution of Man (Thames & Hudson 1970)
Rapaport, D: Psychoanalysis as a Developmental Psychology (N.Y. Int. Univ. Press 1960)
Reed, Bika: Rebel in the Soul: A Sacred Text of Ancient Egypt (Wildwood House 1978)
Reich, Wilhelm: Character Analysis (Vision Press 1950)
Reik, Theodor: Ritual: Psychoanalytic Studies (Farrar Strauss 1957)
—— Myth and Guilt (Braziller 1957)
Richards: The Popes and the Papacy in the Early Middle Ages (Routledge 1979)
Richter, H: Geschichte der Malerei im 20. Jahrhundert (Du Mont, Köln 1981)
Rivers, W. H. R: Medicine, Magic and Religion (N.Y. 1924)
Roheim, G: Psychoanalysis and Psychology (N.Y. 1950)
Romanes, G. J: Mental Evolution in Man (Kegan Paul 1888)
Rorvik, D: As Man Becomes Machine (Souvenir Press 1973)
Roszak, T: The Making of a Counter Culture (Faber & Faber 1970)
Runes, D. D: The War Against the Jews (Phil. Library 1968)
Russell, Bertrand: History of Western Philosophy (Allen & Unwin 1955)
Sandars, N. K: Prehistoric Art in Europe (Penguin 1968)
Sayre, K. M: Cybernetics and the Philosophy of Mind (Routledge 1976)
Schaller, George: The Year of the Gorilla (Penguin 1967)
Sorokin, P. A: Sociological Theories of Today (Harper & Row 1966)
—— Society, Culture and Personality (Harper & Row 1947)
Strachey, A: The Unconscious Motives of War (Allen & Unwin 1957)
Stuckenschmidt, H. H: Twentieth Century Music (World Univ. Library 1969)
—— Die Musik eines Halben Jahrhunderts (Piper & Co 1976)
Sulloway, F. J: Freud: Biologist of the Mind (Burnett Books 1979)
Sweezy, P. M: The Theory of Capitalist Development (Modern Readers Paperback 1970)
Tawney, R. H: Religion and the Rise of Capitalism (Pelican 1940)
Thomson, G: Studies in Ancient Greek Society (London 1949)
Ure, Andrew: The Philosophy of Manufacture (London 1835)
Vaizey, John: Capitalism and Society (Weidenfeld & Nicholson 1980)
Vegh, Sandor: Music as Experience (Eranos Jahrbuch 1960)
Velikovski, I: Mankind in Amnesia (Sidgwick & Jackson 1982)
Washburn, S. L: Tools and Human Evolution (Scientific American 1960)
Washburn, S. L. and Lancaster, C. S: The Evolution of Hunting, in "Man the Hunter" (Chicago 1968)
Weber, Max: The Protestant Ethics and the Spirit of Capitalism (Allen & Unwin 1978)
Wiener, N: The Human Use of Human Beings (Boston 1950)

Yerkes, R. M. and Yerkes, A. V: The Great Apes (Yale 1929)
Young, J. Z: Doubt and Certainty in Science: A Biologist's Reflection on
    the Brain (O.U.P. 1960)
Zilboorg, G: Sigmund Freud. His Exploration of the Mind of Man (N.Y.
    1951)

Index

**This book is to be returned on or before
the last date stamped below.**

FRANKL, george

91-2